PARENTS AS EDUCATORS

PARENTS AS EDUCATORS
Training Parents to Teach
their Children

Keith J. Topping

CROOM HELM
London & Sydney

BROOKLINE BOOKS
Cambridge, Massachusetts

© 1986 Keith J. Topping
Croom Helm Ltd, Provident House, Burrell Row,
Beckenham, Kent BR3 1AT
Croom Helm Australia Pty Ltd, Suite 4, 6th Floor,
64-76 Kippax Street, Surry Hills, NSW 2010, Australia

British Library Cataloguing in Publication Data

Topping, Keith J.
  Parents as educators: training parents to
  teach their children.
  1. Home and school
  I. Title
  371.1'03   LC225

  ISBN 0-7099-2468-2
  ISBN 0-7099-2469-0 Pbk

Brookline Books, PO Box 1046,
Cambridge, MA 02238

Library of Congress Cataloging-in-Publication Data

Topping, Keith J.
  Parents as educators

  Bibliography: p.
  Includes index.
  1. Portage for handicapped children — Handbooks,
manuals, etc.   2. Domestic education — Handbooks,
manuals, etc.   3. Parent-teacher relationships —
Handbooks, manuals, etc.   4. Parents of handicapped
children — Handbooks, manuals, etc. I. Title.
LC4019.15.T67 1986   649'.68   86-14698
  ISBN 0-914797-29-8
  ISBN 0-914797-30-1 (soft)

Typeset in Times Roman by Leaper & Gard Ltd, Bristol
Printed and bound in Great Britain by Mackays of Chatham Ltd, Kent

CONTENTS

For my parents

1 INTRODUCTION

Parents, renouncing their bit part as peripheral irritants in the education system, have moved centre-stage. It has long been known that parental influence is considerably more profound than that of the school. Curiously, it is only in relatively recent years that the creative deployment of this positive force has begun to take place on a large scale.

Not that the notion of parents as educators is a new one. Brim (1965) traces it back to the eighteenth century in the USA, when there were reports of child-rearing advice being communicated to mothers in training pamphlets. This practice is thought to have been imported from Europe, where it had clearly been prevalent for some decades before. However, as Brim notes, there is a sense in which parents acting as educators must be a phenomenon as old as human culture itself, dating back beyond Caxton to oral transmission, and beyond that to the breathless joint guarding of a weak flame in a cave.

In a way, then, the development of formalised education in schools served largely to rob parents of a function they had carried out for millennia — and now the wheel is beginning to come full circle (having been reinvented).

While reports of parents acting as educators are not uncommon in Europe in the seventeenth century, it was not until the rapid growth of the schooling system had consolidated it into a widely available resource that the notion of parental *involvement in school* could be countenanced, and this does not begin to be documented until the nineteenth century.

Current development still reflects a degree of tension and ambivalence in schools about the role of parents. Parental involvement in schools is one thing, and some teachers are happy enough to see parents as the handmaidens of the professionals. However, parents acting as educators in their own right, not necessarily in consultation with the school, is a different ball game entirely. And as for parents having political power over school policy and curriculum — well, that's obviously democracy run amok.

Nevertheless, the times are changing, and the flood of major books since the mid-1970s on the topic of parents as educators

1

must be indicative of a tide in the affairs of men. Thus in the USA, Lamb and Lamb (1975, 1978), Lillie and Trohanis (1976), Arnold (1978), Morrison (1978), Fine (1980), Abidin (1980) and Berger (1981) have all produced substantial landmark works on the subject. In the United Kingdom, Blackstone (1979), Pugh (1981) and Pugh and De'Ath (1984), and Sheila Wolfendale (1983, 1986) have all made notable contributions. All of these works are of significant volume, although some have a higher specific gravity than others, but their sheer numbers are superficially impressive.

It is not the intention here to retread a great deal of ground already amply covered in these publications, which are all easily accessible to the interested reader. So far as parental involvement in school is concerned, the first inroads were undoubtedly made by the corps of mums recruited as volunteers, who subsequently proved themselves worthy of trust. The initial fears of teachers were rarely borne out by experience, while both mothers and children gained. Wilton (1975) had come so far as to be able to report: 'it cannot be over-stressed that we count ourselves fortunate to have the opportunity of working with all mothers, especially those deemed "unsuitable" by middle class standards, because our primary aim is to establish a recognition of common humanity before social convention". Revolutionary stuff. With their usual feeling for sublime paradox, some of the teaching unions have recently begun to express strong antagonism to parental involvement in school (Caudrey, 1985). When institution fights institution, it's only the little people ground between the millstones who actually get hurt.

The UK has an honourable tradition of pioneering work in parental involvement in school, given massive impetus by the Plowden Report and spawning innovative studies like that of Young and McGeeney (1968). By the mid-1970s, Ballard (1975) was arguing forcefully for special attention to be paid to parent–teacher relationships in the case of children with special educational needs, an argument taken up in the Warnock Report and even appearing, albeit deformed, in the bureaucratic fiasco of the 1981 Education Act.

By 1984, however, some writers were beginning to take a pessimistic view of the rate of acceleration of change: 'without further efforts, future progress is likely to remain at the same low level ... more fundamental, system-wide change is unlikely' (Mortimore and Mortimore, 1984). Parker (1985) noted that few teacher training courses were preparing teachers for the notion of 'partnerships with parents', although the archaic concept of education current in Westminster was in favour of parental help with 'homework' (Bayliss, 1985).

In the USA, similar trends are evident. As early as 1974, Magnus was pleading for the involvement of parents in residential treatment programmes for children with special needs. Croake and Glover's (1977) survey of parent education involved a literature search which yielded 5,000 documents on the topic. Further description came from Carnine (1979) and Becker and Epstein (1981). The latter conducted a survey of 3,700 primary school teachers, which overall indicated 'a very positive view and widespread use of several parent-orientated teaching strategies'. However, in 1984 Kasouf reported another attitude survey which indicated that 78 per cent thought their professional colleagues were doing fine, while only 20 per cent thought parents made a good job of parenting.

Despite the great upsurge of interest in parents as educators, and the development of many new initiatives of proven worth, it seems that there are still many parts of the school system the news has yet to reach. Even where change in teachers' attitudes is achieved, behaviour change may be slow to follow. It is hardly surprising that some parents are becoming impatient.

In the USA, parental power has been a significant factor in the educational management equation for some time. Public Law 94-142 gave parents the right to 'due process' in the special educational placement of their children — at least in theory. Proposed education budgets may be subject to referendum, and as like as not thrown out. Direct accountability to those contributing the tax dollars does exist, although how often this happens in practice is more debatable. Stone and Taylor (1976), in *Parent Power in America*, give contact details for relevant organisations. And similar movements are afoot in Europe.

The 1980 and 1981 Education Acts gave UK parents some real say in choosing a school for their children and on how their children's special educational needs were to be met — at least on paper. In practice, over-complex procedures are hedged round with obfuscatory sub-clauses and writing between the lines so that only articulate, influential and determined parents can beat the system. However, some professionals have made strenuous efforts to advocate for parents and coach them in the rules of the game (see Wolfendale (1986) on parental profiling, for instance). Meanwhile, even in the more conservative European countries such as France, various parent power groups are growing rapidly (Heafford, 1984), and the establishment of a European alliance of parent groups is well in hand (Rowan, 1985). On a more immediately practical level, there have been calls in the UK for the establishment of local education advice centres, which could inform parents about their rights in practice by advocacy and direct action.

However, politicking is something of an acquired taste, like eating octopus. Many parents will doubtless prefer quietly to get on with what parents have always done, raising their children the best way they know how. The main theme of what follows is parents as educators in their own right, with or without the co-operation of school. Parents need no longer ape the institution, need not wait for crumbs of wisdom to fall from the teachers' table. Instead of working to make parents pale mechanistic shadows of teachers, operating some transplanted fragment of 'professional' technique, modern projects focus much more on the unique contribution of parents to the development of their children — enhancing the naturalistic skills of parents and taking their views and priorities very much into account (Mittler and Mittler, 1982). This has been referred to by Rich *et al.* (1979), among others, as the 'non-deficit' model of parent education.

This view of the great potential of parents has been put forward in the UK by Yule (1975) and Meighan (1981). In the USA, from the pioneering work of the Minnesota Parent Education Program which involved tens of thousands of parents from 1925 through 1932 (Davis and McGinnis, 1939), wider developments have stemmed, chronicled by such as Fine (1980) and Sherrets *et al.* (1980).

But surely parents who are themselves not well educated cannot possibly facilitate the educational development of their children? Don't working-class parents interact with their children in an authoritarian, unstimulating, closed way, using only 'restricted' language codes?

Parental Teaching Styles

Teachers always knew that lower-class children did poorly in school, so it came as no surprise when Davie *et al.* (1972) found in their longitudinal study of almost 16,000 children that the chances of an unskilled manual worker's child being a poor reader were six times greater than those of a professional worker's child, and the chances of the child's being a non-reader proportionally even greater. (Douglas (1964) had reported a similar finding several years earlier.)

Almost simultaneously, however, an American in Sweden was demonstrating that the home environment was more stimulating for pre-school children than a professionally run nursery environment (Cochran, 1973). As the 1970s progressed, the Newsons (Newson and Newson, 1977) accumulated evidence that both working- and middle-class parents were equally interested in their children's educational progress, even though the former were not so involved with the school. In 1975, Tizard reviewed evidence of high levels of stimulation in working-class families, and noted that 'much of the thinking about parent education seems both psychologically and sociologically simplistic'. Subsequently, Richards *et al.* (1977) demonstrated that parental involvement in child raising did not vary with social class, while social class I and II families were more likely to be socially isolated.

Work on non-directive and intrusive teaching styles of middle- and working-class English mothers by Phinney and Feshbach (1980) ushered in the well-known studies of Tizard *et al.* (1982) and Tizard and Hughes (1984). First, it was noted that the talk of nursery teachers contained a higher proportion of cognitive demands than the talk of either middle- or working-class mothers. But because there was much *more* adult–child talk at home, children received about twice as many cognitive demands per hour at home than they did at school, and this was true across social classes. Furthermore, much of the 'questioning' popular with nursery teachers was ineffective in eliciting spontaneous talk from children — largely because of its lack of naturalism and warmth. The 1984 work confirmed the view that even working-class homes were far richer sources of intellectual growth than nursery classes.

Meanwhile, work in the USA was slower to adapt its pessimistic view of the potential of parents of low socio-economic status (SES). In 1969, Bee *et al.* noted that low-SES mothers tended to be more directive and critical with their children than high-SES mothers, and this was confirmed by Brophy (1970). Schaefer reviewed pertinent research in 1972 and noted that the relationship between SES and stimulation was far from simple, and gender expectations, family process, and degree of emotional support appeared to be equally important factors. However, Zegiob and Forehand (1975) found low-SES mothers to be more directive and less verbal, and white mothers more co-operative than black, but no differential gender factor. The study of Carew *et al.* (1976) did not find SES or ethnicity to be critical variables, however. Sadler *et al.* (1976) noted that income level and parental educational level correlated positively with *some* outcome measures in parental education programmes, but so did both order and pre-treatment rates of compliance.

A detailed review by Clarke-Stewart (1978) covers some cross-cultural work, and it is noted that African infants pass developmental milestones earlier than American infants, while Mayan Indian child-rearing practices which appear severely to restrict exploratory experiences for their infants have no effect at all in delaying milestones. It is noted that the modal behaviour of parents and children is the same at different socio-economic levels, and heterogeneity within social classes is generally greater than that between them. There was evidence that low-SES parents stimulated their children *more* in infancy, but beyond this cultural patterns reversed and tended to favour the high-SES child. Clarke-Stewart notes that much of the research had confounded elements of the composite variable of SES, and many other complexities of interpretation of research findings are noted in this highly recommended paper. The conclusion is that 'children's performance may be related to demographic groupings like SES, [but] these variables alone do not predict children's behaviour as well as parents' actual behaviour does. A range of environments in different sociocultural contexts supports normal development'.

There is certainly a tension in the devising of a parent education programme between a curriculum which is specific and pragmatic without becoming highly technical and unrealistic, and one which is naturalistic and self-reinforcing without becoming loose and woolly. Recent research from the UK and USA seems to indicate that we cannot assume that a programme tending to one or the other approach will necessarily be more or less suitable for groups of a particular SES. The Clarke-Stewart review is not to be missed, and other substantial, wide-ranging reviews of the parent education field are available for those with a broad interest in the area.

Wide-span Reviews

A well-respected and much quoted review of parent intervention programmes for children with a very wide range of difficulties was provided by Levitt and Cohen (1975).

Up to the time of writing, substantial reviews of UK origin were hard to find, with the exception of that of Cave and Maddison (1978), although even here much of the research discussed is inevitably American. Far briefer is the review of Tavormina (1980), who, under the guise of addressing the 'behavioural vs. reflective counselling issue', drags in research on very diverse populations. No prizes for guessing which method wins, in Tavormina's view.

From New Zealand, Parker and Mitchell (1980) offered a commendably thorough review of methods and interventions for children with all kinds of difficulties, while Stanhope and Bell (1981) and Honig (1983) produced something much briefer, but nevertheless worthy, in the USA.

Writers of reviews tend eventually to give away an approach to the task which veers either to the pessimistic or the optimistic. The research on parent education can be readily criticised, but then so can any research, and the dissection and destruction of supposedly clear-cut empirical findings is a long-standing pastime for undergraduates with time on their hands and nothing more creative to do. On the other hand, evangelical fervour for the latest social panacea may do nothing but result in the futile spending of a great deal of taxpayers' money if project evaluation becomes suffused, as it frequently is, with a roseate glow of dissonance reduction and self-satisfaction. Some writers have, of course, criticised the parent education movement on grounds other than the academic — philosophical, moral, political, financial and legal arguments for and against are also very much in play.

Critiques of Parent Education

As early as 1973 Neifert and Gayton were suggesting a categorisation of families who were thought unlikely to be able to respond to home-based parent-education programmes. Included were families where (i) mother felt something was wrong with the child but father disagreed; (ii) a power struggle between mother and child existed; (iii) there were multiple problems; (iv) there was marital conflict; and (v) the family was 'large and disorderly'. This would seem to rule out a large proportion of families, and these views would be supported by few workers today.

Bacon (1976) discussed issues of parent power and professional control at some length, concluding that for many parents, involvement in school merely 'gives an illusion of local participation in the decision-making process'. Perhaps professionals merely become more adept and subtle at manipulating children by manipulating their parents. Schlossman (1978) also addressed this topic, referring to 'the politics of child psychology'. Harmon and Zigler (1980) offer a critique of the Schlossman analysis, clearly feeling that he was tilting at windmills, and worried that the parent education 'issue' would become 'needlessly polarized'.

From a UK perspective, Raven (1980) argues (dialectically) that parent education intervention programmes 'should, at least in some ways, be construed as unjustified interference in the lives of those concerned, ... bringing in its train serious disbenefits'. An article in *Early Childhood* (1981) recorded observations that for some families a home-based programme like Portage is 'far from ideal' — in fact, unworkable and likely therefore to make the mother anxious and guilty. Varying services were necessary to help families with varying needs — an unexceptional conclusion.

In similar vein, Turnbull and Turnbull (1982) argue that programmes and services are often based more on what some advocates and policy-makers think parents ought to be and do than on *parental* preferences for participation. The principle of 'individualised involvement' wherein parents determine the extent of their involvement at different developmental and life stages is advanced. Such a concept clearly implies choice from a continuum of services with varying levels of parent involvement, and few localities — even in the USA — are likely to be able to offer this.

Public agencies must make decisions about the allocation of scarce resources, and parents never will be offered an ideal range of choice. For the sake of parents and children serviced by the programmes that do exist, and for the sake of those whose taxes go to pay for such programmes, it is essential that policy decisions in public agencies about programme implementation should be informed by evidence on programme effectiveness.

What follows is largely an attempt to make such evaluative information more readily available. There is no suggestion whatsoever here that public agencies should take *only* cost-effectiveness evidence into account when making policy decisions, since local cultural and historical factors, ethical considerations and political influences will all, rightly, affect the final outcome. All that is being suggested is that evaluation research should form a larger part of policy deliberation than is currently often the case. Given the existence of this easily accessible review, there is no excuse for ignorance. Some consideration of evaluation methodology and the conducting of the literature search on which this review is based will lead out of this Introduction and into the main body of the assembled evidence.

Evaluation Methods

Schrank (1978) wrote: 'if a program doesn't work, expand it. The bigger it gets, the less notice anyone will take that it isn't working'. It is to counter this tendency that this review has been conducted. Early studies of the effectiveness of training parents as educators tended to rely over-much on self-reports of consumer satisfaction, indications of change in parental attitude, and measures of increased parental knowledge. All of these are fraught with problems. Very few parents say they are dissatisfied with a service for their children, especially if it is free, and especially if asked by someone associated with the programme. Parents may show increased knowledge on a paper-and-pencil test, but that does not mean that the knowledge is maintained at a conscious level during ordinary everyday life, let alone put into practice. The concept of 'attitude' is of similar status to that of 'personality': both imply a consistency in human beings which is rarely demonstrable from one social context to the next, and both suffer grave problems of mensuration. Neither has been demonstrated to correlate well with behaviour. A review by Wicker (1969) found 'little evidence to support the postulated existence of stable, underlying attitudes within the individual which influence actions'.

Subsequent research addressed itself to the reliability and validity of more tangible measures (e.g. Shipman, 1979). Gray and Wandersman (1980) reviewed the methodology of home-based intervention programmes, and concluded that the traditional experimental design was too restrictive, and more longitudinal, interactive research was necessary. The Joint Committee on

Standards for Educational Evaluation (1981) produced a useful checklist of standards for the evaluation of educational projects, which incorporated a range of scientific and value criteria. A series of articles in *Studies in Educational Evaluation* in 1983 addressed problems of research methodology in this field (Powell, 1983; Grotberg and Deloria, 1983). Sponseller and Fink (1983) note the numerous criticisms of traditional procedures, but the alternatives proposed look no more enticing or reliable. The differentiation between process (formative) and product (summative) evaluation is debated *ad nauseam*. Grotberg and Deloria (1983) identify eight components of an evaluation model.

In what follows, product evaluation (i.e. the demonstration of improvements in child well-being) will be considered the most important, with process data being significant only in so far as they are needed to demonstrate beyond doubt that programme products are indisputably the result of programme interventions. While there will be some interest in parent satisfaction, attitudes and knowledge, there will be greater interest in demonstrable changes in parental behaviour, indicated by self-report, self-recording, observation of parents in various settings and other means. There will be even greater interest in demonstrable changes in child behaviour, as evidenced by self-report, self-recording, direct observation, and criterion- and norm-referenced test results relating to pre–post, normative, baseline or control comparisons. The greatest interest of all will be reserved for evidence of generalisation and maintenance of child gains.

The literature search on which this review is based was not without bias and flaws. At the end of 1983, a computer-assisted search of British Education Index, Exceptional Child Education Resources and Educational Resources Information Centre was run, seeking evaluations of the effectiveness of various methods of training parents in techniques of teaching and managing their children at home. In the reference lists, E.R.I.C. (E.D. prefix) and E.C.E.R. (E.C. prefix) retrieval numbers are given. The computer print-out was then supplemented with items retrieved manually and informally. Thus two sources of bias were introduced. First, areas of parent education best known to the writer were inevitably more likely to be easily and fruitfully informally searched, and this may have introduced a bias in favour of the areas of behaviour difficulties and learning difficulties. Second, it took two years to assemble all the material, read, analyse and distil it into the current review. Given that many items are not lodged in computerised search data files immediately they are written, there is thus a sense in which some of this review is already out of date. Furthermore, there is no guarantee that the parameters of the computer search were perfectly specified, or indeed that perfect specification is possible, so many items of relevance may well have been overlooked, although extensive cross-referencing was undertaken in the attempt to eliminate this problem. Some of the items indicated as relevant by the literature search proved unavailable in the UK, although such items were relatively few. Further error may of course have been introduced by the writer simply failing to understand certain texts! Generally, Faber's Law should be assumed to apply, and *caveat emptor* (Faber's Law states that 'the number of errors in any piece of writing is directly proportional to the amount of reliance on secondary sources' — Faber, 1980).

To have produced a review along the lines advocated by Cooper (1984) would have been magnificent, but beyond current resources. Cooper notes that the greater probability of publication for studies which (a) show statistically significant results, (b) are in favour of the programme, and (c) confirm the existing findings or support conventional wisdom, introduces a marked bias tending to exaggerate programme effects. On the other hand, non-significant research is more likely to be the product of students undertaking theses or dissertations, which may reflect incompetence or lack of resources. Cooper's recommendations to tabulate all data with a view to undertaking some sort of conglomerate meta-analysis which pools the significance of small-n studies was rendered impractical by the sheer volume of studies and their prodigious heterogeneity. Instead, a more naturalistic, but nevertheless hopefully methodical, approach has been adopted. This may, of course, have the effect of rendering the review more readable.

At the end of it all, one may be reminded of Dr Johnson's dictum — it may not be done well, but it is remarkable that it should be done at all.

References

Abidin, R.R. (ed.) (1980) *Parent Education and Intervention Handbook* (Springfield, Illinois: Charles C. Thomas)
Arnold, E.L. (ed.) (1978) *Helping Parents Help Their Children* New York: Brunner/Mazel)

Bacon, A.A. (1976) Parent Power and Professional Control — A Case Study in the Engineering of Client Consent, *Sociological Review, 24*, 577-97

Ballard, R. (1975) Special Parents, Special Relations, *Special Education: Forward Trends, 2, 3,* 10-12

Bayliss, S. (1985) Juniors Improve with Homework, *Times Educational Supplement,* 10 May

Becker, H.J. and Epstein, J.L. (1981) *Parent Involvement: Teacher Practices and Judgements* (Baltimore, Maryland: The Johns Hopkins University) (E.R.I.C. ED 206601 SP 018839)

Bee, H.L. *et al.* (1969) Social Class Differences in Maternal Teaching Strategies and Speech Patterns, *Developmental Psychology, 1, 6,* 726-34

Berger, E.H. (1981) *Parents as Partners in Education: The School and Home Working Together* (St Louis, Missouri: C.V. Mosby)

Blackstone, T. (1979) 'Parental Involvement in Education', *Educational Policy Bulletin, 7, 1,* 81-98

Brim, O.G. (1965) *Education for Child Rearing* (New York: Free Press)

Brophy, J.E. (1970) 'Mothers as Teachers of Their Own Preschool Children: The Influence of Socioeconomic Status and Task Structure on Teaching Specificity, *Child Development, 41,* 79-94

Carew, I.V. *et al.* (1976) *Observing Intelligence in Young Children* (Englewood Cliffs, New Jersey: Prentice-Hall)

Carnine, L.M. (1979) 'Parent Involvement in Education: The Follow Through Experience', paper presented at annual meeting of the American Educational Research Association (San Francisco, California) (E.R.I.C. ED 171379 PS 010557)

Caudrey, A. (1985) Volunteer Army Steps Into the Firing Line', *Times Educational Supplement,* 12 April

Cave, C. and Maddison, P. (1978) *A Survey of Recent Research in Special Education* (Windsor: National Foundation for Educational Research)

Clarke-Stewart, K.A. (1978) 'Evaluating Parental Effects on Child Development', in L.S. Schulman (ed.) *Review of Research in Education* (Itaca, Illinois: F.E. Peacock)

Cochran, M.M. (1973) 'A Comparison of Nursery and Non-nursery Child-rearing Patterns in Sweden', doctoral dissertation, University of Michigan

Cooper, H.M. (1984) *The Integrative Research Review: A Systematic Approach* (Beverly Hills, California: Sage)

Croake, J.W. and Glover, K.E. (1977) 'A History and Evaluation of Parent Education', *The Family Coordinator,* pp. 151-8

Davie, R. *et al.* (1972) *From Birth to Seven: A Report of the National Child Development Study* (London: Longman)

Davis, E.A. and McGinnis, E. (1939) *Parent Education: A Survey of the Minnesota Program* (Minneapolis, Minnesota: University of Minnesota Press)

Douglas, J.W. (1964) *The Home and the School: A Study of Ability and Attainment in the Primary School* (London: MacGibbon & Kee)

Early Childhood (1981) Parents as Partners — Are We Sometimes Asking Too Much?, *Early Childhood, 2, 1,* 15-16

Faber, H. (1980) *The Book of Laws* (London: Sphere Books)

Fine, M.J. (ed.) (1980) *Handbook on Parent Education* (New York: Academic Press)

Gray, S.W. and Wandersman, L.P. (1980) 'The Methodology of Home-based Intervention Studies: Problems and Promising Strategies', *Child Development, 51,* 993-1009

Grotberg, E.H. and Deloria, D.J. (1983) 'Changing Strategies in Evaluations of Parent Programs', *Studies in Educational Evaluation, 8,* 281-9

Harmon, C. and Zigler, E. (1980) 'Parent Education in the 1970s: Policy, Panacea or Pragmatism', *Merrill-Palmer Quarterly, 26*, 4, 439-51

Heafford, M. (1984) 'The Growing Voice of Parent Power', *Times Educational Supplement*, 31 August

Honig, A.S. (1983) 'Evaluation of Infant/Toddler Intervention Programs', *Studies in Educational Evaluation, 8*, 305-16

Joint Committee on Standards for Educational Evaluation (1981) *Standards for Evaluations of Educational Programs, Projects and Materials* (New York: McGraw-Hill)

Kasouf, D. (1984) 'Teachers Happy with Their Work but Hold Poor Opinion of Parents', *Times Educational Supplement*, 12 October

Lamb, J. and Lamb, W.A. (1975) *Parent Education and Elementary Counseling* (Ann Arbor, Michigan: ERIC Clearinghouse on Counselling; also by Human Sciences Press, New York, 1978)

Levitt, E. and Cohen, S. (1975) 'An Analysis of Selected Parent-intervention Programs for Handicapped and Disadvantaged Children', *Journal of Special Education, 9*, 4, 345-65

Lillie, D.L. and Trohanis, P.L. (eds.) (1976) *Teaching Parents to Teach* (New York: Walker)

Magnus, R.A. (1984) 'Parental Involvement in Residential Treatment Programs', *Children Today, 3*, 25-7

Meighan, R. (1981) 'A New Teaching Force? Some Issues Raised by Seeing Parents as Educators and the Implications for Teacher Education, *Educational Review, 33*, 2, 133-42

Mittler, P. and Mittler, H. (1982) *Partnerships with Parents* (Stratford-upon-Avon: National Council for Special Education)

Morrison, G.S. (1978) *Parent Involvement in the Home, School and Community* (Columbus, Ohio: Charles E. Merrill)

Mortimore, J. and Mortimore, P. (1984) 'Parents and School', *Education*, 5 October

Neifert, J.T. and Gayton, W.F. (1973) 'Parents and the Home Program Approach in the Remediation of Learning Disabilities', *Journal of Learning Disabilities, 2*, 2, 85-9

Newson, J. and Newson, E. (1977) *Perspectives on School at Seven Years Old* (London: Allen & Unwin)

Parker, M. and Mitchell, D. (1980) *Parents as Teachers of Their Handicapped Children: A Review* (Hamilton, New Zealand: Waikato University) (E.R.I.C. ED 201125 EC 132551)

Parker, S. (1985) 'Preparing for Parents', *Times Educational Supplement*, 25 January

Phinney, J.S. and Feshbach, N.D. (1980) 'Non-directive and Intrusive Teaching Styles of Middle- and Working-class English Mothers', *British Journal of Educational Psychology, 50*, 1, 2-9

Powell, D.R. (1983) 'Evaluating Parent Education Programs: Problems and Prospects', *Studies in Educational Evaluation, 8*, 253-9

Pugh, G. (1981) *Parents as Partners* (London: National Children's Bureau)

Pugh, G. and De'Ath, E. (1984) *The Needs of Parents: Practice and Policy in Parent Education* (London: Macmillan, for National Children's Bureau)

Raven, J. (1980) 'Intervention as Interference' *Scottish Educational Review, 12*, 2, 120-30

Rich, D. *et al.* (1979) 'Building on Family Strengths: The "Nondeficit" Involvement Model for Teaming Home and School', *Educational Leadership, 36*, 7, 506-10

Richards, M. *et al.* (1977) 'Caretaking in the First Year of Life: The Role of Fathers, and Mothers' Social Isolation', *Child Care Health and Development, 3*, 23-36

Rowan, P. (1985) 'Building Pressure for Parents' Voice', *Times Educational*

Supplement, 17 May

Sadler, O.W. *et al.* (1976) 'An Evaluation of "Groups for Parents": A Standardised Format Encompassing Both Behavior Modification and Humanistic Methods', *Journal of Community Psychology, 4,* 157-63

Schaefer, E.S. (1972) Parents as Educators: Evidence from Cross-sectional, Longitudinal and Intervention Research', *Young Children, 27,* 227-39

Schlossman, S.L. (1978) 'The Parent Education Game: The Politics of Child Psychology in the 1970s', *Teachers College Record, 79,* 788-809

Schrank, R. (1978) *Ten Thousand Working Days* (Massachusets MIT Press)

Sherrets, S.D. *et al.* (1980) 'Parent Education Studies: Introduction to an Overview of Parent Education', *Journal of Clinical Child Psychology, 9, 1,* 35-51

Shipman, V. (1979) *Maintaining and Enhancing Early Intervention Gains* (Princeton, New Jersey: Educational Testing Service)

Sponseller, D.B. and Fink, J. (1983) 'Early Childhood Evaluation: What? Who? Why?', *Studies in Educational Evaluation, 8,* 209-14

Stanhope, L. and Bell R.Q. (1981) 'Parents and Families', in J.M. Kauffman and D.P. Hallahan (eds.), *Handbook of Special Education* (Englewood Cliffs, New Jersey: Prentice-Hall)

Stone, J. and Taylor, F. (1976) 'Parent Power in America' *Where, 123,* 315-8

Tavormina, J.B. (1980) 'Evaluation and Comparative Studies of Parent Education', in R.R. Abidin (ed.), *Parent Education and Intervention Handbook* (Springfield, Illinois: Charles C. Thomas)

Tizard, B. (1975) *Early Childhood Education* (Windsor: National Foundation for Educational Research)

Tizard, B. and Hughes, M. (1984) *Young Children Learning* (London: Fontana)

Tizard, B. *et al.* (1982) 'Adults' Cognitive Demands at Home and at Nursery School', *Journal of Child Psychology and Psychiatry, 23, 2,* 105-16

Turnbull, A.P. and Turnbull, H.R. (1982) 'Parent Involvement in the Education of Handicapped Children: A Critique', *Mental Retardation, 20, 3,* 115-22

Wicker, A.W. (1969) 'Attitudes versus Actions: The Relationship of Verbal and Overt Behavioral Responses to Attitude Objects', *Journal of Social Issues, 25, 4,* 41-78

Wilton, V.M.E. (1975) 'A Mother Helper Scheme in the Infant School', *Educational Research, 18, 1,* 3-15

Wolfendale, S. (1983) *Parental Participation in Children's Development and Education* (New York: Gordon & Breach)

Wolfendale, S. (1986) 'Ways of Increasing Parental Involvement in Children's Development and Education', in J. Harris (ed.) *Child Psychology in Action: Linking Research and Practice* (London: Croom Helm)

Young, M. and McGeeney, P. (1968) *Learning Begins at Home* (London: Routledge & Kegan Paul)

Yule, W. (1975) 'Teaching Psychological Principles to Non-psychologists: Training Parents in Child Management', *Journal of the Association of Educational Psychologists, 3, 10,* 5-16

Zegiob, L.E. and Forehand, R. (1975) 'Maternal Interactive Behavior as a Function of Race, Socioeconomic Status, and Sex of the Child', *Child Development, 46,* 564-8

2   PARENTAL INVOLVEMENT IN SCHOOL

Encouraging parents to participate, usually in a minor way, in activities which are essentially school-based is a far cry from a structured programme of parent training which is skill-oriented and home-based, and designed to raise the attainments of children. Although these are arguably the extremes of a 'continuum' of parental 'involvement', the latter is considerably more recent in origin than the former.

The roots of parental *involvement in schools* can be traced back to the early nineteenth century (Adult Learning Potential Institute (hereafter ALPI), 1980) in the USA, albeit somewhat tenuously. By the first decade of the twentieth century, relevant initiatives begin to be documented with some certainty. This development seems to have withstood social pressures resulting from a state of flux in the child-rearing practices advocated by the 'experts'. Shifts in the ethnic and class composition of Western societies have added to the acceleration in the rate of change, as have movements in family composition, such as increased incidence of stepparenthood.

One of the earliest pieces of tangible research in the UK was the survey conducted by Wall (1947), who analysed the views of 262 headteachers on the subject of parent–teacher co-operation (66 per cent response rate). Little difference in *opinions* regarding the value of such co-operation was evident with respect to age of children concerned, about 85 per cent of respondents reacting favourably. The main benefits were seen to be: (i) leading the parents to take a greater interest in the school, (ii) helping the teacher to understand the child, and (iii) encouraging the child in his lessons.

The main drawback of such co-operation was that it might lead to criticism of the teacher in the home. The vast majority of parent–teacher meetings were general gatherings incidental to school life (sports, displays, etc.) or individual meetings between parents and teachers. Other types of contact had many fewer proposers and as many or more antagonists. Wall concluded that despite the expression of vaguely positive attitudes, it was hardly surprising that 'in many schools, co-operation exists only where the

15

need for it arises *on both sides'* (my italics). A repeat of this survey, in the same area and using the same methodology but 40 years on, would be a fascinating undertaking. Would the results be very different?

A major event in the UK history of parental involvement in school was the publication of the Plowden Report (Central Advisory Council for Education (hereafter CACE), 1967). Datagathering included interviewing 3,000 parents in their own homes about their attitudes towards their children's education, and their relationships with the teachers involved. The report concluded that there was certainly an association between parental encouragement and children's educational performance, but it was difficult to extricate the direction of causality. Positive recommendations about action to promote partnership between home and school were made, which served to create a wider acceptance of the principle of parental involvement.

A useful brief review of postwar historical developments in the UK is provided by Sharrock (1980). Coupled with accumulating evidence that parental encouragement was a causative factor in children's learning of more profound significance than IQ, socioeconomic status or school variables, was the growth of organisations committed to parental involvement in school: the Home and School Council, the Advisory Centre for Education, the National Confederation of Parent–Teacher Associations, and the Confederation for the Advancement of State Education. In 1977 strong recommendations about the involvement of parents in the governance of schools were made in the Taylor Report (Taylor, 1977), proposing that half of the governing body be composed of parents of children in the school (elected by the parents) and other representatives of the local community. Children themselves were also to participate where legally possible, and training should be provided for parent governors. How much of this was implemented is another story altogether.

In the USA, similar developments came within a similar timespan. Nursery schools had often worked co-operatively with parents, and early intervention programmes for disadvantaged children came to recognise the need. Thus Project Head Start included objectives and performance standards for parent involvement in its policy manual, and the Home Start Program took this several stages further.

In 1974, Public Law 93-380 arrived on the statute book, requiring that advisory councils be initiated for school districts and individual schools served by federally assisted programmes. Membership of the council was to include a majority of parents of children receiving the services in question. A year later, the Education for All Handicapped Children Act (Public Law 94-142) was even more specific regarding the involvement of parents, at the policy level for handicapped children in general and at the individual level for the parents of particular handicapped children.

The latter aspect of this legislation was echoed in the UK in 1981 by an Education Act concerning children with special needs. A year previously, another Act had given parents statutory rights in choosing a school for their children. Needless to say, not all of this legislation has worked well in practice, and some of the intended effects have not materialised.

Nevertheless, some slow and uneven progress has been made. The catchphrase of 'parental involvement' has become less fashionable, which may reflect the absorption of the idea into the body educative or its slow death. That the former outcome is the more probable is reflected by the advent of a new and more ambitious catchphrase: 'parents as partners'.

Mittler and Mittler (1982) provided an excellent pamphlet on this theme, which is a model of sensibility and clarity. The role of fathers and siblings is reviewed, and issues regarding unsupported and surrogate parents considered. 'Partnership' can be very difficult to establish with ethnic minority parents where a language barrier intervenes, but Tomlinson (1980) notes that many of the stereotypes held by the teaching profession of attitudes to education by various ethnic groups are not supported by the facts. This valuable study, a major contribution to an under-researched area, shows that ethnic minority parents are quite as eager to help in their children's education as indigenous parents, but their own educational experiences have tended to leave them with confused expectations of the educational system in their adoptive country and even more dependent on the schools taking the initiative in encouraging involvement, quite irrespective of language problems.

Although the tide of parental involvement is flowing forward in general, the shoreline is not without its Canutes. Caudrey (1985) reports on political rumblings about parental involvement in classrooms:

Some teachers believe the presence of parents in the classroom can be beneficial and may even enhance the status of the teacher. But others resent amateurs encroaching on their professional territory, as well as claiming the exercise gives local education authorities an excuse to keep down staffing levels ... [One union] branch has told its members to boycott volunteers in classrooms. This has already led to parents being barred from some schools.

Modes of Parental Involvement

A very wide range of possibilities for parental involvement activities exists. There are similarities and differences between countries, and it may be instructive to consider the UK, the rest of Europe, and the USA separately.

United Kingdom

With respect to special events or visits, parents have long been utilised as organisers, fund-raisers and audience. The effect of involvement in establishing social networks and relieving loneliness is emphasised by Laishley and Lindon (1980). At a basic level, information about the school of a detailed nature is increasingly available in written form pre-admittance. Written reports on children's progress when in school are not always provided, particularly with younger children, and when provided may be bland and largely meaningless. To what extent this is to cover a lack of professional clarity and to what extent to guard against misinterpretation and a reduction in face-to-face contact is debatable.

Open days and semi-formal meetings between class teacher (and sometimes headteacher) and individual parents have been a long-standing, if infrequent, feature of primary school life, which are now much more readily supplemented by a home visit from the concerned teacher. In schools with localised catchment areas this may prove little more time-consuming than school-based interviews, and is often considerably more productive — depending on the objectives of the exercise. Schools have often not been too clear about the specific aim and purpose of some of their by now ritualised 'parent involvement' activities.

Parents can prove a valuable educational resource in many ways. Many schools have 'parent helpers', but these may be delegated menial tasks and kept out of classrooms. (None the less, their very presence in the school can have a positive social effect.) In more ambitious and less insecure schools, parents are involved in educative child contact in and out of classrooms, including sometimes in relation to basic academic skills. Many parents have specialist skills, knowledge or experience which can be made available to children both in the classroom and outside it in the process of neighbourhood research. The provision of educational artefacts, supply of rich oral history, brief specialised instruction and the maintenance of widespread community display sites for children's work have all been effectively used.

As a *quid pro quo*, parents can be encouraged to use school facilities outside school hours for their own as well as school-related purposes. Some local authorities have extensively developed the concept of 'community schools', with a wide range of adult education classes, leisure activities, social events and discussion groups taking place in addition to child-focused work.

However, the involvement of parents in school policy-making has not shown such rapid development. One or two headteachers have systematically surveyed 'consumer' opinion, but such efforts are rare. Parental input to school policy has usually been routed through laid-down procedures for school governing bodies. These have often fallen far short of the Taylor recommendations, and have proved a mockery of democratic representation.

Group sessions for parents of an educative nature bearing on the school system or child development have likewise proved less than sweepingly popular with schools, and the situation described by Wall in 1947 still seems to pertain — schools will usually try to be helpful in individual discussions of problems with a particular child, but the sight of parents in groups tends to frighten them. In a situation of lack of clarity about what can be offered this is unsurprising, but, as we shall see in subsequent pages, such a lack is increasingly inexcusable.

Mittler and Mittler (1982) note that, particularly for children with difficulties, there is a need for parental involvement in the assessment and diagnosis of the child's skills, abilities and teaching requirements, and indeed this is now enshrined, albeit in bureaucratic obfuscation, in the 1981 Education Act. The implication is not that parental observations should be acquired and sifted by professionals, but that information-giving be mutual and mutually accountable. Thus parents should have access to school records and the facility for commenting on these. Some schools have review meetings involving parents or home–school notebooks to promote a better quality of parent–school interaction, but these tend to be special schools.

Gillett (1980) notes that home–school liaison teachers have been deployed in some areas, not always concentrating on the families of the youngest pupils. Such workers have sometimes established parents' rooms or centres within schools where falling numbers have freed physical space. Other schools have deployed the extra staffing to teach classes in rotation while the class teachers themselves undertake home visits. This well-written article is recommended reading, as is the useful one-page summary chart of parental involvement activities designed by Broome (1974). Any headteacher who can truthfully tick all the boxes in this chart will have just cause for self-satisfaction.

For those requiring more day-to-day detail to give a real 'feel' for it all, the book by Patrick McGeeney (1969) called *Parents are Welcome* is still the best source, although now perhaps rather dated.

Europe

Much of the scholarly English-language work is by Beattie, who noted in 1978 that there was:

> an obvious trend in Western European education since the end of the Second World War towards formal parental involvement in the management and control of schools. There must exist some sort of conviction, even if only among the elites which make decisions and administer them, that parents are worth taking trouble over.

Beattie (1978b) traces the development of parent groups back to the start of the century, but remarks that many were supportive of the status quo or even reactionary. He argues that even current developments could be seen as reflective of political necessity — in particular, 'the need experienced by western democracies to legitimise the status quo by defining certain areas within which "democratic participation" can occur'. Thus the hasty 'conversion' to parental involvement which occurred in France in the late 1960s is seen by Beattie as fundamentally associated with the events of 1968. Developments in West Germany are associated with pro-democratic and anti-Fascist sympathies following the Second

World War, compounded by student and other unrest in the late 1960s spawning a range of initiatives in the early 1970s.

By comparison, Beattie sees England as lagging well behind in this area, presumably implying the absence of the same degree of political urgency. The French system post-1968 for high schools involved parent representatives sitting on councils operating at class as well as school level. The school management council had, in principle, extensive powers over the school, including budgetary. Elected parents constituted one-sixth of the members, pupils another one-sixth (in high schools), one-third teaching staff and one-third local authority members and co-optees from the community. The class councils involved headteacher and relevant teacher(s), two parents and two pupils, and made proposals of candidates for the school council *and* decisions about promotion or retention of individual pupils in the 'grade' system. Parental involvement in other subsidiary bodies — the standing committee, discipline council and the students' society — was also delineated.

Little of this was new in principle. Secondary school management councils had been established in 1944 and parent representation specified in 1945. In 1968 there was a sudden urgency to implement the structure in practice in a publicly visible manner. Interestingly, contrary to British practice, arrangements for the governance of primary schools were ignored until 1969, and then promulgated as an option but not a requirement. Parent representation for all state schools did not become mandatory until 1975, when incorporated in an Education Act. Beattie (1978a) notes that meanwhile the Catholic schools had achieved a high degree of parent participation without being legally required to do so — in 1967 a full 96 per cent of church schools already had parent representation on management committees.

The considerably more complex situation in West Germany is described in more detail by Beattie (1979), differences between the eleven states or Länder often being more real than immediately apparent. Again, the analysis is preoccupied with statutory requirements and permissions in the context of a politicised process which is largely alien to the British experience.

No less political in tone is the account by Senf (1980) of co-operation between home and school in East Germany, which is remarkable for its high content of 'pedagogical propaganda'.

It seems that group parent meetings play some part in the system, occurring about three times a year and being designed to inform parents about curriculum structure and content, child development and how they can help at home. Parents are encouraged to support the educational process by participating in extra-curricular activities, including attendance at 'after-school' youth centres. Elected parents' committees, parent–teacher councils and class parent–teacher committees also exist.

Senf (1980) reports that 600,000 parents are serving as elected members of parents' committees of one sort or another, and another 40,000 at pre-school facilities. Thus one in every four families has a serving representative on a committee, an astonishing level of formalised participation. Senf notes disapprovingly that 'some parents show a tendency towards concentrating on attainments', and that some teachers fail to 'come up to expectations' by making regular and purposeful use of all forms of co-operation with parents, i.e. parents' meetings, home visits, consultation hours and the like. Specific courses and television programmes for parents are also utilised, but no details are given.

More recently, parent organisations in the ten countries of the European Community ('Common Market') formalised an agreement to co-operate on information and development (Wilce, 1983). It was agreed that parent involvement should at the very least include representation on school councils or governing bodies, but parents should ideally be represented at every level of national education systems. Greater emphasis on home–school partnership was needed in initial teacher training. Parent signatories agreed that the primary concern of involvement should be the education and development of children, rather than the traditional preoccupation with fund-raising and so forth.

United States of America

A interesting political analysis is offered by Taylor (1981) of developments in the USA. At the turn of the century corruption was rife in local government, caused by an 'excess of democracy' which dispersed and fragmented control of services among various groups and individuals. Subsequent legal reforms, the consolidation of school administration into larger districts, and the 'professionalisation' of teaching and administration all subsequently served to decrease lay influence on the educational process. Taylor feels that professional dominance has been slow to weaken its grip in the USA and that parental impact has been confined to protests on isolated issues, such as property tax and desegregation. Describing the situation in California, Taylor never-theless remarked on increasing dissatisfaction among both lay and professional groups, resulting in consideration of the development of school site councils.

Deitchmann *et al.* (1977), reviewing parental involvement in pre-school programmes, observe that the diversity and complexity of programmes can militate against effective parental involvement. They note that the existence of a structure for parent–teacher con-tact does not ensure that two-way communication occurs, and may serve to pacify parents into 'low-involvement' activities focused on their own children, while avoiding parental involvement in wider issues of policy — and decision-making — for all children.

More encouraging reports stem from specific programmes. For example, Project Partnership (Hauser-Cram *et al.*, 1981) was designed to promote parent–professional collaboration in the edu-cation of young 'special needs' children. Some 500 families of low socio-economic status were involved in projects based on various sites, including special needs and Head Start operations and pre-school facilities. Interesting features included the use of 'parent leaders' who liaised with other parents, earning a 'small stipend to defray babysitting and transport fees'. Facilities and activities developed included parent libraries, schemes for parents to act as 'co-teachers' in classrooms, provision for extra teaching time to free class teachers to meet with parents, joint parent–teacher workshops, and so on.

Evaluation research revealed a marked increase in parent–teacher contact in programme groups compared with control groups, associated with a change in the quality of contact, which was much more child-focused and much less administration-focused for the programme parents. Also, programme parents were much more likely to have face-to-face (rather than written or telephone) con-tact with teachers than were control group parents. This additional contact was linked with a marked increase in parents' carrying out educational activities with their children at home. Parents were found to be very eager for advice about home instruction.

A survey of 28 programmes in large cities incorporating parental involvement which catered for children aged 5–18 was conducted by Collins *et al.* (1982). The programmes included pro-vision for parents to act as monitors of homework and/or attendance, tutors in the home, or guides in the use of community educational resources. All of these are what Deitchmann *et al.*

(1977) would characterise as 'low-involvement' projects.

It would seem that parental involvement in the USA is largely restricted to special needs or other specific programmes, and that participation by parents at a policy-making level for individual neighbourhood schools is, in general, ill-developed. It is interesting that East Germany seems considerably more democratic in this respect.

However, the UK has no cause for complacency, lagging considerably behind some of its EEC partners regarding parental involvement in policy.

Incidence and Take-up

Some teachers, doubtful of the value of parental involvement, are frequently heard saying something like: 'Of course, *our* parents wouldn't be interested in/capable of anything like that'. A brief résumé of parental take-up in one primary school in an Educational Priority Area is offered by Fryer (1973), referring to the era immediately post-Plowden.

The more successful means of contacting parents are listed with their respective 'hit rates', thus: (i) parents see headteacher when entering child's name for school (100 per cent); (ii) parents welcomed to enter classrooms, especially at 9.00 a.m. (100 per cent); (iii) special individual interviews with headteacher (small number of children with 'problems'); (iv) parents' library in school where parents and children meet after school (25–50 per cent); (v) paperback sales scheme (10 per cent); (vi) fund-raising sales and fairs (almost 100 per cent); (vii) concerts in school with refreshments and conversation (50–100 per cent); (viii) parental help with school visits, self-help skills training, other menial tasks (10 per cent). Other strategies included frequent short letters from school to home, and home visits in emergencies or when invited. Many of these approaches are much more widespread now than they were in 1973, but the rate of take-up is encouraging. By current standards, also, they represent fairly low-key modes of involvement.

The classic large-scale study of parental involvement in the UK is owed to Cyster *et al.* (1979), who analysed questionnaire returns from 1,400 primary schools (83 per cent response rate). Only 35 per cent of the schools had a parent–teacher association and a further 26 per cent claimed some loose equivalent. However, this compared favourably with the Plowden finding (1967) of merely 17 per cent. Parents' evenings and open days were found in almost all schools, and half the schools claimed attendence of 75 per cent or over. Written information about the school was available to the parents of new children in 65 per cent of cases, while 92 per cent invited preparatory visits prior to admittal. In contrast, less than half the schools produced written reports, this being particularly rare with younger children. Home visits were undertaken by teachers in 22 per cent of schools, especially with respect to nursery children, but more schools preferred to rely on liaison agents.

The most frequent type of parental involvement was that of helping on school visits and outings (78 per cent), followed by sewing and minor repairs (65 per cent), providing transport (54 per cent), imparting specialist knowledge to children, usually of a vocational type (45 per cent), helping with craft, cooking, music, etc., under teacher supervision (36 per cent), helping in school library (29 per cent), hearing children read under supervision of teacher (26 per cent), helping with sports and school clubs (22 per cent), and helping dress children after swimming or physical education (20 per cent). Teacher opinion was (sometimes fiercely) divided on the question of whether parents should hear children read. In the light of evidence we shall consider later, this borders on the absurd.

Problems were associated with parental involvement, but rarely were these of the proportions that might have been expected. The major problems were the unavailability of parents who were working, and attracting parents who did not want or were otherwise unable to visit the school. Of the other problems feared by teachers (breaches of confidentiality, children showing off, complaints from the uninvolved, teachers barricading classrooms, parental unreliability or over-enthusiasm, favouritism of own children, criticism of teachers, etc.), none proved to present significant difficulties in more than one in ten cases. The majority of headteachers felt parental involvement had increased, and would increase further.

The study also found a strong correlation between socioeconomic status and degree of involvement. Cyster *et al.* (1979) note the danger that parental involvement can serve merely to 'add yet another string to the bow of middle-class educational advantage'. Some evidence that the physical layout of a school and the form of teaching organisation adopted can also affect levels of parental involvement is cited, although this does vary with the nature of the parental involvement activity in question. Large schools with poor staffing ratios were particularly likely to encourage parental involvement.

In the USA context, again the information tends to relate to specific, federally aided programmes rather than to the general routine in schools operated solely by the state boards, although some information on the very variable participation rates in the latter will be found in Collins *et al.* (1982). A series of seven volumes on parental involvement in federal programmes is available, of which volumes 3 (Robbins and Dingler, 1981) and 5 (Smith and Nerenberg, 1981) are of particular interest. In the first of these, in all twelve sites sampled a district-wide advisory committee had been established, as required by the 1973 legislation, but none of these actually made decisions. This lack 'was largely attributed to the project directors' failure to encourage parent leadership'. Few sites involved parents in the instructional process, as paraprofessionals, volunteers or tutors at home. However, there was some subjective evidence that where this did occur, parent interest increased, pupil performance improved, and teachers' instructional approaches tended to change.

A different picture is painted in the other volume (Smith and Nerenberg, 1981), which looked particularly at projects funded by the Follow Through Program, which of course incorporated much more structured and explicit expectations about parent involvement. In a survey of 16 sites, all had policy advisory committees, although all were structured differently from what was prescribed in the Follow Through regulations. Most of the committees made decisions about parent activities, but few participated significantly in decisions about student services, budget or personnel. Parents were widely used as classroom aides, and most sites worked to involve parents in teaching their children at home. Utilising parents as volunteers was rare, but where it occurred, the parents enjoyed a 'substantial' role. Parents had a major role in determining the content of parent education activities. Again, subjective evidence that parental involvement 'materially affected the quality of education' is presented.

Surveys of incidence and subjective impressions of impact are interesting, but inadequate to justify further developments in the area. Some substantial empirical research on the effectiveness of parental involvement has been conducted, mostly in relation to nursery and primary (kindergarten and elementary) schools, and this will be reviewed under these two headings (see pp. 27-33). There is little substantial evaluation work on parental involvement in secondary (high) schools, and this will be discussed in a subsequent section (pp. 33-35).

Evaluative Research: Nursery Schools

A controlled study in an Educational Priority Area was reported by Rathbone (1977), who involved the parents of 15 nursery children in attending the nursery for one afternoon per week to participate in all aspects of the teaching work. The parents were also given specific tuition in developing children's language and supplied weekly with books and language-development kits. Tuition was individual, by modelling, verbal and written information and discussion. Assessment of language development utilised the individually administered English Picture Vocabulary Test and Sentence Comprehension Test, carried out by someone familiar to the children. The scores of both experimental and control groups rose during the ten-week programme, but experimentals' scores rose markedly and significantly more than control group scores. The teachers were surprised by the responsiveness and good attendance of the low-SES parents.

A more impressionistic but larger-scale process study is offered by Smith (1980). Fifteen playgroups and/or nursery classes were observed in detail, utilising a fairly general but highly pertinent coding system. The nursery schools were more likely than the playgroups to have relaxed beginnings and ends to sessions, and to welcome parents with problems. The playgroups were more likely than the nurseries to have large numbers of parents present with more interaction occurring between them. The nursery schools, as distinct from the nursery classes in ordinary schools and the playgroups, were more likely to have parents clearing up than working with children. Observation showed staff in playgroups to be more directive about parent activities, although the self-perceptions of the staff were quite different. To some extent, practice varied according to the experience of the parent in working in the setting in question. It was evident that the more open and least hierarchical groups involved parents more fully.

Athey (1981) noted that although much verbal interaction

occurred between adults and children in nurseries, the quality was often poor, not constituting true dialogue and often being pre-occupied with maintenance routines. An 'illuminative' study is described of 20 families of low SES attending an experimental nursery for three hours a day for two years, compared with another group whose children attended a nearby fee-paying nursery. The experimental group included four Asian families, one West Indian, one African, two Armenian and one gypsy family.

The experimental parents attended the nursery minimally twice per week, and some attended all the time. All fathers except one came at least sometimes, and several other relatives visited. Home visits were made, and at the nursery the parents were drawn into a continuous dialogue about their children's learning behaviour and its significance. Parental interest was sustained, if not increased, during the two years, but they did know of the special nature of the project. Observation and coding of parental behaviour showed that they moved from copying teacher behaviour in the early days to increased self-initiated work with the child based on the content of current activities, and furthermore also to work with the child developing abstract concepts (or 'schemata', in Piagetian terms).

Gains on objective tests were also striking. At the end of the project the group members were 20 IQ points ahead of their older siblings, who were also tested. The project children were six months ahead of their chronological age in reading accuracy and three months ahead in reading comprehension (Neale Analysis). By comparison, the older siblings were 14 months *behind* in reading accuracy and comprehension. The control group, of much higher SES, made no significant gains except on the English Picture Vocabulary Test. The experimental group gains were maintained over two years after entry to the primary school.

These results are clearly exciting. It is unfortunate that it is not possible to partial out the parental-involvement effect from the direct teaching undertaken by professionals in the nursery. Also, while the effectiveness of the undertaking is not in doubt, there must be some question concerning issues of replicability and cost-effectiveness.

A project involving the parents of 25 nursery children in a low-SES area is described by Swinson (1985). The nursery had no previous experience of parental involvement beyond fund-raising. The project aimed to promote parental reading of stories to children at home. Training was by verbal and written instruction, video modelling, provision of materials and very simple self-recording. The project ran for two and a half terms. Assessment was via the English Picture Vocabulary Test and the Verbal Comprehension and Naming Vocabulary Scales from the British Ability Scales. The experimental group made significant gains on all measures during the project, while the control group scores remained unchanged. After each child had left the nursery class and had been in infant school for one and a half terms, a follow-up criterion-referenced assessment of 'academic' skills was carried out. No significant differences were found between experimental and control groups on maths and writing tests, but there were differences favouring the experimental group on two reading tests, one of which reached statistical significance.

Evaluative research from the USA is equally encouraging. Irvine *et al.* (1979) report on a parent involvement scheme attached to a pre-kindergarten programme, which incorporated school visits, group meetings, home visits and ancillary contact (e.g. by telephone). Assessment was undertaken of general reasoning (Walker Readiness Test), school-related knowledge (Cooperative Preschool Inventory) and receptive vocabulary (Peabody Picture Test). Results showed that parental involvement had a positive effect on all three measures, which was independent of the child's age, mother's educational background or family's financial status.

Herman and Yeh (1980) likewise demonstrated that the extent of parental interest and involvement in school activities was positively related to pupil achievement. Parents who felt involved in decision-making and able to relate to their child's teacher experienced greater satisfaction with the school — as might be predicted by simple dissonance.

A pre-school programme involving parents in classroom observation, teaching, and group discussions with other parents is described by Benas (1980). The training 'curriculum' included child development and behaviour. Parents from a variety of socioeconomic backgrounds participated, responded positively and subsequently were eager to enrol siblings. Cost-effectiveness is claimed for the project, but supportive data are insubstantial.

A specialised project is reported by Claus and Quimper (1980), aimed at disseminating a traffic safety curriculum among pre-primary children by teachers and parents working together. A multitude of teacher and parent materials were developed and field tested. Teacher, headteacher and parent questionnaires were used to evaluate the level of use of the materials, the effectiveness of the associated in-service programmes, and teacher and parent perceptions of the post-programme behaviour of the participating children. The ratings indicated that project pupils outperformed control pupils in naturalistic compliance to four safety rules — but not on the remaining nine rules. The parental ratings tended to be more optimistic than teacher ratings, but this may have reflected superior knowledge of the children. The reliability of these kind of data is open to question in any event, of course.

Evaluative Research: Primary Schools

An interesting early study in the UK is that of Wood (1974), who established a variety of home–school activities, on an action-research basis, focusing on four 'levels' of parental involvement in the curriculum, viz. observational, instructional, practical, formal. A home–school liaison teacher was deployed in a catalytic role. While the study has inspirational qualities, the outcomes are presented descriptively, and subsequent replication with more tangible outcome measures has not been reported.

By 1976, Terry had documented the impact of bringing into school parent volunteers to 'hear children read'. Reading tests showed an overall increase in reading standards since this practice was implemented, but Terry had not been able to control for the possible influence of other variables.

A well-structured investigation is reported by Rathbone and Graham (1981), who assigned 45 low-SES children to three groups of 15. The experimental group experienced a specific language programme implemented by volunteer parents, the placebo group involved as much parent contact but with simple number work substituted for the language programme, while the control group had no special parental contact but was exposed to the same language programme as part of the normal school curriculum.

A number of parents already had a track record of a half-day's involvement per week in the nursery department of the school, as reported in Rathbone (1977), and ten of these parents were delegated to work with three experimental or three placebo children for three half-hour sessions per week over one term. The language programme was derived from the Breakthrough to Literacy Scheme and incorporated some reading, spelling and writing.

Pre- and post-testing was carried out using the National Foundation for Educational Research's Maths Test A (oral), the English Picture Vocabulary Test (EPVT), and Daniels and Diack's Graded Spelling Test and Reading Test 1. No differences were found on the spelling test. The placebo group scored higher than the others on the maths test, but this difference did not reach statistical significance. The experimental group did better than the others on the reading test and EPVT, reaching statistical significance except for the EPVT comparison with the placebo group.

Rathbone and Graham (1981) reasonably conclude that this kind of input from parent volunteers has curriculum-specific effects over and above any gains accruing from 'extra attention'. The parents involved had much less experience of operating maths programmes than language programmes.

A much wider-ranging programme in Coventry is reported by Widlake and McLeod (1985). For some years a multi-ethnic disadvantaged sector of this local authority has been the target of a community education project designed to involve parents in many ways in the education of their children. Home–school–community links were developed via educational services for parents, children and teachers. A range of pre-school facilities, adult education provision, social events, clubs, parents' rooms and family gatherings, workshops for the joint production of curriculum materials, special packs of resource materials, training courses for parent leaders, a range of schemes and materials for parental involvement in children's reading and language, holiday play schemes, home tutoring for Asian parents and various other initiatives were promulgated.

Eight schools were selected as examples of good practice in the field of parental involvement, and assessment carried out on samples of infant and junior age pupils using the Hunter-Grundin Literacy Profiles, scrutinising attitudes to reading, reading skills, spelling, language and writing. Results generally were considerably higher than normative data indicated could be expected in an area of this kind; in fact, on reading skills the overall means were at least equal and sometimes superior to those of 'middle-class' schools.

While it is claimed that the amount of parental involvement in a school bore a linear relationship (unspecified) to the reading scores, this study has not partialled out the effect of parental involvement from other variables, and the sample of schools was deliberately biased. There are also doubts about the objectivity of some sub-scales of the measure utilised, and information on inter-tester reliability would have been invaluable. However, the generalised results can only be construed as most encouraging.

More detailed evidence on the impact of parental involvement comes from the USA. Gillum *et al.* (1977) tested the reading progress of children aged 7–11 years who were part of a reading programme that entailed performance contracting and a variety of forms of parental involvement. Pupil achievement was greater than predicted by norms on the Stanford and Metropolitan Achievement Tests, and positively related to the degree of parental involvement. Where parents had been integrally involved in deciding curriculum content and had worked closely with teachers and children, achievement was higher than where the parental input had been restricted to attending group meetings or completing forms.

A city-wide parental involvement in curriculum programme is described by Irwin (1979), wherein 'home curriculum specialists and assistants' are deployed. Results from testing pupils at 10 years of age and 13 years of age indicate a continuous steady improvement in reading standards in the city. Yet again, there is unfortunately no partialling out of the effect of the parental-involvement component.

Equally vague are the data cited by Figgures (1980) from the Primary Skills Project for children aged between 4 and 8. Two instructional frameworks were deployed in 17 schools, a behaviour analysis model and a Bank Street model. Parents received a 'stipend' for participation in the classroom. Evaluation was by analysis of rather loose data gathered in the city's standard monitoring procedures, showing that both models yielded higher than expected scores in mathematics, but not in reading. The proportionate contribution of the parental involvement is unclear.

A much smaller-scale exercise is reported by Raim (1980). A reading 'club' for parents at an inner-city elementary school focused on helping the parents produce materials for teaching reading to use with their own children. The children certainly enjoyed the involvement, and the parents felt their own skills had increased, but tangible improvements in children's reading skills were not demonstrated. In another area, merely increasing the amount of generalised parent–teacher contact was found to raise the reading achievement of under-achieving elementary school children (Iverson *et al.*, 1981). However, with older children (12–13 years old), increasing such contact was associated with *decreased* achievement.

Fantini, in Sinclair (1980), reviews evidence on the effects on academic achievement of different kinds of parental involvement in school. He concludes that parental involvement in instruction has been shown to improve pupil achievement, while involvement in school governance enhances pupil self-image.

Another review is provided by Henderson (1981), who analyses 37 research reports on the effect of parental involvement on pupil achievement in the USA. Much of this 'evidence' is of rather poor quality. Henderson concludes that parental involvement in school activities can be as effective as training parents to carry out educational activities at home, provided the parental involvement is comprehensive and well structured and integrates home and school experiences.

Parental Involvement in High Schools

There is very little satisfactory evaluative research in this area, where, arguably, it is most needed. The Collins *et al.* (1982) survey describes some US programmes involving high schools, but evaluation data are very weak, usually being confined to descriptive statistics and grateful testimonials. Even contact between the parents and teachers of secondary school pupils can be hard to achieve. Bynner (1974) found in a survey of 3,000 parents that the majority visited their child's primary school, but far fewer working-class (40 per cent) than middle-class (80 per cent) parents visited their child's secondary school.

A useful study of parental perceptions of secondary schools is provided by Johnson and Ransom (1980). Teachers referred to a small minority of enthusiastic parents and a small minority of 'problem' parents with whom crises generated forcible contact. In between 'lay the silent majority of unknown and invisible parents who were presumed to be apathetic and uninterested'. However, the authors' 109 home interviews with parents of high school pupils in London suggested a different interpretation.

The parents reported feeling that adolescents needed an independent aspect of life, free from parental interference. Many pupils did not want home–school contact. Furthermore, parents' evenings tended to be seen as functions where parents were called to account for the failings of their children. Many parents wished to help children with learning difficulties at home, but felt frustrated by their own lack of expertise. Many arranged and supported a wide range of extra-tuition or extra-mural activities, unbeknown to the school. Some families placed more importance on voluntary activities than on compulsory education. The responsiveness of many parents to a school had been handicapped from the outset by the denial of the parents' supposed right to choose the school the child attended.

Attempts to mobilise the 'silent majority' into contact with secondary schools are described by Gregory (1980) and Gregory *et al.* (1982). Disadvantaged parents are again shown to be much less likely to attend 'open evenings' than non-disadvantaged parents, roughly in the ratio of 1:2. A system whereby parents collected their child's written progress report from school was successful in increasing contact, particularly for first-year pupils. Where this was possible during the day instead of the evenings, the response from low-SES parents was particularly good. Gregory *et al.* (1982) report on the reorganisation of a secondary school's parents' evening system, involving notifying parents by a welcoming and reliably delivered letter, deformalising the procedure, shifting the emphasis to positive reporting, providing staff with a structure for parental interviews, and conducting a needs assessment survey of the parents. Parental attendance was raised from an average of 16 per cent at baseline to 68 per cent, with marked improvements in attendance from the parents of the least able pupils, though not for the parents of the children whose own school attendance was very poor.

Earlier exploratory work of more pessimistic tone is that of Lynch and Pimlot (1976), who researched home–school contact in school clusters based on three core secondary schools. A questionnaire survey of parents was coupled with discussion groups for parents and teachers (separately). Unfortunately, the parent group structure and content were unsophisticated by modern standards, and parental attendance was low, irrespective of socio-economic status of the school catchment. From the questionnaire survey it was clear that substantial numbers of parents had not visited the school in the preceding year, while the overwhelming majority did not know a single governor. The majority of the teachers were unenthusiastic about any greater parental involvement, and unimpressed by the 'community school' concept.

There is clearly a long way to go before parental involvement in secondary schools begins to develop satisfactorily, but the results from primary schools and some of the more recent work in secondary schools indicates that such developments are possible.

How to Do It

For those wishing to read further in the area of parental involvement in school, the National Children's Bureau provides a booklist, *Home–School Relations* (NCB, 1979), and Trippier (1978) offers a select annotated bibliography on parents as a resource in primary education. The Advisory Centre for Education list many practical suggestions in a brief pamphlet entitled *How You Can Help Your Local School.*

In the USA, Kroth and Scholl (1978) have produced a helpful practical manual including a framework for designing a parent education programme, many concrete examples or vignettes, and a parent involvement assessment scale for schools. Rutherford and Edgar (1979) wrote a guide to teacher–parent interaction and co-operation which is very clear and methodical. The application of a problem-solving model, an applied behaviour analysis model, and an interpersonal communication skills model to the area of parental involvement are considered in detail. This volume shows a degree of conceptual sophistication which is unusual in this rather muddled area, coupled with specific systematic procedures to follow.

Back in the UK, Tizard's evangelical work in the area of parental involvement (1978; Tizard *et al.*, 1981a) culminated in the production of a 'source book' for teachers entitled *Involving Parents in Nursery and Infant Schools* (Tizard *et al.*, 1981b), which many teachers working with young children will find a good starting point.

Summary

Encouraging parents to participate in school-based activities is far from new, but the practice has not grown rapidly. More recently, legislation has supported these developments, at least on paper.

A very wide range of parental involvement activities has been tried, incorporating a variety of means of information transfer, individual and group meetings at home and school, deploying parents to help with fund-raising, chores or with learning tasks in and out of the classroom, and establishing sundry community education programmes. Involvement of parents in child assessment and school governance has developed more slowly.

Western Europe can be construed to have been ahead of the UK and USA in this field, partially owing to pressure arising from the politicisation of the education system. In the USA parental involvement has been successfully organised on a large scale in some areas, but often only in relation to federal projects, while the majority of schools continue to lie fallow.

There is evidence that where schools apply themselves methodically to developing parental involvement, good results are possible even in disadvantaged areas. Nevertheless, many schools still have no programme of parental involvement, or one which confines parents to low-level menial tasks. The problems which teachers fear rarely materialise. Where parents are given a say in school policy, they utilise it infrequently.

Evaluative research on the effect of parental involvement on pupil achievement in nursery schools and classes is encouraging. Four controlled studies show good results, including some maintenance of gains at six-month follow-up, but other studies are weak in methodology.

The situation is less clear for primary schools, where many studies have failed to partial out the effect of the parental-involvement component. There is generalised evidence that schools developing parental involvement tend to produce high standards of learning, but the causative linkages may be multiple. Deploying parents as teaching aides raises skill levels in a curriculum-specific manner, independent of the effect of 'extra attention'. Despite the poor quality of data for primary schools, it is nevertheless reasonable to conclude that parental involvement has been shown to have an impact on pupil achievement, although two studies report less than satisfactory results.

There is little evidence that high schools are attempting to involve parents, and virtually none of the success of this practice. Both parents and children may see parental involvement as less appropriate at this level. However, schools which approach the task more positively can greatly improve parental response. A number of helpful practical manuals for schools are now available. Much of the research on the effects of parental involvement has been of limited use from an evaluative point of view. Anecdotal reports of positive spin-off do little to dispel fears about the replicability of many projects and their generalisation to other populations. Aims and objectives are often not well thought out, and schools often dabble in a lot of possibilities and end up doing nothing well. Very few studies have demonstrated control over process variables and causative linkages convincingly, and there is virtually no evidence on maintenance of gains in the longer term. Generalisation to other children or contexts is also unresearched. There are solid grounds for optimism only in the case of parental involvement in nursery schools, and even here much more research of a more methodical nature is required. Not least, experimental comparison of the effects of different forms of parental involvement is required.

References

Adult Learning Potential Institute (1980) *Guide to Parental Involvement: Parents as Adult Learners. Overview of Parental Involvement Programs and Practices* (Washington, DC: ALPI, American University)

Advisory Centre for Education (undated) *How You Can Help Your Local School* (London: ACE)

Athey, C. (1981) 'Parental Involvement in Nursery Education', *Early Child Development and Care*, 7, 4, 353-67

Beattie, N.M. (1978a) 'Parent Participation in French Education, 1968-75', *British Journal of Educational Studies*, 26, 1, 40-53

Beattie, N.M. (1978b) 'Formalised Parent Participation in Education: A Comparative Perspective (France, German Federal Republic, England and Wales)', *Comparative Education*, 14, 1, 41-8

Beattie, N.M. (1979) 'Three Patterns of Parent Participation in Education: Bavaria, Hamburg, Hessen', *Compare*, 9, 1, 3-15

Benas, E.A. (1980) 'How One City Got Parents Involved', paper presented at the International Congress on Early Childhood Education, Tel Aviv (E.R.I.C. ED 187449 PS 011465)

Broome, R.A. (1974) 'Programmes of Parental Involvement', *Remedial Education*, 9, 134-9

Bynner, J. (1974) 'Deprived Parents', *New Society*, 21 February

Caudrey, A. (1985) 'Growing Role of Parents in Class Causes Alarm', *Times Educational Supplement*, 12 April

Central Advisory Council for Education (1967) *Children and their Primary Schools* (London: HMSO)

Claus, R.N. and Quimper, B.E. (1980) *Preprimary Traffic Safety Curriculum Demonstration Project: Evaluation Report 1979-80* (Saginaw, Michigan: Saginaw Public Schools) (E.R.I.C. ED 194596 TM 800727)

Collins, C.H. *et al.* (1982) *The Home–School Connection: Selected Partnership Programs in Large Cities* (Boston, Massachusets: Institute for Responsive Education) (E.R.I.C. ED 219853 EA 014884)

Cyster, R. *et al.* (1979) *Parental Involvement in Primary Schools* (Slough: National Foundation for Educational Research)

Deitchmann, R. *et al.* (1977) 'Dimensions of Parental Involvement in Pre-school Programmes', *Child Care Health and Development, 3,* 213-24

Figgures, C. (1980) *Evaluation of the Primary Skills Program 1978-1979* (Philadelphia, Pennsylvania: Office of Research and Evaluation, Philadelphia School District)

Fryer, K. (1973) 'Parental Involvement Scheme: Infant/Junior', *Remedial Education, 8, 2,* 35-6

Gillett, N. (1980) 'New Trends in Home–School Cooperation in the United Kingdom', *New Era, 61, 1,* 9-16

Gillum, R.M. *et al.* (1977) 'The Effects of Parental Involvement on Student Achievement in the Michigan Performance Contract Program', unpublished paper, Michigan (E.R.I.C. ED 144007)

Gregory, R.P. (1980) 'Disadvantaged Parents and Contact with Secondary School', *Therapeutic Education, 8, 2,* 23-6

Gregory, R.P. *et al.* (1982) 'Parental Involvement in Secondary Schools', *Journal of the Association of Education Psychologists, 5, 8,* 54-60

Hauser-Cram, P. *et al.* (1981) 'Parents and Schools: A Partnership Model', paper presented at annual meeting of the American Educational Research Association, Los Angeles (E.R.I.C. ED 206146 EC 133600)

Henderson, A. (ed.) (1981) 'Parent Participation — Student Achievement: The Evidence Grows', unpublished paper (E.R.I.C. ED 209754)

Herman, J.L. and Yeh, J.P. (1980) 'Some Effects of Parental Involvement in Schools', unpublished paper, California (E.R.I.C. ED 206963)

Irvine, D. J. *et al.* (1979) 'Parental Involvement Affects Children's Cognitive Growth', unpublished paper (E.R.I.C. ED 176893)

Irwin, J.R. (1979) *Annual Evaluation Reports: ESAA Basic Projects Reading Components and Final Evaluation Report: 1978-79. Detroit Objective Referenced Testing Program* (Detroit, Michigan: Department of Research and Evaluation, Detroit Public Schools) (E.R.I.C. ED 208047 TM 810758)

Iverson, B.K. *et al.* (1981) 'Parent–Teacher Contacts and Student Learning' *Journal of Educational Research, 74, 6,* 394-6

Johnson, D. and Ransom, E. (1980) 'Parents' Perceptions of Secondary Schools', in M.Craft *et al.* (eds.), *Linking Home and School* (3rd edn) (London: Harper & Row)

Kroth, R.L. and Scholl, G.T. (1978) *Getting Schools Involved with Parents* (Philadelphia, Pennsylvania: Council for Exceptional Children)

Laishley, J. and Lindon, L. (1980) 'Schemes of Parental Involvement in Pre-school Centres', *Early Childhood, 1, 2,* 16-19

Lynch, J. and Pimlot, J. (1976) *Parents and Teachers* (London: Macmillan Education)

McGeeney, P. (1969) *Parents are Welcome* (London: Longman)

Mittler, P. and Mittler, H. (1982) *Partnership with Parents* (Stratford-upon-Avon: National Council for Special Education)

National Children's Bureau (1979) *Home/School Relations. Booklist No. 98* (London: NCB)

Raim, J. (1980) 'Who Learns While Parents Teach Reading?' *The Reading Teacher, 34, 2,* 152-5

Rathbone, M. (1977) 'Parent Participation in the Pre-school', *Educational Studies,* *3, 1,* 81-5

Rathbone, M. and Graham, N.C. (1981) 'Parent Participation in the Primary School', *Educational Studies, 7, 2,* 145-50

Robbins, A.E. and Dingler, D.D. (1981) *Parents and Federal Education Programs,* vol. 3: *ESAA. The Study of Parental Involvement* (Santa Monica, California: Studies and Evaluation Department, Systems Development Corporation) (E.R.I.C. ED 218785 EA 014813)

Rutherford, R.B. and Edgar, E. (1979) *Teachers and Parents: A Guide to Interaction and Cooperation* (Boston: Allyn & Bacon

Senf, H. (1980) 'Co-operation Between School and Family in the German Democratic Republic', *Prospects, 10, 3,* 340-5

Sharrock, A. (1980) 'Research on Home—School Relations', in M. Craft *et al.* (eds.) *Linking Home and School* (3rd edn) (London: Harper & Row)

Sinclair, R.L. (ed.) (1980) *A Two-way Street: Home—School Cooperation in Curriculum Decisionmaking* (Boston, Massachusets: Institute for Responsive Education) (E.R.I.C. ED 201055 EA 013507)

Smith, A.G. and Nerenberg, S. (1981) *Parents and Federal Education Programs,* vol. 5: *Follow Through. The Study of Parental Involvement* (Santa Monica, California: Studies and Evaluation Department, Systems Development Corporation) (E.R.I.C. ED 218787 EA 014815)

Smith, T. (1980) *Parents and Preschool* (London: Grant McIntyre)

Swinson, J. (1985) 'A Parental Involvement Project in a Nursery School', *Educational Psychology in Practice, 1, 1,* 19-22

Taylor, M. (1981) 'Educational Reform in California: Changing Professional Perceptions of Public Participation', *Journal of Education Administration and History, 13, 1,* 43-53

Taylor, T. (1977) *A New Partnership for Our Schools: Report of the Committee of Inquiry* (London: HMSO)

Terry, J G. (1976) 'The Listeners: Parents Involved in a Reading Project', *Head Teachers' Review, 67,* 8-9

Tizard, B. (1978) 'Carry on Communicating', *Times Educational Supplement,* 3 February

Tizard, B. *et al.* (1981a) 'The Way to Involvement', *Times Higher Educational Supplement,* 19 June

Tizard, B. *et al.* (1981b) *Involving Parents in Nursery and Infant Schools: A Source Book for Teachers* (London: Grant McIntyre)

Tomlinson, S. (1980) 'Ethnic Minority Parents and Education', in M. Craft *et al.* (eds.), *Linking Home and School* (3rd edn) (London: Harper & Row)

Trippier, R. (1978) *Parents as a Resource in Primary Education: A Selected Annotated Bibliography* (Sheffield: Department of Education Management and In-service Education, Sheffield City Polytechnic)

Wall, W.D. (1947) 'The Opinions of Teachers on Parent—Teacher Cooperation' *British Journal of Educational Psychology, 17, 2,* 97-113

Widlake, P. and McLeod, F. (1985) 'Parental Involvement Programmes and the Literacy Performance in Children', in K. Topping and S. Wolfendale (eds.) *Parental Involvement in Children's Reading* (London: Croom Helm/New York: Nichols Publishing Company)

Wilce, H. (1983) 'Parents Agree on Need for Liaison', *Times Educational Supplement,* 8 April

Wood, A.J. (1974) 'Parents and the Curriculum — A Study of Academic Cooperation and its Effects on Children, Parents and Teachers', unpublished D.Phil thesis, University of Southampton

3 HOME–SCHOOL REPORTING

The 'school report' is a long-standing institution, despite the fact that objective information therein which might actually be useful to parents is usually conspicuous by its absence. Meaningless grades and percentages, together with vacuous value judgements, which tell more about the writer than about the child in question, seem to be the order of the day.

If school reports have any purpose, surely it is to promote parental interest in children's education, in order to improve child motivation and foster practice and development of newly learnt skills in the home environment. Given the demonstrably low effectiveness of written communication, additional media for home–school dialogue are clearly necessary, and the 'parents' evening' is the usual format for a (hopefully) more interactive exchange of information. Even this, and associated opportunities to scrutinise books, equipment and facilities in school, may still give parents precious little idea of what their children are actually learning.

Inviting parents into school as observers, participants, helpers or tutors gives them a much more 'real' understanding of what their children are up to, but only a minority of parents will ever be able to do this at all regularly. Both formulating and offering, soliciting and absorbing detailed information about school curricula are highly energy- and time-consuming, and schools and parents who do not demonstrate high attainment in these areas may be forgiven. The existing over-reliance on brief written information is hardly surprising, but there are well-researched ways of rendering such communication much more specific, functional and interactive, which are highly cost-effective. Before considering these, it is worth looking at two more ambitious projects.

Ambitious Projects

Marshall and Herbert (1981) report on an interesting programme which involved six elementary school teachers recording telephone messages for parents as a means of encouraging them to help their children learn basic skills. Every week for 31 weeks, a two- to three-minute message was available which recapped the week's classroom work on basic skills and gave parents suggestions for home activities to consolidate gains. A telephone number was given, to be called if parents wished to arrange a meeting with the teacher or procure supplementary teaching materials.

The response rate to the parental evaluation questionnaire was unfortunately low (47 per cent), but these parents reported using the service frequently and using at least five activities at home to improve child skills. A high level of consumer satisfaction was evident among respondents. However, achievement scores of pupils in the telephone classes did not differ from those of pupils in other classes, and of the pupils in the telephone classes, a direct relationship between pupil achievement and frequency of telephone usage was found only for third graders, and not for the second grade. While this approach seems to have some promise, it seems likely only to have impact in families who are already well motivated, unless considerably more parental preparation, structure and monitoring are built into the system.

A large-scale programme to prepare mainstream schools and teachers for the reintegration of children with special needs is reported by Fine *et al.* (1977). An integral part of the in-service work of the project was training teachers to train parents to develop and apply behavioural techniques in the home to reinforce the academic progress of their newly reintegrated children. Evaluation results indicated that reintegrated children subsequently showed higher than expected gains on the Metropolitan Achievement Tests, but in not all areas did these differences reach statistical significance. The parents were very positive about the programme, and sociometric data indicated excellent acceptance of the special needs pupils by their peers. However, as the impact of the training in home reinforcement was not differentiated from other programme components in the evaluation data, this project is of more significance as a testimony to the effectiveness of mainstreaming than to that of home–school reporting.

Much more precise evaluative evidence is available from more specifically behaviourally oriented projects.

Behavioural Projects

Work under this heading has typically focused on children with difficulties in school, and the home–school report system has been designed to deploy parental influence at home to modify behaviour in school. Some pupils with problems manifest both learning and behavioural difficulties in school, but these are often inextricably intertwined, since if the pupil did more work there would be less time for problematic behaviour, and if the pupil spent less time behaving badly there would be more time to work. Children with combined learning and behaviour problems have thus been managed by home–school reporting which has targeted increased academic behaviour, reduced problematic behaviour, or both. It will be simplest to look first at the use of home–school reporting solely to increase academic behaviour.

Learning Difficulties

One of the earliest studies was that by McKenzie *et al.* (1968), who established a reward system for ten students in a learning disabilities class, involving the reinforcing of good marks on daily assignments with privileges in class *and* weekly pocket money from parents at home. In fact, the researchers found that the children's performance on the in-school rewards alone stabilised after a period, and the introduction of the home-based contingency then produced a further marked increase in academic progress.

A structured system of weekly assignments in reading, spelling, writing skills, written composition and arithmetic, which had to be mastered before the child continued, greatly facilitated the awarding of marks or grades. In-school rewards included play-time out of class, free-time activities in class, special tasks of privilege, status and responsibility, eating lunch in a group social setting rather than privately, and teacher attention. The subsequent in-home rewards were worked out by each family at so much per A grade, less for Bs, even less for Cs, while a 'Work Incomplete' grade resulted in a *subtraction* of the A amount. It was thus possible for a child to end up owing parents money, a debt which the child could 'discharge' by doing extra household chores. The children were not allowed to acquire money any other way than via earning through the programme.

Observational data gathered independently in the classroom showed that pupil attention rose on average from 68 per cent to 86 per cent with the institution of home–school reporting. Significant differences were found for all ten pupils in reading and for eight pupils in arithmetic. The programme continued through the school year; but as the pupils improved, the size and difficulty of the assignments increased. Eventually, some pupils transferred into mainstream classes, and the reporting system was easily transferred also, to good effect.

Hawkins *et al.* (1972) worked with seven elementary school children who showed low motivation and were under-achieving. With children aged 6, 9, 10 and 11 years, three programme phases (baseline; supply of a note of commendation to take home; and supply of note with associated tangible reward and response cost at home) showed clearly that regular reports home were more likely to be effective if paired with tangible reinforcement. It is worth noting, however, that many teachers would feel the second phase as structured by the researchers to be rather mechanical, and would be unsurprised at its relative ineffectiveness. It is perhaps worthwhile to experiment with a home–school report backed up by only social reinforcement at home initially, before deciding whether to resort to tangible reinforcement. Furthermore, as Hawkins *et al.* point out, the issues of likely maintenance of gains, how and when to fade the programme, what behaviours are not susceptible to such a procedure, and what types of reinforcers parents are prepared and able to dispense consistently, all need addressing by any intending user.

A procedure similar to that of McKenzie *et al.* (1968) was described by Trovato and Bucher (1980), who applied it to children with reading difficulties. Sixty-nine second- to fourth-grade pupils were randomly assigned to one of three groups. One group experienced tuition by *peers* using the SRA Reading Laboratory 1b, another group had the same peer tuition plus home-based tangible reinforcement established by contract, and a control group received in-school regular remedial reading programmes. Changes in reading accuracy and comprehension were assessed. Both were improved by the peer tutoring procedure over the 15 weeks of the programme, relative to the control group. However, the addition of home-based reinforcement doubled this increase. The peer tutor and home reinforcement group improved their oral reading accuracy by an average of 1.27 years in 0.29 years of actual time, compared with the control group's increase of 0.19 years. Comprehension gains were similar. The Trovato and Bucher paper is essential reading for all remedial reading teachers.

Harrop and McCann (1983), working with mixed ability 11–12 year-olds in a comprehensive school and also using the SRA Reading Laboratories, showed that with this population the use of tangible reinforcers was not necessary to achieve significant results. Pupils in one class were promised a letter of commendation to take home to their parents if they showed an improvement in their reading comprehension, while pupils in a control class were not given this promise. Evaluation by pre- and post-testing at a five-week interval with the Wide-span Reading test showed a significant increase in standardised score ('reading quotient') for the experimental group; but not for the control group.

Although this work is slightly flawed by the lack of exact matching between experimental and control groups, it nevertheless demonstrates that straightforward verbal reinforcement in a form which can be transmitted to the home is worth at least considering before launching into the use of tangible home-based reinforcers. The dangers of 'behavioural over-kill' are manifold: when not necessary, it may actually reduce intrinsic motivation, and leave teachers with too few shots in the locker. There is substantial evidence that children greatly value a 'favourable report home' (Highfield and Pinsent, 1972; Davies and Thorne, 1977; Burns, 1978), and this seems a useful strategy to deploy before turning to more heavyweight interventions.

That success is not automatic with any approach is demonstrated by Meyers (1976), who found that neither feedback to parents without tangible reinforcement, nor the use of a home-teaching package by parents, nor the home teaching plus feedback with tangible reinforcement for in-school work made any difference to the spelling and mathematics attainment of 14 learning-disabled middle-class children aged 7–10 years, although their parents were convinced the children had improved. The teachers preferred the report-card system as it was much less time-consuming than the home-teaching package.

Behaviour and Learning Difficulties

A daily report card backed up with in-home reinforcers has a wide range of application, as Dougherty and Dougherty (1977) point out. It can provide feedback on classroom behaviour and homework completion as well as schoolwork. It can be used on several different levels of complexity, ranging from simple rating scales to precise behavioural definitions with criteria for target achievement, coupled with unspecified consequences or detailed reinforcement 'menus', carefully 'priced' and involving a balance of long- and short-term reinforcers.

The authors describe the application of home–school reporting and reinforcement in an ordinary fourth-grade classroom in a private school, consisting of 15 pupils. Lack of homework completion and talking loudly and irrelevantly during group instruction were particular problems. A simple one- to four-point scale for both behaviours was adopted for the home report. The parents were asked to discuss the reports with the children, emphasising the positive aspects, but were not required to use tangible reinforcers. As a result, the percentage of children not completing their homework dropped on average from 35 per cent to 17 per cent. After three weeks the children began taking the cards home only weekly, and the improvement was maintained. Likewise, the mean rate for inappropriate talking decreased from 13.5 per hour to 2.3 per hour, and was subsequently maintained by a weekly card.

Schumaker *et al.* (1977a) worked with a 'tougher' population — disruptive and 'remedial' junior high school students — and found tangible reinforcement at home necessary. Target behaviours included school conduct, classwork, daily grades and teacher satisfaction, and the daily report scheme allied to home privileges produced considerable improvement in three students. In a second experiment, the report card was linked only with parental praise for two students, and while this worked for one student, it did not for the other, until contingent home privileges were added. The researchers also demonstrated that school guidance counsellors relatively inexperienced in the use of behaviour modification procedures could be effectively instructed to implement the report-card system independently, with equally problematic pupils.

Schumaker *et al.* also describe a fading system whereby the pupils carry a shortened version of the card daily, then twice week, then weekly, then not at all. The authors claim this has been successful in maintaining adequate school performance in the eventual absence of the card, but cite no data to support this contention. Some students are said to have had to repeat some of the initial fading steps, while others have remained on a particular fading step indefinitely because of repeated failure on the more advanced steps.

Although the procedures were relatively cost-effective, the

counsellor spent approximately one hour per week with each student's parents and teachers to keep the programme running smoothly, and this is more time than most pastoral care staff have for each problematic pupil each week. It is proposed that with more co-operative families and greater school experience, the time commitment could be reduced, perhaps by substituting telephone calls to the parents.

Further data on the effectiveness of a home–school report with back-up reinforcers at home is provided by Drew *et al.* (1982), who worked with two children aged 8 and 9 years with a history of behavioural difficulties when faced with 'desk-work' and academic task completion. Both parents chose to make outside play the back-up reinforcer (presumably in summer-time). The procedure produced immediate significant changes in rates of task completion and task accuracy for both children.

However, one child objected to his first experience of having outside play restricted when he received a poor report, and for several hours argued, tried to sneak out of the house, and made manipulative and hurtful remarks to his mother. Fortuitously, his mother received timely support from the programme, stood fast, and had no more problems. Drew *et al.* warn that many parents may feel guilty when first required to impose deprivation of privileges, and will be strongly tempted to relent — which will, of course, sabotage the programme. Initial feelings of guilt soon subsided when the parents began to see tangible improvements, but parents might need extra support during the child's 'extinction burst', as Drew *et al.* delightfully label the death-throes of the child's unwanted behaviour.

A slight variation on the theme is reported by Witt *et al.* (1983), who used a home–school reporting programme on the academic performance and disruptive behaviour of three fourth-grade boys, but placed tangible home contingencies only on academic performance. Marked increases in academic performance were coupled with large decreases in disruptive behaviour for all subjects. Throughout baseline and treatment conditions there was a strong negative correlation between academic performance and disruptive behaviour, presumably because the two were incompatible. Reinforcing the improved academic performance while merely reporting the disruptive behaviour could well prove more acceptable to parents and teachers who fear that children could become dependent on 'artificial' reinforcement for good behaviour, while still having the same net outcome owing to the incompatibility effect. However, it is possible that a small proportion of pupils will discriminate against the contingencies, and will prove to require tangible reinforcement for both sets of behaviour.

Taylor *et al.* (1984) report a study of a multi-racial third-grade class of 26 children, who had a list of both positively and negatively phrased rules posted in the classroom. Brief notes home informed the parents of a day free of rule violations by their child, to which they responded with verbal praise or tangible rewards at their discretion. After overall class rule-breaking had reduced by 80 per cent, notes were faded out altogether. Results showed a dramatic decrease from baseline violation rates when daily notes were introduced, followed by a slight rise when notes were thinned to weekly, followed by a further rise when notes were completely faded, although violations remained at half-baseline rate to the end of the programme. Considering the lack of clear instruction and monitoring of parental behaviour, a less than perfect degree of temporal generalisation could have been predicted.

Reviews

A thorough review of work in the field is provided by Atkeson and Forehand (1979), including tables detailing the studies under headings noting type of classroom environment, number and age of children, target behaviour, adequacy of research design, whether treatment was varied systematically and multiple outcome measures used, information on monitoring of programme process in school and at home, and details of follow-up.

Practical problems of implementation are also reviewed. It is noted that some pupils 'lose' reports notifying poor work or behaviour, which makes sending only positive reports the procedure of choice (leaving parents to assume the worst if no note arrives, and act accordingly). Use of the telephone can also circumvent this problem, but requires more teacher time. Atkeson and Forehand speculate that non-tangible reinforcement at home may work better with younger children, other things being equal. They also note that home–school reporting should not be used if there are doubts about the quality of teaching, since it may be the school tuition that needs improving, rather than the child's 'motivation'. It is observed that there is little direct comparative information on the importance of the specificity of the report. Some evidence is cited that when using the home–school report system with a whole class, greater effectiveness is achieved when a sample of pupils is picked at random each day to be the subject of a report, rather than all pupils being the subject of a weekly report on Friday afternoon. When sanctions or response costs were included in home reinforcement, they were limited to loss of privileges and were never used without being combined with a reward system.

Atkeson and Forehand conclude that the studies reviewed support the view that home-based reinforcement is effective in changing classroom behaviour. This proved consistent across a wide range of ages, types of classroom, and academic and disruptive behaviours, which 'attests to the general impact of the procedure'. Some of the studies failed to use appropriate research designs, and detailed monitoring of programme process in home and school had rarely occurred, which limited the confidence with which the research findings could be espoused. Long-term follow-up had been widely neglected.

Another review of 'home-based contingency systems' is provided by Broughton *et al.* (1981), who describe the range of reports, from the very simple to the highly detailed, and also note that comparative research on the impact of report format is still unavailable. The authors emphasise the importance of consistent delivery of consequences by the parents and review various researchers' procedures for training parents to play their part, as well as the degree of teacher participation required. There is some discussion of fading procedure, but Broughton *et al.* question whether total fading is actually desirable, except in terms of saving teacher time.

The authors conclude:

> Home-managed contingency programmes can be extremely effective methods for improving the school-related problems of children. Such programmes are effective, easily implemented, and have the additional advantage of opening positive communication channels between home and school.

The steps in developing such a programme are then briefly outlined. Teachers may prefer this more descriptive and pragmatic review to that of Atkeson and Forehand (1979), which is more analytic.

Another review of the field is provided by Barth (1979), and other interesting papers are those of Phillips (1968), Bailey *et al.* (1970), Cohen *et al.* (1971), Karraker (1972), Sluyter and Hawkins (1972), Ayllon *et al.* (1975), Todd *et al.* (1976), Bristol (1976), Lahey *et al.* (1977) and Imber *et al.* (1979). A number of authors have provided helpful suggestions about the implementation of home–school reporting programmes, and Broughton *et al.* (1981) list these. However, the most substantial work of a 'do-it-yourself' nature is undoubtedly the manual by Schumaker *et al.* (1977b), in which step-by-step instructions are provided. Procedures for follow-up and fading are detailed, and practical suggestions are offered for dealing with everyday problems like non-cooperating teachers, pupils who can forge, and the congenitally forgetful.

A considerably briefer action sequence is presented in Table 3.1.

Summary

Relying on parent-initiated telephone contact to improve pupil achievement does not appear to raise pupil attainment. Virtually all the significant work in this area is behavioural in orientation.

The behavioural home–school reporting programmes have linked school performance to parental praise and/or parent-controlled reinforcing privileges (more often both) via simple written messages home (usually daily). Tangible home reinforcement has proved necessary with 'harder' cases. Successful modification of a wide range of academic behaviour and disruptive or problematic behaviour with a broad span of child ages and special needs is reported in the literature, with remarkably few failures noted.

However, there is as yet limited evidence on long-term maintenance of gains and transfer to non-tangible reinforcement or intrinsic motivation, and comparative research on alternative fading procedures is needed. There is virtually no evidence of generalisation to non-target behaviours, or information on the effect on siblings. Comparative data on the relative effectiveness of report formats of varying specificity are needed, and much more research

Table 3.1: Action Cascade for Behavioural Home–School Report
Programmes

Sequential steps	Fault-finding guide
For each step, try positive feedback only first, adding negative feedback if necessary:	If the programme doesn't work try:
	Persisting a little longer
Feedback to parents on academic performance	Reduce time-span of report (weekly becomes daily)
Feedback to parents with parent verbal reinforcement on academic performance	Specify target behaviours more precisely
	Tighten up the recording system
Feedback to parents with parent verbal reinforcement and tangible reinforcement on academic performance	Use phone to check with parents
	Train parents more specifically
Feedback to parents on academic and behavioural performance with parent verbal reinforcement and tangible reinforcement for academic performance	Check parental consistency
	Ensure no alternative access to reinforcers
	Institute specific targets/criteria
Feedback to parents and parent verbal reinforcement on academic and behavioural performance with tangible reinforcement for academic performance	Set lower targets
	Institute more varied reinforcers
	Institute bigger reinforcers
Feedback to parents and parent verbal and tangible reinforcement for academic and behavioural performance	Institute response cost
	Institute heavier response cost

Note on fading: Go through the above steps in reverse, plus: (i) institute reports on isolated random days or weeks; (ii) as (i) direct to the parents by mail or phone; (iii) spot checks with individual class teachers by senior staff.

is necessary to demonstrate experimental control over the dependent variable of parental behaviour. Procedures for parent training and monitoring have been somewhat neglected. Few studies have used multiple-outcome measures, and the degree of client satisfaction (parent *or* child) with such systems is unclear.

Notwithstanding these reservations, home–school reporting is an easily delivered and highly replicable intervention, widely acceptable to parents on account of its simplicity. Its absolute effectiveness in comparison to other methods of changing school behaviour is, of course, dependent on levels of parental co-operation as well as professional competence in organising the programme, but even parents who are not noted for being pro-school may co-operate with a well-structured and explicit scheme. Compared with other methods of changing school behaviour *or* other methods of parent training, there can be no doubt that home—school reporting is highly cost-effective, and as such can be recommended as a strategy of first choice. A summary chart to aid planning is provided.

References

Atkeson, B.M. and Forehand, R. (1979) 'Home-based Reinforcement Programs Designed to Modify Classroom Behavior: A Review and Methodological Evaluation', *Psychological Bulletin, 86*, 6, 1298-308

Ayllon, T. *et al.* (1975) 'The Elimination of Discipline Problems through a Combined School—Home Motivational System', *Behavior Therapy, 6*, 616-26

Bailey, J.S. *et al.* (1970) 'Home-based Reinforcement and the Modification of Predelinquents' Classroom Behavior', *Journal of Applied Behavior Analysis, 3*, 223-33

Barth, R. (1979) 'Home-based Reinforcement of School Behavior: A Review and Analysis', *Review of Educational Research, 49*, 436-58

Bristol, M. (1976) 'Control of Physical Aggression through School- and Home-based Reinforcement', in J. Krumboltz and C. Thoreson (eds.), *Counseling Methods* (New York: Holt, Rinehart & Winston)

Broughton, S.F. *et al.* (1981) 'Home-based Contingency Systems for School Problems', *School Psychology Review, 10*, 1, 26-36

Burns, R.B. (1978) 'Relative Effectiveness of Various Incentives and Deterrents as Judged by Pupils and Teachers', *Educational Studies, 4*, 3, 229-43

Cohen, S. *et al.* (1971) 'The Support of School Behaviors by Home-based Reinforcement via Parent—Child Contingency Contracts', in E. Ramp and B. Hopkins (eds.), *A New Direction for Education: Behavior Analysis* (Lawrence, Kansas: University of Kansas)

Davies, B. and Thorne, M. (1977) 'What Pupils Think', *Times Educational Supplement*, 23 December

Dougherty, E.H. and Dougherty, A. (1977) 'The Daily Report Card: A Simplified and Flexible Package for Classroom Behavior Management', *Psychology in the Schools, 14*, 2, 191-5

Drew, B.M. *et al.* (1982) 'Increasing Assignment Completion and Accuracy Using a Daily Report Card Procedure', *Psychology in the Schools, 19*, 540-7

Fine, J.R. *et al.* (1977) 'A Three-year Evaluation of "Project Mainstream"', paper presented at the annual meeting of the American Educational Research Association, New York (E.R.I.C. ED 143672, TM006243)

Harrop, A. and McCann, C. (1983) 'Behavior Modification and Reading Attainment in the Comprehensive School', *Educational Research, 25*, 3, 191-5

Hawkins, R.P. *et al.* (1972) 'Modification of Achievement by a Simple Technique

Involving Parents and Teachers', in Harris, M.B. (ed.), *Classroom Uses of Behavior Modification* (Columbus, Ohio: Charles E. Merrill)

Highfield, M.E. and Pinsent, A. (1972) *A Survey of Rewards and Punishments in School* (London: Newnes, for NFER)

Imber, S.C. *et al.* (1979) 'Modifying Independent Work Habits: An Effective Teacher—Parent Communication Program', *Exceptional Children, 45,* 218-21

Karraker, R.J. (1972) 'Increasing Academic Performance through Home-managed Contingency Programs', *Journal of School Psychology, 10,* 173-9

Lahey, B.B. *et al.* (1977) 'An Evaluation of Daily Report Cards with Minimal Teacher and Parent Contacts as an Efficient Method of Classroom Intervention', *Behavior Modification, 1,* 381-94

McKenzie, H.S. *et al.* (1968) 'Behavior Modification of Children with Learning Disabilities Using Grades as Tokens and Allowances as Backup Reinforcers', *Exceptional Children, 34,* 745-52

Marshall, G. and Herbert, M. (1981) *Recorded Telephone Messages: A Way to Link Teacher and Parents. Evaluation Report* (St Louis, Missouri: CEMREL, Inc.) (E.R.I.C. ED 211200, PS 012570)

Meyers, J.G. (1976) 'Parents as Change Agents on the Academic Behavior of Learning Disability Students', unpublished doctoral dissertation, University of Kansas

Phillips, S.E. (1968) 'Achievement Place: Token Reinforcement Procedures in a Home Style Rehabilitation Setting for "Pre-delinquent" Boys', *Journal of Applied Behavior Analysis, 1,* 213-23

Schumaker, J.B. *et al.* (1977a) An Analysis of Daily Report Cards and Parent-managed Privileges in the Improvement of Adolescents' Classroom Performance', *Journal of Applied Behavior Analysis, 10, 3,* 449-64

Schumaker, J.B. *et al.* (1977b) *Managing Behavior, Part 9: A Home-based School Achievement System* (Lawrence, Kansas: H. & H. Enterprises, Inc.)

Sluyter, D. and Hawkins, R. (1972) 'Delayed Reinforcement of Classroom Behavior by Parents', *Journal of Learning Disabilities, 5,* 16-24

Taylor, V.L. *et al.* (1984) 'Home-based Contingency Management Programs that Teachers Can Use', *Psychology in the Schools, 21,* 368-74

Todd, D.D. *et al.* (1976) 'Modification of the Extensive Inappropriate Classroom Behavior of Two Elementary School Students Using Home-based Consequences and Daily Report Card Procedures', *Journal of Applied Behavior Analysis, 9,* 106

Trovato, J. and Bucher, B. (1980) 'Peer Tutoring With or Without Home-based Reinforcement, for Reading Remediation', *Journal of Applied Behavior Analysis, 13, 1,* 129-41

Witt, J.C. *et al.* (1983) 'Home-based Reinforcement: Behavior Covariation between Academic Performance and Inappropriate Behavior', *Journal of School Psychology, 21,* 337-48

4 ORDINARY CHILDREN

Surely, if you're an ordinary parent with ordinary children, you don't need any special training? Why interfere with normal spontaneous processes of naturalistic parenting if there are no problems? Parents can always be improved by some specialist training (comes the reply from some of the 'experts'). However, the dangers of contagious 'expertosis' with parents who do not see themselves as having a problem are well demonstrated in a study by Vogel (1975). Thirty mothers were assigned to control or experimental groups, and the latter were given an eight-week training programme in behaviour modification. Attitudinal and observational data showed little subsequent difference between the trained and control groups, except that the control group mothers showed increased warmth towards, and enjoyment of, their children, whereas the trained group did not. Vogel suggests that the behaviour modification training may have had a depressing effect on positive maternal attitudes by increasing the mothers' anxiety regarding their child-rearing practices.

Given that caveat, however, there is considerable evidence that sensitive and sensible parent training for non-problematic families can be well received and effective. Rich *et al.* (1979) review the results of a large number of programmes that are aimed at building positive family interaction and child achievement, without cutting across school experiences. The key success is seen as building on family strengths, in what Rich *et al.* describe as the 'Nondeficit' involvement model for teaming home and school.

However, some parent-training programmes have focused on guiding parents into methods of cognitively stimulating their 'normal' children at home prior to starting school.

Early Stimulation

Thirteen Early Childhood Family Education Programs in one American state are described by Patton (1977). The opinions of 127 participating parents (sampled by telephone interview) are reported,

53

but independent objective evaluation information is lacking.

An interesting account of a Parent/Child Toy Library Program is provided by Nimnicht *et al.* (1977). Built around a set of educational toys and games, the programme included a course for parents, the toy library lending service, and training for the teacher–librarian who taught the course to the parents and operated the library. Toy libraries are not uncommon in North America or the UK, but are usually targeted on families which include handicapped or disadvantaged children, and rarely entail structured, formal training for the parents. Parent self-report findings were very positive. Achievement tests on children immediately after the course showed increases, but these did not reach statistical significance, and longitudinal research was not conducted. A replication in Venezuela produced similar results, with parents frequently reporting learning new intellectual skills themselves.

A considerably more ambitious programme is reported by Kessen *et al.* (1975) and Fein (1977), who were involved in a longitudinal study which compared the effects of three types of home-based parent-oriented curricula. Mothers and children from 108 middle- and working-class families received home visits beginning when the children were 12 months old and ending when they were 30 months. Four assessments of mothers and children were made at 12, 15, 24 and 30 months on a multiplicity of observational, attitudinal and attainment measures at home and in the laboratory, and extensive data on demographic and family life variables were also collected.

The 108 children were assigned to six groups of 18. In three groups a home visitor called regularly to work with both parent and child, following a language-focused, play-focused and social-development-focused 'curriculum' respectively. In the fourth group, the visitor tried to cover all three curricular areas, but only worked with the mother, while in the fifth group all areas were covered, but the visitor worked only with the child. The sixth group was not visited, but assessed, and acted as a control.

The mother-only group proved time-consuming, as conversations of doubtful relevance to programme objectives tended to prolong visits, and the child-only group suffered from the handicap that some very small children are either uninterested in or averse to visitors, particularly those with educational intentions. On the other hand, the 'triadic' groups suffered more postponements, there being a greater probability that one member of the 'team' would be indisposed.

Most of the 351 pages of the Kessen *et al.* report are devoted to results, which are extremely complex. The children's development over time is discussed in detail, and the surges and rests in development discussed for each group. Overall, however, the triadic language curriculum group seemed to do best, followed by the triadic play group, trailed by the triadic social group. Girls tended to do better than boys. The two 'dyadic' groups (mother-only and child-only) performed about equally well.

Gotts (1979, 1980) reports on a related but less complex enterprise labelled HOPE — Home Oriented Preschool Education. This was designed to serve rural families with pre-school children, falling largely into the lower-middle-class range. Services included: daily television lessons in the home for the child associated with weekly printed 'Parent Guides' suggesting follow-up activities, weekly home visits from a local trained paraprofessional who modelled constructive activities and counselled the parent, and a weekly half-day 'playgroup' experience under the supervision of a qualified teacher. One set of children received TV stimulation only, one TV plus home visitor, one TV plus home visitor plus playgroup, and a control group nothing at all.

Initial evaluation results showed that both home-visited groups did better than the TV-only group, which in turn did better than the control group, and this was true on attainment tests *and* measures of social skills. Long-term follow-up studies were carried out later, tracing 50 per cent of the original HOPE children from four counties three or more years afterwards. The home-visited children were found to be significantly outperforming the TV-only children in school attendance and attainment as revealed by school records and test results. Subsequently, 57 per cent of the 600 HOPE children from a wider geographical area were traced, and the HOPE children proved to have higher school attainment in first and second grades, but not significantly in the third. There was evidence from teacher-completed checklists that HOPE children were more self-organised, happier, less aggressive and more responsible than non-HOPE pupils, and were less likely to be held back a year in school. To what extent biased sample attrition was a factor in these findings is open to question.

Another well-evaluated programme is reported by Metzl (1980). Sixty normal first-born children of intact, self-supporting families were allocated to three groups: mothers receiving a specific language-stimulation programme, mothers and fathers receiving the programme simultaneously, and a control group. At 6 weeks and 6 months, the infants were assessed with the Bayley Scales of Infant Development, and the stimulation at home assessed via a specifically designed inventory. Infants whose parents received simultaneous training showed the greatest gain on both measured over time, and both experimental groups gained significantly more than the control group. Unfortunately, no long-term follow-up data are available.

However, by no means all the results of early parent stimulation programmes for normal children have been as positive. For instance, Dusewicz and Coller (1978) evaluated the impact of *Picturepages*, a pre-school readiness programme televised daily in Kentucky. Teaching booklets for the children to use with the broadcast programmes are distributed in advance. Questionnaire returns from over 1,000 families (2 per cent response rate) indicated that the respondents viewed the programme positively. However, a more controlled study in which 110 children were randomly assigned to experimental or control groups and pre- and post-tested on a variety of instruments revealed no evidence of significant programme effects.

Similarly, Payne (1976) evaluated a programme for training parents in the home use of parent–child interaction exercises, intended to promote the cognitive and interpersonal growth of children. The programme had no measurable effect on the children in those directions, as compared with control groups.

Nevertheless, the general picture is positive, as Hess (1976) demonstrates in his review of 28 pre-school intervention programmes. The programmes variously included direct teaching of parents during home visits, modelling with mothers observing teacher–child interaction, and unstructured observation in pre-school nursery classes. Significant gains in children's IQ scores were consistently demonstrated, and school performance and parental behaviour and attitudes often also showed positive shifts.

Some programmes had more dramatic effects than others, and factors in this included the degree of structure in parental educational activities and the subsequent closeness of the relationship between the parents and the child's teachers. Eight of the programmes included follow-up, and of these, seven reported positive differences favouring programme children over controls, although not all these results reached statistical significance. Thus, many of the gains made were maintained into the early years of formal schooling.

Academic Skills

Many parents, possibly the majority, give their children some form of instruction in what could be construed as 'academic' skills prior to official school entry. Often they do this on the basis of fragmentary knowledge and confused objectives, strongly coloured by their muddled reminiscences of their own early schooldays. This is hardly surprising, since rarely are parents given clear, well-structured, pragmatic and systematic guidance about how to prepare their children for school. At best, the earnest parent will be bombarded with a plethora of ill-articulated competing commercial claims by the media.

An exception to this general rule is the work of Niedermeyer (1970), who deployed a highly structured parent-tutored nursery reading curriculum. Practice exercises were provided in pursuit of four reading objectives: the ability to sightread 90 one-syllable words, to recognise and say eleven initial consonant sounds, to recognise and say twelve vowel–consonant blend ending sounds, and to blend learned sounds to 'sound out' new words. Each practice exercise included written materials incorporating 20 separate tasks. Instructions for the child were scripted for the parent to read. The total programme consisted of 80 practice exercises, each exercise to be worked through twice each day. To enrol in the programme, parents were required to attend a 90-minute training session.

In Niedermeyer's study, 91 parents of 74 children in the nursery in question presented themselves for training (83 per cent take-up). Two comparison groups were used, one of children whose parents had indicated willingness to participate in such a programme, but had not been offered it; and one of randomly selected pupils. On criterion-referenced pre- and post-tests, the programme children improved by 24 per cent, the first comparison group improved by 6 per cent, and the second comparison group deteriorated by 2 per cent, a highly significant outcome. Children in the experimental nursery whose parents had declined to participate improved their scores by 6 per cent, despite achievements analogous to those of experimental children at pre-test. Clearly, high levels of parent participation and child learning had been elicited.

Niedermeyer feels that the success of his programme is attributable to clear specification of objectives and clear communication of these to the parents, the provision of structured teaching materials, the incorporation of consistent practice of a highly programmed nature, the inclusion of role-playing of teaching procedures in the training session (with immediate feedback from supervisors), the instruction of the parents in the use of positive reinforcement, and the provision of record cards to help parents monitor a child's performance. When the programme ended, a substantial majority of parents indicated that they would have maintained participation for the rest of the year. However, as Niedermeyer points out, the effectiveness of the programme in an area of socio-economic disadvantage might be considerably less. Nevertheless, he cites nine other studies which support the view that this type of intervention is extremely effective. It is a pity that long-term follow-up data are not cited.

A less labour-intensive project is described by Perlish (1970), who investigated the effectiveness of a television reading programme, along with parental home involvement, in helping 3-year-old children learn to read. Following 39 weeks of exposure to the programme, the children in the experimental group achieved scores on reading tests that were significantly higher than those obtained by the control group. The more competent parents with the more interested children produced the best results on post-test, indicating that it was programme process that affected the outcome rather than random variables.

The experimental group was 135 children and the control group 162. An impressive battery of five individual and group tests of intelligence and reading skill were deployed. The television series consisted of 195 half-hour programmes during which 87 words and 17 sentences were introduced. In the control group, two solitary children read one word each at post-test, while the experimental group demonstrated substantial reading performances. There was no significant relationship between post-test reading performance and pre-test reading level, parental educational level, chronological age, sex, nursery school attendance, verbal ability, socio-economic status, or number of siblings. The programme parents were lower middle to upper middle class, and again the question of generalisation to a population of low socio-economic status arises.

As children grow older and enter 'proper' school, they may or may not be lucky enough to find that their teachers encourage parental involvement in their reading development. A recent survey by Hannon and Cuckle (1984) indicated that while teachers of 7-year-olds showed some interest in, and support for, the idea of parental involvement in reading, this was rarely operationalised, and usually stopped far short of helping parents work constructively with their own children at home. In view of the mounting evidence that guided parental involvement in children's reading development is a highly effective (and extremely cost-effective) strategy (see Topping and Wolfendale, 1985), teachers seem slow to learn this lesson.

Further work in this area will be dealt with in much more detail in Chapter 7 ('Learning Difficulties'), since although all children can benefit from such schemes, those schools which have taken some initiative in this area have tended, not unreasonably, to focus on the weaker readers in the first instance.

There is no doubt of the impact of parental involvement in children's reading, and some evidence that much the same applies to children's writing skills. In a small-scale longitudinal study by Raban (1982), the children were followed at home and school from pre-school to age 9, and data were collected on oral language development, from classroom observations, test results, analysis of examples of written work, and interviews with both parents and children. Those parents who were providing literacy experiences during the pre-school years had a lasting effect, and the differences in outcome attributable to the contributions of the homes were far greater than those attributable to school factors. Interestingly, measures for quality of oral language did not correlate significantly with quality of writing. While this study is indicative of an expected trend, it should be noted that no specific parent training was undertaken, and methods of statistical analysis were weak.

A programme of wider scope is reported by Corno (1980), who devised parent-assisted instruction to help 8–9-year-olds develop greater competence in organising, summarising and remembering information, a competence they could then apply in school. The programme consisted of eight exercises, each lasting 30 minutes. Practice materials included classroom vignettes, but parents did most of the reading involved. Written scripts were provided for parents throughout. The experimental group incorporated 17 school classes and the control group 16 classes. Outcome measures included a criterion-referenced test of programme content, a reading comprehension test, a vocabulary test and a test of non-verbal analytic reasoning. Unfortunately, the samples suffered marked attrition, with only 32 per cent completing the entire programme sequence. The exercises were found difficult by the participants, and the higher-ability pupils were more likely to complete the course unless there was additional motivational input from the school teacher. The programme pupils performed significantly better than controls on the programme curriculum test and the vocabulary test. When discrimination was made between the outcomes for those completing the programme and those who did not, programme 'completers' also did better than controls on reading. This programme would appear to hold promise for high-ability pupils, but further research is needed to disentangle the critical factors. There are similarities with the work of Shure and Spivack (1978) (see below).

Gifted Children

The strategies developed by Corno (1980) and Shure and Spivack (1978) seem particularly relevant to high-ability children, but do not purport to be specifically targeted upon them.

It is astonishing that the literature search has unearthed virtually nothing which offers evaluative evidence of the impact of parent training upon gifted children. It seems improbable that gifted children are so few in number and uninteresting to study that no one has bothered. Perhaps it is assumed that gifted children will have gifted parents whose naturalistic parenting skills are not capable of improvement — but that would be to make two false assumptions.

Leonard (1977) describes the activities of the Chapel Hill Gifted–Handicapped Project, intended to identify gifted children who are disadvantaged or handicapped aged between 3 and 6. The project provided a pre-school programme of enrichment activities, therapy and remediation in dificit developmental areas. Another component was the family programme, and a parent manual, workshop agendas and home visit guidelines are described. Evaluation of child progress is extremely difficult with a high-ability and very various group, but individual test results are cited for eleven children which indicate that half of them markedly accelerated in cognitive development during the programme. Two of the children appeared to have reached a cognitive developmental plateau. Semi-structured subjective feedback from parents is also reported. The differential impact of the in-school activities and the parental involvement were not discriminated.

It is clear that a great deal of further work is needed on the early identification of gifted children, particularly those from disadvantaged homes or ethnic minorities, with a view to training their parents in early stimulation activities and subsequently providing specialist educational facilities. Otherwise a huge reservoir of potential exceptional talent could be wasted. By the time such children enter 'official' school, it may already be too late; self-expectations may already by irremediably conditioned.

General Parenting Skills

The range of skills which the 'experts' have considered parents need to acquire is extremely wide and various. Brim (1965) provides a useful, if now rather dated, review of *Education for Child Rearing*. He notes that the majority of studies have evaluated post-programme parental knowledge and/or parental attitudes, but fewer have looked at subsequent parental behaviour and even fewer at subsequent child behaviour.

The majority of studies evaluating parent knowledge or attitudes had used a group tuition format, although sometimes mass media (including mailing), individual counselling or combined methods were utilised. Of these studies, almost all had been able to demonstrate immediate increments in parental knowledge. When it came to parent attitudes, less than half the studies had demonstrated the predicted positive shift in this area, while the remainder comprised negative or equivocal findings. The group tuition method seemed more likely to produce positive attitude shift — an interesting social psychological phenomenon.

So far as subsequent parental behaviour was concerned, two-thirds of the studies which did not employ control groups claimed to demonstrate positive shifts, while less than half of the studies which did employ control groups could claim unequivocal positive shifts. Of only three studies examining subsequent child behaviour, just one could claim unequivocal positive results.

Many of these studies, however, utilised paper-and-pencil out-come measures, and the 'training' was often brief, cursory (e.g. a mail drop of pamphlets), ill-structured and vague in specified objectives. Even where parental or child behaviour was scrutinised post-programme, this was often done in a way which raises doubts about reliability, e.g. by *post hoc* analysis of generalised progress records. In 1965, Brim concluded: 'the issue of effectiveness of parent education is still unresolved' and he 'looked forward to future studies'. The expectation at the time was that improved research methodology would bring more conclusive results. To some extent that has happened, but far more significant has been the improvement in structure and delivery of parent-training pro-grammes.

Despite recent trends to teach 'parenting skills' in a more thorough and effective manner, the variety of programmes in operation remains vast. A taste of that variety may be obtained by sampling three very different programmes.

Three Sample Programmes

These three programmes may be characterised, in order, as dif-fusive, didactic and pragmatic.

There is a substantial tradition in the USA of parent study groups based on Adlerian principles. The most widely adopted format is that of Dreikurs (Dreikurs and Soltz, 1964), which includes a group leader's guide, and is also used with teachers. The groups typically consist of eight to twelve members, usually led by a parent graduate of a previous group. The leaders do not actually lead, but 'facilitate', and although each meeting has an agenda of specific child-rearing topics, there is very little didactic input. Handouts, homework arrangements and suggestions for further reading are utilised.

The relevant evaluation research on this approach is reviewed by Christensen and Thomas (1980). Much of this consists of paper-and-pencil measures of attitudes or parental self-reports of behaviour change in themselves and/or their children. Again, positive shifts in parent attitudes are a fairly common finding, but there is little of a more tangible nature. One study based on parental self-report at two-year follow-up indicated that a sub-stantial number of parents reported themselves to be still using Adlerian principles, and could list the specific methods in use.

However, there was only a 40 per cent response rate in this questionnaire study, so the representativeness of these findings remains a mystery.

A much more didactic approach was taken by Jackson and Terdal (1978), who describe a parent-education programme within a paediatric medical practice. Seven group sessions, each for about eight couples, were run three times, with good attendance and low drop-out rates. Written, verbal, video and film information were presented, followed by group discussion and reinforced by homework assignments. The curriculum included general child development and behaviour modification approaches. Parental subjective responses were extremely positive, and all but one family subsequently reported successful completion of their 'practice' behaviour modification programme. The reliability of parental self-report data is again a critical feature in the interpretation of this outcome.

A quite different venture, in theory much more attuned to the day-to-day needs of parents, is reported by van der Eyken (1980), who notes that needs assessments showed that a major parental requirement was for information about different forms of provision. Parents were often reluctant to approach statutory agencies for fear of being labelled 'problem families'. Van der Eyken concluded that there was a need for a service which was non-institutional, local, sympathetic in allowing parents time to express their requirements, and was immediately available and readily accessible to a wide community. The solution was to use the telephone, which had the added advantage of 'conspirational anonymity'.

This approach was not new, having originated in the 1960s in the USA with the Parents Anonymous movement, which sparked a number of replications in the UK, including one linked to local radio. The majority of calls to such facilities related to children under 5, and so the Islington pre-school INFOPHONE service was established in North London. The aims were to inform, counsel and interlink young families. Subsequently, the level of usage was rather low, with peaks of usage coinciding with extra publicity. The users tended to regard INFOPHONE very much as an information service and rang during ordinary office hours. Thirty per cent of the callers were from other professional agencies or institutions, and almost half were mothers. No more detailed evaluation is provided, unsurprisingly, as the evaluation of an enterprise of this kind would be a researcher's nightmare.

Transactional Analysis

By no means all parent training is founded on a well-articulated and coherent theoretical base, but this cannot be said of Transactional Analysis. Originating with the books of Berne (1964) and Harris (1969), the theory was subsequently considerably elaborated. Transactional Analysis focuses on human social interaction, postulating a range of basic human needs which are stimulated and/or exacerbated by 'strokes' of positive or negative kinds from other people. Four 'basic life positions' are described, which denote the relationship of self to the world. 'Ego states' of parent, adult and child are defined, not radically different from those of Freud. Flexibility and fluidity between ego states is necessary to cope with the world, but 'exclusions' and 'contaminations' can occur. When interpersonal transactions take place, they can be complementary (ego state addressed is ego state that responds), crossed (wrong ego state responds, communication breaks down), or ulterior (a covert transaction overlaid by a different one). A game is an 'ongoing series of complementary ulterior transactions progressing to a well-defined, predictable outcome' — with a payoff. Berne's work is perhaps most widely remembered for his delightful descriptions of 'games' such as 'Wooden leg', 'Let's you and him fight', 'See what you made me do', 'If it weren't for you' and 'Now I've got you, son of a bitch'.

Parent training based on Transactional Analysis has tended to adopt a simplified theoretical structure. Harris (1969) tends to be less complex and discusses parent–child interaction in some detail, describing the use of 'contracts' to enhance relationships. Later books which dealt with Transactional Analysis in child-rearing were those of Levin (1974), James (1974) and Babcock and Keepers (1976). Transactional Analysis groups typically involve didactic and experiential learning, and part of each session is devoted to 'practising'. A considerable amount of reading may be necessary and homework assignments of a practical nature are often given. Groups have a leader, but tend to evolve in very different ways according to the group composition. Specific problems brought to the group by participants may be 'brainstormed'. A useful summary is provided by Sirridge (1980).

Transactional Analysis is highly cognitive, and much more preoccupied with what people feel about themselves and others than with what they actually do. Specific training objectives are rarely set, and this form of parent training is extremely difficult to evaluate both reliably and validly. In addition, in view of the cognitive demands of Transactional Analysis, its applicability to all sections of the population must be in question. Certainly, parents looking for immediate practical solutions to day-to-day problems are unlikely to find them quickly in a Transactional Analysis group. Likewise, parents with low motivational levels may not stay the course. It is hardly surprising that the literature search uncovered no substantial examples of evaluations of Transactional Analysis groups for parent training. Transactional Analysis does, however, have the redeeming feature of often being enormous fun.

The other two major 'schools' of generalised training for ordinary parents which have a well-developed theoretical infrastructure can now be considered.

Problem-solving Techniques

The most widely known work in training parents to train their children in problem-solving techniques is that of Shure and Spivack (1978). Shure has noted that there is some evidence (Combs and Slaby, 1979) that reinforcement techniques alone sometimes do not produce an effect which lasts beyond the period of training, and suggests that training children to generate novel (behavioural) solutions to their problems is a creative extension of the simple operant paradigm. At the widest level, this might involve parents suggesting to a child that he/she engage in a new positive behaviour instead of the unacceptable behaviour the parents are busy modifying. Shure's implication, that this might be a great deal quicker than the tedious complexities of shaping up new behaviour targeted by the parents, is entirely reasonable, although this may be a misconception of how behaviour modification actually works in the average household.

The work of Shure and Spivack is particularly interesting in that it is targeted on very young children, those aged 4–5. The authors cite their own extensive research which demonstrates that 'alternative solution thinking' is a good predictor of teacher-rated behavioural adjustment in school, irrespective of IQ or socioeconomic status. The good 'problem-solvers' were likely to be less impulsive than their peers, calmer, and more sociable.

Systematic training of children by their parents or by their teachers showed that, relative to controls, children of such tender years could improve their interpersonal problem-solving skills, and those who improved most also improved most in pro-social behaviours, peer popularity and self-control (Shure and Spivack, 1978, 1979, 1980). There is some evidence that this approach is applicable to disadvantaged target groups as well as to 'ordinary' parents, and that boys acquire it as well as girls, despite seeming a potentially more resistant group at pre-test.

The training approach was thorough. See Shure and Spivack (1978) for full details. As mothers were trained in problem-solving thinking skills, they in turn taught their children lessons from a sequenced day-by-day programme script, as demonstrated and role-played in ten weekly workshops. The parents were encouraged to analyse their own behaviour, with a view to increasing awareness of the wide range of different ways to solve problems and sensitivity to the child's point of view, de-emphasising the value of immediate action without thought, and providing a good model of problem-solving behaviour to the child.

As noted above, the results were convincing, and process data (albeit paper-and-pencil vignette analysis) strongly suggest that maternal skill changes mediated the changed child response. It is interesting that the mothers did not generalise their problem-solving skills to interactions which did not involve their children. However, the improvements in child response did generalise to the school, which operant behavioural interventions have repeatedly failed to show (albeit often with older children). This approach clearly has great promise, although wider replication is needed.

Parent Effectiveness Training

Parent Effectiveness Training (PET) is probably the largest parent-training programme anywhere in the Western world, having involved several hundred thousand parents. Originated by Thomas Gordon, a clinical psychologist, the book *Parent Effectiveness Training* (Gordon, 1970) became a bestseller. Involving group training and incorporating theory, skill training and skill practice, a PET course has a leader who models the skills, supervises role-play, gives feedback, manages the social dynamics and assigns written exercises.

Gordon sees the training as dealing with 'the critical issue of power and authority in human relationships'. The courses are designed in the hope that both parents will attend, but have usually been fee-paying in the USA. Many professionals and parents who are graduates of a course have been trained as group leaders, and courses are held in a very wide range of local meeting-places. An instructor's guide is provided to trained group leaders, and practice teaching arranged and back-up support provided.

The course content includes: describing behaviour eschewing value judgements and reference to personality traits, learning to behave congruently with feelings, communicating (via open-ended questions, active listening, and sending feeling statements or 'I-messages'), discriminating between types of authority and various child responses to them, and using a six-step, 'no-lose', problem-solving strategy.

A great deal of research has been conducted on the effectiveness of PET, but is of very disparate quality. Stearn (1971) used a variety of paper-and-pencil (PAP) pre- and post-tests with 18 PET parents and two control groups. The results were said to show that the PET groups become more democratic in attitudes towards the family, but other variables inter-related eccentrically. Lillibridge (1972) used a similar design but different (PAP) measures, and found PET parents became more confident and accepting and trusting of their children. The children perceived the PET parents to be more accepting of them. The two control groups showed no change on any measure.

Larson (1972) compared PET with an Achievement Motivation Program (AMP) and a Discussion Encounter Group (DEG). Five PAP measures, a parental log of child behaviour, and generalised parental verbal feedback were the outcome measures. The AMP and PET groups did markedly better than the DEG group, although the DEG participants reported feeling equally satisfied. On the whole, PET did a little better than AMP. In a similar vein, Hanley (1974) compared PET with a course entitled Family Enrichment Program (FEP). Some significant differences between the groups emerged favouring PET.

Dubey *et al.* (1977) found PET training to have a significant positive effect on the behaviour of hyperactive children, but rather less than in the children of parents having behaviour modification training. More parents in the behaviour modification group reported finding the workshop relevant and fewer of them dropped out. Of course, this comparison is not entirely fair, as PET aims to be more preventive than curative and is not designed for children with specific behavioural dysfunctions. Rob and Norfor (1980) report the results from 152 attitude questionnaires collected after PET courses in Australia. Results were positive, and parents with the lowest initial scores improved most. The authors take this as an indication that low-SES parents can benefit from PET, but cite no evidence that low scorers actually were of lower SES, and appear to have ignored the possibility of regression to the mean artefacts.

A sweeping criticism of PET comes from Doherty and Ryder (1980), who also express their distaste regarding the commercial and media aspects of the programme. The authors complain about the 'technologization' of relationships, the way PET is said to scapegoat parents while appearing to have all the answers, and the 'naive view' PET is alleged to take of family dynamics. A number of possible undesirable side-effects are listed. Unfortunately, this paper lacks coherence to much the same degree as the pro-PET studies.

Gordon (1980) himself lists a large number (25) of outcome studies of PET which have found statistically significant results in favour of the programme. He notes that the quality of the studies varies widely, but does not acknowledge how selectively he has quoted from overall findings. For instance, in one of the few studies which examined parent–child behaviour as well as attitude change, Gordon cites the PAP indication of increased parental confidence without bothering to mention that no change whatsoever was detected in either child or parent behaviour. Bearing this in mind, it is worth noting that these studies are claimed to demonstrate: increased parental confidence, increased parental acceptance of and trust in children, increased understanding of their children, more democratic and less autocratic attitudes to their children, parental improvements in self-esteem and reduction in anxiety, and so on. The vast majority of these studies are based on paper-and-pencil measures of attitudes, and many have been conducted by Gordon's aficionados or relatives. Only one study is cited wherein the children of PET parents are said to have improved their behaviour.

The most thorough review of the research on the effectiveness of PET training was conducted by Rinn and Markle (1977), who noted that the existing research was limited in scope and inadequate in design. Problems were often evident with respect to random assignment of subjects to groups, a lack of objective behavioural measures, inappropriate statistical methods, absent or inappropriate control conditions, and a lack of follow-up. Rinn and Markle conclude that 'the effectiveness of PET as a prevention or intervention strategy is not supported', and provide helpful suggestions as to how adequate evaluative research might proceed. This judgement may seem a little harsh; after all, PET has often demonstrated attitude change in the short term. Whether this kind of outcome justifies the speed with which PET has been adopted over a very large geographical area is another question.

Miscellaneous

A foster family, while by definition atypical, need not be out of the 'ordinary' in terms of relationships, behaviour and developmental problems. There has been a great deal of work on training foster-parents, but the very complexity of the task of foster-parenting makes detailed evaluation of the impact of such courses difficult. Useful guides for foster-parents have been written (Sarason *et al.* 1976; Rutter, 1978) as well as manuals for foster-parent trainers (Stone and Hunzeker, 1974; Panitch, 1977). Marr and Kennedy (1980) provide a summary of work in this field, which will be considered in greater detail in Chapter 8, 'Behaviour Problems', since such problems often pose the greatest threat to placement breakdown.

A much more specific programme is described by van der Molen *et al.* (1983), who trained parents to train their children in safe road-crossing strategies. Previous research had established that parents often provided poor models of road-crossing behaviour, and either left children to walk alone with little supervision, or held their hands — the latter merely leading to stereotyped conformity which did not generalise. Furthermore, where parents taught safety rules verbally, they often broke them themselves.

The programme identified three key tasks, and by modelling, practice together, practice alone and reinforcement, parents were trained to train their children aged 4–6 years. Twelve training sessions lasting between 10 and 15 minutes were provided for the children, preceded by sensitising video material in which a child modelled the required behaviour. The parents received a lecture, video material for modelling, written instruction, group discussion and practice opportunities.

Subsequently, secret observation of 63 children and their

parents indicated significant improvement in parental behaviour, in terms of setting a better example and giving verbal instruction. The children's traffic behaviour also improved. There is, unfortunately, no datum on long-term follow-up, or on generalisation of these gains to situations where parents are not present.

Turning to something completely different, Hinze (1980) describes a large-scale programme designed to help parents and others transmit nutrition education to their pre-school children, with a view to improving their dietary habits. Nutrition education would be seen as part of health education in many countries, but it is not usually targeted on pre-school children in any systematic way, rarely involves parents, and is equally infrequently evaluated. Hinze's (1980) programme established workshops in two family day-care homes, 16 childcare centres and eight schools. The final report is full of detailed description which will be of interest to those wishing to replicate the programme; it is, however, rather light on evaluation. Nevertheless, the programme certainly resulted in great participation in and understanding of nutrition education, although information about longer-term behavioural change is not presented.

Least probable of all, Olympus Research (1977, 1979) reports on a programme designed to 'extend the benefits of career education to pre-school children in the home'. A package of materials was developed for parent training groups, including a parents' guide, films and audio-tapes, to be used by teachers to train parents. Evaluation included pre- and post-tests, recordings of sessions, and interviews with those involved, for 67 programme participants. Results indicated that parents achieved increased knowledge and more definite opinions on the topic. What implications this holds, if any, for long-term behaviour is not clear.

Summary

Parent training for 'ordinary' families must be relevant to their self-perceived needs and build on existing strengths. Programmes to increase the stimulation parents provide to their children pre-school have been found to work well where they were clearly structured, involved both parents, incorporated home visiting and subsequently linked with the receiving school. Long-term follow-up data from several studies are encouraging, although not always statistically significant. Less structured programmes utilising distance teaching have shown less success, but overall the picture is fairly positive.

Structured parent training together with the provision of relevant materials is effective in developing early reading skills in pre-school children. Distance teaching by television associated with written materials has also been found effective. There is also evidence for the impact of parents on writing skills and information processing/retention. A great deal of associated work is referred to in Chapter 7, 'Learning Difficulties'. There is surprisingly little information on education and training for parents of gifted children.

A very wide range of programmes intending to impart general 'parenting' skills exists. Many of these are vague in objectives, weak in structure, and evaluated by paper-and-pencil tests of attitudes which are of doubtful validity and reliability. It seems easy to demonstrate short-term increments in knowledge, less easy to show positive shifts in attitudes, somewhat less easy again to show changed parental behaviour, and very difficult to prove child behaviour had concomitantly changed. Three very different sample programmes are reviewed in detail, none offering very tangible evaluation results.

Of the three general parent-training programmes with a well-developed theoretical base, there is least evaluation information on Transactional Analysis, which does not lend itself to such an exercise. The problem-solving techniques for pre-school children developed by Shure and Spivack show considerable promise, but initial positive evaluation results need wider replication. Parent Effectiveness Training, by contrast, has had too much replication and too little proper evaluation, and its effectiveness remains in question, although many people like it.

Brief reviews of training in traffic skills, nutrition and career education conclude the chapter. The general picture is very various, but the field includes many ill-structured programmes, with muddled curricula and unsophisticated teaching methods, and very weak evaluation measures. Particularly regarding 'general parenting skills', there is little evidence of maintenance of gains, or generalisation to other environmental contexts or children or to parents with special needs or of low socio-economic status. The effectiveness of at least half of the work in this field is in doubt, and its cost-effectiveness even more open to question.

Why should 'ordinary' parents be offered training in many ways worse than that offered various 'special needs' groups? Do potential trainers try less hard, on the assumption that they can't actually do much damage with ordinary parents? Surely, if something is worth teaching at all, it is worth teaching properly? Having said that, there are some examples of good practice in this area, which will be evident from reading the text — other workers, please copy.

References

Babcock, D.E. and Keepers, T.D. (1976) *Raising Kids O.K.* (New York: Grove Press)

Berne, E. (1964) *Games People Play* (New York: Grove Press)

Brim, O.G. (1965) *Education for Child Rearing* (2nd edn) (New York: Free Press)

Christensen, O.C. and Thomas, C.R. (1980) 'Dreikurs and the Search for Equality', in M.J. Fine (ed.), *Handbook on Parent Education* (New York: Academic Press)

Combs, M.L. and Slaby D.A. (1979) 'Social Skills Training with Children', in B. Lahey and A. Kazdin (eds.), *Advances in Clinical Child Psychology* (vol. 1) (New York: Plenum Press)

Corno, L. (1980) 'Individual and Class Level Effects of Parent-assisted Instruction in Classroom Memory Support Strategies', *Journal of Educational Psychology*, 72, 3, 278-92

Doherty, W.J. and Ryder, R.G. (1980) 'Parent Effectiveness Training (PET): Criticisms and Caveats', *Journal of Marital and Family Therapy*, 6, 4, 409-19

Dreikurs, R. and Soltz, V. (1964) *Children: The Challenge* (New York: Meredith Press)

Dubey, D.R. *et al.* (1977) 'Behavioral and Reflective Parent Training for Hyperactive Children: A Comparison', paper presented at meeting of American Psychological Association, San Francisco

Dusewicz, R.A. and Coller, A.R. (1978) *An Evaluation of the Kentucky Picture Pages Program. Technical Report and Appendix.* (Philadelphia, Pennsylvania: Research for Better Schools Inc.) (E.R.I.C. ED 151081, PS 009790)

Eyken, W. van der (1980) 'Under-fives Info-phone: The Implementation and Initial Evaluation of Telephone Based Services to Parents of Young Families', *Early Child Development and Care*, 6, 3, 151-78

Fein, G.G. (1977) 'The Social Context of Mother–Infant Relations: A Study of Home Based Education', paper presented at annual meeting of the American Educational Research Association, New York (E.R.I.C. ED140986, PS 009382)

Gordon, T. (1970) *Parent Effectiveness Training: The 'No-Lose' Program for Raising Responsible Children* (New York: Wyden)

Gordon, T. (1980) Parent Effectiveness Training: A Preventive Program and its Effects on Families', in M.J. Fine (ed.), *Handbook on Parent Education* (New York: Academic Press)

Gotts, E.E. (1979) *Early Childhood and Parenting Research Program. Final Report* (Charleston, West Virginia: Appalachia Educational Lab.) (E.R.I.C. ED183293, PS011292)

Gotts, E.E. (1980) 'Long-term Effects of a Home-oriented Pre-school Program', *Childhood Education*, 56, 4, 228-34

Hanley, D.F. (1974) 'Changes in Parent Attitudes Related to Parent Effectiveness Training and a Family Enrichment Program', *Dissertation Abstracts International, 34*, 7044-A

Hannon, P.W. and Cuckle, P. (1984) 'Involving Parents in the Teaching of Reading: A Study of Current School Practice', *Educational Research, 26, 1*, 7-13

Harris, T.A. (1969) *I'm O.K. — You're O.K.* (New York: Harper & Row)

Hess, R.D. (1976) 'Effectiveness of Home-based Early Education Programs', paper presented at annual convention of the American Psychological Association, Washington (E.R.I.C. ED 133048, PS 008964)

Hinze, L.L. (1980) *SPEAC for Nutrition. Final Report* (Minneapolis, Minnesota: Minneapolis Public Schools) (E.R.I.C. ED 194201, PS 011797)

Jackson, R.H. and Terdal, L. (1978) 'Parent Education within a Pediatric Practice', *Journal of Pediatric Psychology, 3, 1*, 2-5

James, M. (1974) *Transactional Analysis for Moms and Dads* (Reading, Massachusets: Addison-Wesley)

Kessen, W. *et al.* (1975) *Variations in Home-based Infant Education: Language, Play and Social Development. Final Report* (New Haven, Connecticut: Yale University) (E.R.I.C. ED 118233, PS 008302)

Larson, R.S. (1972) 'Can Parent Classes Affect Family Communications?', *The School Counselor, 19*, 261-70

Leonard, J.E. (ed.) (1977) *Chapel Hill Services to the Gifted Handicapped: A Project Summary* (Chapel Hill, North Carolina: Chapel Hill Training-Outreach Project) (E.R.I.C. ED 149549, EC 103865)

Levin, P. (1974) *Becoming the Way We Are* (Berkeley, California: Transactional Publications)

Lillibridge, E.M. (1972) 'The Relationship of a Parent Effectiveness Training Program to Change in Parents' Self-assessed Attitudes and Children's Perceptions of Parents', *Dissertation Abstracts International, 32* (10-A) 5613-A

Marr, P.M. and Kennedy, C.E. (1980) 'Parenting Atypical Families', in M.J. Fine (ed.), *Handbook on Parent Education* (New York: Academic Press)

Metzl, M.N. (1980) 'Teaching Parents a Strategy for Enhancing Infant Development', *Child Development, 51, 2*, 583-6

Molen, H.H. van der, *et al.* (1983) 'Pedestrian Behaviour of Children and Accompanying Parents During School Journeys: An Evaluation of a Training Programme', *British Journal of Educational Psychology, 53, 2*, 152-68

Niedermeyer, F.C. (1970) 'Parents Teach Kindergarten Reading at Home' *Elementary School Journal, 70*, 438-45

Nimnicht, G. *et al.* (1977) 'The Parent/Child Toy Library Program', in M.C. Day and R.R. Parker (eds.), *The Pre-school in Action* (2nd edn.) (Boston: Allyn & Bacon)

Olympus Research Centers (1977) *Supporting Home-based Career Education at the Pre-school Level. Final Report* (San Francisco, California: Olympus Research Center) (E.R.I.C. ED164927, CE019271)

Olympus Research Centers (1979) *Continuation of a Project Supporting Home-based Career Education at the Pre-school Level. Final Report* (Salt Lake City, Utah: Olympus Research Centers) (E.R.I.C. ED183803, CE024350)

Panitch, A. (1977) *Comparative Approaches in Foster Care Training* (Boise, Idaho: Boise State University)

Patton, M.Q. (1977) *An External Review of Early Childhood and Family Education Pilot Programs: Abridged Report* (Minneapolis, Minnesota: Center for Social Research, Minnesota University) (E.R.I.C. ED182041, PS011195)

Payne, G.E. (1976) 'The Effect of a Parent-training Program on the Intellectual and Interpersonal Behavior of Pre-school Children', *Dissertation Abstracts International, 36*, (12B-1) 6396

Perlish, H.N. (1970) 'Early Reading via Television', *Educational Television International, 4, 2,* 110-15

Raban, B. (1982) 'Influences on Children's Writing, 5-9 Years', paper presented at annual meeting of the United Kingdom Reading Association, Newcastle upon Tyne (E.R.I.C. ED222921, CS207255)

Rich, D. *et al.* (1979) 'Building on Family Strengths: The "Nondeficit" Involvement Model for Teaming Home and School', *Educational Leadership, 36, 7,* 506-10

Rinn, R.C. and Markle, A. (1977) 'Parent Effectiveness Training: A Review', *Psychological Reports, 41,* 95-109

Rob, M. and Norfor, J. (1980) 'Parenting — Can Skills Be Learned?', *Australian Journal of Social Issues, 15, 3,* 189-93

Rutter, B.A. (1978) *The Parent's Guide to Foster Family Care* (New York: Child Welfare League of America)

Sarason, I. *et al.* (1976) *A Guide for Foster Parents* (New York: Human Sciences Press)

Shure, M.B. and Spivack, G. (1978) *Problem-solving Techniques in Child-rearing* (San Francisco: Jossey-Bass)

Shure, M.B. and Spivack, G. (1979) 'Interpersonal Cognitive Problem Solving and Primary Prevention: Programming for Preschool and Kindergarten Children', *Journal of Clinical Child Psychology, 8,* 89-94

Shure, M.B. and Spivack, G. (1980) 'Interpersonal Problem Solving as a Mediator of Behavioral Adjustment in Preschool and Kindergarten Children', *Journal of Applied Developmental Psychology, 1,* 29-44

Sirridge, S.T. (1980) 'Transactional Analysis: Promoting O.K.ness', in M.J. Fine (ed.), *Handbook on Parent Education* (New York: Academic Press)

Stearn, M.B. (1971) 'The Relationship of Parent Effectiveness Training to Parent Attitudes, Parent Behavior and Child Self-esteem', *Dissertation Abstracts International, 32* (3-B) 1885-6

Stone, H. and Hunzeker, J. (1974) *Education for Foster Family Care: Models and Methods for Foster Parents and Social Workers* (New York: Child Welfare League of America)

Topping, K. and Wolfendale, S. (eds.) (1985) *Parental Involvement in Children's Reading* (London: Croom Helm/New York: Nicholls Publishing Company)

Vogel, M.D. (1975) 'Maternal Attitude Change Towards Self and Child as a Result of Training in Behavior Modification', *Dissertation Abstracts International, 30* (6-B) 3079-B

5   DISADVANTAGED CHILDREN

Who *are* the disadvantaged? And *why* are they disadvantaged? This whole area of study is fraught with political and moral issues, long before we come to ask the question which concerns us here: what can we effectively *do* about educational disadvantage?

It is undisputed that working-class children tend to have lower school attainments than do middle-class children, and these class differences are already occurring at the infant school stage. This tends to be even more true for pupils from ethnic minorities.

In the 1960s the dominant view was that working-class children suffered from deficits in linguistic and cognitive skills and motivation which were largely environmentally determined. 'Cultural deprivation', associated with poverty, was the problem. 'Compensatory education' was the cure.

Then compensatory education failed — was demonstrated to be ineffective — and interest in the influence of genetic factors increased, fuelling an intense and, at times, furious debate.

A third school of thought then emerged. Working-class children were no longer to be considered deficient, merely 'different'. At variance from the dominant middle-class culture in linguistics, priorities and objectives, it was not to be wondered at that the working classes showed little interest in jumping through the hoops in a circus owned and run by aliens.

Conflicting interpretations spawned many ancillary whirlpools. Are working-class children less intelligent because they do less well on middle-class tests of supposed 'intelligence', administered by middle-class testers? Do different ethnic groupings display idiosyncratic profiles of cognitive sub-skills? Does the interminable discussion of questions like these improve the quality of life of anybody but university academics? Readers wishing to pursue this further will find useful summaries in Pilling and Pringle (1978) and Hinckley *et al.* (1979).

The Westinghouse and other evaluations of the Head Start Program in the USA showed that after three years in school the gains from compensatory pre-school programmes had washed out. A similar pattern emerges from UK studies of the long-term effectiveness of nursery education, albeit slightly less depressing.

More recent studies in both countries have yielded more optimistic results, particularly with respect to 'sleeper' effects which may only emerge in the very long term.

Evidence that highly structured intervention programmes produce the greatest immediate gains is now viewed in the context of longitudinal data indicating that the gains from such programmes are not necessarily the best maintained in the long term. And, perhaps most crucially, attention has of late focused much more on the impact of education at home via the parents. How could so many apparently sophisticated researchers have sustained such a simplistic view of education for so long?

By the mid-1970s Bronfenbrenner (1974) was beginning to suggest that home-based intervention was less susceptible to long-term wash-out, although hard evidence was still scanty. As time went on, it became increasingly evident that the development of more effective and efficient home-based programmes would be likely to bear rich fruit. And so it was.

Let us now examine the developing evidence in more detail.

Head Start and Follow Through

Federally funded Head Start Programmes spread through the USA like a forest fire in the late 1960s and early 1970s. Projects were mainly developed to serve the 'disadvantaged', but many were targeted on children with more specific handicaps as well. Thus, by 1974, Clark and Johnston could report on 14 separate programmes under the Head Start umbrella, offering strategies for delivering services to 'handicapped' children. As the alarm bells began to sound for increasing awareness of the 'wash-out' phenomenon, more emphasis was placed on 'finding out what works'. The Follow Through Program adopted a harder evaluative line from the outset, as it 'followed through' Head Start to scrutinise different approaches to the education of the disadvantaged from nursery to the third year of formal schooling.

Innovative programmes were developed under the aegis of 20 'sponsors', and the programme eventually served 75,000 children from 170 communities at a cost of $59 million. Many of the children involved might have preferred just to take the $787. It was not until 1971 that a clear evaluation strategy was developed, and evaluation contracts awarded. Even then, only nine of the 20 sponsors could be persuaded to adopt control group evaluation designs.

The intervention models compared were very disparate. The Open Education Model was loosely derived from a transatlantic understanding of 'good practice' in British infant schools — individualised discovery learning and personal responsibility. The Tucson Early Education Model (TEEM) used a language experience approach coupled with direct teaching in cognition. The cognitive curriculum associated with the High/Scope Foundation emphasised self-discovery along Piagetian lines. The Responsive Education Model used gadgets but was very eclectic, with a Montessori flavour. The Bank Street Model was based on a *mélange* of Dewey, Piaget and Freud. The Behavior Analysis Model emphasised task analysis and reinforcement. The Direct Instruction Model, based on Bereiter-Engelmann, spawned the DISTAR materials. The Florida Parent Education Model, originated by Ira Gordon, professed some allegiance to Piaget, but differed from the others in that parent educators spent much of their time working with the parents of the target children. Finally, the Language Development Model incorporated a structured and sequenced curriculum taught in English and Spanish and emphasising language development.

A variety of attainment tests, attitude inventories and rating scales were applied to programme children in a variety of programme sites on a yearly basis. Supposed control groups were often less disadvantaged than experimental groups, necessitating the use of ANCOVA (analysis of covariance). Detailed process data were not always collected, and it is thus difficult to tell whether the results evaluate the programme content or how well the programme was actually implemented.

The results given in the final report (Abt Associates, 1977) are highly complex. Basically, however, as Becker (1978) was quick to point out, Direct Instruction did best. The next best were the Language Development and Parent Education Models. Some of the models appeared to have *negative* effects. The two models doing best on *affective* outcomes were the Direct Instruction and Behavior Analysis Models, followed by the Language Development and Parent Education Models. Direct Instruction did best in raising simple test attainment in reading, maths, spelling and language, and the Behavior Analysis Model also did well in all but the latter.

Whether all of this shows much more than that children learn what they are taught, and that the more they are taught the more they learn, is debatable. Bearing in mind that many of the programmes were cobbled together at some speed to catch the funding, it is not altogether surprising that the more subtle programmes which demand a high degree of teacher skill and experience and an all-pervading organisational infrastructure of great clarity, did not emerge well from the evaluation. The results do, however, demonstrate quite convincingly that Direct Instruction is relatively idiot-proof.

As Berman and McLaughlin (1975) note, the assumptions that (i) if schools knew about better methods they would adopt them, (ii) if schools adopted better methods they would do a better job, and (iii) if the government initiated innovation the schools would keep it going, are all unsupportable by the facts. Other evaluative reports, such as that by Toll (1976), note that 'there is some range in practices among centers in terms of extent of model implementation'.

The 'no difference' finding of the notorious Westinghouse evaluation of Head Start (Cicirelli *et al.*, 1969) has been much scrutinised and criticised. In fact, the study found that the positive impact of full-year programmes was balanced by the negative impact of shorter programmes, and the setting of high critical values for significance statistics arguably under-estimated the impact of the interventions. Subsequent reanalyses of the data squeezed positive findings even from the lemons of the data on the short-term programmes.

Subsequently, of course, Follow Through was demonstrated to be capable of preventing 'wash-out', and the now well-acknowledged 'sleeper effects' discovered (e.g. Seitz *et al.*, and Palmer; both in Brown, 1978). The Development Continuity Consortium at Cornell University under the chairmanship of Irving Lazar (Lazar and Darlington, 1979) has generated massive data analyses presenting a more positive picture, as meta-analysis of many studies better enables educational significance to be weighed against statistical significance.

There now seems little doubt that compensatory education can be effective. The questions that remain are: for whom does it work? How does it work? And how can cost-effectiveness be maximised?

Home Start

Beginning in 1972, 16 communities were funded to operate Home Start programmes over a three-and-a-half-year period. The initial intention was to serve 3–5-year-old children in low-income families for whom a centre-based programme was not feasible because of geographical isolation. By 1980, over 400 Head Start grantees were implementing some variant of a home-based option.

Trained home visitors, often paraprofessionals recruited from local neighbourhoods, made weekly or bi-weekly visits, spending time equally focused on parents and children. Toys and equipment were brought and loaned, techniques demonstrated and parents trained. Curriculum included pre-school skills, health, nutrition and socio-emotional development. Monthly group meetings were often incorporated to reduce the social isolation of families, especially in the summer months.

By 1974, the first follow-up evaluations were emerging (e.g. Scott, 1974). Scott's programme evaluation included six monthly tests during Home Start involvement on the Iowa Tests of Pre-school Development for 44 children, with follow-up assessment 19 months later when the children were in school. At the end of the programme the target children were well ahead of their siblings (used as a comparison group), but at follow-up the differences had washed out in verbal skills. However, in perceptual, numerical and spatial skills, the black children in particular had maintained, if not improved, their position.

The most voluminous evaluative work on Home Start is that of John Love and his associates (1975, 1976, 1977). The first of these reports, based on the second year of operation, included a variety of normative attainment tests, attitude scales, self-report inventories, observational checklists, parental interviews and checks on the height, weight and diet of the children. After seven months in the programme, the experimental children significantly outperformed control children on three out of four skill measures, but for children in the programme for twelve months, this was true for only one out of four measures. Experimental children had visited doctors and dentists more than controls. Children in the seven-month programme had more toys and books in the house than controls, but children in the twelve-month programme had only more toys than controls. In contrast, the twelve-month children did better on socio-emotional measures, where they outscored controls on three out of six measures, while seven-month programme children managed this only on one out of six. Seven-month programme children were heavier than controls, while twelve-month programme children were taller than controls, but considering the absence of evidence for radically different diet, this finding is mysterious. Given sufficient multiplicity of measures, almost any intervention will generate *some* statistically significant findings, but the more numerous the measures, the greater also is the probability of silly answers to non-existent questions.

Overall, little significant difference was found between the effectiveness of Home Start and that of Head Start. The two programmes were compared on 54 outcome variables, and significant differences found in only 15 cases — four pro-Home Start and eleven pro-Head Start. However, Head Start tended to be more expensive than Home Start, although Love *et al.* put the cost of Home Start per family in 1974 at $1,660.

Subsequent reports (Love *et al.*, 1976, 1977) used more sophisticated statistical analysis and considered data from more families (370) over more sites (16), although attrition rates as high as 49 per cent were noted. Earlier results were largely confirmed — particularly the finding that periods longer than seven months in the programme yielded no greater effects. The shorter programme was thus clearly more cost-effective. Visits of 90–120 minutes were found to be optimal, but more *frequent* visits were clearly associated with greater child progress. Visits to doctors and dentists tended to tail off in the long term. The Love *et al.* (1976) report includes a series of useful abstracts of research from other home-based intervention projects in an appendix. An impressionistic evaluation oi the Home Start Training Centers (for training home visitors) is offered by Love *et al.* (1979), with loose and, unsurprisingly, fairly positive results.

Data on long-term outcomes is reported by Bache and Nauta (1979) and Bache *et al.* (1979). Ex-Head and Home Start families were 'tracked down' for the purpose, with inevitable problems of sample attrition. The final sample included 199 Home Start families, with comparisons made with 46 Head Start and 137 'control' group families. Standardised tests were used with the children and parents individually interviewed.

Results on maths and reading tests showed that Home Start children tended to be below the national averages (norms) in their first year in school, but by the second year their mean maths percentile was 49 per cent and mean reading percentile 56 per cent. Thus, two years after Home Start ended, these 'disadvantaged' children were holding their own in basic attainments. Although the immediate Home Start outcome data were less than enthralling, the long-term evidence indicated Home Start had just as strong a 'sleeper effect' as Head Start. However, the longer Home Start programmes still had no greater effects than the shorter ones.

Many programmes which originated under the Head Start umbrella subsequently continued to develop, and many refined their methods and evaluative technique. It will be worth while to consider some of these in more detail.

The Florida Parent Education Program

This pioneering enterprise, spanning over a decade of intense activity by Ira Gordon and his associates, was finally marred by Gordon's untimely death in 1978. The work is reported in Gordon (1969), Guinagh (1971), Guinagh *et al.* (1975), Guinagh and Gordon (1976), Gordon *et al.* (1975, 1977, 1978, 1979), and Yahres (1977). Based at the Institute for the Development of Human Resources at the University of Florida in Gainesville, the programme was part of the Follow Through thrust, serving children from kindergarten to third grade (age 9). Community people were hired and trained to work as parent educators, visiting homes weekly to teach parents skills to use at home with their children. The parents were to acquire home-teaching competencies designed to improve their children's intellectual behaviour, self-esteem and motivation.

Curriculum content was flexible, but loosely Piagetian and emphasising language interaction. Raising the self-esteem and sense of control of both parent and child was an important objective. Items and activities from the Gesell, Bayley and Cattell Scales were incorporated. General folklore and a variety of eclectic professional sources yielded other ideas. Home visiting began when the target child was aged 3 months, and different treatment groups stayed in the programme for periods lasting up to three years. The curriculum content was organised into five stages or series, sub-divided into specific single lessons, detailed on simple written sheets which could be left with the family. Sequencing of lessons was individualised. For children in the programme between the ages of 2 and 3 years, an additional component was included — two 2-hour sessions per week in a 'home learning center' with four other children and two adults, the 'center' being the home of a programme mother.

Each parent educator had a 'caseload' of ten parents, and was accountable to a supervisor. Parental training was by verbal explanation, written instruction sheet, and demonstration with the child. The mother was then asked to practise the activity with the child while the visitor watched. If the child was unavailable, the visitor demonstrated by role-play using the parent as simulated child, then roles were reversed for parental practice. There was no specification of the amount of time the parent was to spend teaching the activity, but progress was evaluated at the next visit. Visitors filed a weekly report, scrutinised by their supervisor.

Evaluation was to be via the Stanford-Binet intelligence test and the Caldwell Preschool Inventory at age 5, together with language and self-concept measures and parent interviews. Data were available on 258 mothers, assigned to eight groups with different permutations of experimental and control conditions. Prior to age 5, data were also gathered on Griffiths, Bayley and Leiter Scales.

Results in the long term were encouraging. On the Stanford-Binet, children in the programme over all three years, or for just the first year, just the first two years, or only the third year, all scored higher than controls — only children who were in the programme only in the second year or in the first and third years seemed to miss out. The 'first-year-only' group had left the programme four years before this testing. On the Preschool Inventory, children in the programme for all three, the first two or the last two years did better than controls, as did the 'first-year-only' group. It is concluded that the programme, applied early and/or consistently over the first three years of the life of the child, produces long-term effects on the intellectual performance of the child. The long-term effects of parent education in the first year of the child's life are particularly remarkable.

Subsequently, Guinagh and Gordon (1976) reported a longitudinal extension, involving the scrutiny of the school records of 91 programme graduates then aged 10 years, who had been involved in the programme for one, two or three years. Current class teachers also rated pupil functioning and degree of parental involvement in school. Significant differences in favour of treatment groups were found. Fewer programme graduates had been assigned to special education facilities, and there were significant differences in favour of the experimental children on achievement tests in both second, third and fourth grade, although the teacher ratings showed no differences. It is concluded that there were clear lasting school achievement and performance effects for children who were in the original programme for two or three years, and the effect lasted up to six years. Parental involvement in school was also enhanced for programme graduates (also see Gordon *et al.*, 1978, 1979, on this topic).

The useful paper by Gordon *et al.* (1975) gives details of 44 exemplary parent-oriented early childhood education programmes — a most convenient directory for those interested in the area. An annotated bibliography of resource materials is attached.

The Mother–Child Home Program

Phyllis Levenstein's work, developing out of the Verbal Interaction Project, is reported in Levenstein and Sunley (1968), Levenstein (1970), Levenstein *et al.* (1973), Madden *et al.* (1976), Levenstein (1977, 1978a, 1978b, 1979), Rosenfeld (1978) and VIP (1978). The programme was designed to stimulate the low-income mothers of 2–3-year-old children to improve the cognitive skills of their children by verbally oriented play activity.

In the first study, an average of 32.4 visits per family over seven months in one year was made by a 'Toy Demonstrator', who presented a series of toys and books (Verbal Interaction Stimulus Materials) to the child and demonstrated their use as a focus for language activity to the mother. Eight kinds of verbal stimulation techniques were articulated in the programme's procedures, allowing a form of categorical interaction analysis.

Two control groups were utilised, one of which experienced visits and 'gifts' to control for the effect of mere extra attention. For the 33 experimental children, gains of 17 points on Cattell and Stanford-Binet Scales over the period were recorded, compared with one point and two points for the control groups. Peabody Picture Vocabulary Test scores rose 12.2 points for experimentals, while one control group gained 4.7 points and the other lost four points.

By 1973, well-structured replications were being reported, and the children in the programme were aged 2–4 years. Programme length doubled, home visiting frequency moved to 46 sessions, and a number of stimulus materials changed. Four replications showed that mean IQs for 37 children moved from 90 to 106. Despite the strong verbal emphasis of the programme, there was no evidence that only verbal skills improved as a result.

Long-term follow-up data began to accumulate, and Madden *et al.* (1976) report on 151 experimental and 55 comparison children. Children were tested at around age 5 on the previous measures and also the Wechsler test (WISC) in some cases. Attrition rates averaged 15 per cent. Mean IQs for various sub-groups ranged from 101 to 111. Further follow-up for four sub-groups at age 9 on the WISC showed mean IQs ranging from 95 to 108, although comparability of Cattell, Stanford-Binet and WISC scores must be questionable. It became clear from the follow-up data that paraprofessional Toy Demonstrators had been as effective as the original social work graduate Demonstrators, and that those children who had been in the programme for two years tended to do better than those involved for one year or only seven months.

A short-term study with a true control group involving random allocation to conditions was carried out, with less encouraging results. Of 51 allocated dyads, at the end of the two-year programme 19 experimentals and 16 controls remained, and mean E IQ was 105, while mean C IQ was 101. The researchers were unable to explain the pervasive phenomenon of spontaneously improving control group in their case, or why these short-term experimental results with small n should contradict the long-term quasi-experimental results with much larger numbers.

Training for Toy Demonstrators included an initial eight-session workshop, weekly group conferences, and individual supervision. Guide sheets for each stimulus material were available in the *Demonstrator's Handbook*. A rating scale for child development and a rating scale for parental maintenance of functional child-rearing practices were also used, particularly to assist the Demonstrators in developing the affective components of the intervention. These latter aspects were considered only second in importance to the primary and more tangible objective of verbal interaction. Demonstrator supervisors utilised discussion, audio-visual materials, modelling, and role-play in the training and supervision process. A useful paper for finer detail of day-to-day process is Levenstein (1977).

This was the subject of further study (reported in Levenstein,

1978a, 1978b) based on the Demonstrators' ratings of mother and child behaviour. At age 4, the child's behaviour traits (n = 45) were found to correlate significantly with aspects of the mother's verbal interactions with it. Almost all child task-orientation and cognitive-orientation measures were linked to mother's verbal interactions. The children were rated again at age 6 by school class teachers in comparison to their peers, and some evidence was found that maternal verbal interactive style continued to influence child behaviour in the long term and other environmental contexts.

Furthermore, programme effects in terms of school-based attainment gains were demonstrated for 78 programme graduates (attrition rate 21 per cent). These children reached national norms in their third grade (age 9) reading and arithmetic scores on the Wide Range Achievement Test, significantly outperforming control groups. Programme graduates were less likely to be held back a grade than control group children. The mean IQs of two of the three sub-groups in the experimental sample exceeded the national norm, although this difference did not reach statistical significance.

By 1978 programme replication in 70 settings in 16 states was being reported (see VIP, 1978, for a useful brief overall summary). A further true experimental study had been undertaken, attempting to control for the 'John Henry' effect. Attrition rates of 19 and 26 per cent were noted in the original experimental and control groups of 35 dyads. At pre-test, experimental children's IQs were two points ahead of those of controls, and by post-test this differential had increased to six points, a statistically significant finding. However, the control group still increased its mean IQ to be on a par with national norms! The cost per participant of the MCHP was reported to be $690 on average in 1974 (range $250-1,787 depending on salaries), comparing favourably to other programmes.

High/Scope Foundation Projects

A number of projects under the general auspices of David Weikart have operated in Ypsilanti, Michigan — the Ypsilanti–Perry Preschool Project, the Ypsilanti Home Teaching Project, and the Ypsilanti–Carnegie Infant Education Project, among others. The work is reported in Radin and Weikart (1967), Weikart (1970, 1972), Wittes and Radin (1971), Radin (1972), Lambie *et al.*

(1974), Weikart (1975) and Epstein and Weikart (1977).

The Perry Preschool Project was a two-year programme involving a daily three-hour nursery experience and a weekly 90-minute individualised home-teaching session, for children aged 3–4 years. During the home visits mothers were 'encouraged to observe and participate in as many teaching activities as possible'. During the first year of the programme, IQ gains in the children ranged from −5 to +37 points (median 17 points), but no further gains were made in the second year. Maternal involvement tended to decrease in the second year.

As part of the programme, a 'group work' experience for parents was trialled (Wittes and Radin, 1971). Parent group meetings were activity-oriented to avoid over-reliance on verbal interaction. Sixty-five of the programme's 93 mothers agreed to be involved, and were allocated to experimental or control groups. The group experience consisted of three units, each of six weekly meetings. The curriculum covered learning theory, behaviour management, teaching through household tasks, and promoting positive attitudes in children. Parents were given written handbooks and involved in role-playing, rehearsal, and home assignments. Group feedback at subsequent meetings was a regular feature, as was praise from group leaders. Another experimental group experienced a more traditional lecture–discussion format.

Outcome measures included attitude questionnaires and ratings of maternal behaviour in the home, coupled with Stanford-Binet scores. The paper-and-pencil measures showed some change favouring the experimental groups, but independent observation and test results showed few differences. However, experimental mothers seemed less inclined to be punitive than control mothers. There were no differences between the two group formats.

Subsequently, attempts were made to analyse the significance of the degree of maternal involvement in the programme. Seventy-one children were divided into three matched groups: no maternal involvement, moderate involvement and intense involvement. The first group had centre-based and in-home teaching without the mother being present, the second had mothers present at home tutorials, and the third added a separate group experience for the mothers. Outcome measures were Stanford-Binet and Peabody scores, teacher ratings, and parent questionnaires. Follow-up measures included the Wechsler Preschool and Primary Scale of Intelligence (WPSI).

At the end of the one-year programme there were no significant differences between groups on the Binet or Peabody tests: all had gained between twelve and thirteen points. Gains on other measures likewise were similar across groups. A further year later, the Peabody scores of the 'involvement' groups were ahead of the non-involvement group, but the difference for the highest-involvement group did not reach statistical significance, and there were no differences in Wechsler scores.

The Infant Education Project, by contrast, was totally home-based, and involved the implementation of a 'flexibly structured' Piagetian curriculum by professional teachers working with families in a 16-month home-teaching programme. It was also targeted on younger children, aged 3–11 months on programme entry. More detail is given in Lambie *et al.* (1974), but even then the specifics of programme process are undocumented, e.g. 'in essence, the curriculum was a viewpoint for looking at child development, rather than a package for teaching defined skills'.

Of the 150 families located who met eligibility criteria, 88 began the project and 65 completed it. Families were randomly assigned to three groups, one receiving weekly home visits from professional teachers, one visits from paraprofessionals who were unfamiliar with programme curriculum, and a no-contact control group. Assessment was conducted via the Bayley Scales and Stanford-Binet, an observational language checklist, ratings of maternal behaviour and a maternal attitude test.

Children in the experimental group performed better on tests and were noted to have better linguistic skills than children in the other two groups. However, these differences did not always attain statistical significance. The age of the child on programme entry did not have a consistent effect. Experimental mothers showed more positive and facilitative language interactions.

Long-term follow-up results gathered between four and five years post-project are reported by Epstein and Weikart (1977), who utilised families eligible for, but not participating in, the programme as an untested control group. The three age cohorts were collapsed and the paraprofessional contrast group dropped. Final comparisons were made with only 20 in the experimental group, 19 in the original control group, and 14 in the untested control group. In addition to existing programme measures, an observational assessment of mother–child dyads on a mutual problem-solving task and the reading and mathematics sub-tests of the

Metropolitan Achievement Test were used.

No significant differences were found between groups on the intelligence or attainment tests; all Binet scores were above average. More experimental than control children had been held back a grade. Of 65 analyses of variance carried out on the various behaviour rating scales, only four were statistically significant.

Compared with the long-term follow-up results from other compensatory programmes, the High/Scope outcomes can only be described as disappointing. Weikart and his associates have carried out yet further follow-up, and it is reported that Perry Preschool children show better adjustment to school and greater success in employment at age 19 (Makins, 1984, 1985). Whether a sleeper effect of this order is actually plausible is left to the reader to decide. Notwithstanding, the High/Scope pre-school programme was to be imported to the UK amidst considerable media hyperbole. An independent evaluation of the UK version is being carried out by researchers at Oxford University (Sylva and Smith). Let us hope the UK programme is a little more specific in its objectives and somewhat more methodical in its research design.

DARCEE Early Training Project

Most continually associated with the name of Susan Gray, this work is based at the George Peabody College for Teachers, Nashville, Tennessee. One of the most long-standing programmes, having begun in 1961, it is reported in Klaus and Gray (1967, 1968), Gray and Klaus (1970), Gilmer *et al.* (1970), Forrester *et al.* (1971), Gray and Ruttle (1976, 1980) and Gray (1977).

The initial programme, the Early Training Project, involved disadvantaged children in a ten-week pre-school during three consecutive summers, and delivered weekly meetings with a home visitor between the pre-school centre-based sessions. A second experimental group experienced a two-year programme in similar format. The home visitor, with a teaching and social work background, brought educational materials and showed the mother how to use them effectively with the child, during the hour-long weekly visits.

Random allocation to treatment and control groups was utilised, and outcome measures included the Stanford-Binet and Wechsler Scales, the Peabody Picture Vocabulary Test, the Illinois

Test of Psycholinguistic Abilities, the Metropolitan and Gates Reading Readiness Tests, the Metropolitan Achievement Test and the Stanford Achievement Test.

There were no group differences at the beginning of the study. After treatment, the experimental children were superior to the control children on the IQ tests and the tests of language and reading readiness. Many of these gains endured for four years of longitudinal measurement. However, the absolute size of the gains was modest on the whole, whilst usually managing to reach statistical significance, despite the relative intensity of the programme. However, there was evidence of generalisation of programme impact to younger siblings. In the experimental families the younger siblings showed Binet gains of thirteen points compared with control families.

Numbers of children involved were small, only 61 having been allocated to the two experimental groups and the local control group. A small distal control group was also followed. Details of the curriculum content are vague. There is talk of emphasis on language development, concept formation and achievement motivation within a traditional nursery curriculum which also emphasises reinforcement to encourage persistence and toleration of delay of gratification, but few clues about operational structures.

Although the experimental groups stayed ahead of the control groups by modest amounts (1.1–6.6 points) on IQ tests, the biggest gains tended to be made early in the programme and the two-year programme did better than the three-year programme. The highest scores were not maintained, all groups oscillating and showing some decline. Scores on the Illinois Test of Psycholinguistic Abilities were not significantly better in the third year of comparison, although Peabody Picture Vocabulary Test differences stood up well. At long-term follow-up in first and second grade, Metropolitan Achievement Test scores significantly favoured the experimental groups on five out of nine sub-tests, and on the Stanford tests on five out of twelve sub-tests. However, modest gains which stand up relatively well over four or five years are probably preferable to more spectacular gains which wash out very quickly.

By the end of fourth grade, however, all significant differences on language and achievement tests had washed out, although trends remained favouring the experimental groups. Intelligence test score differences did persist, however (Gray and Klaus, 1970).

Subsequent work tried systematically to separate the possible effects of the home-visiting component. This later study involved three treatments: (a) a special group pre-school programme lasting two and a half years, centre-based; (b) the pre-school combined with weekly home visits; and (c) the home visits alone. For the target children, the pre-school seemed most effective with or without the visiting. Both these groups did better than visited-only or control groups. However, for the younger siblings of the target children, the two groups incorporating visits did best, and results at two-year follow-up post-programme suggested that the mother-involved children had best maintained their early gains. The moral seemed clear — start your programme when the children are younger.

The next move was to work with the mothers of children aged 8–18 months (Forrester *et al.*, 1971). Ten white and ten black children aged 7–9 months on entry to the programme were served via home visits from paraprofessionals who made an average 24 visits in nine months. Toys were lent and mothers encouraged to make their own materials and undertake weekly assignments. The visitors modelled aetivities for mothers and reinforced maternal efforts.

Experimental children did significantly better than control children on a developmental checklist, Piagetian Scale and the Bayley Scales, on which latter the target group gained an average 18 points. Alas, at follow-up six months later, these infants were no longer significantly different from the controls. This caused the programme directors to conclude that the programme had been too infant-oriented and had not left mothers with skills generalisable to the toddler age-range.

This led to the development of the Family-oriented Home Visiting Program, which tried to provide just such generalisable skills, thereby hoping to capitalise on the well-documented generalisation to siblings at the same time. Nine months of weekly visits were made to homes containing two or three children under 5. One group received a nine-month programme specifically designed for the needs and characteristics of the individual families, another received a generic treatment focused chiefly on materials, and a third sub-group of the 69 families involved served as a control. Half the experimental mothers had an additional nine-month treatment of less frequent contacts.

The programme was designed to improve the mother's teaching style, help her with behaviour management and household organisation, and encourage more reciprocal language. The mother was seen as the major client. Mothers and children were pre- and post-tested on the usual range of instruments relating to maternal and child competencies. (Bayley, Binet, language test, Slosson Test, Maternal Behaviour Scales.) Visits were made by professionals, paraprofessionals and volunteers.

Results were again positive but modest, suffering from high attrition rates. Programme mothers certainly seemed to have improved the stimulus potential of the home, and this was well sustained over consecutive post-tests. Individualised home visiting did a little better than materials-only visiting, but ns were very small. Results from language and intelligence tests were likewise positive. Additional less frequent visiting made no significant difference with such small samples. Paradoxically, however, in this study there was no evidence of parallel gains in siblings (programme siblings actually doing slightly worse than control siblings). Further long-term follow-up is reported in Gray and Ruttle (1980).

The DARCEE story is thus generally one of modest gains, well sustained. Any expectation of sustaining very long-term gains in disadvantaged families, often constantly beset with random life events of much more profound seriousness than mere educational matters, needs to be realistic. The evidence here of some generalisation to siblings is encouraging. Who knows what a more structured curriculum and more specific objectives might have brought about?

The Family Development Research Project

Ronald Lally and Alice Honig were the mainsprings of this programme, reported in Lally and Honig (1977a, 1977b), Honig *et al.* (1978) and Honig (1980). Based at the Syracuse University (New York) Children's Center, services were provided for children aged 6 months to 60 months, and indeed extended to unborn children, as weekly home visits by paraprofessionals could start between three and six months before the child's birth. Children aged 6-15 months attend a half-time centre-based programme known as 'Infant-fold', based on the theories of Piaget and Erikson. Toddlers (15–48 months) attend a full-day centre-based programme based on British infant schools' practice, called the Family

Style Program. Parents attend the centre, and meet in small groups either at home or in centre, and a continuous programme of weekly paraprofessional home visits runs throughout.

The programme stipulates curriculum objectives in a degree of detail. For instance, the functioning of children aged 36 months is related to 50 goals in six areas: personal awareness, gross motor skills, social skills, cognition, language, and self-help skills. While more precise than those of some programmes, the goals are still very variable in their specificity, including (for example) 'asks questions in complete sentences' and 'sings songs'.

Goals for parents are also articulated, which home visitors work towards through a wide variety of games and tasks, modelled and discussed with the mother. Toys and books are loaned, and/or made in the home. Nutrition and health information is provided, and liaison with professional agencies facilitated. The visitors (or 'child development trainers') also liaise between the centre and the home, keep records of the children's development, and lead the parent group meetings. Lally and Honig (1977a) give considerable detail of the in-service experiences to which recruited staff are exposed.

Evaluation results on Stanford-Binet and Cattell Scales are cited. At six months, IQ scores of 40 infants whose families had participated in the perinatal home visiting programme were significantly superior (mean IQ = 113.5) to scores of 46 control infants (mean IQ = 101) prior to centre entry. These gains had washed out by the time the children reached 12 months of age, however.

In a further study, of 58 children at 36 months of age, the scores of programme children were well above normal distribution, 57 per cent scoring IQ 110 or better and only 7 per cent scoring below average. A control group (n = 39) had scores which were normally distributed, while a high-education contrast group had scores even further ahead of normal, with a mean and median score in the 120–129 range (n = 31). However, Illinois test (ITPA) data were very variable and showed few significant differences between the groups, although programme children did better than the normative average. Results from the Early Language Assessment Scale were encouraging, and a variety of Piagetian tests indicated that programme children at 12 months of age tended to perform as well as middle-class infants and better than low-income control children on some tasks. Positive results were also found on some items on various rating scales and behaviour inventories. Interviews with parents indicated programme parents perceived their children more positively than did control parents. Parental subjective evaluation of the home visitors was highly positive. Generalised evidence of improvement in parental quality of life is given.

A follow-up study (Honig *et al.*, 1978) of 37 kindergarten and 26 first-grade programme graduates suggested that while some programme gains remained evident in kindergarten, they declined during first grade. The first-grader experimentals smiled less than controls and seemed to seek adult attention in negative as well as positive ways.

While many of the in-programme outcomes are positive, the long-term evaluation results as the children move into first grade are weak in structure and disappointing in nature. No discrimination is made at any stage of the relative impact of the home-visiting and centre-based components of the programme, which was undoubtedly expensive, although costing details are not easy to unearth. While many of the shorter-term results are encouraging and undoubtedly of educational significance, the dearth of information on statistical significance is to be regretted.

Karnes Programmes

Merle Karnes mercifully resisted any temptation to label her work as any sort of pompous or acronymic 'project'. With her associate Reid Zehrbach, Karnes developed three programmes for children sequentially aged 0–18 months, 18–36 months and 36–60 months.

The first significant report was that of Karnes *et al.* (1968), whose subject group of 30 children were aged 39–51 months. A twelve-week training programme was administered to the parents of the 15 randomly allocated experimental children. Training in three groups of five parents included making materials to use at home, learning songs and rhymes, and many traditional nursery activities. Books and puzzles were loaned, and language and fine-motor activities were emphasised. Mothers reported back to the group on their home teaching experiences. Overall attendance was only 53 per cent, although mothers were paid for attending, but where mothers did not attend, home visits were made by professional staff instead. In any event, all families received a home visit every two weeks.

Three months elapsed between pre- and post-testing on the Stanford-Binet and Illinois Psycholinguistic (ITPA) tests. During this period, experimental children showed a mental age gain of 6.5 months (equivalent to a rise of seven points of IQ) while control children showed a 'normal' gain of three months. On the IPTA however, experimental children scored significantly higher than controls on only one sub-test, although eight of nine sub-test scores favoured the experimentals. Details of curriculum, process data and long-term follow-up were lacking in this study. Further work is reported in Karnes *et al.* (1970, 1971). In a two-year programme for 20 mothers, experimental children ended with IQs 16 points above those of control children. Control ITPA scores lagged six months behind those of experimentals.

Subsequently, more detailed curricula were developed: the Karnes Infant Activities (for children aged 0–18 months), the Karnes Early Language Activities (for children aged 18–36 months), and the Karnes Home-based Language Programme (for children aged 36–60 months). A much heavier emphasis on language had developed. Curricula were presented in the form of lesson plans using a game format. Each plan included a behavioural objective, a list of materials and specific suggested procedures. A manual readable by parents was provided. Considerable exemplary detail is given in Karnes and Zehrbach (1977).

An interesting feature of the programme was the extent to which other family members, including grandparents and older siblings, participated. Weekly meetings of about two hours' duration were held. Half the time was devoted to discussion on topics selected by the parents. Written items, films and visits were incorporated. The other half of the time was for parent learning of teaching strategies. Professionals demonstrated strategies and parents made materials. Group size had by now been increased to 10–15. Additionally, home visits were made every two weeks for reinforcement, monitoring and problem-solving.

Studies were designed to investigate the ability of teenage siblings to implement a programme with their 3- and 4-year-old siblings. In the first study, twelve teenagers aged 12–16 years acted as tutors. Their tutees made IQ gains of over ten points in a six-week period, although a classroom programme was also running concurrently. In the second study, 15 teenagers were involved, but subject IQ gains were insignificant at a mean of 1.1 points. The third study showed eleven subjects made IQ gains of 6.7 points in a six-week period, significant at the 1 per cent probability level. Karnes feels there is great potential in this approach, not least as many of the tutors also gained in self-confidence.

Unfortunately, no long-term follow-up results are cited for any of these endeavours.

The Infant Education Research Project

Another of the early programmes, this was initiated by Earl Schaefer in 1965. Reports (Schaefer, 1969; Schaefer and Aaronson, 1977) describe a home-tutoring project involving an experimental group of 31 children under 2 years of age and a control group of 33, all male and black. College graduates were recruited as tutors and briefly trained by lecture, observation and practice. Two tutors alternated weekly in visiting each child in the experiment for an hour a day, five days a week, for 21 months during which the subjects aged from 15 to 36 months. Various activities, materials, trips, toys, etc., were incorporated in a very loose 'curriculum'. This later came to be written down in more detail, but not structured or sequenced. Participation of the mother and other family members was 'encouraged', but not required. The mothers varied widely in their level of participation.

Attrition was low, and the Bayley and Stanford-Binet Scales were administered at seven-month intervals. Initially, mean control group scores were above experimental scores by three points, but at 21 months the experimental group was ahead by seven points, at 27 months by eleven points and at 36 months by 17 points. Highly significant differences were also found on the Peabody Picture Vocabulary Test, a perceptual test and ratings of task-oriented behaviour.

However, by a year after the tutoring was terminated, the scores of the children has dropped significantly. Follow-up tests at 4, 5 and 6 years of age yielded disappointing results. The experimental group's mean IQ decreased, and after school entrance the control group's mean IQ increased. Both common forms of 'wash-out' were thus encountered. At the end of first grade, no significant differences were found between groups on the Stanford Achievement

Test. Schaefer concludes that brief child-centered early education programmes are unlikely to have an enduring effect unless continuing support is in-built. In interpreting the long-term results from this programme, it is necessary to remember that it was not primarily a *parent*-education project, but focused on intensive direct tutoring of the children.

Miscellaneous US Programmes

An early programme with innovative characteristics was the HOPE (Home-oriented Pre-school Education) project reported by Alford (1971). Over a three-year period, 450 children were involved in four West Virginian communities. Daily TV programmes, weekly home visits by paraprofessionals and a mobile classroom for small group sessions were involved. One group experienced all programme components, one TV and home visits, one TV only; the control group was subjected to no intervention. Teaching materials provided included tapes, worksheets and parent guides, and the paraprofessionals brought educational materials into the homes. In the first year, no gains were found, but in the second year gains in language development, cognition, psychomotor and social skills were noted for two groups only — the 'all treatments' group and the TV and home visits group.

Niedermeyer's 1970 work in training parents to help their children with reading will be discussed in Chapter 7, 'Learning Difficulties', but his later work on the same theme (Niedermeyer, 1973) is discussed here as it particularly focused on the problems of recruiting and sustaining the involvement of disadvantaged inner-city parents. The curriculum used was the objectives-based SWRL Beginning Reading Program, which involved practice exercises and games related to classroom procedure. Three ten-minute exercises and one game went home each week. Parents were trained via a slide–tape presentation, written instruction, role-playing and feedback, all carried out within one hour. In addition to training parents in group meetings in school, which had yielded a participation rate of 40 per cent in the past, individual training of parents at school and home was offered. Schools could also opt to: (i) have afternoon *and* evening training sessions; (ii) provide childcare during the meetings; (iii) request parents to RSVP in writing; (iv) provide transport; (v) provide telephone reminders.

Half of the participating parents were required to sign and return completed exercises to the class teacher each week.

The study was conducted in relation to ten classes in four schools, from February to the end of the academic year. Of 271 participating parents, 41 per cent were trained in group meetings, a further 13 per cent in individual meetings in school and a further 7 per cent in individual meetings in their homes. The remaining 39 per cent of parents were merely sent the written instruction. Different schools placed different emphases on methods, and home visits encountered difficulties — many parents were not in. The accountability procedures were effective in promoting a higher level of participation during the year, 50 per cent of 'accountable' parents reporting an 80 per cent exercise completion rate compared with 67 per cent for the other group. Parental subjective feedback was positive. Providing transport seemed to raise participation rates at in-school meetings. It is a pity Niedermeyer used no measures of increased reading skill, and this study is also short on significance testing.

Ketchel (1975) reported on a parent-group based intervention wherein two parent groups were trained in eight two-hour sessions The curriculum stressed verbal stimulation, reinforcement, play and exploration for infants. One group was trained by modelling and discussion without their infants present, while the other group was trained by discussion, guided observation, guided practice and feedback with their infants present. Pre- and post-programme behavioural and attitudinal measures were applied, and again at six-month follow-up. Of the range of outcomes, a modest number favoured the group trained with their infants. The other training group did little better than the control group.

Most programmes in this field have adopted a simple triadic model of dissemination (programme co-ordinator trains parents trains children), but the role of the *child* as a conditioning variable was examined by Falender and Heber (1975). Their extra-familial teaching programme encompassed children aged from 6 months to 6 years, but the reported study relates to 21 children then aged 40-66 months, parented by low-IQ, low-income mothers. The control group numbered 19.

A variety of specific tasks were the outcome measures, and programme participants were video-recorded carrying these out in a 'mobile laboratory'. The experimental children showed significant treatment effects. The detailed recordings indicated they also used significantly more verbal information-processing behaviours and more verbal and physical positive feedback. The control children, by contrast, used more physical information-processing and more negative feedback. On some — but not all — tasks, the experimental mothers used more positive feedback than controls. More 'association' or behavioural predictability was evident in the experimental dyads. In other words, a more positive interaction style was noted in experimental dyads, despite the fact that their involvement in the teaching programme meant they had actually spent less time with their mothers.

The Lennox Early Childhood Outreach Program for parents is described by John (1976). This project, for children aged 2.9 to 3.9 years, trained parents to provide informal learning experiences for their pre-schoolers. Tutors modelled activities and made suggestions, and parent–teacher aides based in the Child–Parent Center in a local elementary school facilitated liaison. Evaluation is largely by opinion survey of teachers and parents and by process data related to programme goals, however.

A computerised system for managing curriculum decisions and tracking child progress in a home-based pre-school education project is described by Lutz *et al.* (1978). Individual Education Plans were incorporated on the CBIS (Child-based Information System). The intervention input was a home-tutoring programme. Outcome measures include two normative tests, a developmental checklist, and a rating of maternal teaching style. CBIS was used with an experimental group and outcomes compared with two control groups. The system appeared to lead to better identification of relevant learning objectives for individuals, and to increased achievement on those objectives. Administrative costs were also reduced.

The Parent Education Follow Through Program (PEFT) is described by Olmstead (1979). PEFT families (n = 63) from two sites in the second year of participation were compared with 46 control families. Parent–child interaction on two tasks was video-recorded, and reading and mathematics sub-tests of the Stanford Achievement Test applied. Results from the two PEFT sites were very different: site A was all-Caucasian, while site B was all-black; in site B the programme's objectives had been 'given less emphasis'. In site A, project children's parents showed the highest use of Desirable Teaching Behaviors (DTB) taught in the programme. The next-highest DTB score was that of site A controls, followed by site B experimentals, followed by site B controls. Correlations between DTBs and achievement test scores reached 0.50 for reading and 0.35 for maths in site A, but were virtually zero in site B, where the range of scores was more restricted. Unfortunately, the author does not cite the range of absolute achievement test score values.

Further work is reported in Olmstead and Rubin (1983), wherein it is noted that PEFT implementation 1969–81 had spread to ten communities involving 8,000 children per year. In a study based in a third programme site (C), 50 per cent of project parents clearly showed a high level of use of Desirable Teaching Behaviors, and many were able to combine or develop modifications of DTBs. These maternal behaviours were significantly related to reading achievement, but not maths achievement.

In another similar study, programme parents were found to ask no more questions of their children than control parents, but framed their questions in a different way, conforming to the DTBs. These differences were positively related to the child's reading achievement. A fourth multi-variate analysis study suggested that socio-economic status influenced home environment strongly but level of parental participation less strongly, length of time in the programme was related to child achievement, and parental language stimulation and ambition was also positively related to child achievement.

A more pessimistic picture emerges from the data of Loveridge and Carapella (1979). Disadvantaged 3–5-year-old pre-school children attended a centre-based programme for two half-days each week. Parent instruction was also provided through seminars, workshops and home visits. Parents participated in class activities and field trips. Booklets were given to parents regularly to help them work with children at home. For each child, developmental growth was assessed via a battery of achievement tests. Results showed that while the overall programme increased developmental growth (more in cognitive than motor areas), the degree of parental involvement was not related to faster child development. In fact, for certain parental activities, significant *negative* correlations were found. This report does not give sufficient detail of process to enable us to speculate on what went wrong, however.

The Multiple Model Preschool Program (MMPP) is described by Waller and Waller (1980). This is a three-year longitudinal intervention, focusing on individualised education, parental involvement and home–school relations. A sample of 134 programme children from three sites was subjected to a battery of achievement and aptitude tests. Significant gains were found on a number of measures.

A multi-media parent instruction programme is reported by Coleman *et al.* (1981). The Parent–Child Interaction Program combined the instructional components of toys, video-tapes, guidesheets, and role-play to enhance mothers' ability to teach their young children specific cognitive and perceptual skills. Children aged 3–4 years and their mothers were recruited (n = 120), and it should be noted that mean socio-economic status was higher than for many studies discussed in this chapter. Pre- and post-testing on the specifically designed Cognitive and Perceptual Skills (CAPS) test was carried out, and a range of attitudinal measures applied to the parents.

Enrolled mothers met in groups for one hour per week over nine weeks. Video and guidesheets related to the 'toy of the week', use of which was role-played (children were not present). Programme children subsequently had significantly larger gain scores on the CAPS test (p < 0.005). Attitudinal variables bore little relationship to child gain scores. The authors note that video-taped instruction has the advantage of consistency. No follow-up data are reported.

Reviews of US Programmes

A large number of useful over-views of the field exist, some more comprehensive and analytical than others. Only selected items will be mentioned here.

An early effort of quality was that of Chilman (1973), who offers a useful historical analysis of the development of the compensatory movement from the beginning of the 1960s, when 'poverty was rediscovered'. The psychological and sociological foundations of the principle of parent participation are examined. Programmes of intervention dating from the 1930s and 1940s are mentioned, and Chilman notes that evaluation results from the early studies of generalised parent education programmes (where available) tended to be disappointing, with 13 out of 15 studies reviewed failing to show unequivocally positive results. (This paper thus constitutes a major source for reportage of 'failed' projects, which is just as instructive as endless listings of successful ones.) More specifically focused programmes which had sought to deploy parents as tutors to provide extra stimulation for their children had, by contrast, shown 'promising results'. Useful summary tables are provided.

The Office of Child Development (1975) subsequently produced a report of a national conference on compensatory parent education programmes, including Home Start, the Florida Parent Education Program, the DARCEE Program, the Mother–Child Home Program, and the High/Scope Infant Education Project. Stevens (1976) reviewed research and compared programmes using individual in-home consultation with those using centre-based group training meetings. The author comments on factors in programme effectiveness.

By the mid-1970s the field had shown considerable development, and the review of Goodson and Hess (1976, 1978) was extremely influential in its further development. The efforts of 28 intervention programmes designed to train parents to teach school-related skills to their young children were examined for evidence of immediate and long-term impact on intelligence test performance and school achievement. Nearly all the programmes produced significant immediate gains, and those programmes that incorporated long-term follow-up had shown largely positive results.

Of the 28 programmes, 25 used intelligence tests as outcome measures, and of these 23 produced either significant gains for programme children or significant differences between experimental and control children, at the immediate end of the intervention. The distribution of gains is represented in Figure 5.1 (adapted from Goodson and Hess, 1976, 1978).

The average pre–post IQ gain over the 28 programmes was 9.3 points. Goodson and Hess note that regression to the mean cannot account for these results, since although children with the initially lowest IQs did tend to make the biggest gains, changes in control groups were near zero irrespective of initial IQ.

Eight programmes had carried out follow-up assessment when the review was written. Seven of these reported positive or significant differences favouring the programme children over follow-up times ranging from three months to five years. Some of these differences were very small, however, and some programmes reported negative as well as positive findings at different terms of

Figure 5.1: Mean Pre–Post Child IQ Gains from Parent Education Programmes

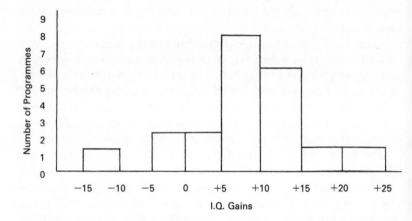

I.Q. Gains

follow-up or with different cohorts. The general trend was for IQ scores to plateau or decline slightly post-intervention. This had the effect of largely sustaining the superiority of the programme children compared with control children who had shown no developmental acceleration. (Indeed, the IQs of many control children had declined at follow-up after school entry.) However, continued acceleration beyond programme end was hard to find. Three programmes incorporated data on school attainment tests or grades. All three showed positive long-term results compared with controls. Goodson and Hess continue in their review to attempt to identify the influence of five factors in programme effectiveness: (i) the amount of instruction to parents, (ii) the curricular content, (iii) the teacher/parent ratio, (iv) the level of structure in the activities, and (v) the degree of structure in the instruction to parents. Useful summary tables of these factors in the programmes reviewed are given, although the authors acknowledge that the categorisation involved is somewhat arbitrary and broad.

Sheer amount of parent instruction did not appear to be predictive of success, but those programmes incorporating home visits tended to produce higher immediate gains. The curricular focus of a programme (verbal, sensori-motor, cognitive) did not predict global effectiveness — unsurprisingly. A high level of teacher–parent contact was clearly associated with larger child gains both in the short term and at follow-up. Home-visiting programmes tend to have high contact levels, and it is unclear whether this alone is the key factor in the impact of home visiting, or whether other factors are at play. Programmes with a high level of structure in parent teaching activities consistently produced short-term gains, but the relationship was not unequivocal. In terms of stability of gains in the long term, the relationship was clearer. Level of specificity in the instruction of parents was not systematically related to programme effectiveness. The authors note that some programmes have included within-programme comparisons of the relative effectiveness of a parental involvement component, and in four separate programmes greater parent involvement was associated with higher child gains.

Also reviewed are miscellaneous data on changes in parental behaviour and attitudes, difficult to summarise owing to the great variety in measures utilised. Three programmes report that maternal feelings of personal efficacy were enhanced. Some programmes reported softening of authoritarianism towards the child and more appropriate developmental expectations. Six programmes showed changes in parental verbal behaviour, but typically not on all sub-scales of the instrument used. Three programmes noted increased parental positive reinforcement and two decreased negative feedback. Two studies noted IQ gains in younger siblings as well as target children. Five programme evaluations incorporated ratings of the stimulatory qualities of the home environment and three of these found programme families scoring higher than control or comparison groups. Generally, the evidence on changed parental behaviour is much less substantial than that on child gains, and much more sophisticated research effort is necessary convincingly to demonstrate that the former mediates the latter.

As the field of parent training developed, reviews began to come thick and fast. Kapfer (1977) provided a broad overview in the proceedings of a national conference on Home Start and Family Resource Programs. Ambron (1977) offered a detailed review of seven programmes, incorporating summary tables and dealing with curriculum in some depth. The consistently positive results in child gains and the good proportion showing long-term maintenance are noted.

A major exercise in meta-analysis resulted from the formation of the Developmental Continuity Consortium, a collaboration of twelve research groups conducting longitudinal studies on the outcomes of early education programmes for low-income infants and pre-school children initiated in the 1960s. Follow-up data collected included information gathered in 1976–7 when the subjects were between 9 and 18 years old. Interviews with parents and children, IQ and attainment tests, and data from school records were all used in this mammoth follow-up effort. The combined results indicated that early education significantly reduced allocation to special classes and grade retention, and Stanford-Binet IQ gains were maintained for up to three years. This was true for both home-based, centre-based and combined programmes. Further details will be found in Lazar *et al.* (1977a, 1977b), Palmer (1977, 1978), Hubbell (1978) and Darlington *et al.* (1980).

Pooling results in this way could be cynically viewed as an attempt to crank up the statistical significance of the longer-term findings, but let us not be uncharitable. Attrition rates were 41 per cent, but there is no evidence that this introduced a consistent bias. Lazar notes that IQ gains wash out eventually, but it may indeed be unrealistic to expect anything else. There is some evidence of improved self-concept in programme graduates in high school, and parental responses to loaded consumer satisfaction questions were overwhelmingly positive. No discrimination was made in the analyses of differential effects of home- and centre-based programmes. No indications emerged of the most effective age or length of intervention, according to Lazar (1977a, 1977b), but Palmer (1977), a consortium member, cheerfully asserts that the evidence 'suggested earlier and longer intervention produced better results'. Palmer also reports that studies which individualised instruction in the home or centre seemed to show positive effects more consistently.

Kuno Beller was also a member of the consortium, but offers a wide-ranging review of the field separately in Beller (1979). Although much of this is descriptive and reiterative, many readers will find it a useful summary, and it includes coverage of centre-based programmes and the Parent–Child Centers funded by the Office of Economic Opportunity. These latter incorporate very various and conglomerate methods and contacts. First-hand reports of the work of these centres is difficult to locate (but see Johnson *et al.*, 1974), and Beller's summary is valuable, if inevitably second-hand.

Other reviews are offered by Haskins *et al.* (1978) and Seager *et al.* (1980). The former reviews daycare programmes as well as home stimulation programmes, and refers to programmes for the 'biologically impaired'. An interesting discussion ensues of the finding of increased febrile illness for infants attending daycare facilities, compared with those staying at home. One section of the Seager *et al.* review is particularly concerned with six early childhood programmes designed to utilise home-based education in rural areas faced with geographic isolation and limited facilities and resources.

Canadian and Latin American Programmes

Relatively little is reported from elsewhere in the Americas. Halpern and Fisk (1978) have produced a survey report on preschool education in Latin America. Home- and centre-based programmes for the families of children aged 3–6 years in Bolivia, Chile and Colombia are documented, and details of organisation and implementation given. Cost-effectiveness is considered, but little hard evaluation data cited.

Waksman (1979) reports from Ontario on the Mother-as-Teacher Program. Nursery-aged children were assigned to experimental (n = 23) or control (n = 25) groups by matching then random allocation. Paraprofessional home visitors were given three weeks' training, then visited weekly to present designated tasks in a simple, uniform style. Verbal instruction and reversal role-playing were coupled with discussion of relevant materials and feedback on subsequent visits. Over 20 weeks, 22 tasks were delivered. Outcome measures included Peabody Picture Vocabulary Test, Metropolitan Readiness Test, teacher observational checklist, and set tasks to enable examination of maternal teaching strategies.

Experimental mothers subsequently introduced tasks better, praised more, gave more reasons, and talked with the child more than control mothers. No greater usage of questioning was noted, however. The experimental group gained six points on the Peabody Picture Vocabulary Test, unlike the controls. Both groups gained on the Metropolitan Readiness Test, the experimentals more than the controls but not significantly on all sub-tests. On the teacher checklist, only four of 24 variables reached statistical significance in favour of the experimental group. A four-month follow-up on the maternal teaching task with a much reduced sample showed four variables still showing significant gains. These results seem encouraging for a relatively lightweight intervention, particularly with respect to the changes in maternal teaching style.

Programmes in Scotland

The massive investment in compensatory parent education programmes in the USA is not matched anywhere else in the Western world. On a smaller scale of relativities, however, Scotland has a distinguished tradition of work in this field. Major projects in Renfrewshire, Govan and Lothian are worthy of attention.

The work in Renfrewshire is largely associated with the name of Donachy (1976, 1979), more simply described in Murphy (1982). A total of 96 children aged 3–4 years were allocated to control and experimental groups, and four matched experimental subgroups formed. The group included disadvantaged children and other children from the locality. Two experimental sub-groups (n = 16 each) experienced a four-month programme of home stimulation, administered by mothers but organised from local schools. A further experimental sub-group (n = 16) experienced a half-time nursery routine *and* the home-based programme, and the fourth sub-group the half-time nursery routine only. Two distal control sub-groups were merely tested.

Outcome measures included the Stanford-Binet, English Picture Vocabulary Test and Reynell Developmental Language Scales, together with unstructured interviews with mothers, maternal self-recording and attitude scales, and rating scales for the nursery groups only. The 'parent training' consisted of parents and children attending centre-based group meetings for child play, refreshments, group discussions 'chaired' by a teacher, and a weekly typed unit of a programme for administration at home. The programme dealt with vocabulary, numbers, time, space and size. Mothers were also given story books, and were asked to spend 30 minutes a day on both activities. Feedback was given to the peer group at the next meeting.

Results were mixed, as might have been expected from such a relatively loosely structured exercise. English Picture Vocabulary Test gains were significant for only one 'home programme' group. All four experimental groups showed significant gains on the

Stanford-Binet, including the nursery-only group with no home programme. In expressive and receptive language (Reynell Developmental Language Scales), programme groups were significantly ahead of the nursery-only group. Gains made by the control groups were not significant on any measure. Stanford-Binet scores were not correlated with socio-economic status, and experimental effects were equally evident with children aged 3 or 4 years.

Parental feedback was very positive, and diffusion of programme effects to siblings was reported by mothers. It should, however, be noted that home programme participants were by definition volunteers, and self-selection may have introduced some bias with respect to the nursery-only group. No long-term follow-up is reported. Attitude scale results were erratic, changes ranging from +6 to −3 in the experimental groups. Maternal records showed that high-gain children were much more likely to have experienced paternal participation in the programme.

A similar exercise in Glasgow is reported by Wilkinson and Murphy (1976), French (1977) and Wilkinson *et al.* (1978). This was located in an unambiguously severely disadvantaged neighbourhood. Sixty children participated in four groups of 15. Experimental and control groups were established for the nursery attendance and home programme treatments, where again client self-selection operated. Considerable sample attrition was experienced (30 per cent), particularly in the home control group.

As might be expected, the home experimental group had the highest pre-test IQs. This group gained 11.4 points while the nursery-only group gained 13.6 points. Nursery and home controls gained 5.6 and 1.5 points respectively. A similar pattern was evident on Reynell Developmental Language Scales, but with the nursery control group doing relatively better. Wilkinson and Murphy conclude that parent training is as effective as expensive professional direct teaching of children.

Extensions of this work in the Govan project included reading workshops, toy library workshops, playgroup workshops, and language-experience field trips. Data on attendance rates is given showing seasonal fluctuations. A relatively small proportion of the population tended to be intensively involved. No relationship between degree of contact with the project and mean IQ, English Picture Vocabulary Test, Reynell Development Language and Edinburgh Reading Test scores was found — thus the project could not be accused of serving 'the parents who didn't really need it'. Other descriptive information on time allocation is given.

The Lothian Educational Home Visiting Scheme is described in Raven (1980) and McCail (1981). Raven's book gives the results of an evaluation of the programme, which deployed home visitors from nursery schools to promote parental involvement in their children's educational development. Six visitors worked with 2–3-year-old children for an average of nine months prior to nursery entry, initially working with the children but increasingly involving the mother in the activities. About ten families were visited per week, thus 180 in the first two years of operation. There was little structured guidance on curriculum content, although visitors usually took a specific play object, and there was considerable variation in visitor practice. Project families were by no means uniformly 'disadvantaged'.

The data subsequently gathered were largely descriptive — or 'illuminative', to use a current euphemism. There is interesting discussion of different 'styles' of home visiting. The data from parent interviews are complex and open to multiple interpretations. Evidence for the effectiveness of the visiting programme is ambiguous, to say the least, although there is some indication that programme mothers self-report teaching and questioning their child more than control mothers. One or two findings which could be construed as negative emerged.

Programmes in England

Educational home visiting was introduced into the UK in 1970 as part of the Educational Priority Area action research project in the West Riding of Yorkshire (Smith, 1975). In ensuing years a number of similar schemes sprang up in various parts of the country, e.g. Home Start in Leicester and Home Link in Liverpool, although both of these utilise volunteer visitors. Other UK schemes include Priority Area Playgroups (Birmingham) and Scope (Southampton).

Even if they are the subject of written report at all, many of these projects are documented only in localised or in-house publications, which may prove very difficult to track down, especially by researchers outside the UK. In any event, the majority of the existing reports contain purely descriptive information, and very few offer tangible evaluative evidence. Poulton and James (1975) reviewed 15 such schemes, noting many common features: regular weekly visits of one hour; books, toys and games taken; visitor works with mother to develop specific skills, but usually not according to sequenced curriculum; visits usually in the year preceding nursery entry, etc.

However, evaluative data are very infrequently recorded. Aplin and Pugh (1983) and Pugh and De'Ath (1984) include several brief reports of schemes. Readers may also care to consult Crow (1983) and Jayne (1976), if they can locate the items. Leicester Home Start is reported descriptively by Harrison (1981, 1982, 1983) and Liverpool Home Link by Bell *et al.* (1977). A description of the Birmingham, Liverpool and Leicester work was given by Haydon (1978) and a wider (but brief) review was offered by Pugh (1977). Van der Eyken (1982) has published a 'four-year evaluation' of Leicester Home Start which consists only of loose description. During 1981 a further survey of home visiting schemes was undertaken by Poulton (1983), which noted over 50 schemes operating in England and Scotland. Despite financial stringencies and the comprehensive lack of evidence to show that such schemes worked, they continued to expand.

However, not all efforts in the field have followed the English tradition of idiosyncratic amateurism. Berry and Wood (1981) discuss the evaluation of parent intervention programmes in the British context and point out that many possible methods exist which have yet to be tried, although the observational analysis which they would particularly like to see more of is, of course, time-consuming. Subsequent reports of the authors' having applied their theories are hard to locate.

The most substantial English evaluation is that of the West Riding Home Visiting Project (Smith, 1975). The project covered 20 children, aged 18–27 months at the start, in the catchment area of one school. A matched distal control group was formed in a similar community. During the course of a year, the project children were visited every week for between one and two hours. Three different kinds of toy or book were presented on each visit, one to develop colour, shape and size knowledge, one to develop fine motor skills, and one to develop perception and memory of language. Mothers were 'encouraged' to take part, but the primary focus seems to have been the child. Games and toys were left with the mother only if they had been particularly enjoyed. Pre- and post-testing on the Merrill-Palmer Scales indicated that in an inter-test period of nine months the project children had made substantial gains and were about four months ahead of controls in mental age. This would roughly approximate to 13 points in IQ, very much in line with the better US projects. There was also some evidence of change in maternal attitude and interaction style. A further home-visiting programme was carried out, and a second post-test undertaken after completion of this. At this time, 14 months after first post-test, both groups had substantially increased their scores, but the experimental group was still about six standard points higher. There are suspicions about inter-tester reliability here.

A follow-up study is reported by Armstrong and Brown (1979), who managed to locate all the original children when they were 8 years old and attending junior schools. Parents were interviewed and children retested on a very brief intelligence test of doubtful reliability (Kent Short Oral) and the Daniels and Diack Reading Test.

Maternal interview reactions were largely positive, visited mothers reporting much more involvement in fine motor skill activities at home in the past than non-visited mothers, and project mothers reported preparing their children for school entry much more than controls, who were more preoccupied with the child learning basic skills quickly *at school.* Visited mothers still seemed more able to engage their children in educational leisure activities at home, and were much more likely to feel they had been able to help in their children's education, and wished to be more involved with schooling. Visited parents were more likely to want further education for their children.

So far as testing was concerned, the gains made at first post-test had been erratic, particularly in the case of the project group, where gains ranged from three to 20 months of mental age in a nine-month inter-test period. At follow-up, the project group was ahead of controls by two months of mental age, which at this chronological age represents approximately two points of IQ and is not significant. Correlations between first pre-test scores and follow-up scores was low, and again the experimental group was more erratic than the control group. Likewise, project children were two months of reading age ahead of controls on the reading test, an insignificant difference. Children in both groups were, on average, reading at a level well below their chronological age. Thus the project gains appeared to have largely washed out.

The development and longitudinal evaluation of a pre-school

home-visiting programme in Halifax, West Yorkshire, is reported by Jungnitz, Stott and Topping (1983). A 52-item criterion-referenced assessment checklist of behavioural objectives covering concentration and motivation, language, fine motor skills, visual/auditory skills and reading, and symbolic and cognitive skills (including mathematics) was specially developed. This outlined the 'core curriculum' of the visiting programme. A supplementary checklist of a further 50 items was devised for follow-up purposes.

Each year 20 children were visited weekly in the year prior to nursery entry, and the project focus was very much on teaching the parents to teach their children. Ancillary events and group meetings were also arranged. The visitor recorded child progress on the checklists, and class teachers continued the assessing and recording blind in subsequent years. In the first year of visiting (1978 cohort) the project children were selected on the basis of being most 'at risk' and in need. Despite this, at assessment midway through nursery, and at the end of nursery, reception and middle infants, the composite scores of visited children were consistently ahead of those of non-visited children, although this difference never quite reached statistical significance (maximum $p = 0.06$).

For subsequent years, the demand for places on the visiting scheme was so great that local politics necessitated the random allocation of children to the programme. For the 1979 cohort, at the end of nursery, visited children were substantially ahead of non-visited children ($p < 0.025$), and the gap was even wider by the end of the reception-class year ($p < 0.005$). For the 1980 cohort, the visited group was again substantially ahead of non-visited children at the end of nursery ($p < 0.005$). Thus this home-visiting programme appears to have made a significant difference which endured over time. The authors note that in addition to being mother-focused, this programme built in subsequent parent liaison with the receiving school, in both cases unlike the West Riding Educational Priority Area project.

Programmes in Europe

Little emerged from the English-language literature search pertaining to parent education programmes in the rest of Europe, and we must perforce rely on the now rather dated observations of Stukat (1976). Some Belgian work exploring interactive processes in the education of the disadvantaged is reviewed. The Mons project involved centre-based professional teaching coupled with parent education for the families of children aged 3–6 years. Parent meetings, open classes, films, discussions and individual consultations with teachers were utilised. On post-testing after four months the project group had gained ten points of IQ and showed increased verbal fluency, while controls made no progress. However, a subsequent re-evaluation after a two-month holiday showed the control group had made gains, while the experimental group had not. Subsequently, the direct teaching was made more structured and the home intervention was intensified. Cross-age peer tutors (aged 9–12 years) were deployed, and closed-circuit television was used to analyse parent educational behaviour in the home. No further outcome data are given by Stukat, however.

In the Netherlands, the Utrecht Compensatory Project includes a family programme wherein home visitors contact families once or twice a week to teach parents to observe, play and read with children, and encourage them to show interest in school activities. According to Stukat, the effects are 'moderate and specific, with little transfer'. Research from France detailing the positive effects of nursery experience is reported, but nothing on parent education.

Research from Finland indicates that children from sparsely populated areas are less ready for school than others, but no outcome data on subsequent intervention are given. In a separate project, correspondence instruction of parents has been explored, the parents receiving weekly sets of guidance for themselves and material for the children, complemented by a four-week summer school for the children. Future plans include widening the range of instructional media and deploying peripatetic teachers to give instruction to small groups in private homes.

A study in Gothenburg, Sweden, compared the relative effectiveness of day-nursery education and education at home. Matched experimental and control groups of children aged 12–18 months (n = 60 each) experienced day nursery or stayed at home. No intervention was provided to the parents. The home children were found to explore their environment more and interact with adults more frequently than the day-nursery children. However, results on the Griffiths Scales showed little difference between the groups. The observational results have since been replicated in England by Tizard (1982) and Tizard and Hughes (1984) (see Introduction for references).

Generally, however, as Stukat points out: 'European research on compensatory pre-school education cannot be described as abundant.'

Programmes in Israel

A report from the Hebrew University (1976) describes HATAF (Home Activities for Toddlers and their Families), which provides home-based enrichment activities for disadvantaged pre-schoolers via their mothers. One pilot project involved trained paraprofessional aides visiting Asian and African immigrant families to deliver and explain pre-planned written materials with appropriate play activities for 1-year-old children. Subsequently, a more active role for the visitors and a more flexible range of materials were incorporated. A second pilot project focused more on cognitive stimulation via mother–child interaction. Evaluation is largely in terms of process goal attainment, however.

The later HIPPY (Home Instruction Programme for Pre-school Youngsters) is perhaps better known (Lombard, 1981; Weil, 1985), being nationally administered. The programme is particularly targeted on immigrant children from Islamic countries. Mothers are taught how to teach their children using highly structured materials focusing on language and perceptual discrimination skills and problem solving. Weil reports that 13,000 families participate in the programme in urban and rural communities. International dissemination workshops are held, and HIPPY has been implemented in three US states and in Turkey, with other far-flung nations showing interest.

Mothers work with their children from age 4 through 6, receiving a weekly packet of materials from a paraprofessional aide, herself the mother of a pre-school child from the local community and often a HIPPY graduate. A professional co-ordinator/supervisor of visitors is in turn monitored by a regional co-ordinator. Weekly meetings alternate between individual home visits and group meetings at a local centre. Visitors use reversal role-play of the activities to teach the mother, or to teach an older sibling of the target child as an intermediary if the mother cannot cope. The mother remains the primary focus of service delivery, however. Subsequently, the aide checks tasks completed in the child's workbook. The (salaried) aides meet in a group weekly for support, supervision and joint problem-solving, and are encouraged to try out materials on their own children first.

Mothers contracting to join HIPPY must commit themselves to regular attendance, and have to pay a (minimal) participation fee. At the group meetings of mothers, additional generalised information input is made, by lecture, activity or demonstration. Between 220 and 240 families is considered the optimum number for a local self-sustaining programme, developing to that size over three years.

The original HIPPY study in Tel-Aviv randomly assigned 161 children to home-instructed, teacher-instructed or control conditions. The teacher-instructed children (n = 42) experienced HIPPY materials in a classroom setting. There were 48 in the home group and 30 controls. Considerable organisational shifts and attrition subsequently occurred during follow-up. Outcome measures included the Columbia Test of Mental Maturity, Goodenough Draw-a-Man, two sub-tests of the Frostig Test of Visual Perception, a shape and colour identification task, a similarity discrimination task, a matrix test, and a home story task. Some differences between groups were noted at pre-test and taken into account in later analyses.

At the end of the first year of the programme, the home-instruction groups performed significantly better than controls on five out of five measures, and also outperformed the teacher-instructed group on four out of five measures. However, imbalance in pre-test scores accounted for 25 per cent of the variance in two of the tests. Subjective feedback from class teachers after the children entered school was very positive.

After a year in nursery, the children were again tested, on one Frostig sub-test, the Minkovich Test of Maths Readiness and the Boehm Test of Basic Concepts. The home group scored highest on four of the six sub-tests and on the total score in the maths test, reaching statistical significance on three of the four. On the Frostig, the home group did better than the teacher group, which in turn did better than the control group. On the Boehm Test, the home group did significantly better on the space and quantity sub-scales, and total score, but not on the time or 'miscellaneous' sub-scales. The poor performance of the teacher-instructed group is explained in terms of the teacher's inability to get through more than 60 per cent of the activities, which were designed for individualised instruction.

After a further year, when the children were in first grade, class teachers were asked to rate the children in six areas. In all 96 children were rated, and the home group excelled in academic achievement, enthusiasm and persistence, but not initiative, sociability or discipline. Additionally, a full Frostig Test, the Milcan Intelligence Test, and report card evaluations were used. The home group excelled on all five sub-scales of the Frostig and all three of the Milcan. Report card evaluations showed the home group did better in reading, writing and arithmetic, but this only reached statistical significance for arithmetic.

Another year later, at the end of second grade, only 76 children were available to take maths and reading tests. The home group scored better at reading ($p < 0.03$) and maths ($p < 0.02$). However, the performance of children who had only been in the programme for a period of up to one year was poor.

This research was subsequently replicated in Jerusalem, using matched experimental home-visited and control groups. Various organisational problems emerged in this different setting. At the end of the first year, on four tests, the effects of chronological age accounted for more of the variance than the effects of treatment on two tests, but the home group did better than the control group on the Frostig V and Matrix Tests. Attempts to determine the relative effectiveness of aide modelling with the child showed no difference. A year later the home group did better on Frostig V and two sub-tests and total score on the Boehm, but not on the rest of the Boehm and the Minkovitch Maths Test. A year later HIPPY children were slightly ahead of controls in reading, but the reverse was true in maths; neither difference reached significance, and teacher reports rated HIPPY children worse than controls on reading and maths. Paradoxically, a year later, HIPPY children were again ahead on both reading and maths tests and teacher reports, though the difference indicated in the teacher reports was not significant for maths.

Long-term follow-up of the Tel-Aviv children was carried out. Reading testing at the end of the third grade showed no significant differences, but the test suffered from a ceiling effect. Maths testing showed HIPPY children ahead, but not significantly. At the end of fifth grade, teacher ratings were solicited, but only 59 children were now locatable. The home group was rated higher, but differences were small. Three further years later, in a major follow-up effort, 99 children were located, and both they and their parents completed questionnaires. HIPPY children had been much less likely to be held back a grade or be placed in special education, had more positive academic self-images, and were reported by teachers to be performing better. Long-term follow-up in Jerusalem has shown HIPPY children consistently ahead of controls, but not significantly.

A third major study by independent researchers examined programme effects on 206 HIPPY children compared with 103 controls, and also considered the possible spin-off effects by simultaneously studying 402 older siblings in these families. Teacher ratings of child variables were solicited in structured interviews, but the exercise appears to have been prone to 'yea-saying' by the interviewees. At the end of first grade, HIPPY children were significantly ahead of controls in reading and maths, but subsequent results were disappointing.

Later follow-up studies have tracked HIPPY graduates through to school leaving age (Weil, 1985), and there is some evidence that programme impact can still be discerned. Parental reactions to the programme are usually positive. However, organisational difficulties have beset the programme's operation in some areas. While the overall results are undoubtedly very positive in comparison to many other programmes, HIPPY has suffered from the dilution and systemic accidents which beset any very widely disseminated work. It will be important to maintain the evaluation effort in new locations, for the final durability test of any project is whether it can survive the withdrawal of its originators.

Programmes in Australia

A series of reports are available on the Queensland Pre-school Correspondence Programme (e.g. McGaw *et al.*, 1975; Grant *et al.*, 1978; Ashby *et al.*, 1979), designed to meet the needs of pre-school children in remote and sparsely populated areas of the state. Parents receive a resource/guide book and an equipment kit with suggested activities in a regular sequence, including booklets to read to the child and audio-tapes of songs and stories. Parents keep in contact with programme co-ordinators by letter and audio-recorded messages. Packages are despatched at intervals of between five and six weeks.

McGaw *et al.* (1975) report an interview study with 34 participating families. Practical problems included delays in mail services of up to a month during the wet season. The majority of parents favoured the addition of home visits to the programme, and complained about the unresponsiveness of their distant 'teachers'. Overall, more than half the parents felt the programme had had no effect on their children's development. Grant *et al.*, (1978) reported on the distance teachers' perceptions of the programme.

Ashby *et al.* (1979) report on an extension of this work known as the Span Programme, wherein parent workshops were conducted, designed to increase parental knowledge, skills and participation with their children. Questionnaire, individual and group interview and observational data were utilised. In general, parents felt that their children benefited from social contact with age peers when attending Span workshop/playgroups, but they did not see any positive programme effects in their home situations.

The other major documented venture in Australia is the Mount Druitt Early Education Project, reported by Ball and Braithwaite (1976), Braithwaite and Healey (1979) and Healey (1980). Comparative evaluation of five pre-school programmes, of which only one was home-based, is discussed. The Mount Druitt area near Sydney is of predominantly lower socio-economic status. The four non-home programmes were oriented towards behaviour modification, cognitive skills and structures, 'competency orientation' and social/affective growth, respectively.

The home-based programme was a year-long experience for children aged at least 3 years 9 months. Weekly home visits were made of up to two hours by a teacher who designed individualised work programmes, with each weekly 'lesson' planned and structured in advance. Parents were intended to copy teacher behaviour in the days between visits. Group sessions for several parents and children were introduced later.

Healey (1980) subsequently reported evaluation data for a home-based programme, a sessional nursery programme, and a mixed programme. Information is unfortunately confined to teacher ratings of mother and child behaviour and interviews with mothers, and is highly impressionistic and inconclusive. Mothers of children in the mixed programme group tended to report a higher developmental level in their children than did other mothers. One or two other Antipodean ventures are mentioned in Parker and Mitchell (1980).

Summary

Provision for the disadvantaged has been an area of conflict in opinion, not least about the interpretation of empirical findings. The widespread Head Start programmes enabled the trialling of different curricula, some of which appeared to have negative effects. Structured behavioural curricula did best in the short run, followed by language development and parent education programmes. Lengthy programmes did better than short ones. Early conclusions of widespread long-term 'wash-out' did not stand up to more detailed scrutiny, and as years passed 'sleeper effects' began to emerge, suggesting programmes could have an enduring impact over decades.

Home-based programmes became more popular as concern over wash-out increased, and the Home Start Program developed. Short-term impact was readily demonstrated, with results paradoxically favouring the shorter programmes. Home Start seemed no more effective than Head Start in the short run, although it was cheaper. However, long-term follow-up data showed Home Start children did well in the long run in school attainments.

As programmes varied enormously between themselves and often within themselves from site to site, some individual programmes are considered in more detail. Gordon's Parent Education Program used paraprofessional home visitors, a loose curriculum, varying programme lengths and (later) group meetings also. IQ gains were significant for children in four of six programme involvement patterns over several years, and longer-term follow-up of school functioning favoured children who had been in the programme for two or three years. Levenstein's Mother–Child Home Program focused on verbal interaction, involving home visits over a period of seven or 14 months. Early studies showed programme children gaining 17 IQ points in the short run, and replications confirmed this. Long-term follow-up at ages 5 and 9 showed these gains to be largely well maintained. School attainments at age 9 were also ahead. However, two studies with a randomly allocated control group showed the controls gained also.

High/Scope Foundation projects included the Perry Preschool Project, combining a daily nursery with weekly parental instruction. IQ gains in the first year were 17 points, but there were no further gains in the second year. An experiment with group meetings for mothers failed to show any impact. Likewise, an experiment manipulating degree of maternal involvement in the programme showed no effects, all groups increasing by 12–13 IQ points. The High/Scope Infant Education Project, by contrast, was totally home-based and targeted on 1-year-olds. Curriculum content was very loose. Experimental children performed better on some outcome measures, but not all. No significant differences were found at follow-up four to five years later, and frequency of grade retention favoured controls. Very long-term follow-up at age 19 has shown some High/Scope children to be better adusted to school and employment, but the plausibility of this finding is questionable.

The DARCEE Early Training Project involved two or three consecutive summer schools with weekly home visits during some of the intervening periods. Experimentals did better than randomly allocated controls on IQ, language and reading tests, and although gains were modest they endured for four years of follow-up. Effects of generalisation to siblings were more striking — they gained 13 IQ points. Achievement test scores in first and second grade put experimentals ahead of controls on at least half of the sub-tests. By the end of the fourth grade, attainment test gains had washed out but IQ still had not. Subsequent experimentation with home- and centre-based programmes showed a nursery placement seemed most effective in the short run, but generalisation to siblings was far better in the home-visited group and this group maintained gains better. A programme of home visiting for 1-year-olds was developed which showed substantial gains in experimentals (18 points), but these had washed out at six-month follow-up. The Family-oriented Program was thus developed with an emphasis on teaching mothers enduring and generalisable skills over nine months of visits to households with at least two children under 5 years of age. Results were again consistently positive but modest; paradoxically, however, there was no evidence of parallel gains in siblings.

The Family Development Research Project offered a variety of facilities for children of different ages, which combined home visiting with parent group meetings and a nursery experience for children aged 18 months to 4 years. Curriculum goals for children and parents were quite well articulated. Children involved in the perinatal visiting programme were twelve points ahead of controls at age 6 months, but this had washed out by 12 months. A study of 58 children at 3 years of age showed IQs well above normal, and although ITPA results were not significant, language and Piagetian tests showed the experimentals were performing as well as middle-class infants on some tasks. Follow-up studies showed gains declining through kindergarten and into first grade.

Karnes also developed three sequential programmes for children of increasing age. Early studies utilised a twelve-week group parent training programme, coupled with bi-weekly home visits. Over three months experimentals gained IQ points twice as fast as controls, who proceeded 'normally', but ITPA results were disappointing. A subsequent replication as a two-year programme saw experimental IQs 16 points ahead of controls, and even comparative gains on ITPA. No follow-up is reported. More detailed curricula were developed. Teenage sibling tutees were demonstrated to be able to produce a ten-point IQ gain in a six-week period. One replication study confirmed this but another did not. Again no long-term follow-up is reported.

Schaefer's Infant Education Research Project initially deployed visitors as direct teachers of infants, while 'encouraging' maternal involvement. At 21 months experimentals were ahead of controls by eleven IQ points and by 36 months 17 points, also doing well on other tests. However, follow-up at 4, 5 and 6 years of age showed both forms of 'wash-out' operating. The HOPE project used TV programmes, home visits, kits of materials and a mobile nursery, and showed gains in the second year only for the 'all treatments' group and the 'TV and home visits' groups. No follow-up is reported. Niedermeyer's reading programme raised the recruitment level from 40 per cent to 60 per cent of eligible parents by offering one-to-one tuition at home or school, and there is some evidence that parent accountability procedures raised task-completion rates modestly.

There is some evidence that training parents with their children outside the family can improve the interaction within the family. The PEFT programme's attempts to modify intrafamilial interaction met with very mixed results, while another study finding some short-term programme effects was unable to demonstrate any correlation with degree of parental involvement. However, significant short-term gains are reported by two other programmes. The positive general trend is confirmed in a 1976 review of 28 programmes which notes a mean overall IQ gain of 9.3 points for programme children. Most programmes incorporating long-term follow-up had recorded maintenance of gains in at least some respects. Meta-analysis of pooled data by the Developmental Continuity Consortium also yields a positive picture.

A relatively lightweight but well-structured Canadian programme showed modest but encouraging gains which were maintained on four-month follow-up. In Scotland, Donachy's programme was tight in research design but loose in curriculum, and IQ gains were as good for nursery-only as for nursery-plus-home-visit and home-visit-only groups. However, language tests markedly favoured home programme children. No follow-up is reported, and home-visited programme clients were self-selected. A similar effort found nursery-only children as good on all measures as home-visit-only groups, and degree of parental involvement did not correlate with outcome. Other data from Scotland are impressionistic. A very low proportion of schemes in England have been satisfactorily evaluated. The West Riding Home Visiting Project involved sequenced materials, but was more child- than mother-focused. After nine months, programme children were approximately 13 IQ points ahead of controls. Home visiting continued, and at second post-test 14 months later, controls had improved to narrow the gap to six points. In a follow-up study when the children were aged 8, gains had washed out, although some effects on maternal interactive style may have endured. A longitudinal study, also in Yorkshire, indicated a year's visiting prior to nursery entry could raise disadvantaged children to 'normal' levels and keep them there during three subsequent years of schooling. This programme was mother-focused and had strong links with the receiving school, offering continuing support. Subsequent random allocation to programme and control groups resulted in control children lagging well behind at programme termination and follow-up.

There is little relevant research from the rest of Europe, and the few outcomes noted have been modest and unenduring. The HIPPY programme in Israel is long-standing and well developed. Home visits alternate with group meetings and structured kits of materials are used in sequence. In the first studies, the home visit group outperformed control and teacher-instructed groups on four out of five measures. At one-year follow-up, gains were maintained on a majority of several measures, and after a further year, test results and (to a lesser extent) teacher ratings all favoured the home visit group. After yet a further year, experimentals were still ahead on reading and maths tests. Follow-up through to the end of eighth grade showed programme effects were still discernible. However, a replication of this programme in another location was beset with organisational difficulties, and results were not so good, though still bearing comparison favourably with some of the US work. Programmes in Australia have tended to rely on subjective feedback, which has not been uniformly positive.

Overall, the programmes with the most positive results seem to be Gordon's, Levenstein's, DARCEE and HIPPY, with promising developments in Canada and the UK. It is easy to produce short-term gains, but much more difficult demonstrably to sustain them. Nevertheless, long-term maintenance is undoubtedly possible. Among the other programmes, the lack of follow-up, or evidence of wash-out, the extraordinary lack of attention to curriculum detail, and the failure to separate out the respective effects of programme components are all worrying. The use of intelligence tests as outcome measures is far more prevalent in the area of 'disadvantage' than in any other and the reliability and validity of such usage must be in doubt, although it does have the advantage of enabling swift (if superficial) comparison between studies.

References

Abt Associates (1977) *Education as Experimentation: A Planned Variation Model* (vol. 4) (Cambridge, Massachusets: Abt Associates Inc.)

Alford, R. (1971) *Home-oriented Pre-school Education* (Charleston, West Virginia: Appalachia Educational Laboratory)

Ambron, S.R. (1977) A Review and Analysis of Infant and Parent Education Programs', in M.C. Day and R.K. Parker (eds.), *The Pre-school in Action* (2nd edn.) (Boston: Allyn & Bacon)

Aplin, G. and Pugh, G. (eds.) (1983) *Perspectives on Pre-school Home Visiting* (London: National Children's Bureau)

Armstrong, G. and Brown, F. (1979) *Five Years On: A Follow-up Study of the Long-term Effects on Parents and Children of an Early Learning Programme in the Home* (Oxford: Social Evaluation Unit, Department of Social and Administrative Studies, University of Oxford)

Ashby, G. *et al.* (1979) *Evaluation of the Span Parent Workshop and the Operation of Span Groups* (Brisbane: Department of Education, Queensland University) (E.R.I.C. ED 183253 PS 011224)

Bache, W. and Nauta, M.J. (1979) *Home Start Follow-up Study: A Study of Long-term Impact of Home Start on Programme Participants. Executive Summary* (Cambridge, Massachusets: Abt Associates Inc.) (E.R.I.C. ED 192904 PS 011728)

Bache, W. *et al.* (1979) *Home Start Follow-up Study: A Study of the Long-term Impact of Home Start on Program Participants. Final Report* (Cambridge, Massachusets: Abt Associates Inc.) (E.R.I.C. ED 192903 PS 011727)

Ball, S. and Braithwaite, J. (1976) *The Mt. Druitt Early Education Project: Evaluation Study* (North Ryde, Australia: Macquarie University) (E.R.I.C. ED

129434 PS 008842)

Becker, W.C. (1978) 'The National Evaluation of Follow Through: Behavior-theory-based Programs Come Out on Top', *Education and Urban Society, 10, 4*, 431-58

Bell, S. *et al.* (1977) 'Home Link: The Parents' Home-visiting Project', *Where, 124*, 10-12

Beller, E.K. (1979) 'Early Intervention Programs', in J.D. Osofsky (ed.), *Handbook of Infant Development* (New York: Wiley)

Berman, P. and McLaughlin, M.W. (1975) *Federal Programs Supporting Education Change*, (vol. 4): *The Findings in Review* (Santa Monica, California: Rand)

Berry, I. and Wood, J. (1981) 'The Evaluation of Parent Intervention with Young Handicapped Children', *Behavioural Psychotherapy, 9*, 358-68

Braithwaite, J. and Healey, M. (1979) 'Home-based Pre-school Programs — A Viable Alternative', *Australian Journal of Early Childhood, 4, 1*, 21-4

Bronfenbrenner, U. (1974) *A Report on Longitudinal Evaluation of Preschool Programs*, vol. 2: *Is Early Intervention Effective?* (Washington, DC: US Department of Health Education and Welfare). Also in summary as: Bronfenbrenner, U. (1976) 'Is Early Intervention Effective?', in A.M. Clarke and A.D.B. Clarke (eds.), *Early Experience: Myth and Evidence* (London: Open Books)

Brown, B. (1978) 'Long-term Gains from Early Intervention: An Overview of Current Research', in B. Brown (ed.), *Found: Long-term Gains from Early Intervention* (Boulder, Colorado: Westview Press)

Chilman, C.S. (1973) 'Programs for Disadvantaged Parents: Some Major Trends and Related Research' in: B.M. Caldwell and H.M. Ricciati (eds.) *Review of Child Development Research*, vol. 3: *Child Development and Social Policy* (Chicago: University of Chicago Press)

Cicirelli, V.G. *et al.* (1969) *The Impact of Head Start: an Evaluation of the Effects of Head Start on Children's Cognitive and Affective Development*, vols. 1 and 2 (Columbus, Ohio: Westinghouse Learning Corporation, Ohio University)

Clark, V.L. and Johnston, S.P. (1974) *Description of Projects: Developing Strategies for Integrating and Delivering Services to Handicapped Children in Head Start Programs* (Chapel Hill, North Carolina: North Carolina University)

Coleman, M. *et al.* (1981) 'Effects of Multi-media Instruction on Mothers' Ability to Teach Cognitive Skills to Preschool Children', *Journal of Social Psychology, 115, 1*, 89-94

Crow, G. (1983) *An Evaluation of the Manchester Low-cost Pre-school and Parent Education Unit* (Coventry: Community Education Development Centre)

Darlington, R.B. *et al.* (1980) 'Preschool Programs and Later School Competence of Children from Low-income Families', *Science, 208*, 202-4

Donachy, W. (1976) 'Parent Participation in Pre-school Education', *British Journal of Educational Psychology, 46*, 31-9

Donachy, W. (1979) 'Parental Participation in Pre-school Education', in M.M. Clark, and W.M. Cheyne, (eds.), *Studies in Pre-school Education* (London: Hodder & Stoughton)

Epstein, A.S. and Weikart, D.P. (1977) *The Ypsilanti–Carnegie Infant Education Project: Longitudinal Follow-up* (Ypsilanti, Michigan: The High/Scope Press)

Eyken, W. van der (1982) *Home Start: A Four Year Evaluation* (Leicester: Home Start Consultancy)

Falender, C.A. and Heber, R. (1975) 'Mother–Child Interaction and Participation in a Longitudinal Intervention Program', *Developmental Psychology, 11, 6*, 830-6

Forrester, B.J. *et al.* (1971) *Home Visiting with Mothers and Infants* (Nashville, Tennessee: George Peabody College for Teachers)

French, S. (1977) 'Helping Society into Education', *Scottish Education Journal,* 60, 11, 4-5

Gilmer, B.R. *et al.* (1970) *Intervention with Mothers and Young Children: A Study of Intrafamily Effects* (Nashville, Tennessee: George Peabody College for Teachers) (E.R.I.C. ED 050809 PS 004661)

Goodson, B.D. and Hess, R.D. (1976) *The Effects of Parent Training Programs on Child Performance and Parent Behavior* (Stanford, California: School of Education, Stanford University) (E.R.I.C. ED 136912 PS 009152). Also under the same title in: Brown, B. (ed.) (1978) *Found: Long-term Gains from Early Intervention* (Boulder, Colorado: Westview Press)

Gordon, I.J. (1969) *Early Child Stimulation through Parent Education. Final Report* (Gainesville, Florida: University of Florida)

Gordon, I.J. *et al.* (1975) *Parent Oriented Home-based Early Childhood Education Program. Research Report* (Gainesville, Florida: University of Florida) (E.R.I.C. ED 148466 PS 009678)

Gordon, I.J. *et al.* (1977) 'The Florida Parent Education Infant and Toddler Programs', in M.C. Day and R.K. Parker (eds.), *The Pre-school in Action* (2nd edn.) (Boston: Allyn & Bacon)

Gordon, I.J. *et al.* (1978) 'Continuity Between Home and School: Aspects of Parental Involvement in Follow Through', paper presented at fifth biennial SE Conference on Human Development, Atlanta, Georgia (E.R.I.C. ED 154931 PS 009953)

Gordon, I.J. *et al.* (1979) *Aspects of Parent Involvement in the Parent Education Follow Through Program* (Chapel Hill, North Carolina: School of Education, North Carolina University) (E.R.I.C. ED 170024 PS 010491)

Grant, J. *et al.* (1978) *Teachers' Perceptions of the Pre-school Correspondence Program* (Brisbane: Queensland Department of Education) (E.R.I.C. ED 151101 PS 009817)

Gray, S.W. (1977) 'Home-based Programs for Mothers of Young Children', in P. Mittler (ed.), *Research to Practice in Mental Retardation,* vol. 1: *Care and Intervention* (Baltimore, Maryland: University Park Press)

Gray, S.W. and Klaus, R.A. (1970) 'The Early Training Project: A Seventh-year Report', *Child Development, 41,* 908-24

Gray, S.W. and Ruttle, K. (1976) *The Family-oriented Home Visiting Program: A Longitudinal Study* (Nashville, Tennessee: George Peabody College for Teachers) (E.R.I.C. ED 164083 PS 009962). Further reported in: Gray, S.W. and Ruttle, K. (1980) 'The Family-oriented Home Visiting Program: A Longitudinal Study', *Genetic Psychology Monographs, 102,* 2, 299-316

Guinagh, B.J. and Gordon, I.J. (1976) *School Performance as a Function of Early Stimulation. Final Report* (Gainesville, Florida: University of Florida) (E.R.I.C. ED 135469 PS 009098)

Guinagh, B.J. *et al.* (1971) *Florida Parent Education Program* (Berkeley, California: Far West Laboratory for Educational Research and Development) (E.R.I.C. ED 125750 PS 008602)

Guinagh, B.J. *et al.* (1975) *The Florida Parent–Infant Education Program* (Gainesville, Florida: University of Florida) (E.R.I.C. ED 111497 PS 008012)

Halpern, R. and Fisk, D. (1978) *Preschool Education in Latin America: A Survey Report from the Andean Region* (Ypsilanti, Michigan: High/Scpe Educational Research Foundation) (E.R.I.C. ED 208941 PS 012384

Harrison, M. (1981) 'Home-Start: A Voluntary Home-visiting Scheme for Supporting Young Families', *Early Childhood, 1,* 5, 5-8

Harrison, M. (1982) 'Working with Young Families in their Homes', *Adoption and Fostering, 6,* 3, 15-18

Harrison, M. (1983) 'The "Home-Start" Scheme', *Midwife, Health Visitor and Community Nurse, 19,* 8, 328-30

Haskins, R. *et al.* (1978) 'Infant-stimulation Programs and their Effects' *Pediatric Annals, 7, 2,* 123-44

Haydon, C. (1978) 'Chameleons in the Community', *Times Educational Supplement,* 24 April

Healey, M. (1980) *Report on the Evaluation of Bidwell Community School's Preschool Programs 1979* (North Ryde, Australia: School of Education, Macquarie University) (E.R.I.C. ED 198900 PS 011843)

Hebrew University (1976) *Home Activities for Toddlers and their Families (HATAF): An Interim Report* (Jerusalem: School of Education, Hebrew University) (E.R.I.C. ED 218368 UD 022214)

Hinckley, R.H. *et al.* (1979) *Student Home Environment, Educational Achievement and Compensatory Education: Technical Report No. 4* (Santa Ana., California: Decima Research) (E.R.I.C. ED 213783 UD 022122)

Honig, A.S. (1980) 'Working with Parents of Preschool Children', in R.R. Abidin (ed.), *Parent Education and Intervention Handbook* (Springfield, Illinois: Charles C. Thomas)

Honig, A.S. *et al.* (1978) 'Personal Social Adjustment of Children after Five Years in a Family Enrichment Program', paper presented at the biennial Conference on Human Development, Atlanta, Georgia (E.R.I.C. ED 167244 PS 010377)

Hubbell, V.R. (1978) 'The Developmental Consortium Study: Secondary Analysis of Early Intervention Data', in B. Brown (ed.), *Found: Long-term Gains from Early Intervention* (Boulder, Colorado: Westview Press)

Jayne, E. (1976) *Deptford Educational Home Visiting Project* (ref. RS 645/76) (London: Inner London Education Authority)

John, T. (1976) *Lenox Early Childhood Outreach Program for Parents: An Evaluation Study* (Washington, DC: DC Public Schools) (E.R.I.C. ED 131920 PS 008921)

Johnson, D.J. *et al.* (1974) 'The Houston Parent–Child Development Center Model: A Parent Education Program for Mexican–American Families', *American Journal of Orthopsychiatry, 44, 1,* 121-8

Jungnitz, G. *et al.* (1983) 'The Development and Longitudinal Evaluation of a Pre-school Home Visiting Programme', *Journal of Community Education, 2, 1,* 3-8

Kapfer, S. (1977) *Report of Selected Sessions from the 'Parents, Children and Continuity' Conference (El Paso, Texas, May 23-25, 1977)* (Washington, DC: Dingle Associates Inc.) (E.R.I.C. ED 153731 PS 009894)

Karnes, M.B. and Zehrbach, R.R. (1977) 'Educational Intervention at Home', in M.C. Day and R.K. Parker (eds.), *The Preschool in Action* (2nd edn.) (Boston: Allyn & Bacon)

Karnes, M.B. *et al.* (1968) 'An Approach for Working with Mothers of Disadvantaged Preschool Children', *Merrill-Palmer Quarterly, 14,* 174-84

Karnes, M.B. *et al.* (1970) 'Educational Intervention at Home by Mothers of Disadvantaged Infants', *Child Development, 41,* 925-35

Karnes, M.B. *et al.* (1971) 'A New Professional Role in Early Childhood Education', *Interchange, 2,* 89-105

Ketchel, M.F. (1975) 'Infant Enrichment Program: Focus on Parental Training, Curriculum and Assessment', *Dissertation Abstracts International,* 35 (8-B) 4181-B

Klaus, R.A. and Gray, S.W. (1967) *The Early Training Project for Disadvantaged Children: A Report after Five Years* (Nashville, Tennessee: George Peabody College for Teachers). Also as: Klaus, R.A. and Gray, S.W. (1968) 'The Early Training Project for Disadvantaged Children: A Report after Five Years', *Monographs of the Society for Research in Child Development, 33, 4* (Chicago, Illinois: University of Chicago Press)

Lally, J.R. and Honig, A.S. (1977a) 'The Family Development Research Program', in M.C. Day and R.K. Parker (eds.), *The Preschool in Action* (2nd edn.) (Boston: Allyn & Bacon)

Lally, J.R. and Honig, A.S. (1977b) *The Family Development Research Program: A Program for Parental, Infant and Early Childhood Enrichment. Final Report* (Syracuse, New York: Syracuse University) (E.R.I.C. ED 143458 PS 009487)

Lambie, D. *et al.* (1974) *Home Teaching of Mothers and Infants* (Ypsilanti, Michigan: High/Scope Educational Research Foundation)

Lazar, I. and Darlington, R.B. (1979) *Lasting Effects after Preschool* (ref. 79-30178) (Washington, DC: US Department of Health, Education and Welfare)

Lazar, I. *et al.* (1977a) *The Persistence of Preschool Effects: A Long-term Follow-up of Fourteen Infant and Preschool Experiments. Final Report* (Denver, Colorado: Education Commission of the States) (E.R.I.C. ED 148470 PS 009691)

Lazar, I. *et al.* (1977b) *The Persistence of Preschool Effects: A Long-term Follow-up of Fourteen Infant and Preschool Experiences. Summary Report* (Denver, Colorado: Education Commission of the States) (E.R.I.C. ED 148471 PS 009692)

Levenstein, P. (1970) 'Cognitive Growth in Preschoolers through Verbal Interaction with Mothers', *American Journal of Orthopsychiatry, 40, 3,* 426-32

Levenstein, P. (1977) 'The Mother–Child Program', in M.C. Day and R.K. Parker (eds.), *The Preschool in Action* (2nd edn.) (Boston: Allyn & Bacon)

Levenstein, P. (1978a) *The Parent–Child Network: The Verbal Interaction Component* (Freeport, New York: Verbal Interaction Project) (E.R.I.C. ED 167265 PS 010418)

Levenstein, P. (1978b) *Third Grade Effects of the Mother–Child Home Program: Developmental Continuity Consortium Follow-up Study. Final Report* (Freeport, New York: Verbal Interaction Project)(E.R.I.C. ED 156361 PS 010011)

Levenstein, P. (1979) 'The Parent–Child Network', in A. Simmons-Martin and D.R. Calvert (eds.), *Parent–Infant Intervention: Communication Disorders* (New York: Grune & Stratton)

Levenstein, P. and Sunley, R. (1968) 'Stimulation of Verbal Interaction between Disadvantaged Mothers and Children', *American Journal of Orthopsychiatry, 38,* 116-21

Levenstein, P. *et al.* (1973) 'From Laboratory to Real World: Service Delivery of the Mother–Child Home Program', *American Journal of Orthopsychiatry, 43, 1,* 72-8

Lombard, A.D. (1981) *Success Begins at Home: Educational Foundations for Preschoolers* (Lexington, Massachusets: D.C. Heath & Co.)

Love, J.M. *et al.* (1975) *National Home Start: Interim Report VI* (Ypsilanti, Michigan: High/Scope Educational Research Foundation)

Love, J.M. *et al.* (1976) *National Home Start Evaluation: Interim Report VII* (Cambridge, Massachusets: Abt Associates Inc.) (E.R.I.C. ED 134315 PS 009040)

Love, J.M. *et al.* (1977) *National Home Start Evaluation: Final Report, Findings and Implications* (Ypsilanti, Michigan: High/Scope Educational Research Foundation)

Love, J.M. *et al.* (1979) *An Evaluation of the Home Start Training Centers* (Ypsilanti, Michigan: High/Scope Educational Research Foundation) (E.R.I.C. ED 184717 PS 011361)

Loveridge, R.L. and Carapella, R. (1979) 'Parental Involvement in Preschool Education: Asset or Liability?', paper presented at annual meeting of the American Educational Research Association, San Francisco, California (E.R.I.C. ED 176849 PS 010588)

Lutz, J.E. *et al.* (1978) 'An Analysis of a Computerized System for Managing Curriculum Decisions and Tracking Student Progress in a Home-based Pre-school Education Project', paper presented at annual meeting of the American Educational Research Association, Toronto, Canada (E.R.I.C. ED 165740 IR 006602)

McCail, G. (1981) Mother Start: An Account of an Educational Home Visiting Scheme for Pre-school Children (Edinburgh: Scottish Council for Research in Education)

McGaw, B. *et al.* (1975) *Parents' Perceptions of the Pre-school Correspondence Program* (Brisbane: Queensland Department of Education) (E.R.I.C. ED 125764 PS 008667)

Madden, J. *et al.* (1976) 'Longitudinal I.Q. Outcomes of the Mother–Child Home Program', *Child Development, 47, 4,* 1015-25

Makins, V. (1984) 'American Way to Give the Young a Head Start', *Times Educational Supplement,* 5 October

Makins, V. (1985) 'High Scope: The Pre-school Curriculum', *Times Educational Supplement,* 5 July

Murphy, F. (1982) 'Primary Schools and their Work with Parents of Preschool Children', *Remedial Education, 17, 1,* 18-22

Niedermeyer, F.C. (1973) 'Parent-assisted Learning in the Inner City', *Urban Education, 8, 3,* 239-48

Office of Child Development (1975) *Report of a National Conference on Home Start and other Programs for Parents and Children (St Louis, Missouri)* (Washington, DC: Department of Health, Education and Welfare) (E.R.I.C. ED 125769 PS 008672)

Olmstead, P.P. (1979) *An Observational Study of Parental Teaching Behaviors and their Relationship to Child Achievement* (Chapel Hill, North Carolina: School of Education, North Carolina University) (E.R.I.C. ED 168721 PS 010490)

Olmstead, P.P. and Rubin, R.I. (1983) 'Linking Parent Behaviors to Child Achievement: Four Evaluation Studies from the Parent Education Follow Through Program', *Studies in Educational Evaluation, 8,* 317-25

Palmer, F.H. (1977) 'The Effects of Early Childhood Intervention', paper presented at annual meeting of the American Association for the Advancement of Science, Denver, Colorado (E.R.I.C. ED 143427 PS 009447). Also under same title in: B. Brown (ed.) (1978) *Found: Long-term Gains from Early Intervention* (Boulder, Colorado: Westview Press)

Parker, M. and Mitchell, D. (1980) *Parents as Teachers of Their Handicapped Children: A Review* (Hamilton, New Zealand: Waikato University) (E.R.I.C. ED 201125 EC 132551)

Pilling, D. and Pringle, M.K. (1978) *Controversial Issues in Child Development* (London: Elek)

Poulton, G.A. (1983) 'Origins and Development of Pre-school Home Visiting', in G. Aplin and G. Pugh (eds.), *Perspectives on Pre-school Home Visiting* (London: National Children's Bureau)

Poulton, G.A. and James, T. (1975) *Pre-school Learning in the Community* (London: Routledge & Kegan Paul)

Pugh, G. (1977) 'Educational Home-visiting Schemes', *Where, 132,* 251-3

Pugh, G. and De'Ath, E. (1984) The Needs of Parents: Practice and Policy in Parent Education (London: Macmillan, for National Children's Bureau)

Radin, N. (1972) 'Three Degrees of Maternal Involvement in a Pre-school Program: Impact on Mothers and Children', *Child Development, 43,* 1355-64

Radin, N. and Weikart, D. (1967) 'A Home Teaching Program for Disadvantaged Preschool Children', *Journal of Special Education, 1, 2,* 183-90

Raven, J. (1980) *Parents, Teachers and Children: A Study of an Educational Home*

Visiting Scheme (London: Hodder & Stoughton, for the Scottish Council for Research in Education)

Rosenfeld, A.H. (1978) *Mother–Child Home Program* (Mineola, New York: Family Service Association of Nassau County) (E.R.I.C. EC 120039 ED 175184)

Schaefer, E.S. (1969) 'A Home Tutoring Program', *Children, 16, 2,* 59-61

Schaefer, E.S. and Aaronson, M. (1977) 'Infant Education Research Project: Implementation and Implications of a Home Tutoring Project', in M.C. Day and R.K. Parker (eds.), *The Preschool in Action* (2nd edn.) (Boston: Allyn & Bacon)

Scott, R. (1974) 'Home Start: Follow-up Assessment of a Family Centred Preschool Enrichment Program', *Psychology in the Schools, 11, 2,* 147-9

Seager, D.D. *et al.* (1980) *Important Issues in Rural Education: A Collection of ERIC/CRESS Fact Sheets and Mini Reviews* (Las Cruces, Mexico: ERIC Clearinghouse on Rural Education) (E.R.I.C. ED 191648 RC 012241)

Smith, G. (1975) 'Pre-school: The Home Visiting Project', in G. Smith (ed.), *Educational Priority,* vol. 4: *The West Riding Project* (London: HMSO)

Stevens, J.H. (1976) *Training Parents as Home Teachers: A Review of Research* (E.R.I.C. ED 147014 PS 009656)

Stukat, K-G. (1976) *Current Trends in European Pre-school Research: With Particular Regard to Compensatory Education* (Windsor: National Foundation for Educational Research)

Toll, S. (1976) *Evaluation of Prekindergarten Head Start* (Philadelphia, Pennsylvania: Office of Research and Evaluation, Philadelphia School District) (E.R.I.C. ED 132170 TM 005880)

Verbal Interaction Project (1978) *MCHP/VIP: Mother–Child Home Program of the Verbal Interaction Project* (Freeport, New York: Verbal Interaction Project) (E.R.I.C. ED 167266 PS 010419)

Waksman, M. (1979) 'Mother as Teacher: A Home Intervention Program', *Interchange, 10, 4,* 40-52

Waller, S.P. and Waller, M.I. (1980) 'A Multi-dimensional Approach to Successful Early Childhood Intervention', paper presented at annual meeting of the American Educational Research Association, Boston, Massachusets (E.R.I.C. ED 184679 PS 011318)

Weikart, D.P. (1970) 'A Comparative Study of Three Preschool Curricula', in J. Frost (ed.), *The Disadvantaged Child* (2nd edn.) (New York: Houghton Mifflin)

Weikart, D.P. (1972) 'Relationship of Curriculum, Teaching and Learning in Preschool Education', in J.C. Stanley (ed.), *Preschool Programs for the Disadvantaged* (Baltimore, Maryland: The Johns Hopkins University Press)

Weikart, D.P. (1975) 'Parent Involvement: Process and Results of the High/Scope Foundation's Projects', paper presented at biennial meeting of the Society for Research in Child Development, Denver, Colorado (E.R.I.C. ED 113041 PS 008085)

Weil, S. (1985) 'The Benefits of Having a Hippy Mother', *Times Educational Supplement,* 12 April

Wilkinson, E. *et al.* (1978) *Strathclyde Experiment in Education: Govan Project — A Public Report* (Glasgow: Department of Education, University of Glasgow)

Wilkinson, J.E. and Murphy, H.F. (1976) 'Differential Methods of Enhancing Cognitive Growth in Urban Preschool Children', *Child Care Health and Development, 2,* 1-11

Wittes, G. and Radin, N. (1971) 'Two Approaches to Group Work with Parents in a Compensatory Preschool Program', *Social Work, 16,* 42-50

Yahres, H. (1977) *Teaching Mothers Mothering* (Rockville, Maryland: National Institute of Mental Health) (E.R.I.C. ED 150803 EC 103929)

6 ETHNIC MINORITIES

The literature search yielded extraordinarily few items relating to parent training programmes specifically for ethnic minority groups. The few items retrieved all originated from the USA. Considering the large number of countries, including the UK, where ethnic minority children are automatically educationally handicapped (if only by low proficiency in the main language of their country of residence), it seems astonishing that well-structured and evaluated programmes of parent training are not more widely reported. To some extent, ethnic minority children are included in general programmes for the 'disadvantaged' (see Chapter 5); but, arguably, the nature of the second-language problems often involved calls for a *specialist* type of intervention.

Furthermore, scrutiny of the few relevant reports available rapidly reveals that most programmes have combined an in-school component with a parent-training component, but have failed to discriminate the relative effects of these components in the evaluation. Substantial and tangible outcome measures have often been used, and many programmes have demonstrated considerable success. None the less, information is sorely lacking on the proportion of variance attributable to the parent training components

However, making the best of what is available, various ethnic minority groups will be considered in turn.

Afro-Caribbean

Families of Afro-Caribbean origin are less likely to be recent immigrants and much less likely to experience second-language difficulties than families of some other ethnic groups. Perhaps for these reasons, large-scale parent training provision tends not to be ethnically differentiated specifically for the Afro-Caribbean community, which is catered for, *inter alia*, by the other kinds of provision detailed in this volume. In particular, many of the programmes for 'disadvanted' groups cater for a significant proportion of low-income Afro-Caribbean families.

However, some small-scale provision does exist which is

targeted specifically on this group, and this is well described by Comer and Schraft (1980). Some of this has a 'black conscious-ness' orientation, and deals with cultural inheritance and the mani-festations and management of racial discrimination in some detail. Handbooks and guides which deal specifically with child-rearing in Afro-Caribbean families are available (e.g. Ross and Wyden, 1973; Comer and Poussaint, 1975; McLaughlin, 1976). Evaluative data on the impact of these efforts are unfortunately very difficult to find.

North American Indian

All of the programmes reviewed here which are targeted on this population are school-based, with varying degrees of parent train-ing, and none has partialled out the effectiveness of the parent-training component. Hall and Orcutt (1980) report on an educational programme for pre-school and nursery children which compared three different curriculum models with different ethnic groups. None of the curricula was structured, and all tended to emphasise 'discovery' learning. On the 'Montessori' and 'Piagetian' curricula, white children did better than Indian children. On the curriculum based on Indian culture, the Indian children did better than the white children. This is unsurprising but the pointed finding is worth bearing in mind as we proceed to consider other programmes designed by an alien dominant culture for the uplifting of the ethnic minority.

A programme designed to explore ways of co-ordinating school instruction with Indian heritage education is reported by Chevalier *et al.* (1982). Classroom teachers participated in workshops with Indian parents, pupils and 'heritage instructors', designed to for-mulate a multi-cultural curriculum and develop home–school communication strategies. Workshop activities are described in some detail, and subjective feedback from participant interviews is summarised. No evaluative data on action outcomes are given.

A programme which purports to include a parent liaison com-ponent is described by Norris and Wheeler (1981). The Indian Education Program included remedial teaching, Indian youth advisers offering counselling, field trips to cultural events as part of an Indian Studies supplemental curriculum, and a special summer school. The programme also aimed to 'implement home–school liaison services' and 'increase parental involvement in the educational and social development of Indian students'. The reality appears to have been a shambles. Parents were merely sent information of doubtful comprehensibility about their children's educational attainment and got invited to the occasional tea-party. There is no evidence in the report of any real liaison. Attendance at parental events was very variable, but mostly poor. A needs assessment survey produced only an 11.5 per cent response rate from the parents and 15 per cent from the pupils. The 'evaluation' data are sloppy and impressionistic.

A very different picture is painted by the National Indian Training and Research Center (NITRC) (1978). A needs assessment survey to determine the kinds of activity that would best serve the motivational and academic needs of Apache students was submitted to 900 parents. The six top-priority items suggested by the parents were: provision of home-reading material, tutoring aides, school pictures, a school monthly newspaper, a counsellor programme, and a parent committee. All of these ideas were implemented in the school programme, and the parent committee of 38 members elected to set policies and operating guidelines. Subsequently, however, only one-third of the parents attended meetings with any regularity, and opposing viewpoints between teaching staff and parents became evident. Unfortunately, no objective external evaluation data are cited, merely descriptive statistics.

A programme for members of the Yavapai tribe is described by Wurster (1980). Gathered on a reservation round a decommissioned fort, the tribe had witnessed the collapse of its traditional social structures. Few educational facilities were available locally, and academic failure and drop-out rates were high. Mainly school-based, the programme had very loose educational objectives (e.g. 'to develop an attitude of curiosity', 'to develop reading readiness'). It also aimed to develop culturally relevant curriculum materials, involving tribal elders and historians. Parents were involved as classroom aides, in reassessment tribal and staff meetings, in a pre-school parent association, and in workshops. The structure of the workshops was equally loose, incorporating fragmentary inputs on childbirth, the needs of children, child development, discipline, and so on. The workshops were run for the parents of pre-schoolers.

The overall evaluation results were based on a mixture of

objective and subjective tests, and were mostly positive. Significant improvements in the language, reading and maths skills of the children were noted. Social skills also seemed improved, although the measuring instrument was weak. A measure of attitudes towards child-rearing was completed by a small and doubtfully representative sample of parents, and *no* programme effect was demonstrated. Although no component analysis of the outcome data on academic attainment is offered which reflects on the impact of the parental involvement, it seems implausible that any such effect would be large.

Native Americans appear to have been extremely ill-served by the dominant culture.

Hispanic

Evaluation results for programmes designed to serve Hispanic (including Mexican) populations are considerably more encouraging, although still little attempt has been made to partial out the effect of parent training. Martinez *et al.* (1982) describe a programme designed to train 5-year-olds in English, while maintaining their Spanish-language skills. Classroom activities within a Piagetian framework are supplemented with home-based 'instructional support', but few evaluative data of substance are cited.

More tangible is the work reported by Greene (1975) in the context of the Experimental Bicultural Early Childhood Program, which coupled nursery teaching with a system of 'parental orientation and training' in the home. Educational toys and other materials were made available to the project families, using the child's dominant language. Sixty-five per cent of families were Spanish-speaking. Parental involvement activities included social events and discussions on homemade educational equipment, child-rearing practices and Spanish television broadcasts. Evaluation data indicated significant overall gains in language skills, numerical concepts and social insight, but the children from Spanish-speaking homes did not tend to do as well as children from homes where English was the primary language in use. Unfortunately, there are no data on the relative contribution of parent training to programme outcomes.

A substantial programme spanning several years is reported by the Austin Independent School District (1977, 1981). Again, this was predominantly school-based, but some information is available on the relative benefits of the use of at-home study units by parents. By 1981 the programme had developed to serve ethnic minority pupils grouped in six schools in classes of 18 children. Three of the children in each class were *not* Limited English Proficient (LEP), and served as English-speaking models for their LEP peers. Instruction was provided in English and/or Spanish, as needed. At home, parents conducted at least two 15-minute lessons for their children each week using the materials and instructional format provided. Additionally, there were parenting 'seminars' of an unstructured nature where ideas for home education were discussed, and a parent/community advisory council was formed. Evaluation results showed that the English-language skills of programme children improved significantly, and this finding was supported by a control group comparison. Spanish-language skills also improved. However, no satisfactory partialling of outcome with respect to the parental component is evident.

A very different kind of programme is reported by McConnell (1976). This early education programme used paraprofessional teachers to provide bilingual multi-cultural education to the children of migrant and seasonal farmworkers, the vast majority of whom are of Mexican origin. Migrant children are followed around by mobile project staff who work co-operatively with any local schools. Parents and community members are active in programme management, including hiring and firing, financial policy and evaluation. Family members assist by acting as teachers or teaching assistants, often helping with cultural heritage activities.

Substantial educational gains are reported. For 169 children over 293 tests and retests of mathematical skill, 71 per cent increased by 1 month of 'maths age' for each full month in the programme, with a median gain of 1.4 months of attainment per month in programme. In reading, on a similar base, 60 per cent of children improved by increments which were normal or greater (median 1.5, tests n = 193). On tests of (bilingual) language skill, 83 per cent improved likewise (n = 71), and gains were also shown on tests of knowledge of cultural inheritance. A small-scale comparison showed programme children (n = 23) to be better than controls (n = 45).

However, the contribution of the ordinary school's teaching and the parental input are not partialled out. In addition, the validity of comparing attainment gains to time in contact with the programme rather than chronological time passed must be questioned. Nevertheless, these results are encouraging from a programme deploying paraprofessional tutors working with parents. Interesting features of the parental involvement aspect were 'family fun nights', where educational games were formulated, made and played, and the practice of awarding parents who helped the programme vouchers which were exchangeable for pecuniary incentives from the 'parents' fund'. A very high level of parental participation in activities is reported despite obvious difficulties of working with a transient population.

The one project which has satisfactorily partialled out the effect of parent training is the pre-school programme based on the Community Education Center (El Centro Educativo de la Comunidad) in Redwood City, California, which has been developing for well over a decade. Both school and home programmes are provided, and in the former mother-tongue teaching in an open classroom is the general rule. Members of the community are trained as teachers and teacher aides, parents participate in the school programme, and English classes are offered for adults. In addition, teachers go into the home to train parents to teach their children specific activities and related principles of child development. The parent trainers are all mothers who are graduates of the programme and members of the Spanish-speaking community.

Comparative data were gathered by Hahn and Dunstan (1975) for children experiencing three different kinds of input: (a) three mornings per week in nursery plus weekly home visit (n = 22); (b) five days in nursery plus monthly home visit (n = 17); and (c) weekly home visit only, with no other provision (n = 20). Test results indicate all three groups made significant gains. Group (a) did least well, perhaps because pre-testing was unfortunately delayed for this group. However, groups (b) and (c) showed very large gains, of a very similar order. Thus the children who had only a weekly home lesson with their mother and teacher made gains similar to those made by children who had a five-day-a-week school programme and a monthly home lesson. The implications for cost-effectiveness are clear.

Follow-up data are reported by Read (1979), but sample attrition was heavy, and only 62 of 189 children were locatable and generated data. Teacher questionnaire ratings were the measure adopted, and home interviews with parents were conducted on a small sub-sample. Overall, the Community Education Center children were rated average for the class. Twenty-three per cent had been held back at some point since starting school, whereas the retention rate for all children of Spanish extraction in these schools was 85 per cent. Those parents who participated most tended to be parents of highest-rated children. The parental involvement intrinsic to the centre's programme did not appear to have given the parents the skills and motivation to generalise their input to the (presumably rather different) state school system.

Multi-ethnic

Project Parents caters for Spanish, Greek, Afro-Caribbean, Chinese, and other ethnic groups. Operative in Brooklyn, New York, and based on local schools, the programme aims to complement in-school activities with 'reinforcement of education in the home' and encouragement of 'parental involvement in their children's schooling'.

As described by the New York City Board of Education (1981), the programme offers parental classes, workshops and trips, together with a 'parent network' system. English (as a second language) teaching for parents is organised in local schools, as is tuition in reading and mathematics of a quite formalised and didactic nature. Language teaching incorporates lessons in survival 'bureaucratese'. The programme operates for the parents of children aged 4 through 10 years, but the parents are self-selected (and therefore presumably well motivated). Recommendations for programme evaluation are made, but there is no evidence of their having been followed.

Summary

There seems to be very little evaluative evidence concerning parent training for ethnic minorities, and what there is comes from only one country. In view of the problems of these groups, this is surprising, and indeed alarming. Evaluation research on the existing projects has almost entirely failed to partial out the effect of parent training from the effect of a parallel school programme.

Large-scale parent-training programmes specifically for Afro-Caribbean populations are rare, although many such families receive service under programmes for the low-income 'disadvantaged', which are discussed elsewhere. Programmes for North American Indians have demonstrated the value of teaching based on Indian culture, but many have been ill-evaluated and/or badly organised. Native American parents can respond to parental involvement programmes, but schools are not always prepared to accept this, even where they are well enough organised to support such a development.

Provision for Hispanic minorities has been considerably better, and the deployment of paraprofessional tutors from the Spanish-speaking community has been successful. Combined school/home programmes have shown good results, although not all home-based programme components were well thought out and sequentially structured. Bilingual or mother-tongue teaching has featured regularly in school-based programme components. Good results are also demonstrated by a mobile programme for migrant families. One programme demonstrated that once-weekly home visits to train the parents of pre-school children to teach them pre-prepared activities was as effective as a five-day nursery experience coupled with monthly parent training visits. The cost-effectiveness implications are clear. A project catering for a multiplicity of ethnic groups is described, but no evaluation data are available.

Although there is some evidence that gains made by the children generalise subsequently into the ordinary school setting, parental involvement stimulated at the pre-school level may well not generalise or be maintained, especially in the absence of encouragement or support from the school system. Existing long-term follow-up data are inadequate, and longitudinal controlled studies are necessary. Systematic replication of the quality programmes is essential, and competent replication of well-structured programmes with the Native American population is particularly needed. There is evidence that the effectiveness and cost-effectiveness of parent training programmes *can* be high, but a great deal more research of adequate design is necessary before any general conclusions could be made.

References

Austin Independent School District (1977) *Interim Evaluation Report, 1977-8. ESEA Title 7 Bilingual Project* (Austin, Texas: Office of Research and Evaluation, Austin Independent School District) (E.R.I.C. ED 172577, FL 010431)

Austin Independent School District (1981) *Title 7 Bilingual Preschool Project, 1981-2. Final Technical Report* (Austin, Texas: Office of Research and Evaluation, Austin Independent School District) (E.R.I.C. ED 228247 TM 820718)

Chevalier, Z.W. *et al.* (1982) 'Responsive Evaluation of an Indian Heritage Studies Program: Analyzing Boundary Definition in a Suburban School Context', paper presented at annual meeting of American Educational Research Association (E.R.I.C. ED 220226, RC 013526)

Comer, J.P. and Poussaint, A.F. (1975) *Black Child Care* (New York: Simon & Schuster)

Comer, J.P. and Schraft, C.M. (1980) 'Working with Black Parents', in R.R. Abidin (ed.), *Parent Education and Intervention Handbook* (Springfield, Illinois: C.C. Thomas)

Greene, J. (1975) *Experimental Bicultural Early Childhood Program. Annual Evaluation Report* (Bridgeport, Connecticut: University of Bridgeport) (E.R.I.C. ED 128104, PS 008815)

Hahn, J. and Dunstan, V. (1975) 'The Child's Whole World: A Bilingual Preschool that Includes Parent Training in the Home', *Young Children, 30, 4,* 281-8

Hall, T.A. and Orcutt, L.E. (1980) 'Evaluation of a Comprehensive Early Education Program for Urban American Indian Children', paper presented at annual meeting of American Educational Research Association, Boston (E.R.I.C. ED 189124, TM 800289)

McConnell, B. (1976) *Bilingual Mini-School Tutoring Project. Final Evaluation, 1975-76 Program Year* (Ephrata, Washington: Washington State Intermediate School District 104) (E.R.I.C. ED 135508, RC 009647)

McLaughlin, C.J. (1976) *Black Parents' Handbook: A Guide to Healthy Pregnancy, Birth and Child Care* (New York: Harcourt Brace Jovanovich)

Martinez, J.A. *et al.* (1982) *Project P.I.A.G.E.T.: Promoting Intellectual Adaptation Given Experiential Transforming with Hispanic Bilingual Five-year-old Children and their Families. A Summary* (Pennsylvania: Bethlehem School District and State University) (E.R.I.C. ED 217091, UD 022189)

National Indian Training and Research Center (1978) *Evaluation — Title 4 Program Indian Education Act. Rice School District No. 20* (Tempe, Arizona: NITRC) (E.R.I.C. ED 161572, RC 010751)

New York City Board of Education (1981) *Project Parents: Awareness, Education, Involvement Program. E.S.E.A. Title 7. Final Evaluation Report, 1980-81* (Brooklyn, New York: Office of Educational Evaluation, New York City Board of Education) (E.R.I.C. ED 215070, UD 022249)

Norris, C.A. and Wheeler, L. (1981) *Title 4 - A/Johnson O'Malley Indian Education Program. Final Evaluation Report, 1980-81* (Phoenix, Arizona: Department of Research and Planning, Phoenix Union High School District) (E.R.I.C. ED 207771, RC 012949)

Read, M. (1979) *How Do the Preschool Children of the Community Education Center Perform in the Public School System?: An Evaluation of Children's Performance and Parent Participation* (Redwood City, Caliornia: Community Education Center) (E.R.I.C. ED 171367, PS 010505)

Ross, P.H. and Wyden, B. (1973) *The Black Child — A Parent's Guide* (New York: Wyden)

Wurster, S.R. (1980) *Ft. McDowell Indian Community Preschool Program* (Tempe, Arizona: Arizona State University) (E.R.I.C. ED 188829, RC 012099)

7 LEARNING DIFFICULTIES

Parent training programmes in this area differ from those targeted on behavioural difficulties in two interesting ways. First, the quantity and quality of work on learning difficulties has been markedly less than that on behaviour difficulties, although it might be presumed that learning difficulties were more prevalent. Perhaps they do not impose as much stress on the primary care-givers, and fail to generate the same motivation to 'solve the problem'. Second, although the work on behaviour problems in the USA is markedly better in quality than that conducted in the rest of the English-speaking world, for learning difficulties it can be argued that the converse applies.

By far the greatest volume of work in the area has focused on reading skills, and this will be reviewed with reference to its geographical origin: USA, Australasia and UK. Descriptive work will be considered first in each section, then more robust evaluative studies. After encompassing reading, other skill areas and the impact of parent-powered 'summer schools' will be considered.

Reading: USA

Descriptive Work

A broad review of the influences of parents on their children's reading achievement was produced as long ago as 1968 by Della-Piana *et al.* (1968). By 1973 Neifert and Gayton (1973) were reviewing some of the difficulties involved in implementing home programmes for children with learning disabilities and identified four types of family social dynamic which usually seriously impeded the successful implementation of a programme. McLouglin *et al.* (1978) identified five major stages of service delivery to the learning disabled in which parents could play a significant role.

A *Catalogue of Parent Involvement Projects* was provided by Cruz *et al.* (1981), intended to be 'a collection of quality parent projects for assisting children in the achievement of basic skills'. Projects are categorised according to whether they provide multiple services to parents, educational materials and information, or a home-based parent training service. There is considerable detail about access to materials, but much less about evaluative outcomes. Friedlander (1981) provides a useful annotated bibliography on parental involvement in reading, but few studies cite evaluation data.

Duncan (1979) also surveyed efforts of schools to involve parents in reading programmes, and noted several recurring problems: programmes reflected professional rather than parental values, were not sufficiently flexible to cope with varying parental competence, presented lists of suggestions rather than utilising demonstration or role-play, tended to exclude care-givers who were not full-time natural parents, and often neglected to include formative and summative evaluation. Too little emphasis was placed on needs assessment and establishing interpersonal contact.

A large-scale programme designed to improve the reading achievement of elementary school pupils is described by Leckie *et al.* (1978), who worked with 283 pupils aged 6–12 years in seven different schools. Extra tuition was provided in school from teachers and also from paraprofessionals, and parents were involved in activities at home. Unfortunately, no partialling out of relative effectiveness of these components is reported. A large proportion (89 per cent) of the pupils achieved their reading score targets on criterion-referenced tests, but comparison with other studies is very difficult in the absence of mutual calibration of measures.

Another interesting model of service delivery is described by Neel *et al.* (1973). A behaviourally oriented teaching programme, implemented at school and home, was supported by home visitors who were usually programme graduate parents. At weekly visits, individualised specific learning objectives were set, materials provided, and attainment of the previous week's objectives checked. A 'co-ordinator' visited monthly to monitor the home visitor. This programme bears marked similarities to the Portage programme which will be reviewed in Chapter 11, 'Development Delay'. Unfortunately, no evaluative data are cited. Data collected from programmes operating in this way tend, in any event, to be extremely difficult to synthesise and compare.

Evaluative Work

The excellent early work of Niedermeyer (1970) and Perlish

(1970) with 'ordinary children' has already caught our attention. Parent programmes for children with marked reading *problems* were somewhat slower to develop. An early case study was reported by Hall *et al.* (1970), who supported a mother in arranging for a 10-year-old girl to go to bed one minute early for each minute less than the required 30 minutes she spent on home reading practice. The procedure was certainly effective in increasing reading practice to the scheduled amount. What it did for the child's enjoyment of reading, one dreads to think — not to mention the mother's feelings about sitting for hours with a stopwatch.

Meanwhile, in Hawaii, Arthur Staats had been working since the early 1960s on token reinforcement in the remediation of reading deficits, and the extension of the procedures to parents was bound to come. Ryback and Staats (1970) reported on the use of the SMART (Staats Motivation-Activating Reading Technique), based on the SRA (Science Research Associates) Reading Laboratories, with four children whose reading skills were delayed. The parents were trained by verbal instruction, demonstration, and practice over four hours, and their performance monitored for the next two weeks. Evaluation by normative and criterion-referenced reading tests after between five and seven months of teaching by the parents showed marked gains on all measures. Tangible reinforcers (money) were used less as the children improved. It is a pity that baseline or control data are not available, but interesting to note that the children had improved their reading skills in a way that was generalisable from the very specific training to performance on ordinary norm-referenced reading tests.

The approach began to spread. Coe (1971) reported on a parental programme in which 18 children aged 8 years were tutored for 30 minutes each day for five months. Significant gains in reading ability accrued. Koven and LeBow (1973) developed the Staats approach using a more thorough research design with three boys, aged 7-8 years. Role-play and live demonstration with the child were added to the training procedure, and the reading programme had work on spelling added to it. Results were evaluated via multiple baselines, and marked gains in reading (and spelling) were demonstrated. Follow-up data at two months was less encouraging — two of the children maintained 'a good proportion' of their gains, but the third regressed appreciably.

By the end of the decade, much larger-scale programmes were

being instituted. Rodick and Henggeler (1980) assigned 56 low-achieving 13-year-old pupils in an inner-city area to one of four groups. One group experienced SMART tutored by para-professionals, one group remedial help in schools, the third no intervention, and the fourth a home-based programme called PUSH. This latter consisted of parents and children working together for one hour per week-night on a variety of academic tasks, which could include reading, homework, or material relating to other interests. Follow-up support was by weekly telephone contact and bi-weekly home visits.

A battery of standardised educational and attitudinal tests was administered to each pupil at the beginning and end of the ten-week intervention, and at six-month follow-up. On the whole, SMART produced the biggest short-term acceleration, with PUSH doing better than the remaining two groups. However, at six-month follow-up, the SMART group showed marked regression on some measures, while the PUSH group proved more effective at maintaining its gains. Considering the weakly structured nature of the PUSH programme, these results were highly creditable.

A very different programme is described by Lengyel and Baghban (1980), who combined a daily 15-minute period of 'sustained silent reading' in class every day with a family reading programme designed to encourage parents to read *to* their children for five minutes each day, seven days a week. The programme ran for nine weeks. Participation in both programmes was associated with more positive attitudes to reading, but the direction of causation is unclear. Students who participated in both programmes also scored higher on reading tests.

A study of 150 low-SES pupils aged 9 to 11 years was conducted by Shuck *et al.* (1983), who formed an experimental and a control group. Self-explanatory materials and recording charts were sent to the parents of the 'experimental' group. Activities could include reading a book, completing assigned homework, working on a word-recognition task, or playing reading games. Children were awarded points for work at home (by parents) and at school (by teachers) and were 'paid off' each month at school in tangibles, local stores and parents having donated 'prizes'. Parent–teacher contact was limited to three meetings per year. The group experiencing parental help made markedly greater gains on reading tests than control children. This project appears to have produced a successful outcome despite limited structure and very little specific training for parents. Follow-up data would have been most useful.

Reading: Australasia

The work with token economies in the USA was soon taken up in New Zealand, predominantly by Fry (1973, 1977, 1985). After an initial study had demonstrated the effect of the procedure with brief tuition from a teacher on the word recognition *and* reading comprehension of retarded readers in comparison with two control groups, the approach was extended to parents. Word recognition skills were taught to 30 reading-retarded children for a two-month period in a reversal research design. Parent training consisted of three group meetings in school and two individual sessions in the home with each set of parents. Each child worked to learn individually unknown words from a list of high-frequency words. Each family established a reward menu for token exchange. Words were read in isolation and in context, and frequently rechecked.

The children made normal gains during the baseline and reversal phases on standardised reading tests. During the programme phase, they gained at over four times that rate, on average, with 26 of the 30 children showing the treatment effect. Fry acknowledges that accelerated short-term gains ceased when the programme ended, but notes there was no regression, as has been reported elsewhere. She also acknowledges that word recognition is just the first, if essential, step on the road to reading.

Also with a behavioural flavour, but more in the applied behaviour analysis tradition, is the work of Ted Glynn and his associates (Glynn, 1980, 1981; Glynn *et al.*, 1979, 1980), who have taken great care with experimental design in order to demonstrate unequivocally that changed parental behaviour mediates changed child reading behaviour. Their interactive technique — 'Pause, Prompt and Praise' (PPP) — has the great virtue of flexible applicability to a wide range of reading material, and owes as much to miscue analysis and a psycholinguistic view of reading as it does to behaviourism.

Reading material is graded to be neither too hard nor too easy. Parents are asked to listen to children reading out loud, pausing to allow self-correction if errors are made. If self-correction does not occur, the parents make a tripartite discrimination as to the nature of the error made. If the mistake makes no sense, the parent prompts the child with clues about the meaning of the story. If the mistake does make sense, prompts refer to the visual appearance of the word. If the child says nothing, prompts of asking the child to read on to the end of the sentence, or reread from the beginning of the sentence, are used. Praise is given liberally for correct reading, self-correction and successful reading after prompting.

Parent training is by verbal and written instruction, modelling, practice, feedback and reinforcement. This was initially carried out individually in homes, but now is increasingly commenced at centre-based group meetings and subsequently followed through into homes. In the first small study (n = 8) generalisation of improvements to school was not achieved, but subsequent studies have not found this a problem. Scott and Ballard (1983) instituted this form of tutoring at home and in school simultaneously, and the experimental children recorded gains at three times 'normal' rates. A recent review by Glynn (1985) documents many replications of positive results. The technique is now gaining ground in the UK (Winter, 1985), where a not dissimilar technique had already been used to great effect by Traxson (1980). The main lack with research into the PPP technique has been with respect to long-term follow-up data, and hopefully this will be remedied before too long.

A most interesting study from Malaysia (Atan *et al.*, 1982) was wider in scope and larger in scale, though less sophisticated in research design. Evaluation was by simple pre- and post-test measures, although multiple outcome criteria were employed. From the worst 10 per cent of 8-year-old readers in eleven schools, 146 low-SES children were taken and enrolled in a parent training programme which lasted seven months. Seven 'learning units' were deployed, covering visual discrimination, reading letters, syllables, words and sentences in a graded and sequential manner. Criterion-referenced tests were applied at the end of each unit, and a standardised reading test at the completion of the programme, together with a home background questionnaire, parent interview schedule, teacher questionnaire and teacher–pupil interaction observation schedule. Weekly or fortnightly workshops were held between teachers and parents to give parents guidance in the use of the teaching format and in the production of supplementary materials.

Reading test results showed mean post-test scores higher than pre-test scores by about one standard deviation. Observational data from classrooms showed marked positive shifts in pupil reading behaviour. The quantity of books read more than doubled. These positive results had been achieved despite poor attendance at the workshops by the parents, although partial process data suggested the parents were reasonably positive in approach to reading at home, if not very specific in technique. There was some evidence that the higher-SES parents responded more, and girls received more tutorial attention than boys. No follow-up data are reported.

Reading: United Kingdom

Operant conditioning techniques for remediating severe reading problems were imported into the UK at an early date by one or two enterprising souls (e.g. McKerracher, 1967), but were never deployed with parents. The use of reinforcement *per se* as the major feature of an intervention technique has never become popular with reading specialists in Britain, who usually prefer reinforcement to be social and naturalistically integrated with the overall procedure. This preference does, of course, bring the associated risk that reinforcement may then not occur as often as it should.

Governmental reports had urged the greater involvement of parents for some years, but many schools felt reluctant or too pressured to respond. However, examples of good practice began to be reported in a descriptive manner.

Jackson and Hannon (1981) and Hannon *et al.* (1985) describe the five-year Belfield Project in a primary school in the north of England. Via written information and group meetings, parents were encouraged to hear their children read at home on a regular basis. Extra books, folders for transportation of books and self-recording charts were supplied. Although the school was in a low-SES area, 38 per cent of the children were said to be heard reading at home frequently before the project began, and reading tests indicated these were the more competent readers. The project enrolled parents when their children were aged 5, and many families participated for two or three years. A wider range of books and reading games increasingly went home. Descriptive statistics in Hannon *et al.* (1985) indicate large numbers of families reading very frequently at home.

A very different approach is outlined by Smith and Marsh (1985). Again in a disadvantaged area, reading workshops involving the parents of 5–6-year-old children were run during school hours. Parents took part in a variety of reading activities with their own children, including talking about books, hearing the children read, playing reading games, helping with phonic work, and so on, for one hour each week. So successful was this that the project was extended to involve both younger and older children. For even older children a 'reading at home' project on Belfield lines was designed to follow on from the workshops.

Yet another joint parent–teacher programme, this time for the reading instruction of poor and non-readers, is described by Daines (1978). Townsend (1981) reviewed a range of possible programmes, and referred to the establishment of parent libraries, book clubs, and bookshops in schools.

The major impetus to widespread development in the UK came at the beginning of the 1980s with the publication by Hewison and Tizard (1980) of research in London which demonstrated that whether parents heard children read at home was a major factor in subsequent reading ability, even when socio-economic status and other variables were controlled. Subsequently, Tizard *et al.* (1982) established a controlled study in a low-SES area which compared a parental involvement input on Belfield lines to extra reading tuition in school with a control group. Children of all ability levels in the parental input group made highly significant improvements on reading tests, irrespective of initial level or intelligence, while the 'extra tuition in school' and control groups did not. Hewison (1985) subsequently reported that gains made by the parental input group were well maintained at follow-up, and indeed had not 'washed out' four years later.

Given this tangible evidence that parental involvement was not just a passing fashion, many more schools became interested, and a massive growth in the numbers of parent programmes was seen in the UK in the ensuing years. As this occurred, much more evaluative data accumulated, and more structured and methodical approaches developed.

Expansion and Evaluation

The outcome of a number of smaller scale studies of projects involving 'Parent Listening' to children read is reported in a collection of papers edited by Topping and Wolfendale (1985). Work in Liverpool showed that children in parental input groups improved at least twice as much as control groups, and kept accelerating at an only slightly reduced pace for the term after the project ended. Younger children made greater gains than older children, and the approach has now been extended to nursery children.

Subsequently, work in Somerset with learning disabled children of low cognitive ability showed average gains of 9 months in reading age during a four-month project. Training was via six group meetings, four of which also involved the children, and utilised verbal and written information of a general and specific nature, live modelling, practice, detailed individual feedback, and charting and token reinforcement at home. (The tokens were not exchanged for tangibles, only for social reinforcement in school.)

A broader approach, involving various forms of community education and parental involvement in school, has been adopted in Coventry. Test results from low-SES schools with well-developed parent involvement programmes have proved far better than normative data would lead one to expect. The effect of other factors (e.g. teacher enthusiasm) has not been partialled out, however.

As parental programmes became more widespread, greater attention was paid to structuring the training in both content and delivery. A popular vehicle for this has been the technique of 'Paired Reading', invented by Morgan (1976) in the mid-1970s but never deployed on any scale until the 1980s.

The technique is applicable to books of any level of reading difficulty, and has two phases. During the first, 'simultaneous reading', the parent and child read out loud together in close synchrony, and errors are corrected merely by the parent remodelling the word for the child to self-correct. The second phase, 'independent reading', involves the child making a non-verbal signal for the parent to be silent, and continuing to read alone until an error is made, when the parent corrects as before and joins in the reading again. Regular praise is greatly emphasised and children are not left to struggle with words for more than five seconds.

Training is most commonly done in one or two group meetings, involving parents and children. After a humorous demonstration of 'how *not* to do it', verbal and written instruction is combined with live or video modelling, and individualised practice, feedback and reinforcement. Some projects also involve contracting, on a more or less formal basis. Where a project is targeted on a 'hard-to-reach' population, all the training may be done individually in the home. Virtually all projects incorporate monitoring and continuous feedback, whether by self-recording, further group meetings or home visits. It is most usual for the intensive phase of a project to last about eight weeks, at which point a large group meeting of all concerned can serve to feed back evaluation data about the success of the project to the participants, and articulate the alternatives for those wishing to carry on (almost always the majority).

Paired Reading has been used with children aged between 5 and 14 years, and the children have included non-readers, the severely and mildly reading retarded, average and even above-average readers. Similar acceleration of reading progress has been found in all cases. Likewise, the assumed cognitive ability of the child has not been found to correlate with acceleration resulting from the use of the technique, and children with IQs of 60 and 120 have benefited equally (Topping and McKnight, 1984). Participants of all levels of socio-economic status have been successfully involved, including Asians (Jungnitz, 1985), and parental and child motivation has proved sustainable, with support, for as long as a year (Jungnitz *et al.*, 1983).

Evaluation results to date are encouraging. The procedure has proved highly replicable in a variety of contexts and there has always been an integral emphasis on the worth of evaluative data as an additional motivator for the participants. A very large number of projects have thus generated data. Topping (1986) has compiled the data from 56 such projects at the time of writing, involving almost 1,000 children. Gains on a wide variety of reading test show average gains of three-and-a-half times 'normal' progress during the initial intensive phase of projects, and even more acceleration on reading tests focusing particularly on comprehension.

Project gains are compared with baseline gains in an AB design for twelve sets of data, with identical acceleration demonstrated. Project gains are contrasted with comparison or control group gains for 16 sets of data, with the usual result that findings are less optimistic than for other research designs. Nevertheless, project children still make, on average, twice the gains of the control groups. Short-term follow-up results (for nine data sets) gathered between two and three months after the intensive phase of a project show that the test performance of participant children is *continuing* to accelerate, at three times 'normal' rates. Bearing in mind the findings of Hewison (1985) with a less structured technique, the prognosis for longer-term follow-up seems good.

Other interesting data are emerging from this meta-analysis. The Paired Reading technique has been 'delivered' by age peer tutors, cross-age peer tutors and adult volunteers as well as natural parents. Results to date suggest that natural parents are the most effective (73 data sets), followed by peer tutors (nine data sets), followed by adult volunteers (six data sets), although this finding may be contaminated by natural parents often being able to use the technique more frequently and for longer during the intensive phase of the project.

Furthermore, projects which have included follow-up home visits (35 data sets) have not produced significantly better outcomes on tests than projects which have not included such visits (38 data sets). However, this finding is almost certainly contaminated by selective deployment of home visits — in many cases they are included specifically for the purpose of making contact with 'hard-to-reach' groups, and their effect may be to raise the gains in such participants to the levels attainable by other groups without the visits. Home visits also generate positive subjective feedback from participants and can have other desirable spin-off effects.

There is some evidence that projects catering for children aged 5–7 years do significantly better than those catering for older children, but this may be partially because the former are more likely to offer project involvement on a mixed-ability basis. In addition, there are early indications that single projects which attempt to cater for a very wide age-span (four years or more) are the least likely to have favourable test outcomes.

Heath (1985), working with small samples, demonstrated that a Paired Reading group gained more in reading attainment than a 'social reinforcement' group, who gained more than a non-intervention group. Miller *et al.* (1985) report a multiple baseline control study (n = 23) with children who were two years retarded in reading. During the first stage, the active Paired Reading group gained at 2.4 times normal rates while the passive control group gained at 0.8 times normal rates. The control group families were then trained, and in *their* active phase gained at 4.9 times normal rates!

Bush (1985) notes that in one multi-racial school, the proportion of West Indians participating in Paired Reading projects was the highest and the proportion of white parents the lowest, with Asian families somewhere in between. Data on follow-up twelve months after conclusion of the intensive phase are reported by Carrick-Smith (1985), who studied a project (n = 28) which partly used natural parents and partly peer tutors, wherein participants were instructed to *stop* using the technique at the end of the intensive phase. Although the acceleration of the intensive phase was (unsurprisingly) not maintained during the year, the experimental group remained far ahead of the control group. Thus the experimentals had not regressed and the control group had not caught them up. Jungnitz (1985) reports a comparison group study demonstrating that Paired Reading plus home visiting yielded higher gains than a less structured Parent Listening project without home visits — although the families in the latter group had much higher level skills in speaking and reading English at home.

It is clear that the evaluation research on Paired Reading is very positive, although much of it is not of the most rigorous design and highest scientific quality. This is because the bulk of it has been conducted by practitioners in education rather than research workers from university settings. Nevertheless, compared with other fields of endeavour reviewed in this book, it has been relatively well researched.

The replicability of the technique and results is obviously satisfactory. Generalisation to a wide range of populations is also satisfactory. Generalisation to school is in-built as virtually all the evaluative testing has been conducted in schools by teachers. Class teachers typically observe significant differences in participant children's reading behaviour in class, in addition to the test outcomes (Topping, 1986). There is much anecdotal evidence of generalisation of the use of the technique to siblings, but this has not yet been studied in detail. The evidence for short-term maintenance of gains is good, and the limited evidence for longer term maintenance satisfactory to date. Control and comparison group studies, as well as baseline studies, have demonstrated the impact of the procedure.

The effectiveness of the technique is now unquestioned. Its cost-effectiveness is high in terms of usage of professional time, and parents do not usually find the time costs too onerous, with only one or possibly two or three meetings to attend, and these always in a neighbourhood school. Further research is needed, utilising random allocation to control groups and scrutinising long-term outcomes for more participants over longer periods. Most crucially, detailed demonstration of experimental effects on tutor behaviour in the home settings is necessary, and current research is exploring this area.

Topping and Wolfendale (1985) also review projects which have trained parents in Precision Teaching and Direct Instruction methods. Work in these areas is as yet in its early stages, although Engelmann *et al.* (1983) have produced a Direct Instruction manual for parents. In the UK, Pennington (1982), Solity and Reeve (1985) and Holdsworth (1985) report on projects which have trained parents in Precision Teaching techniques. In the case of Holdsworth, the effects of that training are not partialled out from the effects of other parallel training, and in the case of Solity and Reeve the results for particular children are wholly criterion-referenced and so individualised that summary and comparison is difficult. Pennington's work has positive outcomes, but with a small sample.

Levey and Emsley (1982) describe a project which trained parents in Direct Instruction procedures, but hard evaluative data are lacking. Holdsworth (1985) incorporated similar training, but again did not differentiate the effect of that component of the total training programme.

A series of variations on the procedures so far described is given in Topping and Wolfendale (1985). For example, Bryans *et al.* (1985) tried a variant of Paired Reading with children aged 11–12 years. The variant technique involved the parent reading a paragraph, the parent and child simultaneously re-reading the paragraph, followed by the child reading the paragraph alone. Testing indicated that the children's reading accuracy improved, but there was no change in comprehension or speed of reading. A second study using a baseline period showed significant gains on reading accuracy and spelling, but not on phonic skills or recognition of high-frequency words.

Cooknell (1985) describes a 'mixed-technique' project which appeared to improve participants' reading accuracy, but not their comprehension. Young and Tyre (1985) combined a Bryans-like variant of Paired Reading (utilised for a whole year) with 'holiday schools' for 'dyslexic' pupils, in a control group design. Supportive home visits were provided, and a further variant, called 'Prepared Reading', was introduced for the older participants.

(Prepared Reading entails the parent reading a passage aloud, child reading silently, child reading aloud.) The experimental group made very significant gains in reading ability on test, as did another group whose members had not been diagnosed as 'dyslexic', but who were equally reading retarded and had been exposed to the same procedures; the non-intervention control group lagged well behind.

Buckley (1985) reports on a project which individually trained the parents of eleven Down's Syndrome children aged 5–7 years (developmental quotients 38–94, mean 65). As part of a broad Portage-type home educational programme supported by regular home visits, reading activities were introduced, involving visual discrimination tasks, sight vocabulary on flashcards and simplified Precision Teaching techniques. Reading of phrases and sentences was developed in turn, and generalisation activities incorporated. Results are cited ranging from a child with a sight vocabulary of 700 words to a child who as yet still merely names pictures.

The emergence of reading skills bore little relationship to chronological age, language development or developmental quotient. The reading children made semantic as well as visual errors. Thatcher (1984) has produced a guide to teaching reading to mentally handicapped children which suffers from a plethora of unfounded assumptions, but has some useful practical hints, although no evaluative data.

There have as yet been relatively few direct experimental comparisons of diferent techniques in this field, and those that exist have often been undermined by serious methodological flaws. However, Jungnitz (1985) cites data implying the superiority of Paired Reading over unstructured Parent Listening, while Winter (1985) gave parents a choice of Paired Reading or Pause, Prompt and Praise, and found them equally successful within the technique they had chosen.

Other Skill Areas

Perceptual

An interesting perceptual training programme for nursery children, delivered by parents, is described by Slater (1971a,b). Three consecutive workshops covering visual–motor skills involved 33 mothers. Parents were asked to work with their children for 15 minutes each day, and lists of activities and some teaching materials were provided. Parent training relied on verbal and written instruction and group discussion, and there was little follow-up. Evaluation was via the Bender-Gestalt, Draw-a-Man and Metropolitan Readiness Tests. Participating children scored better than non-participators on all three, but only significantly so on the Bender-Gestalt. The nature of bias introduced by self-selection into the comparison group is not explored.

A later endeavour in the same field is reported by Sabatino and Abbott (1974) and Abbott and Sabatino (1975). Twenty-five 'perceptually handicapped' 4−5-year-old children were volunteered by their mothers to work for 20 minutes five days per week at home. Training included three group sessions incorporating verbal and written instructions and live demonstration, followed up with weekly one-hour group training sessions backed up with self-recording (and telephone contact, if necessary). Teaching materials for the children were made available each week during the ten-week project. Compared with a randomly assigned control group, the experimental children made significant gains on the Frostig test of visual perception, but there were no significantly greater gains on the Metropolitan Readiness Test. This reflects the common finding of lack of generalisation to 'academic' skills of this kind of training. The parents attended well, felt their children had benefited, and were keen to do more.

Spelling

The afore-mentioned work of Koven and LeBow (1973) with three boys aged 7−8 years included parent tutoring in spelling as well as reading, the spelling programme following on from the reading programme. Training was by verbal and written instruction, live modelling, and role-play between the mothers in group sessions, followed by further live modelling in the home, supervised practice and feedback. During the programme, the three subjects learned to spell between 55 and 60 new words, 47−58 per cent of which were retained at short-term follow-up, and 28−65 per cent of which were retained at two-month follow-up. The children disliked the spelling programme.

Broden *et al.* (1978) report the generalisation to school of improvements in spelling resulting from tuition at home by a parent. In the UK, the PAIRS project has trained a number of parents to tutor their children in spelling using Precision Teaching techniques (White *et al.*, 1984; Solity and Reeve, 1985). However, results of individual programmes are difficult to synthesise. This area of work appears to hold promise, but requires a great deal more detailed research.

Mathematics

It is astonishing that even less work has been carried out in the mathematics than the spelling area. McKinney (1975) described the development and implementation of a tutorial programme for parents to improve the mathematics as well as reading of their children, but few evaluation data are cited. Similarly, Jennings (1983) described a programme of support involving parents for mathematics learning in the secondary school, but evaluation data are not detailed.

Perhaps schools assume that 'modern' mathematics is beyond the grasp of most parents, or perhaps the non-specialist teacher's own grasp of mathematics is so insecure as to inhibit schools in 'giving away' any techniques. Mathematics, like spelling, is often seen as a less important skill area than reading, but even so the lack of attention paid to this subject is surprising.

Multiple and Various

A description of the University of Washington's Parent/Child Learning Clinic is offered by Townes *et al.* (1979). This facility for learning disabled children arranges for the observation of children at home and school as part of its assessment procedure. Subsequently, home-based programmes in visual–motor skills, language, memory and problem-solving are generated, among other interventions. However, programme content and training procedure are unsophisticated, and no evaluative data are cited.

Doleys *et al.* (1976) approached parent training on a broad front with five mothers of children with specific learning difficulties. Attempts were made to change the parents' usage of questions, commands and reinforcement. Observational measures were taken while the mother directed the child's play activities in a laboratory setting. An initial training procedure involving verbal and written instruction, modelling and role-play, coupled with a test of knowledge, produced increases in reinforcement and reductions in questioning, but a further training period involving feedback from other parents and self-rating from audio-recordings of play sessions resulted in even more marked effects. These changes were well sustained at three-week follow-up. No data on the impact on the learning difficulties of the children are given.

A large-scale project of a similar nature is reported by Bergan *et al.* (1983). Forty-nine middle-class parents and their pre-school (2½–5-year-old) children participated, assigned randomly to control and experimental groups, and training was given in teaching the children two particular learning tasks they had failed to perform previously. For the experimental group, parent training was by verbal and written instruction, video modelling, role-play and feedback, and child training was to be via modelling, verbal and physical prompting, and positive reinforcement. The control group parents received largely similar training, except that no reference to modelling, prompting and reinforcement was made, and control parents received no feedback on their performance.

After in-laboratory teaching of the two tasks by the parents, the children were immediately post-tested for skill acquisition by professionals. Observation of parent behaviour indicated differential application of modelling, prompting and reinforcement between tasks within groups. Thus behaviourally oriented parent training influenced parent behaviour and child learning on one task, but not the other. What we usefully learn from this, other than that behavioural parent training will not always work if the curriculum content is arbitrary and the setting artificial, is not entirely clear.

Summer Schools at Home

The work of Young and Tyre (1985), cited above, incorporated a home reading programme with 'holiday schools' which were centre-based group experiences. Overall, the project was highly successful, but the impact of the holiday schools was not partialled out in the evaluation.

Many teachers complain that children forget and regress during holidays, particularly the summer holidays, and home-based programmes to counter this for learning disabled pupils seem a good idea in principle.

Gambrell and Jarrell (1980) describe a six-week Summer Book Program which involved teachers and aides visiting 230 homes of 4–8-year-old children weekly. The visitors underwent a three-day in-service course covering 'appropriate' books, activities and strategies. Appropriate strategies included reading to and with the children, auditory cloze and reading several pages from different books. Follow-up activities included children retelling story highlights verbally or by acting or drawing. Unfortunately, evaluation relied on attitude surveys of children and parents.

Welsh *et al.* (1981) and Doss *et al.* (1980) report on a 'summer school at home' for 333 children, aged pre-school to 11 years, mainly black and Hispanic low-achievers. Different kits of materials were prepared for children of different ages. These were 'administered' by the parents over ten weeks and sent back to the project headquarters for marking and grading. Reinforcers available included certificates, T-shirts and banquets!

Compared with control groups, the programme had 'no discernible impact' on the participants' reading achievement on standardised tests (Iowa Test of Basic Skills). There was considerable variation in outcome according to age of child. Six-year-old experimentals did better than controls, 8-year-old experimentals worse than controls, and 7- and 9-year-old experimentals as well as controls. The inter-test period (six months) was much greater than the project period. However, the parents showed a high rate of participation in the programme and were enthusiastic about it.

The effectiveness of summer home programmes thus remains 'not proven'. This field of work has not yet been tackled in a way which deploys the full range of parent training techniques, however.

Summary

The quality and quantity of research on training parents to remediate their children's learning difficulties has been less than that in the area of behaviour problems. Fewer programmes have in-built evaluation, and many have failed to partial out the parent training component effect in multi-faceted programmes. Reading is the main target of programmes. Some relevant work with 'ordinary children' has been reviewed elsewhere.

In the USA early work with the SMART reading programme was behaviourally oriented and showed good effect, although follow-up results at between two and six months tended to show some regression. Training methods become more sophisticated, and one programme using self-explanatory kits of materials, home

recording and school-linked reinforcement with relatively little
parent–teacher contact showed good results, although follow-up
data were lacking. Another programme withh loose curricular
content but follow-up home visits showed good maintenance of
gains.

In New Zealand, work using token economy procedures (like
SMART) showed short-term success, but the same failure in
spontaneous generalisation over time. From the same country, the
Pause, Prompt and Praise procedure derived from Glynn and his
associates has proved effective in changing parental behaviour and
consequent child reading behaviour. Initially, generalisation to
school was not achieved, but later this has proved no problem.
Work with PPP has tended to lack control groups and long-term
follow-up data, but the approach clearly holds promise and is
being adopted in the UK.

Work in Malaysia using kits of materials, weekly skill-
acquisition tests and weekly workshops for parents and
teachers demonstrated satisfactory results over a seven-month
project with a large group of 8-year-olds with marked reading
difficulty. Behavioural changes were noted in pupils in class,
although parental attendance at workshops was poor.

A great deal of work on parental involvement in reading has
been carried out in the UK. Research has shown that whether
parents hear their children read at home is a major factor in children's reading development, irrespective of other factors. A
programme to encourage parents to do this showed marked gains
for participating children in comparison with other children who
received extra remedial tuition in school or no intervention, and
these advances endured satisfactorily at follow-up as much as four
years later.

Subsequent work replicated this design and finding, and
demonstrated equal effect with children of low cognitive ability,
provided well-structured training and follow-up were supplied.

The technique of Paired Reading derived from Morgan has also
become popular, much replicated and well researched. Training is
typically brief, although well structured; intensity of follow-up is
tailored to meet the needs of the target group. Children varying
widely in age (5–14 years) and ability have been shown to make
average gains of three and a half times 'normal' rates. A number of
baseline and control group studies substantiate the effectiveness of
the technique, and follow-up at between two and three months has

shown only slightly reduced acceleration. Longer-term follow-up data are relatively scarce, but evidence to date indicates control groups are still left well behind one year post-intervention. Follow-up home visits have not proved necessary in many cases to sustain effectiveness, and cost-effectiveness of the procedure is high. All ethnic groups have proved able to benefit, irrespective of language difficulties.

Also in the UK, work has developed in training parents in Precision Training and Direct Instruction procedures. Early studies are small scale, with limited, conglomerated or not readily summarised evaluation data, but the approach holds promise.

Variants on the Paired Reading procedure have shown some success, sometimes only in raising reading accuracy, but the combination with the technique known as Prepared Reading and supportive holiday schools has shown very good results over a one-year programme. Mixed techniques have not tended to produce better results than single techniques. Training parents to teach reading to Down's syndrome children has been remarkably effective for some of them. Few adequate direct experimental comparisons of techniques are reported.

Very little work has been carried out on other skill (or 'subject') areas. Parent-powered training in visual perception for 4–5-year-olds has been shown to improve performance on tests of such skills in the short term, but does not generalise to wider attainments. There is a little work on spelling which seems to hold promise, but detailed research is lacking. In the mathematics area an even greater lack is evident. There is as yet no satisfactory evidence that holiday home-teaching programmes are effective, but further research is required.

References

Abbott, J.C. and Sabatino, D.A. (1975) 'Teacher–Mom Intervention with Academic High-risk Pre-school Children', *Exceptional Children, 41*, 4, 267-8
Atan, N.bt *et al.* (1982) 'Remedial Reading Support Program for Children in Grade 2 in Malaysia', *Evaluation in Education, 6, 1*, 137-60
Bergan, J.R. *et al.* (1983) 'Effects of Parent Training on Parent Instruction and Child Learning of Intellectual Skills', *Journal of School Psychology, 21*, 31-9
Broden, M. *et al.* (1978) 'In-class Spelling Performance: Effects of Home Tutoring by a Parent', *Behavior Modification, 4*, 511-30
Bryans, T. *et al.* (1985) 'The Kings Heath Project', in K. Topping and S. Wolfendale (eds.), *Parental Involvement in Children's Reading* (London: Croom Helm/New York: Nichols Publishing Co.)

Buckley, S. (1985) 'Teaching Parents to Teach Reading to Teach Language: A Project with Down's Syndrome Children and Their Parents', in K. Topping and S. Wolfendale (eds.), *Parental Involvement in Children's Reading* (London: Croom Helm/New York: Nichols Publishing Co.)

Bush, A. (1985) 'Paired Reading at Deighton Junior School', in K. Topping and S. Wolfendale (eds.), *Parental Involvement in Children's Reading* (London: Croom Helm/New York: Nichols Publishing Co.)

Carrick-Smith, (1985), 'A Research Project in Paired Reading', in K. Topping and S. Wolfendale (eds.), *Parental Involvement in Children's Reading* (London: Croom Helm/New York: Nichols Publishing Co.)

Coe, M.A. (1971) 'Parental Involvement in Remedial Reading Instruction', *Academic Therapy Quarterly, 6, 4,* 407-10

Cooknell, T. (1985) 'An Inner-city Home Reading Project', in K. Topping and S. Wolfendale (eds.), *Parental Involvement in Children's Reading* (London: Croom Helm/New York: Nichols Publishing Co.)

Cruz, N. *et al.* (1981) *A Catalog of Parent Involvement Projects: A Collection of Quality Parent Projects for Assisting Children in the Achievement of Basic Skills* (Rosslyn, Virginia: Inter America Research Associates) (E.R.I.C. ED 226842, PS 013380)

Daines, R. (1978) 'A Joint Parent–Teacher Programme for the Reading Instruction of Poor and Non-Readers', *Remedial Education, 13, 4,* 188-92

Della-Piana, G. *et al.* (1968) 'Parents and Reading Achievement: A Review of Research', *Elementary English , 45, 2,* 190-200

Doleys, D.M. *et al.* (1976) 'Parent Training Techniques: Effects of Lecture-role Playing Followed by Feedback and Self-recording', *Journal of Behavior Therapy and Experimental Psychiatry, 7,* 359-62

Doss, D. *et al.* (1980) *1980 Summer At-home Reading Program. Interim Evaluation Report* (Austin, Texas: Office of Research and Evaluation, Austin Independent School District) (E.R.I.C. ED 204713, CS 006147)

Duncan, P.H. (1979) 'Family Education in Reading: A School-initiated Model', paper presented at annual meeting of the National Reading Conference, San Antonio (E.R.I.C. ED 184070, CS 005314)

Engelman, S. *et al.* (1983) *Teach Your Child to Read in 100 Easy Lessons* (New York: Simon & Schuster)

Friedlander, J. (1981) *Early Reading Development: A Bibliography* (London: Harper & Row)

Fry, L. (1973) 'Token Reinforcement and the Reading Ability of Retarded Readers', *New Zealand Journal of Educational Studies, 1,* 165-76

Fry, L. (1977) 'Remedial Reading Using Parents as Behaviour Technicians', *New Zealand Journal of Educational Studies, 12, 5,* 29-36

Fry, L. (1985) 'Remedial Action Using a Home-based Token Economy', in K. Topping and S. Wolfendale (eds.), *Parental Involvement in Children's Reading* (London: Croom Helm/New York: Nichols Publishing Co.)

Gambrell, L.B. and Jarrell, M.E. (1980) 'Summer Reading: Description and Evaluation of a Program for Children and Parents', *Reading World, 20, 1,* 1-9

Glynn, T. (1980) 'Parent–Child Interaction in Remedial Reading at Home', in M.M. Clark and T.Glynn (eds.), *Reading and Writing for the Child with Difficulties* (Birmingham: Faculty of Education, University of Birmingham)

Glynn, T. (1981) 'Behavioural Research in Remedial Education: More Power to the Parents', in K. Wheldall (ed.), *The Behaviourist in the Classroom* (Birmingham: Faculty of Education, University of Birmingham)

Glynn, T. (1985) 'The Mangere Home and School Remedial Reading Procedures: Continuing Research on their Effectiveness', *New Zealand Journal of Psychology, 15,* 66-77

Glynn, T. *et al.* (1979) *Remedial Reading at Home: Helping You to Help Your*

Child (Wellington: New Zealand Council for Educational Research)

Glynn, T. *et al.* (1980) *Training Parents as Remedial Reading Tutors* (Wellington: New Zealand Council for Educational Research)

Hall, R.V. *et al.* (1970) 'Teachers and Parents as Researchers using Multiple Baseline Designs', *Journal of Applied Behavior Analysis, 3, 4,* 247-55

Hannon, P. *et al.* (1985) 'Implementation and Take-Up of a Project to Involve Parents in the Teaching of Reading', in K. Topping and S. Wolfendale (eds.), *Parental Involvement in Children's Reading* (London: Croom Helm/New York: Nichols Publishing Co.)

Heath, A. (1985) 'A Study of the Effectiveness of Paired Reading', in K. Topping and S. Wolfendale (eds.), *Parental Involvement in Children's Reading* (London: Croom Helm/New York: Nichols Publishing Co.)

Hewison, J. (1985) 'Parental Involvement and Reading Attainment: The Implications of Research in Dagenham and Haringey', in K. Topping and S. Wolfendale (eds.), *Parental Involvement in Children's Reading* (London: Croom Helm/New York: Nichols Publishing Co.)

Hewison, J. and Tizard, J. (1980) 'Parental Involvement and Reading Attainment', *British Journal of Educational Psychology, 50, 3,* 209-15

Holdsworth, P. (1985) 'Parental Involvement in Mowbray School', in K. Topping and S. Wolfendale (eds.), *Parental Involvement in Children's Reading* (London: Croom Helm/New York: Nichols Publishing Co.)

Jackson, A. and Hannon, P. (1981) *The Belfield Reading Project* (Rochdale: Belfield Community Council)

Jennings, D. (1983) 'Mathematics in the Secondary School: A Programme of Support Involving Parents', *Remedial Education, 18, 4,* 171-3

Jungnitz, G. (1985) 'A Paired Reading Project with Asian Families', in K. Topping and S. Wolfendale (eds.), *Parental Involvement in Children's Reading* (London: Croom Helm/New York: Nichols Publishing Co.)

Jungnitz, G. *et al.* (1983) 'The Development and Evaluation of a Paired Reading Project', *Journal of Community Education, 2, 4,* 14-22

Koven, J.T. and LeBow, M.D. (1973) 'Teaching Parents to Remediate the Academic Problems of their Children', *Journal of Experimental Education, 41, 4,* 64-73

Leckie, S. *et al.* (1978) *Development and Implementation of Procedures to Improve the Reading Achievement of Underachieving Elementary Students* (Virginia: Nova University) (E.R.I.C. ED 184059, CS 005273)

Lengyel, J. and Baghban, M. (1980) 'The Effects of a Family Reading Program and S.S.R. on Reading Achievement and Attitudes' (West Virginia: unpublished document) (E.R.I.C. ED 211925, CS 006423)

Levey, B. and Emsley, D. (1982) 'Involvement of Parents in the Teaching of DISTAR Reading to Slow-Learning Children', *Occasional Papers of the Division of Educational and Child Psychology, British Psychological Society, 6, 1,* 43-6

McKerracher, D.W. (1967) 'Alleviation of Reading Difficulties by a Simple Operant Conditioning Technique', *Journal of Child Psychology and Psychiatry, 8,* 51-6

McKinney, J.A. (1975) 'The Development and Implementation of a Tutorial Program for Parents to Improve the Reading and Mathematical Achievement of their Children', unpublished paper (E.R.I.C. ED 113703)

McLoughlin, J.A. *et al.* (1978) 'Perspective on Parental Involvement in the Diagnosis and Treatment of Learning Disabled Children', *Journal of Learning Disabilities, 11, 5,* 291-6

Miller, A. *et al.* (1985) 'The Development of Paired Reading in Derbyshire', in K. Topping and S. Wolfendale (eds.), *Parental Involvement in Children's Reading* (London: Croom Helm/New York: Nichols Publishing Co.)

Morgan, R.T.T. (1976) 'Paired-reading Tuition: A Preliminary Report on a Technique for Cases of Reading Deficit', *Child Care Health and Development*, 2, 13-28

Neel, J.H. *et al.* (1973) *Process Evaluation in the Behavior Oriented Prescriptive Teaching Approach*, symposium presented at annual meeting of the Mid South Education Research Association (E.R.I.C. ED 100977, TM 004095)

Neifert, J.T. and Gayton, W.F. (1973) 'Parents and the Home Program Approach in the Remediation of Learning Disabilities', *Journal of Learning Disabilities*, 6, 2, 31-5

Niedermeyer, F.C. (1970) 'Parents Teach Kindergarten Reading at Home', *Elementary School Journal*, 70, 438-45

Pennington, A. (1982) 'Parental Involvement in Precision Teaching', *Occasional Papers of the Division of Educational and Child Psychology, British Psychological Society*, 6, 1, 39-42

Perlish, H.N. (1970) 'Early Reading via Television', *Educational Television International*, 4, 2, 110-15

Rodick, J.D. and Henggeler, S.W. (1980) 'The Short-term and Long-term Amelioration of Academic and Motivational Deficiencies among Low-achieving Inner-city Adolescents', *Child Development*, 51, 1126-32

Ryback, D. and Staats, A.W. (1970) 'Parents as Behavior Therapy-technicians in Treating Reading Deficits (Dyslexia), *Journal of Behavior Therapy and Experimental Psychiatry*, 1, 109-19

Sabatino, D.A. and Abbott, J.C. (1974) 'Home Instruction Utilizing Teacher–Moms with Academic High-risk Pre-school Children', *Psychology in the Schools*, 11, 4, 433-40

Scott, J.M. and Ballard, K.D. (1983) 'Training Parents and Teachers in Remedial Reading Procedures for Children with Learning Difficulties', *Educational Psychology*, 3, 1, 15-30

Shuck, A. *et al.* (1983) 'Parents Encourage Pupils (PEP): An Innercity Parent Involvement Reading Project', *Reading Teacher*, 36, 6, 524-8

Slater, B.R. (1971a) 'Perceptual Development at the Kindergarten Level', *Journal of Clinical Psychology*, 27, 263-6

Slater, B.R. (1971b) 'Parental Involvement in Perceptual Training at the Kindergarten Level', *Academic Therapy*, 7, 2, 149-54

Smith, H. and Marsh, M. (1985) '"Have You a Minute?": The Fox Hill Reading Project', in K. Topping and S. Wolfendale (eds.), *Parental Involvement in Children's Reading* (London: Croom Helm/New York: Nichols Publishing Co.)

Solity, J. and Reeve, C. (1985) 'Parent-assisted Instruction in Reading and Spelling', in K. Topping and S. Wolfendale (eds.), *Parental Involvement in Children's Reading* (London: Croom Helm/New York: Nichols Publishing Co.)

Thatcher, J. (1984) *Teaching Reading to Mentally Handicapped Children* (London: Croom Helm)

Tizard, J. *et al.* (1982) 'Collaboration Between Teachers and Parents in Assisting Children's Reading', *British Journal of Educational Psychology*, 52, 1-15

Topping, K.J. (1986) 'Training Parents as Reading Tutors: Effective Service Delivery', *School Psychology International* (in press)

Topping K.J. and Wolfendale, S. (eds.) (1985) *Parental Involvement in Children's Special Education: Forward Trends*, 11, 3, 12-15

Topping, K.J. and Wolfendale, S. (eds) (1985) *Parental Involvement in Children's Reading* (London: Croom Helm/New York: Nichols Publishing Co.)

Townes, B.D. *et al.* (1979) 'Parent-directed Remediation for LD Children', *Academic Therapy*, 15, 2, 173-84

Townsend, D. (1981) 'Reading and the Home', *Reading*, 15, 2, 48-55

Traxson, D. (1980) 'Working with the Parents of Seven Year Old Children Who Are Slow in Developing Reading Skills — An Individualised Approach', unpublished MA thesis, University of Nottingham

Welsh, D.J. *et al.* (1981) 'Title 1 Parents as Compensatory Reading Instructors: Is There No Place Like Home?', paper presented at annual meeting of the American Educational Research Association, Los Angeles (E.R.I.C. ED 204073, RC 012789)

White, P.G. *et al.* (1984) 'Teaching Parents to Teach Reading', *Special Education: Forward Trends, 11, 1,* 11-13

Winter, S. (1985) 'Giving Parents a Choice: Teaching Paired Reading and Pause, Prompt and Praise Strategies in a Workshop Setting', in K. Topping and S. Wolfendale (eds.), *Parental Involvement in Children's Reading* (London: Croom Helm/New York: Nichols Publishing Co.)

Young, C. and Tyre, P. (1985) 'Parents as Coaches for Dyslexic and Severely Reading-retarded Pupils', in K. Topping and S. Wolfendale (eds.), *Parental Involvement in Children's Reading* (London: Croom Helm/New York: Nichols Publishing Co.)

8 BEHAVIOUR PROBLEMS

Training parents in the management of their children's problematic behaviour is one of the three major areas in the field, and rightly so. A very large proportion of the parent referrals to welfare agencies and mental health professionals involve difficulties with child behaviour. Without practical, systematic and effective help for the family, some of these children will subsequently be emotionally and/or physically abused. In those families lacking help, if it were possible for the parents to 'do nothing', spontaneous remission or natural maturation would in time resolve many of the problems. However, by taking action of an over-reactive and confused nature without advice, parents can damage relationships with their children irretrievably, and thereby store up many more problems for the future. For a small minority of parents, their anger, frustration, and eventually desperation spills over into physical damage to their children.

Child Abuse

Recent work has shown that competency-based parent training for child abusers compares well with traditional social work support in terms of both effectiveness and cost-effectiveness. Wolfe *et al.* (1982) report an interesting case study with a low-IQ epileptic single parent who displayed very high rates of verbally and physically aversive behaviour towards her three children. Training was provided in a clinic playroom setting with the mother in miniaturised radio communication (bug-in-the-ear) with the professional workers. This arrangement permitted constant verbal prompting and reinforcement of the mother without the children being aware that external influences were at work. The mother's hostile verbal and physical behaviours were markedly reduced, and the frequency of positive behaviours increased, although less markedly. The radio device was faded out. Generalisation to the home setting was demonstrated, and maintenance of gains following the withdrawal of the training procedure was found at follow-up two months later. The family had previously been supervised unsuccessfully by child welfare agencies for five years.

A useful review of behavioural interventions in child abuse is provided by Isaacs (1982). Eleven studies which include baseline and post-intervention data, and a description of technique sufficiently thorough to enable replication, are discussed. Many other, less adequate, studies are also noted, and useful summary tables provided.

Of the eleven substantial studies, only three dealt with large numbers of families, the remainder being case studies of one or two families. Training was most frequently carried out in the home, but sometimes in a clinic setting and sometimes in both. Method of training included verbal and written information, desensitisation, modelling, role-playing, rehearsal, reinforcement, contracting, and radio-transmitted communication. Few of the studies utilised group training. Curriculum content included the standard principles of applied behaviour analysis, time-out and contracting, stress indentification and relaxation, problem-solving techniques, self-control techniques and general child development — all usually individualised to suit the needs of the trainees.

All these studies reported positive effects, and the majority of effects indicated a shift of a substantial nature on an adequately reliable and tangible measure (generalised parental self-report having notoriously low reliability). It has often proved easier to reduce aversive behaviour than increase positive behaviour. A weakness of many studies was a relatively short follow-up time-span, anything longer than three months being exceptional. A one-year follow-up reported in Wahler (1980) showed a high degree of wash-out of training effects, particularly with mothers who were socially isolated. The positive findings at shorter-term follow-up may thus be beguilingly optimistic. Whether it is reasonable to expect families under high stress levels to be able to maintain their newly learnt behaviour over long periods without continued behaviourally oriented support and reinforcement is debatable. However, this question is crucial if we are to prevent abused children from becoming abusive parents.

By no means all efforts to improve parental skills in managing child behaviour have been directed at such high-need populations, however, and approaches other than the behavioural have been taken. Nevertheless, the bulk of the work in the field has had a behavioural orientation. It may therefore be useful to consider the non-behavioural interventions as a group.

Non-behavioural Interventions

There are *a priori* grounds for optimism about almost any well-organised intervention involving parents. D'Angelo and Walsh (1967) and Glavin and Quay (1969) compared the effectiveness of 'therapeutic' interventions with disabled children, with their parents, and in combination, and found that work with the parents alone was actually the most effective.

The Social Work Tradition

Supportive work with parents has traditionally stemmed from a base in social work, and some efforts in the area have tended to be characterised by the amorphousness of eclectic social work practice, with multi-disciplinary overtones. Kirk (1979) describes services offered to emotionally disturbed children in their homes delivered from a base in a residential treatment centre. One of the aims of the home programme is to prevent any need for placement for residential treatment, and follow-up studies after between one and four years show that this was achieved in 84 percent of cases. The average length of time in the programme was 11.2 months, and the cost was $8.63 per day compared with a cost of $43.26 per day for residential treatment. Paraprofessional 'home management specialists' were employed to support families, under the guidance of social workers. The paraprofessional personnel often had difficult backgrounds themselves. The range of input was extremely wide, encompassing a prodigious scope of activities. A 'foster-grandparent' scheme also operated. Unfortunately, evaluative information is not detailed.

A study by Murphy (1976) also suffered from over-reliance on nebulous dependent variables. A ten-week course, meeting for two and a half hours per week, enrolled 139 parents who were instructed by 'three professionals with varied backgrounds in the human services field'. Parents showed significant changes in their *perceptions* of the severity of their children's problem behaviour and of their own problems and feelings when taught by one of the professionals, but less so when taught by the other two. The moral here — that it's not just what you do but how well you do it — will be worth bearing in mind in relation to other studies which *appear* highly structured and fail-safe with respect to personal idiosyncrasies.

In the UK, Kolvin *et al.* (1981) evaluated a combined parent and teacher consultation programme operated by social workers and aimed at reducing disruptive behaviour in early adolescents. The results were not very encouraging. Karn (1972) describes a residential group project for mothers of children referred to a Child Guidance Clinic. Mothers and children participated together, and a variety of activities were organised, including play, art and music therapy. Interesting detail of the dynamics of the group is offered, and reference made to growth in the confidence and maturity of the mothers, but no objective evaluation data are available.

Training Foster-parents

Education and training for foster-parents have been even more firmly rooted in the social work tradition, and Rosmann (1980) provides a useful review of work in this area. He notes that by 1978 there were at least two dozen published curricula for educating foster-parents, and numerous articles and books describing model training programmes. It is now well documented that the nurturing qualities of enlisted foster-parents are highly variable, and it is necessary to examine the interaction between pre-training qualities and training effects. Even where training programmes are available, participation rates are often less than one-third of all foster-parents, which may be little different from the attrition rate.

There is evidence that training for the whole family (including the foster-child) is more effective than training for the foster-parents alone, and this contrasts with the previously cited findings for natural parents. Loosely structured discussion groups for foster-parents seem to have a social and cathartic effect on the parents, but no impact on foster-parental interaction with their foster-children. Follow-up individual consultation in the foster-home has been shown to produce some generalisation, albeit limited. Experimental comparison of the impact of both behavioural and 'reflective' approaches indicates that both have beneficial effects in relation to control groups, but (unsuprisingly) the behavioural training produces more behavioural change in the foster-parents. Unfortunately, very few data are available on long-term follow-up of benefits accruing to the foster-children themselves.

Behavioural Counselling and Relaxation

It is not always easy to determine where a particular training programme stands on the behavioural/non-behavioural continuum.
Some programmes incorporate 'behavioural' in their title when
there is very little evidence of applied behavioural analysis in the
content or structure of the programme. Alternatively, as for
example in the study by Brown (1976), a programme called
'Parent Counselling' turns out to be 'concerned with systematically
training parents to observe and modify child behaviour via operant
learning principles'. Brown found his programme enabled parents
to change specific target behaviours of their children, but also
resulted in more positive 'attitudes' and feelings in the parents
towards the target children and themselves. Parental feelings of
confidence and personal effectiveness were enhanced, and the
family perception of locus of control tended to shift from without
to within the family. While the programme did not result in
improved attitudes towards spouses or non-target children, this
study is nevertheless an interesting example of how a superficially
mechanistic behavioural training programme can have strong
psychodynamic implications.

Returning to the theme of 'non-behavioural' interventions,
Lupin *et al.* (1976) developed a programme using relaxation tapes
with families including a hyperactive child. Different tapes were
provided for parents and children, to be used for about 20 minutes
per evening over a period of two months. At the end of the
programme the parents rated the children as happier and less
inclined to provocative social behaviour, but otherwise not significantly changed. Observation in the classroom suggested significant improvement on three out of five target behaviours. Lupin
et al. are aware of methodological inadequacies in their study, but
feel, with some justification, that these results indicate the
approach adopted is worth further investigation.

Conflict-resolution and Problem-solving

'Relationship Enhancement' is the name of a programme designed
to teach parents and adolescents means of improving personal
relationships. Skills in self-expression, empathic response, and
problem-solving are taught. The programme is said to lend itself to
a variety of formats, from weekly meetings of one or two hours to
intensive marathon sessions. Facilitator skills to promote generalisation to everyday life at home are included in the programme.

Vogelsong and Guerney (1980) provide a useful summary, and cite three research studies which have demonstrated the effectiveness of the programme, on behavioural as well as self-report measures. Comparisons with other programmes and follow-up data seem encouraging, but wider replication is obviously necessary. There are considerable similarities to Parent Effectiveness Training, which is dealt with in Chapter 4, 'Ordinary Children'.

Conflict Resolution Skills Training has a similar flavour. Six reports on programmes run under this heading are summarised in Wells and Forehand (1981). The aims of such programmes are to reduce the use by parents of arbitrary power, blaming and long lectures. Expression, listening, reflection, problem-solving and negotiation were developed via modelling, role-play, practice and brain-storming. Improvements in negotiation skills were demonstrated on self-report and centre-based and *in vivo* audio- and video-taped measures, but not all studies could show generalisation to the home, and long-term follow-up data are scanty. Holstein (1975) reports a similar programme with fairly uninspiring results.

More encouraging is the work of Robin (1981) in this area. Thirty-three families received problem-solving communication training to resolve parent–adolescent conflict, or alternative family therapy, or a waiting-list condition. Both treatments resulted in significant reductions in self-reported disputes at home, but only the problem-solving training produced increments in problem-solving behaviour objectively coded during discussions at home. Some of the treatment effects had washed out at ten-week follow-up, but most had endured at least that long.

Individualised Interactive Training

A considerably more thorough methodology was adopted for the Mother-instruction Programme reported in Kogan and Gordon (1975), and Gordon and Kogan (1975). Thirty mothers self-referred to the programme. Baseline observations were video-taped and rated according to maternal dominance/submission, warmth/hostility and involvement (or interaction). Individualised modification guidelines for each mother were then developed, and the mothers trained in eight weekly sessions using verbal prompting via a radio device. Further verbal and written instruction was intended to facilitate generalisation to the home. Ten measures of mother and child behaviour were made post-treatment. No significant change had occurred in about 35 per cent of mother behaviours measured, and about 15 per cent of child behaviours measured. It is debatable whether this implies success or failure for the programme, since it may have been more realistic to scrutinise fewer and more specific change targets for each family. There was ancillary evidence that mother–child interaction had become more positive, and maternal self-report suggested the children had reduced their unwanted behaviours by about half.

Of the 30 participants, 15 engaged in the programme immediately and 15 waited eight weeks, when another baseline observation was taken. Overall change was about the same for both groups, and both changed more during instruction than during no-contact periods. The 'waiting' group showed some improvement during their waiting period. The 'immediate' training group continued to improve in the 'no-contact' weeks after training. Gordon and Kogan (1975) draw some encouragement from this latter finding and discuss the role of spontaneous remission in therapeutic intervention in general. Other researchers would do well to bear this in mind.

Behavioural versus Non-behavioural Intervention

A number of interesting studies have compared the effectiveness of behavioural strategies in parent training with a variety of alternatives. An early example is documented by Walder (1968), who compared operant training with non-operant training and a minimum contact group. Data-gathering included audio- and video-tapes of parent–child interaction and psychological tests of parents, but the number of families involved was very small. There was no evidence of a significant difference in effectiveness between the operant and the 'eclectic' programme, despite the inexperience of some of the 'eclectic' therapists.

A classic study by Alexander and Parsons (1973) compared 46 families of delinquents receiving short-term behavioural intervention with 19 assigned to a client-centred family groups programme, and ten assigned to a no-treatment control group. Presenting child problems included absconding, truancy, theft, abuse of drugs and alcohol, and generally being beyond parental control.

The behavioural programme included training in communication and negotiation, discrimination of rules from requests, social reinforcement, and (for some families) the provision of a behaviour modification manual and the institution of a token economy. Process evaluative measures showed the behavioural intervention to be significantly superior to the other three conditions in quality of family interaction and subsequent recidivism rates, despite twelve of the 46 families not completing the programme. The recidivism rates in the client-centred and control groups were similar to national and local averages, while that for the psychodynamic group was markedly higher.

In 1974 Tavormina reviewed parent counselling techniques and discriminated behavioural interventions from the 'reflective counselling' approach, which emphasised parental awareness, understanding and acceptance of the child's feelings. It was noted that both approaches had demonstrated effectiveness in soundly designed studies. Tavormina then conducted a direct comparison for parents of mentally retarded children (Tavormina's 1975 paper is also discussed in Chapter 11, 'Developmental Delay'.) Both approaches resulted in improvements greater than the control group, but the behavioural intervention produced a significantly larger improvement than the reflective method on most criteria, including direct observations, attitudinal scales and maternal self-report. How generalisable this finding is to parents of all children is another matter.

The most substantial comparative review in this area is that of Reisinger *et al.* (1976a). This excellent paper summarises work under behavioural, client-centred and psychodynamic headings, which are accepted to be loose and unspecific. It is noted that psychodynamically oriented professionals tend to be more doubtful about the value of fully involving parents in the therapeutic process, and it is in this field that the majority of failures have been reported. This need not mean that this is where the majority of failures have actually occurred, of course. The authors decline to come out specifically in favour of the client-centred or the behavioural method, however, since at that time much of the research was still based on single case studies or used inadequate methodology.

Veltkamp and Newman (1976) described an interesting two-stage parent training programme. During each weekly two-hour session the parents spent the first hour in a group of 10-15 parents, focusing on general principles of child-rearing; the second hour was in a group of between two and four parents, focusing on the application of the principles to their specific family situation. The initial curriculum content was behaviour modification, but when parents had demonstrated the ability to modify one target behaviour, they were allowed to graduate to the 'advanced' group, where the emphasis was on Adlerian psychology. Training methods included written information, homework assignments, group discussion, role-playing, and didactic presentations verbally and on video and film. Parents stayed in the programme for approximately nine months on average.

Evaluative research encompassed objective recordings of child behaviour, observation, teacher and parent self-report. Significant improvement was reported for 84 per cent of the children, who had previously been highly dysfunctional. It is most unfortunate that no data are presented on the relative effectiveness of the different components of the training model.

No such problem arises in the work of Bernal *et al.* (1980), where a direct comparison was made between behavioural parent training, client-centred parent counselling and a waiting-list control group. Thirty-six families were randomly assigned to the three conditions. After ten training sessions, the behavioural group showed a superior outcome on parental self-report, but not on direct observation. There was no difference between the other two groups. Furthermore, at 6-, 12- and 24-month follow-up, although continued improvement in behaviour was noted, the superiority of the behavioural group, even on parental self-report, was not maintained. Yet again the doubtful reliability of parental self-report and the pervading influence of spontaneous remission are demonstrated.

It seems clear that although there is a strong tendency for behavioural programmes to produce the best results, this is by no means universally the case, and there are major doubts about the long-term durability of gains. However, the range of human variability is wide, and this seems a useful juncture at which to look at some model behavioural programmes in more detail.

Specimen Behavioural Programmes

Many of the early studies were of one or a few children, often in a laboratory setting, using ABAB designs. (ABAB: an evaluation research design comparing measurements/observations of behaviour during a baseline pre-intervention period (A_1) with same during intervention/ treatment (B_1) and subsequent removal of intervention (A_2; also known as 'reversal condition'), followed by reinstitution of intervention (B_2).) This approach still persists, even in these days of large-scale parent training programmes, especially with rare or exotic behaviours.

Early Studies

One of the first significant reports was that of Wahler *et al.* (1965), involving three boys aged 4 to 6 and their respective mothers. Baseline observations were made in the playroom of a university Child Development Department. Systematic attempts to change the mothers' reactions to their children's behaviour were then made via verbal instruction and reinforcement and a signal light which was used for cueing and then for reinforcement. The basic aim was to establish maternal reinforcement of desired behaviour and ignoring of undesired behaviour. In two out of three cases changes in maternal behaviour were clearly demonstrated to result in changed child behaviour, but in the third case this only occurred when an additional punishment strategy (social isolation) was included.

A year later, Hawkins *et al.* (1966) described the transference of these techniques from the laboratory to the natural environment (i.e. the child's home). Problem behaviours of the 4-year-old male subject — biting, kicking, hitting, verbal abuse, non-compliance with instructions, threats to damage objects or persons, removing clothing and throwing objects — were all recorded at baseline. The mother was trained via three gestural signals for: instructing the boy to desist from a behaviour; instituting time out; emitting praise, attention and physical contact. The frequency of objectionable behaviour fell markedly during the first experimental period, rose slightly during second baseline, fell again during the second experimental period, and was maintained at this low level at one-month follow-up.

Johnson and Brown (1969) reported on two case studies. A hyperactive 2-year-old had her behaviour modified in the 'laboratory' by changed parental management resulting from training by verbal and written instruction, modelling and a signal light to cue reinforcement for the child (and subsequently to act as reinforcement for the parents themselves). It was noted that the child's improvement was by no means steady, however. The second case was an overactive 6-year-old who was demanding and manipulative, whose behaviour likewise improved. The modelling component of the training was felt to be the most effective aspect by researchers and parents alike.

One of the first studies involving a larger number of children was that of Mira (1970), who reported on 82 cases seen at least once in a medical centre. The programmes varied considerably: one month of weekly sessions; one week of daily instructions; eight months of weekly sessions. Using stringent evaluative criteria, it is noted that 39 per cent of the cases demonstrated no *satisfactorily recorded* modification. Teachers and social workers were clients of the programme as well as parents, and by and large they proved less successful than the parents. Contrary to reports from other workers, Mira found it more cost-effective to work with the managers of the children individually, rather than in groups. At this time, of course, methods of group training were in their infancy.

A successful example of group training was soon provided by Hall *et al.* (1972), the instructional input being a 'Responsive Teaching' course which met for a three-hour session every week for 16 weeks. Factual and illustrative information about applied behaviour analysis was presented via lectures, films, quizzes and discussions. The number of participants in these classes varied from 40 to 70. However, Hall *et al.* report on only four cases, where the modification was of fairly mild difficult behaviours and where the parents had the additional support of an observer in the home. These were successful, and in two cases long-term duration of gains is reported.

Finally, it is worth mentioning the work of Rekers and Lovaas (1974), who demonstrated reinforcement control over pronounced feminine behaviours in a male child who 'manifested cross-gender identity'. Programming in the clinic and at home via the use of social and token reinforcement respectively by the mother resulted in marked changes in behaviour. Initially, these were highly stimulus- and response-specific, and generalisation to associated behaviours had to be programmed. Follow-up three years later indicated that the boy's sex-type behaviours had normalised.

The Work of Tharp and Wetzel

The book *Behavior Modification in the Natural Environment* (Tharp and Wetzel, 1969) was a major landmark in the development of large-scale programmes. Evaluation data are presented on 77 cases in which intervention took place via individual training of primary care-takers of the problem children. Problem behaviours included defiance, fighting, truancy, damage, eneuresis, encopresis, stealing and poor schoolwork.

Of the total problem behaviours targeted, 16 per cent were totally eliminated, 73 per cent improved by at least 50 per cent from baseline, 7 per cent showed a lesser improvement, and 4 per cent showed no change. For a programme of this size dealing with problem behaviours of this severity, these results were highly creditable, even taking spontaneous remission into account. Of the 26 cases with a criminal record prior to intervention, only five committed offences between termination of the programme and six-month follow-up. Tharp and Wetzel also gave data based on ratings by the primary care-takers, who considered 75 per cent of problem behaviours to be improved at follow-up. This book remains essential reading for those interested in effective service delivery.

An extension of this kind of work was reported by Stuart (1971), who outlined the process of behavioural contracting within the families of delinquents — but, unfortunately, evaluative data are cited on only one sample case.

The Work of Patterson

Gerald Patterson is one of the giants in the work in this area. His evaluative output is summarised in Patterson (1974a, 1975), Patterson *et al.* (1975, 1982), and Horne and Patterson (1980). Many of his co-workers have used his methods and reported on them under their own names, e.g. Wiltz (1969; Wiltz and Patterson, 1974).

Beginning with a single case report in 1966 (Patterson and Brodsky, 1966), Patterson had produced by 1968 the instructional text for parents which was to become the basic tool for many subsequent interventions (Patterson and Gullion, 1968). Wiltz reported in 1969 on the use of the programmed text with associated telephone calls and group meetings for a group of six children over a five-week training period. Problem behaviour decreased by 60 per cent, significantly different from baseline observations and a control group, and these gains were maintained at two-month follow-up.

By 1974 the Oregon workers were considerably more fluent

and practised. Wiltz and Patterson (1974) reported on a programme involving six boys. The experimental group improved significantly on targeted behaviour in comparison with the control group, and also improved on many non-targeted behaviours, although these latter improvements did not reach statistical significance.

In the same year Patterson (1974a) summarised the outcome results of similar treatment programmes for 27 boys exhibiting varieties of 'conduct disorder'. Half of the group also had programming in school. Assessment was via direct observation, together with self-reports from primary care-takers. The group meetings had developed to include modelling, role-playing and contracting. At termination of the programme, two-thirds of the boys showed reductions of at least 30 per cent from baseline levels; six showed increases. Some children regressed during the early part of the follow-up period, and their parents were given brief 'booster' training, but at three-month follow-up the families remained significantly improved over baseline levels. Similarly positive results were evident from the classroom observations and reports. The Patterson (1975) paper documents extensions of this enterprise.

Horne and Patterson (1980) note that this level of success was achieved without the client population suffering large attrition rates. Only 23 per cent of clients dropped out during intake or baseline, and while six others left the programme prematurely, their results were included in the reportage. Given the demographic and clinical characteristics of the referral population, the low attrition and relatively high effectiveness are encouraging.

The work at Oregon was subsequently extended to include children with low-rate target behaviours, such as stealing, with equal success. Further replications using new therapists demonstrated essentially similar results. Comparable results were later achieved with a 50 per cent reduction in professional time input. A useful summary of the refined Patterson procedure is included in Horne and Patterson (1980). Further evaluative evidence of effectiveness in comparison with a control group is provided in Patterson *et al.* (1982).

The Token Economy

Procedures involving token economy, although often used in institutional settings, have not been widely employed in parent training programmes, but some interesting examples of successful incorporation are reported. Christophersen *et al.* (1972) worked with two sets of parents with a total of five children to ameliorate relatively minor behavioural problems (bickering, refusal to help with chores, etc.). Training methods were via verbal, written and filmed instruction and some role-playing in an office base, backed up with home visits and telephone contacts. The system proved successful, but as the parents were known to be co-operative and the problem behaviour not highly dysfunctional, there is little of surprise here.

This work was then developed into a Family Training Programme which relied heavily, though not exclusively, on token economy procedures, and was summarised in Christophersen *et al.* (1976). By this stage, intervention was much more home-based and relied more on the therapist modelling appropriate management with the children in the home. The therapist continued to visit to monitor the programme and provide feedback and reinforcement. Behavioural rehearsal or 'practising' by the parents and children received more emphasis, and a training manual was provided for the parents. Token economy was widely used except with toddlers (ages 1–3 years), backed up with time-out.

Christophersen *et al.* (1976) report on a comparison of their programme with a traditional Child Guidance input. A total of 19 families were randomly allocated to the two conditions. The Child Guidance sample showed markedly less reduction than the Family Training Programme group showed in problematic behaviour. No long-term follow-up data are reported, and it is noted that the Family Training Programme was slightly more expensive in professional time than the traditional intervention.

Modifying Non-compliance

The parent training programme developed by Hanf aims to alter the interaction of parents with their non-compliant children, and was the subject of an evaluation by Peed *et al.* (1977). Modelling, role-play and verbal prompting of the parent while in interaction with the child are used to shape parental behaviours, particularly discriminant attending and rewarding, and effective command and time-out implementation. Clinic-based practice with the child takes place in simulated situations.

Initial evaluations used AB designs and did not investigate generalisation into the home. Peed *et al.* utilised a control group, scrutinised generalisation to the home, and used multiple outcome measures (observational and self-report data from home and clinic settings). Experimental and control groups contained twelve families. Baseline observations were also made prior to the treatment period of approximately 43 days. The treatment included use of a radio device and the setting of tasks of practising at home during 'game' sessions.

Observational data showed that substantial change in parent behaviour and subsequent child behaviour in comparison with control groups was demonstrated within the clinic, and these gains generalised to the home environment. Detailed evidence that changed parental behaviour produced the changed child behaviour is given. However, the parent self-report data were considerably less encouraging. It is rare that there is a mismatch between observational and self-report data in this direction. Sirridge (1976) noted a similarly paradoxical finding, when parents were clearly demonstrated to improve their management skills and child behaviour after training, but their attitudes to child-rearing became more conservative and inflexible.

Programmes with a Residential Component

While the general trend is to base training programmes increasingly in homes and/or neighbourhood centres, one or two programmes have incorporated or been based upon a residential foundation.

Goodman (1975) reports on a training programme for the parents of children resident in a treatment centre on account of consistently unacceptable behaviour in the school or community. Many of the parents had long since despaired of managing their children effectively, and tended to hold extreme stereotyped views about them and resort too readily to physical punishment.

Detailed problem specifications were taken from the parents and matched with observations of the children in the centre. Specific target behaviours were identified for each family, and the parents were shown videos taken in the centre of their children behaving well. The parents were asked to look for instances of such behaviour when the child was at home, and to practise positive reinforcement as taught via modelling and role-play by the therapists. Very frequent telephone calls were made to check on progress.

At this stage, group meetings for 15 of the 17 families in the programme commenced. These meetings involved verbal information, a written or role-play task, and development of a homework assignment. The usual principles of applied behaviour analysis were dealt with in this format. Reinforcement for the parents was dispensed by the therapists. After each group meeting, the parents saw their children in the centre to practise their new skills immediately. The parents began to devise their own strategies for modifying particular problem behaviours, and increasingly took the children out of the centre for day trips to try out these schemes. If the plan worked and the trip was successful, more trips and home visits were arranged — but if not, scheduled home visits were reduced.

Few evaluative data are reported, except that parent programme children were discharged from the centre an average of three months before control group children, but long-term follow-up was planned. Nevertheless, the programme is an interesting example of a variation on normal procedures.

A less institutional residential experience combined with parent training was reported by Blackmore *et al.* (1976), who combined an environmental activity camping programme with a home-based reinforcement system anchored to school activities and achievement. The programme involved males, aged 8–11 years, who had not responded to previous treatment for chronic maladaptive behaviour: non-compliance, tantrums, encopresis, stealing, etc.

The total programme included six parent group training sessions, 18 two-hour simulated classroom sessions aimed at improving class behaviour, 18 days of backpacking in the Rocky Mountains, and follow-up consultation and observation done in each subject's ordinary classroom, at the mental health centre and by telephone. Attempts were made to reinforce similar behaviours in the three different environments and interlock contingencies to promote generalisation. A home–school report scheme during the classroom simulation could result in earning extra goodies to take on the mountain trip, and so on. Contingencies during the backpacking tended to be naturalistic — loss of equipment meant doing without! Considerable detail is provided in the report.

The evaluation evidence suggests that the subjects' behaviours improved in all settings, and follow-up data at six months suggests enduring gains. However, the real significance of some of the changes in on-task behaviour reported in the simulated classrooms must be in doubt, and there is no independent observational data on changes in the home environment. While requiring replication with wider measures, this novel project has much to commend it.

Reviews

This important field of work has been subject to regular critical review over the years.

Berkowitz and Graziano (1972) reviewed 34 studies which had involved training parents to act as behaviour therapists for their children, although at this time relatively few of these involved more than a few children. Useful discussion is included of work which is difficult to access elsewhere, e.g. that of Hanf and Walder. The reviewers note that parent training approaches had already been applied to virtually all possible child problem behaviours. Most work had been with mothers to reduce behavioural excesses, and almost all had used operant techniques. Training had been individual and group, and had included lectures, assigned reading, programmed materials, group discussions, modelling and direct prompting. Aids used included telephones, video- and audio-tapes, films, radio communication devices, and hand, sound and light signals. Many of the papers contained methodological flaws, but later studies provided 'convincing and well-validated evidence for the efficacy and desirability of the parent-training approach'. The reviewers concluded: 'this development provides a new frame-work for clinical intervention, which has important implications for future use in a systematic and prevention-oriented model of mental health intervention'.

A year later Johnson and Katz (1973) produced a much wider-ranging review, covering parent training in the remediation of anti-social and non-compliant behaviour, speech dysfunction, school phobia, encopresis and eneuresis, self-injurious behaviour and seizures. Various combinations of home and laboratory training were noted, still largely with small numbers in each study. Summary tables are provided and methodological criticisms are quite detailed. Criticisms were made of the rarity and quality of follow-up work. Wide variations in the amount of time necessary for successful training were found, and parent training was by no means always cheaper than traditional methods. The reviewers conclude: 'evidence indicates that parents can be used effectively to modify their children's disruptive behaviour'. Further work was needed on identifying critical variables to improve cost-effectiveness, and a widespread failure systematically to programme generalisation of treatment effects required correcting.

A contemporaneous review was that of Cone and Sloop (1973), who offered a historical perspective on the use of parents as change agents dating back to Freudian times. A discussion of the effectiveness of traditional child psychotherapies noted 'rather bleak results'. The inadequacy of existing mental health professionals to deliver a traditional service to all those in need had led to shifts in the service delivery system which coincided with the development of applied behaviour analysis into a form which was transmissible to parents. Various strategies of training are reviewed, design considerations discussed, and the move towards dealing with large numbers of clients noted, in the context of discussing in some detail a large number of studies completed up to 1970.

The field continued to expand, and O'Dell (1974) reviewed 70 articles in a brief but incisive paper. While parent training was 'a very promising area', more investigation was necessary of the links between training, changed parent behaviour, consequent changed child behaviour, and generalisation and maintenance of gains. Experimental comparisons of different training formats were also needed, including the development of means for effective mass dissemination of the techniques. His colleagues could be forgiven for thinking that O'Dell was asking for a great deal in a short space of time.

A review with a different emphasis was then provided by another of the major names in the field, Robert Wahler (1976). This reflected Wahler's interest in the effect of family dynamics on the take-up, generalisation and maintenance of parent training efforts. Wahler discussed the question of care-taker motivation to change child deviant behaviour (which is often difficult to establish), and described the 'positive reinforcer trap' and the 'negative reinforcer trap' into which families often fall. He emphasised the need to consider child behaviour deficits as well as excesses, and to analyse situational aspects of deviant child behaviour (environmental antecedents) as well as parental behaviour precipitants. Detailed discussion of assessment of family needs and developing uniquely relevant intervention strategies then follows, and this material is highly pertinent to family case workers. A section on maintenance of behaviour change concludes the paper.

One of the most helpfully structured and readable reviews is that of Graziano (1977), healthily shot throughly with a pragmatic sensibility. Graziano noted that 'mental health services for children are still of doubtful effectiveness, limited availability and exorbitant cost', and remarked that the pattern of traditional service provision seemed to meet the goals of the professionals rather better than the goals of the clients. Graziano proceeded to review studies in the areas of somatic problems (including toileting), various complex 'syndromes' (e.g. schizophrenic, autistic), noncompliance and aggression, anxiety reduction, language and speech disorder, and various minor behavioural problems. There are useful sections on the selection of parents and training settings and methods, and some discussion of the level of parental participation. Issues of evaluation methodology are considered, with particular reference to replicability. Graziano noted that some training formats with some problem behaviours show good cost-effectiveness, while others do not. Graziano concluded that behavioural parent training was 'highly promising'. While it had at that time only met the minimum criteria of scientific evaluation, in that respect it appeared to be at about the same level of validation as other major, and far older, approaches. Over the next decade, 'highly effective, efficient child treatment approaches' would be 'developed and validated', he predicted.

Just four years later, Gordon and Davidson (1981) were writing that 'behavioural parent training has burgeoned to a massive body of literature reporting the successful treatment of thousands of children with a wide variety of problems. No longer viewed as experimental, this mode of treatment has become increasingly effective, accepted and popular.' Gordon and Davidson, like Wahler, consider practical issues of service delivery in more detail than most reviewers, particularly with respect to parent characteristics. Discussion of structure, content and method of parent training is also extensive. The authors conclude that 'behavioural parent training has moved beyond adolescence and is clearly into early adulthood'.

A contemporaneous review by Wells and Forehand (1981) is a little more cautious. While it was clear that 'behavioural interventions are effective with conduct disorders, ... even though the actual procedures have varied greatly', readers were reminded that the data reported in journals represented a biased, positive view of the field, as negative results are rarely accepted for publication.

Further work on generalisation and maintenance, the development of multiple outcome measures, and the effects of parental characteristics and family dynamics, were all essential. (Also see Moreland *et al.* 1982.)

More recently, Milne (1986) has produced a useful chapter on 'Parents as Therapists'. Training methods and format are reviewed, with extensive discussion of training 'manuals'. A variety of methods for evaluating behaviour change in the parent and the child are detailed, together with means of assessing parental knowledge and attitudes. Selection of parents and the impact of parent characteristics and patterns of social support are considered in the context of 'making it [the intervention] stick'. Milne concludes that 'parent training is a complex process, involving subtle interactions'.

The message from these last two reviews is clear. Parent training can certainly be effective, but that doesn't mean it will automatically be effective right there where you are. Being effective is not the same as being idiot-proof.

Training Format

In addition to the sections on training methods cited in the reviews above, other sources are worth consulting on this topic, particularly those studies which have attempted direct comparisons of different formats.

Reports of successful parent training can give such an endeavour the appearance of being deceptively simple, but the real world is not like that. Problem behaviour is maintained, by definition, by a family system in equilibrium. Producing change can be difficult, particularly where the impetus for change is external to the family, perhaps via relatives, schools or the courts.

A good example is reported by Sajwaj (1973), where in four cases of highly co-operative parents undergoing behavioural training, serious resistances and difficulties were encountered. Two mothers were successfully trained in the clinic, but could not generalise this to the home. A simple disciplinary technique had to be substituted, and this was successfully used in one case of the two. Another very reserved parent found it impossible to interact more frequently with her child as required by a differential attention procedure, but substitution of a punishment procedure was effective. Thus, a blanket parent-training curriculum cannot be relied upon to 'fit' each parent's predilections (or previous reinforcement history, to be more precise).

The first question that arises in the planning of a parent training programme is that of location — where is the training to take place?

Home versus Centre-based Training

Worland *et al.* (1980) randomly assigned the parents of 20 children to one of three conditions: (a) eight sessions of group training; (b) group training plus individual training at home; (c) group training plus in-home observation, but not training. Evaluations were carried out at baseline, termination, and at six-month and two-year follow-up. It should be noted that the 20 families were drawn from an initial pool of 87 intakes, of which 32 were rejected as inappropriate, a further 19 did not commence training and a further 12 dropped out during the training.

The first four sessions of training taught general applied behavioural analysis principles and the next four worked on generating family-specific programmes. Lecturing, modelling and role-play were used. Six-month follow-up included home observation, but two-year follow-up did not. The families paid a fee for participation, and also deposited sums of $8–50 which were refunded only if programme commitments were met. Daily reports were taken from parents by telephone.

Results showed that there was no difference between the conditions on parents' knowledge of behavioural principles, and much of this knowledge had washed out at two-year follow-up. Furthermore, there was no significant difference between conditions on child behaviour measures, all treatments showing significant improvement in behaviour which was maintained at two-year follow-up. Given these findings, clinic-only treatment appeared the most cost-effective, although whether this would also apply to the 67 referred parents who did not participate fully in the training programme is a matter for speculation. The total professional time expended on families in the clinic-only condition was 14.3 hours, comparing very favourably with other forms of intervention.

Siegert and Yates (1980) had four conditions: (a) individual in-office; (b) individual in-home; (c) group in-office; and (d) measurement and contact control. Training was brief (five weeks), and a follow-up was in-built four months after termination. All the experimental conditions produced significant improvements compared to the control condition: 86 per cent reduction in problem behaviours in experimental conditions, but only 38 per cent reduction in the control condition. The three experimental delivery systems did not differ significantly on any measure. At follow-up, 23 of the 25 responding parents reported maintenance of gains. Thus the in-office condition appeared more cost-effective from the professional viewpoint, as it consumed less professional time. However, the in-office service delivery shifted costs of time and money on to the clients, as well as restricting client opportunity to participate, so cost-effectiveness from the clients' point of view could have been a very different story.

Individual versus Group Training

The Siegert and Yates (1980) work found no differences in effectiveness between group and individual training in the office, although it should be borne in mind that the demographic and educational characteristics of their parents were above average. Group training was much cheaper for the professionals, but considerably more expensive in costs to the clients, who had to make a regular commitment at a specific time not necessarily suited to them. The professional and client costs of the two forms of training ended up virtually equal.

Earlier work had been preoccupied with the relative effectiveness of group and individual training *per se.* Hanson (1975) reported assigning ten parents to group training, ten to individual and ten to a control condition. Parental behaviour shifted in the required direction in both experimental groups compared with the control group, and in a sub-sample of both experimental groups significant changes in child behaviour were also demonstrated. All changes were maintained at three-month follow-up, but no differences were found between experimental conditions.

Kovitz (1976) assigned 14 carefully selected families to group and individual conditions, and a remaining six to a control condition. Contracting and cash deposition were employed with the parents. Training included verbal and written information, videotape modelling, discussion and home assignments, lasted six weeks and was office-based and generalist in nature. Virtually no significant differences were found between the group and individual training conditions, and although the group training was cheaper in professional time and cost, it was much more expensive for the programme recipients. However, no differences were found in client satisfaction with the programme between the two groups.

Christensen *et al.* (1980) assigned 36 families to group, individual or minimum-contact control conditions. Observational data and parent records (but not generalised parent ratings) demonstrated the superiority of the experimental conditions over the control conditions, with no difference between experimental conditions in effectiveness. The group programme was much less costly in professional time. No data are given on client costs. There was some evidence of greater client satisfaction with the individual programme.

Generalised versus Specific Training

A group of four mothers receiving combined generalised and specific training was compared with a similar group experiencing only specific target-related training by Glogower and Sloop (1976). Parents in both groups had ten weekly two-hour sessions. The combination group mothers subsequently proved able to deal with a wider range of problems, and their interactions with their children became generally more positive and effective. At five-month follow-up the improvements achieved by the combination group proved more enduring and had generalised more. It should be remembered that this study utilised very small numbers of clients who were selected from a referral pool of 75.

A larger number of subjects were involved in the study by O'Dell *et al.* (1977). All participants experienced a six-session group workshop covering general applied behavioural analysis principles, but a third experienced didactic pre-training in behaviour modification principles, a third placebo pre-training and a third no pre-training. No independent observation of implementation of skills in the home setting was undertaken. The pre-training in behavioural principles produced no significant improvement in parent performance. Indeed, differences tended to be in favour of the briefer training which focused only on behavioural performance skills (but without strong emphasis on developing individual programmes). This programme may well have suffered from offering participants too much of the same thing.

Teaching Methods

The first systematic comparison of different instructional techniques was reported by Nay (1975), who instructed 77 mothers of young children of doubtful demographic representativeness in the use of time-out procedures via five instructional conditions: (a) written presentation, (b) lecture presentation, (c) video-tape modelling presentation, (d) video-tape modelling coupled with role-play, (e) no treatment control. All four experimental groups showed similar knowledge increments for all groups. However, the assessment of subjects' ability to apply time-out in a simulated situation indicated the two conditions incorporating modelling to be equally superior.

Using mothers' behaviour during parent–child interaction as a criterion, Doleys *et al.* (1976) found that feedback consisting of post-interaction critiques by the experimenters, self-recording from audio-tape and recording of other parent–child interactions was more effective than a procedure consisting of written materials, lectures and role-play.

Flanagan *et al.* (1979) extended Nay's (1975) study by collecting observational data in the home. Similar treatments to Nay's were utilised, but a sample of 48 parents of wider demographic characteristics were the subjects. All treatment groups were superior to control on knowledge. While skill performance in the simulated situation was best in the role-play group (not exactly in line with Nay's finding), in terms of application to the home situation the modelling condition came out best.

Following the same theme, O'Dell *et al.* (1979) found that video-tape plus individual checkout was superior to written training as well as to training by live modelling and rehearsal. This work was continued by O'Dell *et al.* (1980). Twenty-four parents were assigned to four conditions: (a) written take-home manual, (b) a film plus take-home manual, (c) individual modelling and rehearsal plus manual, (d) no-treatment control. Outcome was assessed by knowledge increment and home assessment of parental implementation of time-out. All training methods were superior to control, but there were no significant differences between the experimental treatments. O'Dell *et al.* (1980) construe this to emphasise the usefulness of take-home manuals.

Webster-Stratton (1981) worked with 35 well-motivated middle-class mothers, and found they responded well on a wide range of measures to a video-tape modelling and group discussion format with very low professional time cost. Parental behaviour seemed to shift more readily than parental attitude.

The relative effectiveness of written instruction, audio-tape instruction, video-taped modelling and live modelling and rehearsal with their own children on parents' reinforcement skills was studied by O'Dell *et al.* (1982) with 100 parents. Outcome was assessed via home observation. The audio-taped manual proved least effective, but there was little difference in outcome between the other three experimental methods. However, the video-tape group appeared to train a wider range of parents more consistently, whereas parental demographic characteristics and/or reading level were significantly related to outcome in the other groups, where successful outcome was associated with higher socio-economic status and reading level.

Self-recording

Parental self-recording as an adjunct to training, to help establish new parental behaviours in the home setting, has already been referred to in discussing the work of Doleys *et al.* (1976).

This procedure had originally been explored by Herbert and Baer (1972), who taught two mothers to count their episodes of attention to appropriate child behaviour in their homes, using wrist counters. Observational data showed increased appropriate maternal attention, which did not wash out on removal of the counters. Parent self-recording was not very accurate, but nevertheless seemed effective, as the behavioural gains endured over five-month follow-up. However, a third parent was unaffected by the self-recording procedure.

Sanders (1980) reports the use of self-recording in a single case study, where three phases of training were instituted. The first was verbal and written instruction in a group setting, the second self-recording of aversive behaviour to the child in the home with feedback from the professional worker, and the third involved feedback without self-recording. The self-recording phase produced better results than all other phases.

It seems that self-recording as part of training procedures holds promise, and clearly requires further comparative research.

Other Factors

A variety of other variables in the training process have been explored by other workers.

Eyberg and Johnson (1974) worked with 17 families of various ages, demographic status and problem behaviours. Parents in the 'contingency contracting' group made cash deposits, forfeitable in the event of non-cooperation, and did not receive scheduled treatment sessions or phone checks unless they had completed assigned tasks. In a four-cell design, half of the parents were also required to deal with an easy problem behaviour first, while the other half were assigned to deal with the most difficult. Outcome data were positive in terms of parent-collected data, but more modest in terms of independent observational data. Parents subject to contingency contracting completed more assignments, dealt with more problems and were seen as more co-operative by therapists. There was no evidence that order of problems treated had any significant effect. Whether these findings would apply to a study which demonstrated a higher all-round level of effectiveness from training is another matter.

Exploration of an unrelated but equally pertinent variable is reported by Firestone *et al.* (1977). Behaviour modification techniques were taught in an office base to the parents of twelve conduct-problem children. In one group mothers only participated (n = 6), while in another mothers and fathers participated. There was also a control group. After an average of 11.5 hours' training per family, behavioural ratings showed improvement in both experimental groups, with no significant difference between them. The changes were maintained at four-month follow-up according to parental self-report.

How conclusive this finding might be is questionable, however. Numbers were small, and in all twelve cases both parents were *willing* to attend for training. The families were all pre-selected for cohesiveness, and it seems likely that there was some contamination of fathers in the mother-only group.

Before concluding this review of training formats, readers may wish for something a little more tangible than experimental comparative studies — such as a more detailed description of a particular training format — and for this we return to Oregon.

The Patterson Program

A most useful source for those wishing to replicate this work is Patterson *et al.* (1975). This gives detail at the level of fee schedules, telephone interview schedules, rating charts, and standardisation tables for deviancy scores, as well as background reviews of the literature.

Detailed guidelines for instructing parents in pinpointing, tracking and recording problem behaviours are given, down to when to supply the pencils. Training in the use of wrist counters is given. The parents are required to focus on two deviant and two pro-social behaviours initially, and both are required to observe. The problem child participates and is asked for comments and questions. Daily telephone checking is instituted.

The next stage is the setting up of the first contingency contact. Positive reinforcement, negotiation and punishment skills are covered at this juncture. Initial contracts often include a token economy aspect, which is faded as weeks pass, to be superseded by natural consequences. The use of time-out is dealt with, and role-play utilised by the therapist at this juncture. Telephone checking continues.

Work with academic behaviours is often also carried out, and teachers are trained in the procedures as well as parents. Parents are also trained to function as remedial reading teachers, using programmed reading materials, a diluted Precision Teaching approach and naturalistic reinforcement. Unfortunately, few evaluative data are cited for this aspect of the programme.

As the Patterson Program developed, less reliance was placed on tangible reinforcers and contingent parental attention, and observation training and structured data-collection by parents became more prominent as token systems were more widely used. Parental incentives were introduced. In time, it became important to see whether the average treatment time of 31.5 hours per client could be reduced and whether newly recruited therapists could prove as effective as the original team.

Weinrott *et al.* (1979) described replicatory work using the Patterson model with 18 families. Ten core instructional sessions were provided for groups of three to four families, incorporating video-taped presentation, lecturing and discussion. Daily telephone contacts and occasional home visits were included. Curriculum content comprised: (i) pinpointing, observing and recording behaviours; (ii) developing a point incentive system for one deviant behaviour, one pro-social behaviour and one chore, using both verbal and tangible rewards; (iii) time-out, using video modelling; (iv) parent recording and programme evaluation; (v) programme presentation, where all parents describe their programme to the group; (vi) training in ignoring and attending discriminately; (vii) shaping behaviours by task analyses and approximation; (viii) problem-solving, again using video modelling; (ix) contingency contracting (for children aged 10 or more) —

all family members are present at this session; and (x) fading. Following this core programme, the more successful families faded contact with the therapist over the next six weeks, but in ten successful cases further individual sessions were held with the family.

Further details of evaluation procedures, including observer coding categories, and the structure for results analysis are given. Average reductions of over 50 per cent in *all* deviant behaviours for all families completing the programme are reported, with a continuing reduction through the follow-up period. Differential attrition did not occur, and overall a large proportion of previously very troubled families experienced substantial improvement.

Generalisation

Does training a parent successfully to modify one behaviour in one child in one place at one time increase the probability that the parent can subsequently change other behaviours in other children in other settings at other times? If not, the parent has been taught a skill so restricted in application as to be virtually useless.

The immediate question for centre-based training is whether skills learnt in the laboratory or clinic generalise to the home, and, as we have seen, the research on this topic is reassuring. Peed (1976) addressed this question directly in his study of twelve mothers assigned at random to treatment and control groups. Observations in the home were conducted before and after a clinic-based, ten-hour, six-week training programme for the experimental group. Parent and child behaviours shifted for the experimental group in clinic and home settings, while control behaviours did not.

Sibling Generalisation

An early case study by Lavigeur *et al.* (1973) involved training a parent in differential reinforcement and time-out to control the disruptive behaviour of a 3-year-old boy. Similar behavioural changes were observed in the boy's 5-year-old sister, although she had not been considered a problem or subject to specific pro-gramming. Follow-up observations over ten months indicated that changes were maintained in both children, but in the boy's case did not generalise to school.

Arnold *et al.* (1975), using the Patterson model, reported changes in the behaviour of the siblings of 27 pre-delinquents whose parents were involved in a training programme. The target children showed significantly reduced deviant behaviours, and the improvement was maintained at twelve-month follow-up. At termination of treatment, there were significant reductions in rates of deviant behaviour for the 55 siblings in the families. The sibling generalisation was maintained at six-month follow-up, with attrition affecting the twelve-month sibling follow-up. Humphreys *et al.* (1978) found similar effects.

Whether the parents are learning a set of skills they apply to other children, or whether a reduction in deviant behaviour by the target child provides fewer cues for deviant behaviour by the siblings and frees parental time for more positive interaction with the siblings, is a moot point. Either way, these results are encouraging.

Home–school Generalisation

As noted previously in this chapter, improvements in behaviour at home by no means stimulate improvements in behaviour at school, and vice versa.

In Wahler's (1975) study of two boys, a cluster of co-varying deviant behaviours at home did not coincide with the cluster of co-varying deviant behaviours found at school. These latter clusters generalised over different school settings, but not to the home. Curiously, a puzzling treatment effect did occur across settings. In both cases, planned changes in behaviour in one setting were accompanied by unpredictable changes in the other setting, not always of a positive nature.

Forehand *et al.* (1979) investigated home–school generalisation with eight mother–child pairs in a training programme, compared with eight in a control group. Independent observations at home and school showed that behaviour improved significantly at home, but not at school. In fact, inappropriate behaviour at school increased in both the experimental and control groups, though not significantly. McMahon and Davies (1980) report a replication of this study in a larger sample of 16 subjects, again using the Hanf training programme. The expected changes in parent and child behaviour occurred in the home setting, but decreases in deviant behaviour in school were also noted, although these failed to reach statistical significance. It seems clear that behavioural gains at home do not automatically generalise to the classroom, although a 'behavioural contrast' effect does not always apply either.

General Generalisation

A review of evidence on the generality of treatment effects (temporal, setting, behavioural and sibling) was provided by Forehand and Atkeson (1977). The reviewers made the point that evidence for setting generality might be dependent on the method of data collection. While some investigators had shown generalisation from home to school, the more thorough studies (cited above) had failed to show this phenomenon.

Similar complaints about measurement adequacy were made about many studies purporting to show behavioural generalisation beyond immediate target behaviours. It was noted that the Patterson Program has rarely shown significant generalisation, but then behavioural generality is not specified as one of its goals.

More recent evidence is reported by Sanders and Glynn (1981). Data were collected from five families undergoing a three-phase training programme in the home, particularly at the family breakfast, and a variety of generalisation settings in the community. The first phase of training (instructions plus home-based feedback) proved sufficient to reduce target problem behaviour in the home, but generalisation effects out of the home were equivocal. Subsequent self-management training phases (involving training in planning, goal setting and self-monitoring) maintained reduced levels of problem behaviour at home and, in addition, resulted in generalisation effects in community settings for both children and parents. The generalisation data were based on indpendent time-sampling observation in settings chosen by the parents for which they had devised management procedures. Maintenance probes at three-month follow-up showed that the effects had been maintained.

Maintenance

Long-term maintenance or durability of gains is obviously a desirable feature of interventions, although few of the more traditional therapies provide such evidence. 'Temporal generalisation' is another way of expressing this requirement, and Forehand and

Atkeson (1977) review evidence on this topic. The reviewers are dismissive of the value of parental opinion obtained via interview, telephone contact or questionnaire, with some justification. Paradoxically, it tends to be only small-scale studies, with their inherent failings, that are able to undertake detailed follow-up by observation, and even here sample attrition can be a problem. Parental recordings of behaviour tend to be more reliable, and some workers have used tape-recorded assessments. An increasing number of studies have managed to employ independent observation for follow-up.

Reference has already been made to the maintenance of gains reported by Lavigeur *et al.* (1973) in a single case over twelve months, by Arnold *et al.* (1980) in 27 cases over twelve months, and by Sanders and Glynn (1981) in five cases over three months.

Patterson (1974b) cites follow-up data for 14 families over twelve months based on parental records of behaviour, reporting that levels of problematic behaviour at follow-up were below those pertaining at termination of the propgramme, which were themselves much below baseline.

Rinn *et al.* (1975) described follow-up procedures for a training programme which instructed 1,128 parents of 639 children during ten-hour, five-session courses. A random sample of parents who had completed the course at least six months previously were interviewed by telephone for follow-up data. Of 240 calls made, 154 were completed — what bias this introduced is unknown. The follow-up period thus ranged from six months to three years. Of responding parents, over 50 per cent reported the child was 'much improved' (between one-third and two-thirds goal attainment). Sixteen per cent of the famiies sought further professional help. Rinn *et al.* (1975) note that the costs of parent training were about one-third of traditional treatment. As they point out, these data (however unreliable) compare favourably with spontaneous remission rates.

Eleven mother–child pairs were followed up post-training by Forehand *et al.* (1979), who collected behavioural data at six and twelve months on both parent and child. Convincing evidence of maintenance of gains on both occasions is presented, with the exception of parental use of contingent attention, which had declined at both follow-ups from post-treatment levels. There was little contact with the therapists during the follow-up period, and the sample attrition during follow-up was only 9 per cent.

Forehand *et al.* (1979) compare their results favourably to Patterson's (1974), but note that they were dealing with families of higher mean socio-economic status.

Patterson and Fleischman (1979) presented a review of maintenance of treatment effects from the Oregon work. Of 114 cases, 86 received full training and subsequent attrition reduced the follow-up pool to 50 families. Follow-up drop-out was demonstrated *not* to relate to success/failure status at treatment termination. Rates of deviant behaviour were less at twelve-month follow-up than at termination; 84 per cent of the children were functioning within the normal range. Patterson and Fleischman also refer to the encouraging follow-up data in the work of Christophersen *et al.* (1972, 1976) and Alexander and Parsons (1973), already cited above. An interesting discussion of how family inter-relationships might promote maintenance of gains is offered, but little supportive data cited.

A study of 34 mother–child pairs who had completed training one to four and a half years earlier was reported by Baum and Forehand (1981). Evaluation measures included home observational data, parent perceptions of child adjustment and parent consumer-satisfaction measures. Change in child behaviour was maintained at follow-up, although only some parental behaviour change was so maintained. This presumably either reflects spontaneous remission or some children finding their new behaviours self-rewarding. No decrements over longer follow-up periods were found.

Even longer follow-up periods were utilised by Strain *et al.* (1982), who followed up 40 children who three to nine years previously had been infant clients of a programme to train their parents. Observational and checklist report measures were utilised in home and school settings. Results showed that the children's behaviour in both settings was largely normalised, and parental and child behaviour changes seemed to be holding up well.

Thus follow-up results appear to be largely positive, at least as far as published results are concerned. However, high training group and follow-up sample attrition rates remain a cause for concern. As Clark and Baker (1983) point out, parent training programmes do not benefit all families — some are never selected, some fail to complete training, some do not achieve proficiency or relapse after training ends. In a study of 103 families of lower socio-economic status, those who had feared greater problems in applying the trained principles, and had less previous experience with behavioural concepts, were less likely to attain proficiency during the programme. Families doing poorly at follow-up at six months were less likely to have tried management strategies with their children before training, to have achieved proficiency before training, or to have had intact marriages.

Social Psychological Factors

Reference has already been made at several points to the influence of family dynamics on sustaining deviant behaviour and potentially sabotaging the effects of training programmes. These issues must now be considered in greater depth.

An immediate question is whether or not the extra attention and stimulation involved in participating in a parent training programme does not of itself produce changes in the family dynamic, arousal and anxiety levels which could account for behavioural changes. The marked superiority of behavioural training compared with traditional therapy suggests this is not so, but in any event Walter and Gilmore (1973) set out to test this very contention. Twelve families were allocated at random to treatment or 'placebo' conditions. The placebo condition emphasised high status attention and high expectancy of success, but had none of the other features of the training programme. Evaluation was by independent observation. Both groups received equal contact time. Significant decreases in deviant behaviour were only found for the treatment group, while the placebo group children showed slight but not significant increases in deviant behaviour.

An interesting study which deliberately manipulated the family dynamic was reported by Lavigeur (1974), who trained siblings as well as parents to attend discriminately to behaviours in the target child in two families. Results suggested that working with siblings could be effective in combination with parent treatment where the siblings responded consistently to instruction and their attention was valued by the target child (i.e. was actually reinforcing). Sibling relations improved concomitant with the siblings treating the target child in a more positive manner. Taking into account the considerable body of work on using peers as behaviour modifiers in school settings, it is perhaps surprising that siblings have not featured larger in family training programmes.

That training parents successfully to manage their children better has spin-offs for the quality of the family milieu was shown by Karoly and Rosenthal (1977). Nine families in a training programme were compared with a control group. The target children of the trainee parents improved their behaviour at home as measured by direct observation, and the parents' perceptions concurred with this. The programme parents also reported a significant increase in family cohesion and positive interaction.

It may be that a certain minimum level of stability in the family is necessary for this to occur, however. Reisinger *et al.* (1976b) noted that of six mothers who responded equally well to in-office training while *in situ*, mothers who had reported marital difficulties proved less able to sustain the impact of the techniques at twelve-month follow-up.

A relevant consideration here is the group dynamic of the training sessions themselves, and the setting in which they are conducted. Miller and Ellis (1980) describe the establishment of a parent training group in a neighbourhood social and community education centre with a tradition of close parental contacts. Outcome data were based on parental behavioural records, and were moderately encouraging, but perhaps the most significant feature was that the parents felt very relaxed in the centre and ideally placed to support each other. The educational orientation of the centre, embedded in a nexus of neighbourhood relationships, made it ideal as a base for such programmes. Perhaps here we see the beginnings of a British tradition of less determinedly didactic training based in less fearsomely professional settings than clinics, laboratories and offices.

Wahler (1980) has been preoccupied with the role of family dynamics in maintaining behavioural gains after training. A training programme for 18 mothers of low socio-economic status in which the participants reported themselves relatively isolated from social contacts in their communities was conducted. Significant improvement in child behaviour was obtained during treatment, but there was regression to baseline levels during bi-weekly follow-up observations over a period of one year. Self-report data indicated that the more isolated a mother was, the more likely problems were to occur. While no firm conclusions about directions of causality could be drawn, the implications for the long-term success of parent training programmes must be borne in mind.

This theme was amplified in Wahler and Graves (1983), who noted that 'in some cases, environmental events temporally distant from the child's behaviours and their stimulus contingencies appear to exert some control over the stimulus–response inter-actions'. This will hardly be news to many workers with families, who often find parents unable to grasp the most obvious oppor-tunity to help themselves when stressed, depressed or distracted by other events. Wahler and Graves counsel against a narrow and rigidly behavioural view of parent training, and argue that the wider interaction of contingencies in the overall family system must be considered. This will certainly be the case when working with unselected families of low socio-economic status. The intake procedures of some programmes (e.g. Patterson's) attempt a fairly detailed assessment of these factors. An interesting discussion of 'entrapped mothers' and their modification will be found in Wahler and Graves (1983). It may be that studying parent training 'failures' will prove as valuable in the fullness of time as studying the 'successes'.

In this context, it is worth considering the ethics of parent training programmes, an area well reviewed by Sapon-Shevin (1982). An obvious question relates to the appropriateness of target behaviours selected by the parents: are the professionals justified in supporting the parents in crushing their children into submission? Who adjudicates in any conflicts between parents' and children's rights? Some programmes seem to have emphasised the elimination of behavioural excesses and have given little weight to building pro-social behaviours to compensate for deficits. A third issue relates to the morality of ABA research designs with parents who enter the programme to improve the quality of life for their family, not to be tinkered with. This paper is recommended to intending practitioners, but it would be a pity of the faint-hearted used its cautions to justify their inertia.

Training Therapists

A variety of training courses for parents has been referred to in the foregoing text, and their continued proliferation will not make the research and evaluation effort any easier. For instance, Hall and Nelson (1981) have shown enthusiasm for developing a pro-gramme known as 'Responsive Parenting', which they have modified to take into account the needs of participating single parents, but show less enthusiasm for gathering hard evaluation data despite having implemented the programme with over 3,000 parents. (In this context, mention is also made of the Parenting Alone Successfully programme — PALS.)

Quite apart from curriculum context, a training programme may stand or fall by the quality of its therapists and *their* training, and remarkably little research has been conducted on this topic, although some studies have been quick to allude disparagingly to the qualities of the therapists in an attempt to explain away unsatisfactory results. Adequate therapist recruitment and training procedures are obviously crucial, to be neglected at the programme's peril.

Isaacs *et al.* (1982) offer a noteworthy contribution here, having carried out an evaluation of a therapist training format using a multiple baseline design. The training involved a written manual, video modelling, rehearsal, role-play, and feedback on performance. Each therapist worked immediately with a parent and child, and target behaviours in therapist, parent and child showed improvement in every case. If only more workers were as methodical!

Some attention has been paid to training non-professionals or paraprofessionals to act as parent programme deliverers. Gardner (1975) reviews the developments in this field, emphasising the need for stringent selection procedures. Gardner cites evidence that more experienced recruits may sometimes be more resistant to training although more stable on-task, and that low-SES recruits prove just as effective as middle-class paraprofessionals. Gardner distinguishes five different levels of behaviour modification worker, and reports on training programmes for the different levels, giving details of the mastery criteria and evaluative data. Interesting data are cited on the use and ordering of lecture and role-play in training aides: lecturing improved knowledge of principles, role-play improved application skills, but there was little cross-fertilisation and it did not matter in which order the training components were presented.

Gardner goes on to detail various strategies for the supervision of paraprofessionals, emphasising the significance of 'psychological ownership' of responsibility as a motivating factor. A review is made of studies of reinforcing staff for on-task behaviour — for example, by offering a half-day off work for each five weeks of perfect attendance — but the results seem equivocal. The danger of debilitating intrinsic motivation by instituting such contingencies should be considered. Finally, Gardner points out that ethical issues are likely to confront a paraprofessional in regular contact with a family much more immediately than a distant supervisor, and that training in dealing with such issues is essential.

A more recent review of the field is offered by Ingersoll and Eastman (1980), who note the problems of role definition that paraprofessional workers can face. The specific tasks to be performed need to be clearly delineated, task analyses undertaken to identify requisite target skills, and mastery criteria established. Following a useful review of training methods, Ingersoll and Eastman place considerable emphasis on the question of evaluation of the workers' skill levels.

A study is described which used paraprofessionals to implement a programmed parent training package with non-problematic ('normal') families. Eighteen families were assigned to training or control groups. The paraprofessional received only three training sessions in the use of the package of materials, then proceeded over six weeks to conduct a two-hour weekly training programme for the parents. Results showed that the paraprofessionals adhered to programme format more closely than did professional leaders, being more on-task and maintaining more eye contact. Positive but non-significant behaviour changes in the children were found, but this is hardly surprising when working with a normal population. Parent compliance with programme requirements and knowledge gains were very satisfactory. There seems to be no doubt that, given adequate training, paraprofessionals can be as effective as professionals.

Summary

Training parents in the management of their children's problem behaviour is a large and rapidly expanding area of work. Such programmes reduce the incidence of child abuse, although without continued support these gains may wash out. Evaluation of a traditional social work input yields less clear and less encouraging findings. Behavioural training for foster-parents is more effective than other types. Relaxation training for parents and children has shown equivocal results. Training in conflict resolution and problem-solving has also produced ambivalent results, with doubts about maintenance of gains; nevertheless, the area shows promise. Individualised interactive training also merits further investigation, although there must be doubts about specificity of impact and replicability.

In direct comparisons of behavioural and non-behavioural interventions, behavioural programmes do best in the majority of cases. A variety of specimen behavioural programmes is reviewed, including early studies, the classic work of Tharp and Wetzel (1969) and Patterson (1966–82), token economy methods, modifying non-compliance, and programmes with a residential aspect. A review of reviews of behavioural research is presented.

Research on training formats is considered. In-home training seems not to be more effective than centre-based training, although it does shift more participation costs from the client to the professional agency. Likewise, little difference in effectiveness has been found between individual and group training, although the latter shifts a larger proportion of the cost burden from the professionals to the clients. Evidence is equivocal on the relative effectiveness of generalised versus specific training, and may vary with the characteristics of the training group. Teaching methods have included lecture, written instruction, live and video modelling, role-play, feedback, self-recording and subsequent monitoring. Some studies have found no difference between methods, but others have found role-play, feedback, self-recording and subsequent monitoring more effective, and video modelling has done consistently well.

Generalisation of training effects to siblings in the family has been demonstrated to occur. However, generalisation of improved behaviour from home to school does not seem to happen. There is some evidence of generalisation to community settings outside the home. There is no longer any doubt about the durability of gains accruing from parent training programmes, which has been satisfactorily demonstrated over long periods as well as short.

The impact of family dynamics and other social psychological factors on training effectiveness is reviewed, and while there is some initial evidence that marital instability and low socio-economic status militate against programme effectiveness, much further work in this area is needed. Ethical considerations are mentioned.

Procedures for training professional and paraprofessional

therapists are reviewed, and it is noted that with adequate training, paraprofessionals can outperform some professionals.

References

Alexander, J. and Parsons, B. (1973) 'Short-term Behavioural Intervention with Delinquent Families: Impact on Family Process and Recidivism', *Journal of Abnormal Psychology, 81*, 219-25

Arnold, J. *et al.* (1975) 'Changes in Sibling Behavior Following Family Intervention', *Journal of Consulting and Clinical Psychology, 43, 5*, 683-8

Baum, C.G. and Forehand, R. (1981) 'Long-term Follow-up Assessment of Parent Training by Use of Multiple Outcome Measures', *Behavior Therapy, 12*, 643-52

Berkowitz, B.P. and Graziano, A.M. (1972) 'Training Parents as Behavior Therapists: A Review', *Behavior Research and Therapy, 10*, 297-317

Bernal, M.E. *et al.* (1980) 'Outcome Evaluation of Behavioral Parent Training and Client-centered Parent Counseling for Children with Conduct Problems', *Journal of Applied Behavior Analysis, 13, 4*, 677-91

Blackmore, M. *et al.* (1976) 'Summer Therapeutic Environment Program — STEP: A Hospital Alternative for Children', in E.J. Mash *et al.* (eds.), *Behavior Modification Approaches to Parenting* (New York: Brunner/Mazel)

Brown, D.D. (1976) 'Directive Parent Counseling: An Appraisal of its Effect on Extra-conditioning Variables', *Dissertation Abstracts International, 36* (9B) 4680-B

Christensen, A. *et al.* (1980) 'Cost Effectiveness in Behavioral Family Therapy', *Behavior Therapy, 11*, 208-26

Christophersen, E.R. *et al.* (1972) 'The Home Point System: Token Reinforcement Procedures for Application by Parents of Children with Behavior Problems', *Journal of Applied Behavior Analysis, 5, 4*, 485-97

Christophersen, E.R. *et al.* (1976) 'The Family Training Program: Improving Parent–Child Interaction Patterns', in E.J. Mash *et al.* (eds.), *Behavior Modification Approaches to Parenting* (New York: Brunner/Mazel)

Clark, D.B. and Baker, B.L. (1983) 'Predicting Outcome in Parent Training', *Journal of Consulting and Clinical Psychology, 51, 2*, 309-11

Cone, J.D. and Sloop, E.W. (1973) 'Parents as Agents of Change', in A. Jacobs and W. Spradlin (eds.), *The Group as an Agent of Change* (New York Behavior Publications)

D'Angelo, R.Y. and Walsh, J.F. (1967) 'An Evaluation of Various Therapy Approaches with Lower Socioeconomic Group Children', *Journal of Psychology, 67*, 59-64

Doleys, D.M. *et al.* (1976) 'Parent Training Techniques: Effects of Lecture-Role-playing Followed by Feedback and Self-recording', *Journal of Behavior Therapy and Experimental Psychiatry, 7*, 359-62

Eyberg, S.M. and Johnson, S.M. (1974) 'Multiple Assessment of Behavior Modification with Families: Effects of Contingency Contracting and Order of Treated Problems', *Journal of Consulting and Clinical Psychology, 42, 4*, 594-606

Firestone, P. *et al.* (1977) 'Are Fathers Necessary in Parent Training Groups?', unpublished report: Children's Hospital of Eastern Ontario (E.R.I.C.EC 120307, ED 162751)

Flanagan, S. *et al.* (1979) 'A Comparison of Four Instructional Techniques for Teaching Parents How to Use Time-out', *Behavior Therapy, 10*, 94-102

Forehand, R. and Atkeson, B.M. (1977) 'Generality of Treatment Effects with Parents as Therapists: A Review of Assessment and Implementation Procedures', *Behavior Therapy, 8,* 575-93

Forehand, R. *et al.* (1979) 'Parent Behavioral Training to Modify Child Non-compliance: Treatment Generalization across Time and from Home to School', *Behavior Modification, 3, 1,* 3-25

Gardner, J.M. (1975) 'Training Nonprofessionals in Behavior Modification', in T. Thompson and W.S. Dockens (eds.), *Applications of Behavior Modification,* (New York: Academic Press)

Glavin, J.P. and Quay, H.C. (1969) 'Behavior Disorders', *Review of Educational Research, 39, 1,* 83-102

Glogower, F. and Sloop, E.W. (1976) 'Two Strategies of Group Training of Parents as Effective Behavior Modifiers', *Behavior Therapy, 7, 2,* 177-84

Goodman, E.O. (1975) 'Behavior Modification as a Therapeutic Technique for Use with Parents of Emotionally Disturbed Children in Residential Treatment', *Child Psychiatry and Human Development, 6, 1,* 38-46

Gordon, B.N. and Kogan, K.L. (1975) 'A Mother Instruction Program: Behavior Changes with and without Therapeutic Intervention', *Child Psychiatry and Human Development, 6, 2,* 89-106

Gordon, S.B. and Davidson, N. (1981) 'Behavioral Parent Training', in A.S. Gurman and D.P. Kniskern (eds.), *Handbook of Family Therapy* (New York: Brunner/Mazel)

Graziano, A.M. (1977) 'Parents as Behavior Therapists', in M. Hersen *et al.* (eds.), *Progress in Behavior Modification* (vol. 4) (New York: Academic Press)

Hall, M.C. and Nelson, D.J. (1981) 'Responsive Parenting: One Approach for Teaching Single Parents Parenting Skills', *School Psychology Review, 10, 1,* 45-53

Hall, R.V. *et al.* (1972) 'Modification of Behavior Problems in the Home with a Parent as Observer and Experimenter', *Journal of Applied Behavior Analysis, 5, 1,* 53-64

Hanson, T.R. (1975) 'Training Parents as Reinforcement Therapists for their own Children', *Dissertation Abstracts International, 35* (8B) 4174-B

Hawkins, R.P. *et al.* (1966) 'Behavior Therapy in the Home: Amelioration of Problem Parent–Child Relations with the Parent in a Therapeutic Role', *Journal of Experimental Child Psychology, 4,* 99-107

Herbert, E.W. and Baer, D.M. (1972) 'Training Parents as Behavior Modifiers: Self-recording of Contingent Attention', *Journal of Applied Behavior Analysis, 5, 2,* 139-49

Holstein, S.J. (1975) 'The Modification of Maladaptive Mother–Child Interaction through Modeling and Behavior Rehearsal', *Dissertation Abstracts International, 36* (1B) 444-B

Horne, A.M. and Patterson, G.R. (1980) 'Working with Parents of Aggressive Children', in R.R. Abidin (ed.), *Parent Education and Intervention Handbook* (Springfield, Illinois: C.C. Thomas)

Humphreys, L. *et al.* (1978) 'Parental Behavioral Training to Modify Child Noncompliance: Effects on Untreated Siblings', *Journal of Behavior Therapy and Experimental Psychiatry, 9,* 235-8

Ingersoll, B.D. and Eastman, A.M. (1980) 'Paraprofessionals in Behavioral Parent Training', in R.R. Abidin (ed.), *Parent Education and Intervention Handbook* (Springfield, Illinois: C.C. Thomas)

Isaacs, C.D. (1982) 'Treatment of Child Abuse: A Review of the Behavioral Interventions', *Journal of Applied Behavior Analysis, 15, 2,* 273-94

Isaacs, C.D. *et al.* (1982) 'Training Family Therapists: An Experimental Analysis', *Journal of Applied Behavior Analysis, 15, 4,* 505-20

Johnson, C.A. and Katz, R.C. (1973) 'Using Parents as Change Agents for their

Children: A Review', *Journal of Child Psychology and Psychiatry, 14, 3,* 181-200

Johnson, S.M. and Brown, R.A. (1969) 'Producing Behavior Change in Parents of Disturbed Children', *Journal of Child Psychology and Psychiatry, 10,* 107-21

Karn, E. (1972) 'Residential Group Project for Mothers of Children Referred to a Child Guidance Clinic', *British Journal of Social Work, 2,* 2, 175-86

Karoly, P. and Rosenthal, M. (1977) 'Training Parents in Behavior Modification: Effects on Perceptions of Family Interaction and Deviant Child Behavior', *Behavior Therapy, 8,* 406-10

Kirk, M. (1979) *Services in Counseling/Intervention and Life Skills Education* (Philadelphia, Pennsylvania: Southern Home for Children) (E.R.I.C. EC 123968, ED 185781)

Kogan, K.L. and Gordon B.N. (1975) 'A Mother-instruction Program: Documenting Change in Mother–Child Interactions', *Child Psychiatry and Human Development, 5, 3,* 189-200

Kolvin, I. *et al.* (1981) *Help Starts Here: The Maladjusted Child in the Ordinary School* (London: Tavistock)

Kovitz, K.E. (1976) 'Comparing Group and Individual Methods for Training Parents in Child Management Techniques', in E.J. Mash *et al.* (eds.), *Behavior Modification Approaches to Parenting* (New York: Brunner/Mazel)

Lavigeur, H. (1974) 'The Use of Siblings as an Adjunct to the Behavioral Treatment of Children in the Home with Parents as Therapists', *Dissertation Abstracts International, 34* (12-B, 1) 6214-B

Lavigeur, H. *et al.* (1973) 'Behavioral Treatment in the Home: Effects on an Untreated Sibling and Long-term Follow-up', *Behavior Therapy, 4,* 431-41

Lupin, M. *et al.* (1976) 'Children, Parents and Relaxation Tapes', *Academic Therapy, 12, 1,* 105-13

McMahon, R.J. and Davies, G.R. (1980) 'A Behavioral Parent Training Program and its Side-effects on Classroom Behavior', *B.C. Journal of Special Education, 4, 2,* 165-74

Miller, A. and Ellis, J. (1980) 'A Behaviour Management Course for a Group of Mothers: The Importance of the Course Setting for Effective Use of Available Resources', *Child Care Health and Development, 6,* 147-55

Milne, D. (1986) *Training Behaviour Therapists: Methods, Evaluation and Implementation with Parents, Nurses and Teachers* (London: Croom Helm/Cambridge, MA: Brookline Books)

Mira, M. 81970) 'Results of a Behavior Modification Training Program for Parents and Teachers', *Behavior Research and Therapy, 8,* 309-11

Moreland, J.R. *et al.* (1982) 'Parents as Therapists: A Review of the Behavior Therapy Parent Training Literature, 1975-81', *Behavior Modification, 6,* 250-76

Murphy, P.L. (1976) 'Relationship of a Multidisciplinary Parent-Education Course to Changes in Parent/Child Problems', *Dissertation Abstracts International, 37* (4-B) 1920-B

Nay, W.R. (1975) 'A Systematic Comparison of Instructional Techniques for Parents', *Behavior Therapy, 6,* 14-21

O'Dell, S. (1974) 'Training Parents in Behavior Modification: A Review', *Psychological Bulletin, 81, 7,* 418-33

O'Dell, S. *et al.* (1977) 'A Comparison of Parent Training Techniques in Child Behavior Modification', *Journal of Behavior Therapy and Experimental Psychiatry, 8,* 261-8

O'Dell, S.L. *et al.* (1979) 'Media-assisted Parent Training: Alternative Models', *Behavior Therapy, 16,* 103-10

O'Dell, S.L. *et al.* (1980) 'An Assessment of Methods for Training Parents in the Use of Time-out', *Journal of Behavior Therapy and Experimental Psychiatry, 11,* 21-5

O'Dell, S.L. *et al.* (1982) 'Predicting the Acquisition of Parenting Skills via Four Training Methods', *Behavior Therapy, 13*, 194-208

Patterson, G.R. (1974a) 'Intervention for Boys with Conduct Problems: Multiple Settings, Treatments and Criteria', *Journal of Consulting and Clinical Psychology, 42*, 471-81

Patterson, G.R. (1974b) 'Retraining of Aggressive Boys by their Parents: Review of Recent Literature and Follow-up Evaluation', *Canadian Psychiatric Association Journal, 19*, 142-58

Patterson, G.R. (1975) 'Multiple Evaluations of a Parent-training Program', in T. Thompson and W.S. Dockens (eds.), *Applications of Behavior Modification* (New York: Academic Press)

Patterson, G.R. and Brodsky, G. (1966) 'A Behavior Modification Program for a Child with Multiple Problem Behaviors', *Journal of Child Psychology and Psychiatry, 7*, 277-95

Patterson, G.R. and Fleischman, M.J. (1979) 'Maintenance of Treatment Effects: Some Considerations Concerning Family Systems and Follow-up Data', *Behavior Therapy, 10*, 168-85

Patterson, G.R. and Gullion, M.E. (1968) *Living with Children: New Methods for Parents and Teachers* (Champaign, Illinois: Research Press)

Patterson, G.R. *et al.* (1975) *A Social Learning Approach to Family Intervention*, vol. 1: *Families with Aggressive Children* (Eugene, Oregon: Castalia Publishing Co.)

Patterson, G.R. *et al.* (1982) 'A Comparative Evaluation of a Parent-training Program', *Behavior Therapy, 13*, 638-50

Peed, S.F. (1976) 'Generalization to the Home of Behavior Modified in a Parent Training Program for Non-compliant Children', *Dissertation Abstracts International, 36* (9-B) 4703-B

Peed, S.F. *et al.* (1977) 'Evaluation of the Effectiveness of a Standardised Parent Training Program in Altering the Interaction of Mothers and their Non-compliant Children', *Behavior Modification, 1, 3*, 323-50

Reisinger, J.J. *et al.* (1976a) 'Parents as Change Agents for their Children: A Review', *Journal of Community Psychology, 4*, 103-23

Reisinger, J.J. *et al.* (1976b) 'Toddler Management Training: Generalization and Marital Status', *Journal of Behavior Therapy and Experimental Psychiatry, 7, 4*, 335-40

Rekers, G.A. and Lovaas, O.I. (1974) 'Behavioral Treatment of Deviant Sex-role Behaviors in a Male Child', *Journal of Applied Behavior Analysis, 7, 2*, 173-90

Rinn, R.C. *et al.* (1975) 'Training Parents of Behaviorally-disordered Children in Groups: A Three Years' Program Evaluation', *Behavior Therapy, 6*, 378-87

Robin, A.L. (1981) 'A Controlled Evaluation of Problem-solving Communication Training with Parent–Adolescent Conflict', *Behavior Therapy, 12*, 593-609

Rosmann, M.R. (1980) 'Working with Foster Parents', in R.R. Abidin (ed.), *Parent Education and Intervention Handbook* (Springfield, Illinois: C.C. Thomas)

Sajwaj, T. (1973) 'Difficulties in the Use of Behavioral Techniques by Parents in Changing Child Behavior: Guides to Success', *Journal of Nervous and Mental Disease, 156, 6*, 395-403

Sanders, M.R. (1980) 'The Effects of Parent Self-recording and Home Feedback in Systematic Parent Training', *The Exceptional Child, 27, 1*, 62-71

Sanders, M.R. and Glynn, T. (1981) Training Parents in Behavioral Self-management: An Analysis of Generalisation and Maintenance', *Journal of Applied Behavior Analysis, 14, 3*, 223-37

Sapon-Shevin, M. (1982) 'Ethical Issues in Parent Training Programs', *Journal of Special Education, 16, 3*, 341-57

Siegert, F.E. and Yates, B.T. (1980) 'Behavioral Child-management Cost-effectiveness: A Comparison of Individual In-office, Individual In-house, and Group Delivery Systems', *Evaluation and the Health Professions, 3, 2,* 123-52

Sirridge, S.T. (1976) Parent Training: Assessment of Parent Attitudes, Parent Management Skills and Child Target Behavior', *Dissertation Abstracts International, 36* (7-B) 3627-B

Strain, P.S. *et al.* (1982) 'Long-term Effects of Oppositional Child Treatment with Mothers as Therapists and Therapist Trainers', *Journal of Applied Behavior Analysis, 15, 1,* 163-9

Stuart, R.B. (1971) 'Behavioral Contracting with the Families of Delinquents', *Journal of Behaviour Therapy and Experimental Psychiatry, 2,* 1-11

Tavormina, J.B. (1974) 'Basic Models of Parent Counseling: A Review', *Psychological Bulletin, 81,* 827-36

Tavormina, J.B. (1975) 'Relative Effectiveness of Behavioral and Reflective Group Counseling with Parents of Mentally Retarded Children', *Journal of Consulting and Clinical Psychology, 43,* 22-31

Tharp, R.G. and Wetzel, R.J. (1969) *Behavior Modification in the Natural Environment* (New York: Academic Press)

Veltkamp, L.J. and Newman, K. (1976) 'Parent Groups: How Effective?', *Journal of Family Counseling, 4,* 46-51

Vogelsong, E.L. and Guerney, B.G. (1980) 'Working with Parents of Disturbed Adolescents', in R.R. Abidin (ed.), *Parent Education and Intervention Handbook* (Springfield, Illinois: C.C. Thomas)

Wahler, R.G. (1975) 'Some Structural Aspects of Deviant Child Behavior', *Journal of Applied Behavior Analysis, 8, 1,* 27-42

Wahler, R.G. (1976) 'Deviant Child Behavior within the Family: Developmental Speculations and Behavior Change Strategies', in H. Leitenberg (ed.), *Handbook of Behavior Modification and Behavior Therapy* (Englewood Cliffs, New Jersey: Prentice-Hall)

Wahler, R.G. (1980) 'The Insular Mother: Her Problems in Parent–Child Treatment', *Journal of Applied Behavior Analysis, 13, 2,* 207-19

Wahler, R.G. and Graves, M.G. (1983) 'Setting Events in Social Networks: Ally or Enemy in Child Behavior Therapy?', *Behavior Therapy, 14,* 19-36

Wahler, R.G. *et al.* (1965) 'Mothers as Behavior Therapists for their Own Children', *Behavior Research and Therapy, 3,* 113-24

Walder, L.O. *et al.* (1968) *Teaching Parents and Others Principles of Behavioral Control for Modifying the Behavior of Children: Final Report* (Silver Spring, Maryland: Institute for Behavioral Research) (E.R.I.C. EC011540, ED029442)

Walter, H.I. and Gilmore, S.K. (1973) 'Placebo versus Social Learning Effects in Parent Training Procedures Designed to Alter the Behaviors of Aggressive Boys', *Behavior Therapy, 4,* 361-77

Webster-Stratton, C. (1981) 'Modification of Mothers' Behaviors and Attitudes through a Videotape Modeling Group Discussion Program', *Behavior Therapy, 12,* 634-42

Weinrott, M.R. *et al.* (1979) 'Systematic Replication of a Social Learning Approach to Parent Training', in P. Sjoden *et al.* (eds.), *Trends in Behavior Therapy* (New York: Academic Press)

Wells, K.C. and Forehand, R. (1981) 'Childhood Behavior Problems in the Home', in S.M.Turner *et al.* (eds.), *Handbook of Clinical Behavior Therapy* (New York: Wiley)

Wiltz, N.A. (1969) 'Modification of Behaviors of Deviant Boys through Parent Participation in a Group Technique', unpublished doctoral dissertation, University of Oregon

Wiltz, N.A. and Patterson, G.R. (1974) 'An Evaluation of Parent-training Procedures Designed to Alter Inappropriate Aggressive Behavior of Boys', *Behavior Therapy, 5,* 215-21

Wolfe, D.A. *et al.* (1982) 'Intensive Behavioral Parent Training for a Child Abusive Mother', *Behavior Therapy, 13,* 438-51

Worland, J. *et al.* (1980) Does In-home Training Add to the Effectiveness of Operant Group Parent Training? A Two-year Evaluation', *Child Behavior Therapy, 2, 1,* 11-24

9 LANGUAGE DYSFUNCTION

Language development work is commonly one of the features of broad parent training programmes for the 'disadvantaged', 'ethnic minorities', the 'sensorily impaired' and the 'developmentally delayed', and as such is referred to elsewhere. In this chapter, the focus will be on programmes specifically targeted only on language. Consideration will be given in turn to programmes for children with 'compensatory' language needs, those with a specific language dysfunction, the developmentally delayed and autistic children.

Compensatory

An excellent study is reported by Fowler and Swenson (1979), who note that compensatory language training may often start too late to have real impact. Their own investigation was designed to determine the cumulative effects of a parent-tutored programme lasting seven months and beginning before 6 months of age. Four parallel groups of three or four infants were established, in which the language spoken at home was respectively English, Italian, Chinese and English. Three control groups were also monitored.

Assessments included pre-, post- and follow-up testing on a range of measures (Griffiths and Receptive Expressive Emergent Language (REEL)) and process data from parental logs and audio-recordings. The language programme taught by adult modelling and prompting, and moved gradually from concrete object and process labelling to other parts of speech and the introduction of syntax, variation in referents for the same label, timing labelling to action and semantic orientation. There was considerable emphasis on experimental stimulus for language, and sensorimotor play, exploratory excursions, and language in routine household activities were all covered. Parents were given written instruction and guided in weekly home visits via demonstration, feedback and general discussion. Vocabulary lists and record forms were supplied, and kits of toys were given to some families. The written guidance and professional training at home were all given in the mother tongue, although most of the Italian and Chinese parents were bilingual.

Results showed that the subjects as a total group gained an average of 38 quotient points on the language scale of the Griffiths from pre- to post-test, triple the average mean gain for other scales. Mean quotients remained stable at above-average levels (or improved further) at follow-up, 6, 12, 18 and 24 months later, although reduction of the sample size cast some doubt on the reliability of this finding. Similar initial patterns of change were seen in all groups, despite the Italian families tending to have working mothers, receiving home visits less frequently than other groups, and having much less educated parents — which resulted in their experiencing great difficulty with the written instructions. This group did markedly less well at maintaining gains at 18-month follow-up, however. Girls gained substantially more than boys in language. The Chinese group showed the largest overall increases in Griffiths quotients. Control group comparisons were similarly positive. Process measures revealed a similar pattern of development as outcome measures, and underlined the impact of the parental activity.

Fowler and Swenson (1979) boldly conclude:

> Language development can apparently be routinely accelerated through intensification of stimulation during early infancy. Continuing even limited parent guidance of stimulation may have cumulative effects in accelerating language development, while terminating parental guidance at 12 months may produce variable effects. It would appear that parents with less formal schooling need continuing guidance and support to maintain high levels of stimulation.

The authors jusifiably feel they have demonstrated the importance of initiating parent-mediated language training in the early stages of a child's life.

Intervention at a later stage (4 years) was, however, a feature of the work of Beveridge and Jerrams (1981). Four matched groups of ten nursery children were selected. A Parental Assistance Plan wherein parents worked on language with their children at home for 20 minutes each day and came into school one half-day per week for training themselves, was implemented with two of the groups. Children in one of these groups also received the DISTAR language programme in school. The third group received only DISTAR, while the fourth group merely played with toys in the presence of a teacher for an equivalent period.

The parent programme ran for twelve weeks, and included verbal instruction and demonstration. Details of curriculum content are provided, and course structure appears to be modular rather than consisting of highly sequenced objectives. Pre- and post-testing on the Reynell Language Scales and the English Picture Vocabulary Test were carried out, and also at follow-up 18 months later. Parents and teachers completed attitude questionnaires and had individual interviews. Teacher logbooks were also analysed.

Teacher and parent subjective feedback was positive about the parental input, but some teachers were negative about DISTAR. Results on the English Picture Vocabulary Test at post-test showed that the two groups with parental input had made markedly greater gains than the DISTAR-only and control groups. This superiority was maintained at follow-up, although both DISTAR-only and control groups had caught up a little. Unfortunately many children hit the ceiling of the Reynell Test, rendering the results unanalysable, but similar trends were found on this measure.

A related programme which trained three women of limited formal education to act as paraprofessional tutors of language and cognitive skills is described by Ayllon and Roberts (1975). A multiple baseline research design was used to assess the relative effectiveness of different procedures. The target children did not learn when merely exposed to the stimulus material. When reinforcement was introduced in the form of paired praise and consumables, the children learned. The mothers could generalise the procedures to children other than the one with whom they first practised. Substantial detail of the programme, which some teachers would view as rather restricted and mechanical, is available in the Ayllon and Roberts report, but the numbers of children involved are small.

Specific Language Dysfunction

About half of the work with parents in this area has focused on expressive language, and the remainder on children with a variety or multiplicity of language problems.

Expressive Difficulties

An early study which testified to the effectiveness of paraprofessionals was that of Bailey *et al.* (1971), who reported how the articulation errors of two boys aged 12 and 13 years were modified by systematic programming from their peers.

A single case study of a non-speaking child of 3 years 6 months was subsequently described in detail by Whitehurst *et al.* (1972). No specific training programme was provided for the parents, but two different types of parental behaviour to facilitate language were manipulated in a multiple baseline design. The level of parent-initiated conversation and level of use of initiative prompts were systematically varied separately and together, with other types of relevant parental behaviour held constant. Observational data showed that when either behaviour was present at a high level, the child's use of language accelerated; when both were used simultaneously, the child's language accelerated most of all. Reversal conditions emphasised the impact of these parental behaviours. Asking the child questions appeared to have negligible stimulatory impact.

Miller and Sloane (1976) reported a more substantial study, in which five parents of non-verbal children were trained in home settings to modify antecedents and consequences to their children's vocalisations. Parent training was by verbal instruction, live modelling, feedback, reinforcement and self-recording in a one-to-one situation with the child concerned. Training content revolved round parent use of modelling sounds, prompting and positive and negative reinforcement for accurate imitation or vocalisation on the child's part.

Observational data showed that parents rapidly learned to carry out this restricted range of tasks effectively, but that this did not generalise entirely satisfactorily to other times and settings of the day, although how realistic an expectation this was on the part of the investigators is open to question. None the less, improvements in child vocalisations *did* generalise to other times and settings in the home. However, there was minimal generalisation of child vocalisations to either free play or speech therapy sessions conducted in the school. At follow-up two months later all generalisation effects had disappeared, but the specific training effects had been maintained in the setting in which they were originally established, albeit at a somewhat lower rate than during training itself. However, the rather restricted and mechanistic nature of the training should be taken into account, and the cynical reader may be forgiven for thinking that the main thing this study demonstrates is that if you treat people like rats, they usually behave like rats.

A more naturalistic study, with unfortunately confusing results, was conducted by Stevenson *et al.* (1982). Twenty-two children aged 2 years 6 months to 3 years 6 months, and of below average socio-economic status, without hearing loss but with substantive expressive language delay on the Reynell Scales, were allocated to matched experimental and control groups. The experimental families were subsequently visited at home by a speech therapist approximately 22 times over a six-month period. Pre- and post-testing on the Reynell Expressive Scale, English Picture Vocabulary Test, and co-ordination and performance sub-scales of the Griffiths Scale were carried out.

Programme content was individualised, as the experimental group was highly heterogeneous. The therapist worked with the child in the mother's presence, and lent toys and books for use between visits. Significant pre-test to post-test differences were found only on the Reynell Scale, but both the experimental and control group made some gains. Generally, the experimental group did better than the control group, but not statistically significantly. Details of the degree of involvement of different parents are not given. Some of the apparent 'spontaneous' improvement in the control group may reflect practice or Hawthorne effects.

Various Difficulties

An interesting small-scale study is reported by Spiegel *et al.* (1982), who worked with two parents of language-disordered children. Both parents had six hours of training, but training content differed. One parent was trained with respect to language form (mean length of utterance, repetitions, sentence types and other structural aspects), and the other with respect to communicative style (pragmatic aspects of conversational turn-taking, attention and topic agreement). Pre- and post-training assessment was by observational analysis of video-tapes taken in the home. Both parents showed positive changes in the behaviour domain of their own training, and spontaneously in the other domain as well. While this study provides interesting data on the possibility of parent training generalising into other parent behaviours, it was small in scale and little information is provided about the nature of the experimental parents.

An early parent training programme is described by Carpenter and Augustine (1973). Four mothers of children with a variety of communication disorders received training in behaviour change techniques at a two-day workshop. The mothers were selected for motivation and ability to benefit from such training. Written and verbal instruction, video-tape observation and analysis, role-play, modelling, practice, video and verbal feedback and group discussion were included. Home lesson plans were prepared by the professionals, with specific objectives and criteria for each day written out, together with appropriate parental responses and a chart for recording. When children reached a criterion of 80 per cent correct performance on two consecutive days, the next lesson was supplied. The mother returned their charted data weekly and kept in contact by telephone. After about ten weeks, the parents returned to the centre for further direct observation of their work with the children.

Detailed case study information is given by Carpenter and Augustine on two children. Overall, three of the four parents proved able to modify their children's communicative behaviour over the period in question. The fourth mother felt uncomfortable with the technique and was not successful — although her records showed improvement, observation of the child told a different story. She seemed incapable of following instructions, no matter how finely the requisite behaviour was task-analysed — an inability that was not ascribable to any cognitive limitations. Some of the other parents had deviated slightly from the format, but had done so successfully and were now confident enough to challenge the professionals' opinion on certain programme aspects. Generally, the parents of the child with the severest difficulties had been least successful, having had least encouragement in child response. Nevertheless, these results are better than might have been expected from a purely centre-based programme with very little supportive structure to ensure generalisation to the home other than self-recording and telephone contact.

The question of generalisation of parent training was addressed comparatively in some detail by Mulac and Tomlinson (1977). Nine children aged between 4 and 6 years were assigned to one of three conditions: (a) programme with large home component, (b) programme with small home component, and (c) a control programme (articulation training). The programme was specifically designed to establish appropriate use of interrogative syntactical structures. Baseline and post-treatment language samples were collected both in and out of the clinic on a variety of preformulated language tasks.

The highly structured in-centre activities for the children were dealt with by a professional. The programme included 35 imitative steps, each requiring 20 consecutive correct responses; the stimulus, response and reinforcement were precisely defined. This was coupled with a home carry-over activity in which the parent was trained by the professional, consisting of eight ten-minute sessions within a two-week period. Group (a) additionally each received eight sessions within a further two-week period, conducted in the family home and out 'on location', during which the professional modelled the required procedures with the child and then monitored parental practice.

About three to three and a half weeks after the final programme activity, all the children were post-tested on the trained tasks. All members of groups (a) and (b) demonstrated a pre-criterion score of 0 per cent and a post-criterion score of 100 per cent correct on the tasks assessed in the centre. However, performance on the same tasks in the home setting was quite different, with the extended home programme group (a) doing significantly better than the predominantly centre-based programme group (b). Neither group (b) nor group (c) — control — showed significant out-of-centre improvement. However, parents from both groups reported equal satisfaction with their programmes on evaluative questionnaires.

Developmental Delay

Children who are generally developmentally delayed (mentally handicapped, severely educationally subnormal, etc.) nevertheless frequently have erratic profiles of skills, and this is nowhere more true than with Down's syndrome children. Some of these children have certain abilities above the average for 'normal' children. A frequent finding with Down's children, however, is language delay, not helped by a high incidence of ear, nose and throat disorders. Thus most of the work on specific language remediation via parents of the developmentally delayed has focused on Down's children.

An articulate introduction to this area is offered by McConkey (1979), who remarks on the mistake professionals have made in over-estimating their influence in dealing with communication disorders, while parents have under-estimated theirs. The result, he says, is that 'we are in the paradoxical position of calling for a reinstatement of parental involvement in the development of communication skills with the atypical child'. Without parent involvement, McConkey argues, the chance of generalisation of skills is low.

If parental training effects are to generalise and be maintained, it is obviously necessary for the procedures to become integrated into, while to a degree transforming, everyday spontaneous routine interactions in the home. The promulgators of some of the 'high-tech' approaches would do well to remember this, for they fall too readily into the disenfranchisement of parents of which the medical profession has been so guilty. Cheseldine and McConkey (1979) report an interesting study of parental *style* of language interaction with Down's syndrome children. Research is cited which demonstrates that parents who consciously model good language with short mean length of utterance and eschew demands and questions facilitate the language performance of their children. Cheseldine and McConkey therefore set out to determine whether parents, given a language objective to work towards but no instructions on how to attain it, might discover more effective interaction styles for themselves.

The study was home-based, but to enable some standardisation one set of play materials was provided. The parents audio-recorded free play sessions themselves, to limit the effect of 'observer presence'. Seven Down's children aged 4 years 6 months to 6 years, all at the one- to two-word level, were involved. The families were of middle socio-economic status, and in five of the seven only one parent in each family was involved in the programme. Language objectives set revolved round increasing the frequency of two-word utterances, and specific target utterances were stipulated for individual children. At least four ten-minute sessions were to be carried out over between one and two weeks.

Subsequently, the parent and child language was transcribed from the audio-tapes and analysed. The parents of the children most improved had reduced their mean length of utterance significantly more than the other parents. The improver parents had increased their use of statements and decreased their use of questions, while the non-improvers showed the reverse pattern, although the differences were not significant. Improver parents used the target words significantly more in statements, while non-improvers used them more in questions.

Two of the less successful parents were then given specific training to help them modify their language strategies, via written instruction, modelling in the home with the child, and discussion. Both parents changed in the desired direction, although in different ways, and the child's language improved accordingly. The two remaining non-improvers, acting as controls, showed no changes in parent or child language behaviour. The authors conclude that some parents need little training, only targets, while others need targets and brief home training. Whether these results would generalise to a lower-SES group is another matter.

However, a previous study from the same stable had shown that success is not always so easy. Jeffree and Cashdan (1971) also worked towards restructuring adult–child interactions to facilitate language learning at home. The training programme was fairly broad and gave a general grounding in behavioural techniques. Fifteen children of mean age 11 years were studied, but compared with controls, differences did not emerge on most of the group measures used. Both experimental and control groups went up on the Reynell Scales, while both went down on the Columbia and Peabody Tests. Experimental scores on a test of articulation rose more than control scores, but articulation was not a specific target of the programme. The authors — understandably confused — query whether qualitative changes in language might not have occurred, even though quantitative changes were not detected on tests.

Jeffree (1978) later reported on the work of the Parental Involvement Project at the Hester Adrian Research Centre. This project was concerned with developmentally delayed children between the ages of 2 and 5. Of 263 notified families with children conforming to these criteria, 261 were visited for developmental assessment of the children. Forty-five per cent of the parents were chiefly concerned about lack of communication skills: 68 per cent of the children had not yet acquired 20 clear words. From this sample, a sub-sample of parents able to attend the centre was formed; and from this, 20 parents were chosen at random.

Twelve individual sessions were held for each family lasting between one and one and a half hours; usually only mother and child attended. In addition, six group sessions were held in the evening. Individual objectives were set for each child. Audio-recordings were made at home and video-recordings made in the centre, in addition to the completion of developmental checklists. The training emphasised the context of language learning, and all learning took place in an active play situation, taking account of the child's preferences. The parents were taught to model words and minimise questions and demands via a process of modelling, practice, feedback and self-recording in their home.

Baseline and programme frequencies of usage of target words, usage of two-word utterances, and child initiation of utterances are given for sample children. The graphs of these data are dramatic and highly persuasive. However, process data are not reported for parental behaviour for all cases, and neither are full outcome data on all cases given.

Encouraging work is reported from the USA by MacDonald *et al.* (1974). Six Down's children aged 3 to 5 years were assigned to experimental and control groups. The parent training programme was designed to result in increased mean length of utterance and greater syntactical complexity. Parents were trained by modelling, practice, feedback, self-recording and role-play in a two-stage pro-gramme. During the first two months both parents and pro-fessionals worked with the children; during the subsequent three months the parents worked alone at home, supported only by monthly meetings with professional staff. The training procedures specifically included coverage of how to transfer centre-based training to the home. Very detailed activity guidelines were supplied.

Results from the two-month stage indicated marked increases in mean length of utterance and grammatical complexity in experi-mental children, but not in controls. Results from the three months of in-home programming indicated continuing language incre-ments for the experimental subjects compared with controls. The language growth in the programme children during the in-home phase was similar to rates of acceleration for 'normal' children. Subsequently, the training programme was run for the 'control' children, who made entirely comparable gains. It should be noted that none of the study families was of low socio-economic status, however, and the replication of this work with a wider range of families might not give such positive results.

Warnings about a different kind of generalisation are given by another US study, authored by Salzberg and Villani (1983). A multiple baseline design was used to investigate the acquisition and subsequent generalisation of vocal imitation training skills by the parents of two 3½-years-old Down's children. Parents were trained by modelling, prompting, feedback and reinforcement, and they subsequently readily increased their correct use of prompts and praise and decreased their use of tangential statements. Improved vocal imitation and decreased disruptive behaviour resulted from the children. However, the newly acquired parental skills did not extend to free play sessions in the home.

Subsequently, the parents received 'generalisation training'. Instructions were given on how to use the relevant skills at home, and parents were taught how to adapt these to a free play situation, and given feedback based on audio-recordings of in-home sessions. This resulted in rapid increases in the required parental behaviour at home as well as increases in the children's vocal imitation and spontaneous vocalisation.

Autism

Although autism is most popularly conceptualised as a communication disorder, children so diagnosed are characterised by associated behavioural excesses and/or deficits. The need to deal with a complexity of inter-dependent behaviours has resulted in many parent training programmes targeted on 'autistic' children giving as much weight to behaviour management as to language development. Nevertheless, all programmes for autistic children will be reviewed here for simplicity's sake.

Lovaas (1977) provides an introduction to the field, documenting some of the problems. Traditional clinic-based behaviour therapy gains were often situation-specific, long-term follow-up results were often disappointing (depending on the post-treatment environment), and treatment was typically slow and vastly expensive in professional time. Autistic children were often largely indifferent to normal 'reinforcing' stimuli. Artificial reinforcers often had to be used, inevitably automatically limiting contextual generalisation. Follow-up data on 13 children showed that children whose parents were trained to help them continued to improve after treatment, while children who were discharged to untrained parents, foster-homes or institutions, often regressed. However, as autistic children have extensive behavioural retardation, their parents probably need extensive training to be of significant help.

The heavy commitment necessary from the parents in his own approach is detailed by Lovaas (1977; Lovaas *et al.*, 1973). One of the main care-givers will be expected to work with the child for most of the day for at least one year. A contract is signed by both parties. This stipulates that the family may miss a maximum of two centre visits, and must meet various performance criteria during the course of training. Failure to meet these can result in termination of the training. The professionals contract to spend at least ten hours per week in the parental home, provide service to the child's school teacher, and so on.

Training in the clinic proceeds by live demonstration of the target technique with the child, which the parent then imitates, subsequently receiving feedback and reinforcement. Novice student volunteers are sometimes trained in parallel to give the parents more confidence. 'Virtuoso' performances by skilled experts are discouraged, since they present too distant a model for shaping. Dealing with tantrum behaviour is often an early target, as the behaviour is so stressful for the parent. Attention, non-verbal imitation and receptive language goals usually follow. Gradual steps which virtually guarantee success for both parent and child are considered essential. As parents become more competent, the training input fades to a more consultative input, with the parent assuming the main responsibility. However, extensive home visits continue, as there is so much to be done with the children.

Thus the training for parents operates on an 'apprenticeship' basis. Not until parents are already skilful is didactic theoretical material introduced. The framework Lovaas describes is a fascinating blend of appallingly rigid single-mindedness and sensitive practicality, still retaining a quasi-medical colouration. Lovaas accepts that many familes could not cope with the training procedure, and introduces the concept of 'teaching homes', in which a heterogenous peer group containing autistic children could be managed by model (professional) parents from whom the natural parents would learn on visits.

After this introductory sample of the nature of work with autistic children, consideration can be given to the evaluation research, commencing with some early studies.

Early Studies

One of the earliest efforts in this field was that of Risley and Wolf (1967), who trained the mother of a 6-year-old autistic boy to conduct a labelling session similar to those the child experienced in his special school. The professional modelled the procedure for the mother, who then took over, receiving intermittent feedback and further instruction. The mother was also trained to prompt the child to use correct verbal requests instead of 'chanting'. The chanting behaviour was eliminated in the home, but there are no data on generalisation of training effects at home to child behaviour in school.

Another individual case study was presented by Goldstein and Lanyon (1971), who worked with the parents of a 10-year-old autistic boy with some expressive vocabulary, but bizarre articulation. The authors note that in order to screen for personal factors which might interfere with their ability to respond to training, the parents were given an intelligence test and the Minnesota Multiphasic Personality Inventory (MMPI). The parents' intelligence seemed at least average and no obvious emotional difficulties emerged in the MMPI profiles, but the authors appear surprised that the parents responded 'in a highly defensive manner'.

Written and verbal information of a general nature was given over the first four sessions, then role-playing of speech training began. This was later conducted by both parents at mealtimes, using food as a reinforcer, and working through the child's commonly misarticulated words. The father then suggested audio-recording the sessions, and the parents kept a log, which was discussed with the professionals. Occasionally the child was brought for a demonstration session in the clinic. The parents had some difficulty with attention control (in the child), immediacy of reinforcement, graduality of shaping, and appropriate sequencing of words to be taught. After 125 days, the child could correctly articulate 83 words, all of which he grossly misarticulated initially. The beginnings of sentence usage, imitation of simple conversation, willingness to answer questions and a tendency to self-correct also developed. While this rate of development is painfully slow, it was clearly a marked acceleration on previous progress.

A vastly more sophisticated study is described by Howlin *et al.* (1973), who deployed two professionals to work with up to 14 cases at a time, visiting once or twice a week fading to once every two weeks. A time-sampling observation schedule to monitor 23 child behaviours and 27 parent behaviours was deployed. Daily recording of problem behaviours was supplemented by standard assessment procedures at six-monthly intevals. Attempts to assess quality as well as quantity of change were made. Much emphasis was placed on adaptation of treatment to the needs of the child and parents. Analysis of behavioural problems with the parents led to agreement on programme target priorities. Detailed treatment schemata with clear objectives and task-analaysed steps were drawn up. The authors give details of nine treatment plans with outcomes. These lasted from eight to 68 weeks with austistic children aged 5 to 11 years, and related to language skills (two cases), ritualistic behaviour, phobias, hyperactivity, road safety, self-help skills, toilet training and social behaviour. Children had also been taught reading and number skills and a range of imitative behaviours, and temper tantrums had been eliminated.

Techniques used included positive reinforcement, time-out (with tantrums), desensitisation (with phobias) and gradual withdrawal of transitional objects with which the child was obsessed. To be effective, behavioural management techniques needed to be applied consistently throughout each day's household happenings, but specific skill increments had to be built through short periods of intensive one-to-one work. Howlin *et al.* (1973) differ from Lovaas (1977) on the use of reinforcers. They report having found tangible reinforcers of limited use, and prefer to use social reinforcers with children who are at all in social contact with their parents. Social reinforcers are sometimes paired with tangible reinforcers, but edibles are used with caution as they are said to have proved difficult to fade out.

Training includes the general principles of behaviour modification. Programmed written instruction is provided and simultaneous explanation and modelling are utilised, coupled with detailed discussions. Parents are taught to make their own functional analyses of behaviour and devise their own programmes. Daily recording in charts or diaries serves to monitor effectiveness and gives the parents reinforcing feedback on visible progress. Removal of behavioural problems often renders work on educational goals more feasible. After six months of intensive training, the intention was to fade out professional input, but this had not always proved easy in practice. Counselling to deal with other family problems and stresses is provided as part of the programme, particularly in terms of dealing with parental guilt. (This latter is a frequent problem in families with autistic children, since the problems are so severe and mysterious and there was once a fashion for implicating parental personality as a causative factor.) Various kinds of practical advice were also given — such as where to find a babysitter who could cope! Schools are also given management advice by the programme.

Various forms of control comparison had been built into the programme. Multiple baseline techniques enabled children to serve as their own controls, but control groups of non-served families were also established. Attempts were also to be made to compare behaviourally oriented training with other types of training. It is worth noting that this programme was completely home-based, and specifically trained generalisation, with behaviours often being deliberately established in varying contexts. This latter made the procedure very time-consuming, particularly as a wide range of behaviours was often encompassed. The authors concluded that they had demonstrated that behavioural techniques, delivered in this helpful and sensitive way, were effective in the treatment of autistic children:

> Results suggest that marked changes can be effected in the child's behaviour by teaching parents to become therapists in their own homes. Improvements in specific problem behaviours as well as in the whole style of communication between parents and children can be documented and analysed with reliability and precision.

The way was open for rapid development of this highly cost-effective approach.

General Studies

However, not all workers in the area of parent training with autistic children managed to be as methodical as Howlin *et al*. Work in the USA at North Carolina University is documented by Rosenfeld (1978), Marcus *et al.* (1978), and Davis and Marcus (1980) among others. In this programme, after a 'diagnostic' period lasting between six and eight weeks, parents attend the centre to observe professionals modelling required procedure. The professionals then supervise parental practice, and there are individual discussions and group monthly meetings. Individualised programmes are developed, sometimes focusing on specific behaviours but otherwise apparently rather loosely structured, and reviewed and extended during weekly visits to the centre. Emphasis is placed on developing behaviours which seem to be 'emerging' (i.e. are already quite well shaped). 'Exercises' for completion at home are given to the parents, who are encouraged to keep a daily log and complete a weekly rating of child behaviour. Rosenfeld (1978) cites few evaluative data, other than that many children are integrated into ordinary school and 'some' show IQ gains, but it is nevertheless reported that the model is now used statewide, with five centres and 20 special classrooms.

Further details are given in Marcus *et al.* (1978), who pursued families who had been involved in the extended service. The children were aged 2–5 years, 'moderately' psychotic; median IQ was 44, and socio-economic status distribution was normal. Each mother was asked to work with her child on an unfamiliar specified non-language task on two occasions: pre-training and post-training. Video-recordings of these sessions were subsequently analysed, and showed that parental interaction skills and child compliance were significantly better at post-test. Lower SES parents did not do any worse than higher; in fact, the trend was in the opposite direction. The authors cite this as evidence for the generalisation of the training programme, but no evidence on generalisation to home or other tasks is offered, nor is evidence of longer-term maintenance of gains. During test tasks, the children were cued attentionally by working with professional therapists prior to parental take-over. At the worst, this study may demonstrate only parental habituation to video-recording.

The same programme is described further in Davis and Marcus (1980), but no further evaluation data are cited. The authors' conclusion is worth quoting:

> parental involvement should not be limited to home-based application of clinic activities. It should include the parents' concerns and priorities, their interpretation of the child's handicap, their unique capabilities and limitations, and their special role in long-range planning for their child. Communication is a social as well as cognitive process.

How this is operationalised obviously varies from programme to programme.

Baseline Studies

Evaluative research of more adequate design will be reviewed here. Casey (1978) reports on a programme wherein mothers of four 6–7-year-old autistic children were taught to use manual signs with verbalisations to aid the development of appropriate communication. During 20 daily sessions of 45 minutes in the children's school, the parents were taught signed English, concentrating on nouns and verbs. Mothers then practised under observation in school and in the home, adding social reinforcement for improved verbalisation from the children. The class teachers had previously implemented signing and met with the parents weekly.

The manual sign treatment was added successively by weeks to the children's programmes in a multiple baseline across-subjects design. The data on all four children show marked increases in communicative behaviour and marked decreases in inappropriate behaviour after implementation of signing. The authors argue that training in signing can be coherent, straightforward and deployable in a wide range of situations, and the resultant improved communication decreases inappropriate behaviour. The children's pre-project behaviour included hyperactivity, ritualism, tantrums, destructiveness, screaming, and self-injury — they could not be described as only showing mildly problematic behaviour. No evidence emerged with these four children that signing impeded verbal communication.

More detailed investigation of the generalisation of parent training results was reported by Koegel *et al.* (1978). Four parents and seven autistic children participated in a brief training programme, in which the adults first attempted to teach a child a randomly assigned behaviour alone (i.e. without training or help). If unsuccessful, a brief demonstration was given to the parent, who tried again. Success brought a new target behaviour, failure another demonstration. After a predetermined exposure to this form of training, an alternative form incorporating lectures and video-tape modelling designed to teach generalisable skills was instituted. Detailed results showed clearly that the parents' untrained attempts produced no changes in child behaviour. The modelling procedure resulted in changed parent behaviour and changed child behaviour which was in both cases specific to the modelled task and did not generalise, but the broader (and lengthier) training resulted in the parents developing the skills to teach many tasks effectively, with excellent rates of change in child behaviour.

In the second phase of this project, Koegel *et al.* attempted to discriminate the relative effect of the different components of the generalised training programme (the first video-tape on ante-cedents, the second video-tape on consequences, with and without the lectures). Subjects were three miscellaneous adults and six autistic children, aged 8–13 years. Adult teaching behaviour improved after training, but in a way which was specific to the con-tent of the training input. The children's behaviour showed some improvement, but none of the adults produced consistent improve-ments in the children without having seen *both* video-tapes. However, the video-tapes did seem effective without lectures or the presence of a human teacher. Whether video materials alone would be effective with less well-motivated adult subjects is a matter for conjecture. Koegel *et al.* note that the parents trained via human contact seemed much more confident.

The question of temporal generalisation (maintenance of gains) is addressed by Harris *et al.* (1981). The mothers and fathers of eleven pre-school autistic children were taught to use operant procedures to develop speech in their children. The parents were trained in two small groups, each meeting weekly for ten weeks, covering behaviour modification and speech training skills and utilising lecture, written texts, live and video demonstration, revision sessions, discussion, and review of specific programmes (the children were never present).

At post-treatment, the children showed significant gains in pre-speech and speech skills as indicated by observational data. Children who had acquired at least verbal imitative skills made greater progress than those who had not. At follow-up assessment one year later, the children had maintained their gains, but had not improved significantly from immediate post-treatment levels. The importance of ongoing support for parents is thus underlined.

An even briefer training programme is described by Simpson (1978). Titled the 'Severe Personal Adjustment Program', it incor-porates three sequential audio-visual presentations and a work-shop manual for group leaders, and is designed to impart behaviour modification skills. Knowledge tests to check participant understanding level at each session are included. Procedures for follow-up sessions are provided. Simpson reports data showing that 85 per cent of programme parents were able to effect behaviour changes in the children that the parents targeted. Data on generalisation and maintenance are less forthcoming, however.

Controlled Studies

Evaluation utilising control groups seems to be the speciality of the London group associated primarily with the name of Patricia Howlin, who described (1981a, b) the results of an 18-month parent training programme for 16 autistic boys aged 3–11 years, using the procedures reported in Howlin *et al.* (1973). A short-term untreated matched control group of 16 boys was used to assess the effectiveness of the programme over the first six months, and a second matched control group — members of which had received hospital treatment, but not home training — was compared with experimentals at 18 month follow-up.

At six-month follow-up, the control group showed no improvement, while the experimental group had made substantial gains in use of communicative speech and decreased use of non-verbal substitutes. However, improvements in the experimental group's use of more syntactically complex utterances did not reach statistical significance compared with the control group.

The subsequent follow-up at 18 months related to a period of a year during which contact between professionals and programme parents had been faded to a minimum. The improvements found at six months were maintained over the longer period, but few signs of continuing acceleration were evident. Comparisons with the second control group showed experimental children to be superior, although they were on average considerably younger. However, this difference did not reach statistical significance, possibly owing to large group variances in small samples. Qualitative analyses of language (other than syntactical complexity) favoured the experimental group throughout. It should be remembered that the programme aimed to modify many other skills in addition to language, and progress in this area is reported by Hemsley *et al.* (1978). As in other studies, the least verbal children at the outset made least progress.

Hemsley *et al.* give examples of cases in which detailed data demonstrate marked changes in parent behaviour and consequently child behaviour as a result of involvement in the programme. Attention control, attachment to transitional objects, phobias and tantrums were all successfully modified. At six-month follow-up, the experimental group showed half as much ritualism and twice as much co-operative behaviour, while the control group showed no change.

Process data indicated that the experimental parents had spent no extra time with their children, but had merely utilised available time in a more effective way. Experimental parents had increased their interaction with the child during available time spent together by 50 per cent, while controls showed no change. Experimental parents had doubled their use of praise and correction, gesture and physical prompts, while controls showed no change, and programme parents had improved the quality of their language interaction with their children. Given the variousness of the experimental children, the consistency of these findings is remarkable.

At 18-month follow-up, parents were asked systematically about the frequency and severity of various social and behavioural abnormalities. The findings indicated that the experimental children showed significantly less deviant behaviour than the control group, including much less ritualism and stereotyping, and much more normal peer relationships.

As these workers point out, generalisation is (by definition) more difficult to establish with autistic children than it is with any others; set against that, however, autistic children do tend to improve spontaneously with age. Hence the necessity of control groups, but the results shown are highly creditable — if not the best possible given a perfect world. Although the programme was lengthy, time devoted per week per family was relatively short, and certainly much less than that deemed necessary by Lovaas (1977). Compared with institutionalisation or outpatient professional treatment, the approach is clearly highly cost-effective.

Reviews

Additional early studies are mentioned in Carpenter and Augustine (1973), viz. those of Tufts and Holliday (1959), Sommers *et al.* (1959), Sommers (1962), and Carrier (1970), all of whom successfully trained mothers to assist in the remediation of articulation disorders.

Substantive reviews are provided from a North American perspective by Schumaker and Sherman (1978) and Howlin (1980). The most recent and recommendable review, however, is that of Howlin (1984). This suffers a little from insufficient discrimination between the extremely various subjects in the studies reviewed (from children with specific articulation problems to severely autistic children), but includes several additional references not mentioned here and useful summary tables.

Howlin considers the language environment of normal children (and the effect of parental speech) as compared with that of linguistically handicapped children. Her review of the involvement of parents in language 'therapy' covers techniques used, type of child involved, levels of parental involvement, evaluation research designs, different treatment effects, and the influence of parental competence. It is noted that operant programmes have been by far the most popular.

As is usual, the studies with the most sophisticated research designs draw the least sweeping conclusions, with control group studies being most pessimistic. Well discussed is the doubtful relevance of traditional statistical analysis to small samples, and the need for more detailed consideration of individual differences in response to treatment (aptitude × treatment interaction). Howlin notes that the evidence supports the view that parents can be trained to act effectively as therapists for their own children, but wonders whether 'the key question should be, not *whether* language training works, but for whom it works'. Given our present state of knowledge, this is a highly pragmatic question, but considering the rate of development of knowledge in this field over the last decade, it may reflect a pessimistically static view of the universe.

Summary

There is evidence that parent training in language development is effective when commenced before the children are 6 months old. With 4-year-olds, parental tutoring proved more effective than Direct Instruction procedures. Paraprofessionals using reinforcement also proved successful and could generalise skills to other children.

Parents and peers have been successfully trained to remediate articulation problems in children. Parents have successfully initiated vocalisation in non-verbal children by modelling, prompting and reinforcing, although generalisation post-programme was suspect. A traditional speech therapy format operated as a demonstration in the home does not appear to be effective.

Brief centre-based training can be effective with some well-motivated parents, providing a detailed structure is provided for work at home. Programmes with home-based support built in are much more likely to show generalisation to the home, however good performance may be in the centre.

Parents who present good speech models by using short statements and avoiding questions facilitate language development in children with Down's syndrome. Given objectives to work towards, some such parents discover this for themselves, but others can be successfully trained. An earlier (controlled) study of this kind produced disappointing and confusing results, but a later one (uncontrolled) reinforced the *positive* findings.

Specific centre-based training in generalisation of parent skills to the home has proved successful, resulting in gain rates for Down's children comparable to those of 'normal' children. Generalisation training to ensure transfer of procedures from specific 'teaching' sessions to free play situations has also proved successful.

Autistic children are few in number, but have attracted much research attention as they constitute a difficult population to remediate. Early individual case studies reported were optimistic, inevitably. Some rather loosely structured work from the USA is reported.

Training parents in signing has been found to be straightforward and effective in improving communication and consequently reducing deviant behaviour. There is considerable evidence that very specific and narrow training is unlikely to produce generalisation, except with particularly competent parents. Generally, parents learn what they are taught, and broad training is required to give parents wide-ranging and flexible skills.

The substantial work of the London group suggests that parental training can be extremely effective in improving children's language in several respects in the short run (six months), but in the longer run — with the fading of professional support — acceleration slows and becomes specific to simpler features of language, particularly in relation to control groups. However, associated training to remediate deviant behavioural features of autism shows better long-term maintenance in comparison with controls.

Generally, the work in this field has been methodical. Both lengthy, highly detailed training and relatively brief, naturalistic training have shown success — the latter not necessarily with the most challenging population, and the former sometimes showing poor generalisation. Children with the highest initial level of skills tend to improve most. Training methods have been largely behavioural, very frequently featuring modelling, practice and feedback, with considerable use of video and parent recording at home. Much of the work has been largely home-based, with good control shown over process variables.

Generalisation results have been reasonably positive, particularly if facilitating procedures are built into the programme and support is faded rather than suddenly terminated. Generalisation to a wide range of socio-economic status and parent motivation has not been well demonstrated. Long-term follow-up results are reasonably positive, with gains at least maintained in most cases, even if programmes do not result in continued acceleration. This compares very favourably with the results from institutional placement, and cost-effectiveness is very much greater.

References

Ayllon, T. and Roberts, M.D. (1975) 'Mothers as Educateurs for their Children', in T. Thompson and W.S. Dockens (eds.), *Applications of Behavior Modification* (New York: Academic Press)

Bailey, J.S. *et al.* (1971) 'Modification of Articulation Errors of Pre-delinquents by their Peers', *Journal of Applied Behavior Analysis*, 4, 265-81

Beveridge, M. and Jerrams, A. (1981) 'Parental Involvement in Language Development: An Evaluation of a School-based Parental Assistance Plan', *British Journal of Educational Psychology*, 51, 3, 259-69

Carpenter, R.L. and Augustine, L.E. (1973) 'A Pilot Training Program for Parent—Clinicians', *Journal of Speech and Hearing Disorders*, 38, 48-58

Carrier, J. (1970) 'A Program for Articulation Therapy Administered by Mothers', *Journal of Speech and Hearing Disorders*, 35, 344-53

Casey, L.O. (1978) 'Development of Communicative Behavior in Autistic Children: A Parent Program Using Manual Signs', *Journal of Autism and Childhood Schizophrenia*, 8, 1, 45-59

Cheseldine, S. and McConkey, R. (1979) 'Parental Speech to Young Down's Syndrome Children: An Intervention Study', *American Journal of Mental Deficiency*, 83, 6, 612-20

Davis, S. and Marcus, L.M. (1980) 'Involving Parents in the Treatment of their Severely Communication-disordered Children', *Journal of Pediatric Psychology*, 5, 2, 189-98

Fowler, W. and Swenson, A. (1979) 'The Influence of Early Language Stimulation on Development: Four Studies', *Genetic Psychology Monographs*, 100, 1, 73-109

Goldstein, S.B. and Lanyon, R.I. (1971) 'Parent—Clinicians in the Language Training of an Autistic Child', *Journal of Speech and Hearing Disorders*, 36, 4, 552-60

Harris, S.L. *et al.* (1981) The Acquisition of Language Skills by Autistic Children: Can Parents Do the Job?', *Journal of Autism and Development Disorders, 11,* 4, 373-84

Hemsley, R. *et al.* (1978) 'Treating Autistic Children in a Family Context', in M. Rutter and E. Schopler (eds.), *Autism: A Reappraisal of Concepts and Treatment* (New York: Plenum Press)

Howlin, P. (1980) 'The Home Treatment of Autistic Children', in L.A. Hersov *et al.* (eds.), *Language and Language Disorders in Children* (Oxford: Pergamon Press)

Howlin, P. (1981a) 'The Results of a Home-based Language Training Programme with Autistic Children', *British Journal of Disorders of Communication, 16,* 2, 73-88

Howlin, P. (1981b) 'The Effectiveness of Operant Language Training with Autistic Children', *Journal of Autism and Developmental Disorders, 11,* 1, 89-105

Howlin, P. (1984) 'Parents as Therapists: A Critical Review', in D.J. Muller (ed.), *Remediating Children's Language: Behavioural and Naturalistic Approaches* (London: Croom Helm/San Diego: College-Hill Press)

Howlin, P. *et al.* (1973) 'A Home-based Approach to the Treatment of Autistic Children', *Journal of Autism and Childhood Schizophrenia, 3,* 4, 308-36

Jeffree, D.M. (1978) 'Language and Learning: Parental Involvement Project', *Journal of the British Association of Teachers of the Deaf, 2,* 1, 28-31

Jeffree, D.M. and Cashdan, A. (1971) 'Severely Subnormal Children and their Parents: An Experiment in Language Improvement', *British Journal of Educational Psychology, 41,* 184-94

Koegel, R.L. *et al.* (1978) 'Generalization of Parent-training Results', *Journal of Applied Behavior Analysis, 11,* 1, 95-109

Lovaas, O.I. (1977) 'Parents as Therapists', in M. Rutter and E. Schopler (eds.), *Autism: A Reappraisal of Concepts and Treatment* (New York: Plenum Press)

Lovaas, O.I. *et al.* (1973) 'Some Generalization and Follow-up Measures on Autistic Children in Behavior Therapy', *Journal of Applied Behavior Analysis, 6,* 131-66

McConkey, R. (1979) 'Reinstating Parental Involvement in the Development of Communication Skills', *Child Care Health and Development, 5,* 1, 17-27

MacDonald, J.D. *et al.* (1974) 'An Experimental Parent-assisted Treatment Program for Preschool Language-delayed Children', *Journal of Speech and Hearing Disorders, 39,* 4, 395-415

Marcus, L.M. *et al.* (1978) 'Improvement in Teaching Effectiveness in Parents of Autistic Children', *Journal of the American Academy of Child Psychiatry, 17,* 4, 625-39

Miller, S.J. and Sloane, H.N. (1976) 'The Generalization Effects of Parent Training Across Stimulus Settings', *Journal of Applied Behavior Analysis, 9,* 3, 355-70

Mulac, A. and Tomlinson, C.N. (1977) 'Generalization of an Operant Remediation Program for Syntax with Language Delayed Children', *Journal of Communication Disorders, 10,* 3, 231-43

Risley, T.R. and Wolf, M.M. (1967) 'Experimental Manipulation of Autistic Behaviors and Generalization into the Home', in S.W. Bijou and D.M. Baer (eds.), *Child Development: Readings in Experimental Analysis* (New York: Appleton-Century-Crofts)

Rosenfeld, A.H. (1978) 'Parents as Cotherapists with Autistic Children', (Chapel Hill, North Carolina: North Carolina University) (E.R.I.C. ED175186, EC120041)

Salzberg, C.L. and Villani, T.V. (1983) 'Speech Training by Parents of Down's Syndrome Toddlers: Generalization Across Settings and Instructional Contexts', *American Journal of Mental Deficiency, 87,* 4, 403-13

Schumaker, J.B. and Sherman, J.A. (1978) 'Parents as Intevention Agents', in R.L.
    Schiefelbusch (ed.), *Language Intervention Strategies* (Baltimore: University
    Park Press)
Simpson, R.L. (1978) *Parenting the Exceptional Child* (Kansas: University of
    Kansas Press)
Sommers, R. (1962) 'Factors in Effectiveness of Mothers Trained to Aid in Speech
    Correction', *Journal of Speech and Hearing Disorders, 27*, 178-86
Sommers, R. *et al.* (1959) 'Training Parents of Children with Functional
    Misarticulation', *Journal of Speech and Hearing Research, 2*, 258-65
Spiegel, B.B. *et al.* (1982) 'Training Parents of Language Disordered Children:
    Language Form vs. Communicative Style', *Perceptual and Motor Skills, 54, 2,*
    650
Stevenson, P. *et al.* (1982) 'The Evaluation of Home Based Speech Therapy for
    Language Delayed Children in an Inner City Area', *British Journal of Disorders
    of Communication, 17, 3*, 141-8
Tufts, L. and Holliday, A. (1959) 'Effectiveness of Trained Parents as Speech
    Therapists', *Journal of Speech and Hearing Disorders, 24*, 395-401
Whitehurst, G.J. *et al.* (1972) 'Delayed Speech Studied in the Home',
    Developmental Psychology, 7, 2, 169-77

10 SENSORY IMPAIRMENT

The literature search in this area has yielded little work of real sub-stance, particularly with respect to visual impairment. To some extent this might have been expected, given the very small numbers of children with visual impairment. Even allowing for that, this area of parent training seems grossly under-researched, especially since it is now widely accepted that pre-school detection and intervention are crucial for handicapped children, particularly those with hearing impairment.

Hearing Impairment

There are a number of papers describing possible or actual parent training programmes, but few cite hard evaluative data. Rossett (1974) describes a programme designed to facilitate communi-cation between hearing parents and their hearing-impaired adolescents, which is based on group discussions stimulated by pictorial representations of everyday problems faced by such families. For the parents of a hearing-impaired child there is a danger of falling into the habit of making fewer communication overtures to the child. When this is compounded by the self-preoccupation which is often a feature of non-handicapped ado-lescents, let alone the hearing impaired, severe tensions in the family can result. All this may be true, and Rossett's projective visual materials are certainly interesting, but no evidence on their effectiveness is cited.

The role and style of the parent educator is discussed by Simmons-Martin (1975), who proceeds to describe a programme of weekly one-hour sessions of parent training in a simulated apartment. Teaching methods included some modelling and video-tape feedback (micro-teaching), together with written instruction. Individual and group sessions were scheduled. However, the objectives of the programme as described are somewhat nebulous and no evaluative data are mentioned.

Stibick (1972) reports on a programme for five families which included 13 hearing and five hearing-impaired children. All the children were present at the sessions, and the hearing siblings taught the hearing impaired according to a curriculum determined by the sibling tutors as they went along. The subjective view of the participants was that relationships between the children in a family greatly improved, but no objective data are cited.

A more substantial programme is reported by Clark and Watkins (1978): the SKI-HI Model is a model for identification, language facilitation and family support for hearing-impaired children aged 0–6. Home visits were used to cover a curriculum which included hearing aid tolerance and management, auditory training, language training and multi-media communication. Information was also delivered about other support services. Again, the evaluative component is weak.

With the work of Smith and O'Reilly (1981), we begin to approach programmes with some empirical validation. Rural Newfoundland parents of 27 pre-school children with severe or profound hearing impairment were introduced to a one-year parent training programme during a four-day residential workshop with their children. The parents were then loaned a video playback unit and monitor to take home, enabling them to view a series of teaching video-tapes sent to them monthly. The parents were also loaned an auditory trainer ('speech trainer'), which they were to use at least once a day with the child in a language teaching session modelled on one seen on the video-tapes. A teacher of the deaf visited each parent at home once, and subsequently conducted weekly telephone counselling sessions with the parents.

During the one-year programme, the children on average gained 8.6 months in language age for receptive skills and 5.6 months for expressive skills. These results still imply marked delay in speech and language, but are better than those normally expected from this population, particularly in a rural setting where services are hard to deliver and feedback and monitoring difficult and expensive to arrange. The small, cohesive families where a parent was in employment did best. This project is an interesting example of the imaginative and thorough use of 'distance teaching' in a rural area with difficulties of client access.

Equally thorough, but reported on a smaller scale, is the work of Mira (1972), based on the Parent Home Centre or Preschool for the Deaf at the University of Kansas Medical Centre. Part of the work of the centre is to train the parents of hearing-impaired youngsters in operant behaviour managment techniques. These techniques were found more successful with hearing-impaired children than with some other groups. Children who cannot hear have more reason than most to be frustrated and angry, and their parents are at a marked disadvantage in attempts to admonish or 'reason' with them, particularly from any distance. In addition, some parents try to compensate for a child's handicap by relaxing normal disciplinary expectations, and hearing-impaired children can turn a deaf ear to an unwelcome instruction just as much as an ordinary child, if not more so. Mira reports on five specimen case studies, with striking AB design results presented graphically, in which absconding, hitting and tantrum behaviours were reduced and aid-usage and social behaviours increased via parent training on a one-to-one basis.

In addition to parent training, there is a substantial body of research on using children to modify the behaviour of other children with special needs. Professionals training parents to train siblings to train target children may sound an unduly complex quaternary system of service delivery, but Bennett (1973) demonstrated the feasibility of this most convincingly. Previous work by Guess *et al.* (1968) and Sailor (1971) had demonstrated the successful use of operant techniques in teaching mentally retarded children the generative use of the allomorphs -s and -z, but Bennett effectively taught a $4^{1}/_{2}$-year-old girl to teach her 3-year-old sister the expressive use of the plural -s — a sound which she could only *hear* within a range of three feet.

The training utilised pictorial materials for initial stimulus and also for generalisation probes. The tutor was taught by modelling to teach the tutee in the same way, using a Precision Teaching format and edible reinforcement for the tutee and tutor which was contingent upon the tutee's success. The tutor dispensed token reinforcement to the tutee for success on each trial, but was only rewarded herself if the tutee met the criterion target for that session. Subsequent generalisation probes were presented by the author without reinforcement, with entirely satisfactory results. Training the tutor had involved three sessions of 20 minutes, and the elder girl had successfully taught her sister the use of the plural allomorph in seven sessions of 20–35 minutes. The tutor's maximum procedural error rate was 12 per cent, despite signs of her becoming bored towards the end of the (necessarily repetitive) programme.

A larger scale programme is reported by Luterman (1971),

which served 44 children over three years. A nursery programme for pre-school deaf children which emphasised parallel parent training was established, but because of its passive recruitment policy had a distinct middle-class bias in its clients. The parents attended the nursery two days per week over two terms, the time being devoted to observing their children in the nursery, tutoring their own and other children, and participating in group discussions. Two hearing children also attended the nursery, serving to give the parents a normative model for comparison.

Luterman gives little detail of parental training format and curriculum adopted, and the evaluation data given are likewise weak. Parental questionnaire data indicated that the vast majority of parents were satisfied with the programme. A very large proportion of the children were subsequently enrolled in ordinary school classes. Classroom teachers rated the performance of programme children in comparison with non-programme deaf children, and marked superiority was indicated for the former. To what extent this reflects the socio-economic bias of the programme participants is debatable. Luterman also provides an interesting discussion of practical problems encountered, including professionals' inflexibilities, the uselessness of written instruction, and the low participation of the low-SES parents in the face of middle-class dominance and insufficiently structured training.

By far the most substantial work in this area is that of McConnell and Horton (1970), who report on a three-year home teaching programme for 94 deaf pre-schoolers of mean age 2 years and 4 months. McConnell and Horton note how services for the hearing impaired still tend to be clinic-based. They feel that clinicians are often quite unclear about the educational needs of the child, while educators are often unclear about the potential of a child's residual hearing, and thus tend to over-emphasise the visual modality. The authors regard early screening, detection and the experimental investigation of the most effective hearing aid and its management as crucial. Thus the initial period of involvement in the programme was preoccupied with trials of aids and parent training in their management, coupled with evaluation of the effectiveness of the aid in the natural environment (i.e. home).

Subsequently, the parent curriculum covered: selection and constant repetition of sounds to develop; modelling attention and visible response to sound stimuli; consistent sound-source association and positive reinforcement; talking to the child in simple, structured phrases about current high-interest topics; talking close to the child and into the aid microphone; the use of inflection, intonation and gesture; expanding child utterances; maintaining ear- and eye-contact with the child; and establishing 'talking times'. The emphasis was firmly upon language intertwined with everyday experience and serving an immediate useful function for the child. The training was largely individual, but included some group sessions. Contact with the programme was weekly, and training was via verbal and written instruction and demonstration in the context of a domestically furnished simulated home. The parents practised on their own children in the 'Home', and were guided, monitored and reinforced by the teacher and audiologist working with them. Fathers were required to attend at least once. Specific goals were set for each family to work towards at home.

Evaluation data are presented on only 28 children, classed in three groups. During a period of 27 months, one group gained over 35 months on language tests, another group almost 19 months, and the least successful group over 8 months. This represented acceleration and considerably exceeded normal expectation, and it was noteworthy that the non-verbal (performance) development of the children remained linear. Their performance on one language test was twice that of a small non-programme comparison group. The children's ability to *utilise* the amplification from their aid improved, with an improved mean threshold response to spoken voice of 20db. The parents pressured for continuance of the programme when federal aid ended, and were successful. The authors note that the more middle-class parents tended to produce the largest language gains, but their general conclusion seems entirely justified: 'the project demonstrated that early intervention in childhood deafness can substantially reduce the degree of handicap in later years'.

McConnell (1974) gives a more recent review of the work of the 'Parent Teaching Home', which is followed on by a specialised nursery programme incorporating much parental involvement and training. In this report, a more detailed account of the day-to-day process of the work of the 'Home' is offered. McConnell reports further work in which the utterances of programme children were compared with non-programme hearing impaired children and normal children. On many aspects of language analysis, the early intervention group was very similar to the normal hearing group, and significantly different from the non-programme group. Data on subsequent educational achievement as measured by the Metropolitan Achievement Tests is also outlined, demonstrating that a small sample of programme children perform significantly worse in general attainment only in mathematics. McConnell further notes that the combined cost of his parent training programme and ordinary school placement is only one-third of the cost of placement in the State Residential School for the Deaf.

Visual Impairment

A programme for ten blind infants who were not otherwise handicapped was conducted by Fraiberg *et al.* (1969), wherein home visits were made twice monthly to work with mother and child. Focusing on the first 18 months of life, the programme attempted to train mothers in non-visual communication with their infants, reinforcing actions with words in a tactile–auditory modality. No evaluative data are cited.

Jackson *et al.* (1971) ran a two-year project for 15 pre-school rubella deaf–blind children. Mothers and teachers periodically completed rating scales on the children, covering self-help and gross motor skills and activities that stimulated visual and auditory responses. Parents received home visits from teachers, visited the special nursery class weekly, and worked as paid aides. The children showed some cognitive gains at the conclusion of the programme — although in the absence of a control group or normative comparison data, it is difficult to know how much of this was attributable to programme effects.

An early education programme for visually and otherwise handicapped children is described by Robinson (1980) in what is termed a 'Replication Manual'. Project ForSight aimed to help parents teach their children at home through a curriculum labelled 'Vision-up'. No evaluation evidence is given.

Davis (1980) outlines a similar project, describing procedures for the first day of parent participation in the classroom, an initial package of written information, charting of adult–child activities, training modules, home visiting, parent meetings and counselling groups, and so forth. Again, no supportive objective data are supplied.

Summary

There is a paucity of evaluative evidence in this area. Parents of hearing-impaired children in rural areas can be effectively served by mailed training videos combined with an initial residential training and telephone monitoring. Parents can be trained to use operant techniques to modify problematic behaviour in hearing-impaired children. There are examples of highly successful training of such children carried out by siblings under parental supervision. Parent training in conjunction with child attendance at special nursery classes has been a popular model, but rarely well evaluated. A more clearly structured programme operating from a simulated 'home' has produced the most convincing results so far, but the impact on low-SES families remains in doubt. Parent training can improve effective acuity using aids and markedly accelerate language development. Some programmes for the visually impaired are described in the literature, but the search has not located any parent programmes for such children which cite outcome data. A great deal more methodical evaluation research requires to be conducted in the area of sensory impairment.

References

Bennett, C.W. (1973) 'A Four and a Half Year Old as a Teacher of her Hearing Impaired Sister: A Case Study', *Journal of Communication Disorders, 6*, 67-75

Clark, T.C. and Watkins, S. (1978) *The SKI HI Model: A Comprehensive Model for Identification, Language Facilitation and Family Support for Hearing Handicapped Children through Home Management, Ages Birth to Six* (3rd edn.) (E.R.I.C. EC 112418, ED 162451)

Davis, J.A. (1980) *Working with Parents of Visually Impaired, Multihandicapped Infants. Peabody Model Vision Project* (Chicago, Illinois: Stoelting Co.) (E.R.I.C. EC 140582)

Fraiberg, S. *et al.* (1969) 'An Educational Program for Blind Infants', *Journal of Special Education, 3*, 121-40

Guess, D. *et al.* (1968) 'An Experimental Analysis of Linguistic Development: The Productive Use of the Plural Morpheme', *Journal of Applied Behavior Analysis, 1*, 297-306

Jackson, E. *et al.* (1971) *An Experimental Education Program Combining Classroom and Home Instruction for Preschool Deaf–Blind Children* (San Francisco, California: San Francisco State College): Cited in: E. Levitt and S. Cohen (1975), 'An Analysis of Selected Parent-Involvement Programs for Handicapped and Disadvantaged Children', *Journal of Special Education, 9, 4*, 345-65

Luterman, D.M. (1971) 'A Parent-oriented Nursery Program for Preschool Deaf Children: A Follow-up Study', *Volta Review, 73, 2*, 106-12

McConnell, F. (1974) 'The Parent Teaching Home: An Early Intervention

Program for Hearing-impaired Children', *Peabody Journal of Education, 51,* 162-70

McConnell, F. and Horton, K.B. (1970) *A Home Teaching Program for Parents of Very Young Deaf Children. Final Report* (Nashville, Tennessee: School of Medicine, Nashville University) (E.R.I.C. EC 022722, ED 039664)

Mira, M. (1972) 'Behavior Modification Applied to Training Young Deaf Children', *Exceptional Children, 39,* 225-9

Robinson, L.W. (1980) *Project For Sight: Early Education Program for Multihandicapped Visually Impaired Children. Replication Manual* (Austin, Texas: Texas School for the Blind) (E.R.I.C. ED 209814, EC 140328)

Rossett, A. (1974) 'Special Strategies for a Special Probem: Improving Communication between Hearing Impaired Adolescents and their Parents', *Volta Review, 76,* 231-8

Sailor, W. (1971) 'Reinforcement and Generalization of Productive Plural Allomorphs in Two Retarded Children', *Journal of Applied Behavior Analysis, 4,* 305-10

Simmons-Martin, A. (1975) 'Facilitating Parent–Child Interactions Through the Education of Parents', *Journal of Research and Development in Education, 8, 2,* 96-102

Smith, C.N. and O'Reilly, B. (1981) 'Home Centred Video-tape Counseling Program for Parents of Pre-school Hearing Impaired Children', *ACEHI Journal, 7, 4,* 172-84

Stibick, M. (1982) 'Pilot Program for Siblings of Acoustically Impaired Children', *Volta Review, 74, 6,* 352d-352f

11 DEVELOPMENTAL DELAY

In Britain, the term 'developmentally delayed' is used to refer to a child who might otherwise be called 'mentally handicapped', 'severely educationally subnormal' or having 'severe learning difficulties', and this group is the subject of what follows. In the USA, 'developmental delay', 'developmental disability' or 'mental retardation', are often used as labels for this population, but occasionally 'developmental delay' is also applied to children with quite minor skill deficits, thereby generating confusion. Although most of the work on mentally handicapped or retarded populations will be found here, some relevant work also appears in the chapters on 'Language Dysfunction', 'Learning Difficulties', 'Behaviour Problems' and 'Physical and Multiple Handicap'.

Severe mental and/or physical handicaps differ from some of the less immediately obvious problems discussed elsewhere in this volume in that the emotional impact on the parents at the birth of the child is often immediate and shattering. This is often compounded by the paucity of accurate information and lack of empathetic counselling which is still all too common in medical institutions. However, parent training and support programmes in this area are typically preoccupied with raising skill levels in the child, rather than offering emotional support to the parents which might enable them to function better all round, including as teachers of their children. Tymchuk's (1975) description of a parent training programme combining psychodynamic and behavioural strategies is thus something of a rarity, although Attwood (1979) lists others which are oriented towards family therapy. Of course, some apparently skill-based programmes do incorporate a substantial strand of socio-emotional support, whether planned or not.

For those relatively new to this area, the book by Mittler and McConachie (1983) on approaches to partnership between parents, professionals and mentally handicapped people is highly recommended for giving a feel for the work in a lucid and non-technical way. Those wishing to read more widely would do well to consult the reading list prepared by the British Institute of Mental Handicap (1981) on parental training.

Relatively little English-language literature of any substance from exotic climes was turned up in the literature search, which seems curious in view of the universality of developmental delay. Descriptive accounts of work in Western Europe (excluding the UK) and the Indian sub-continent are available in McConachie (1983) and Chacko (1981) respectively. A small number of relevant items from Canada and Australia/New Zealand were retrieved and, purely for the sake of simplicity, these are included under the discussion of work in the USA and UK respectively.

Surveys of provision in the US are provided by Stock *et al.* (1975), who cover eight programmes; the Coordinating Office for Regional Resource Centers (1976), who name 25 different programmes; and Noone (1980), who names 92 different programmes. The vast majority of these do not appear to have generated any publicly available evaluation data. In the UK, a survey of Portage-type provision has been reported (Bendall *et al.*, 1984; Bendall, 1985), providing little evidence of any greater consciousness of the need for evaluation.

Nevertheless, a large bulk of evaluative data does exist on *some* programmes, most notably the Portage and related systems, and for assimilation purposes these studies are grouped into those utilising a weak research design and those using a more robust evaluative framework. Inevitably, categorisation into one or the other sector becomes arbitrary at the margin. Within these groupings, sub-sets of studies considering UK and US, Portage and 'other' studies will be found.

Weak Evaluation Research

Portage Programme

The Portage Program was first established in Portage, Wisconsin, in 1969 (Shearer and Shearer, 1972). Professional or paraprofessional home teachers visit families weekly, identify and agree new skills the parent would like to teach the child, agree strategies for teaching the skills, write these down in a programme, demonstrate the teaching procedures, supervise parental imitation of the model, give feedback and reinforcement, then return the next week to review progress towards agreed criteria of success as indicated by records kept by the parents and a probe administered by the visitor as necessary. The general procedures are very much within a framework of behavioural objectives, behaviour modification and Precision Teaching.

Associated materials are the Portage checklist (developmentally sequenced behavioural objectives in language, cognitive, self-help, locomotor and social skills), a kit of cards providing specific teaching suggestions for each of the checklist objectives, and 'activity charts' on which each teaching programme is specified in detailed Precision Teaching terms. The work of the home visitors is monitored by a supervisor at weekly meetings, and the whole project is advised and monitored by a management team, which is usually multi-disciplinary.

Portage costs little to operate in comparison with other facilities and services for the pre-school developmentally delayed. Holland and Noaks (1982) estimated that compared with a year's Portage involvement, special fostering would be five times more expensive, residential special school 14 times more expensive, hospital placement 17 times more expensive, and placement in a social services residential establishment 19 times more expensive — although it should be noted that these figures were cited for political purposes.

Given the structured behavioural nature of Portage, one might expect consistently robust evaluation research designs. This is unfortunately not the case, and many programmes cite no data at all. The original results of Shearer and Shearer (1972) keep cropping up in a much abbreviated form in non-technical articles (e.g. Boyd and Boyd, 1974), and the distortions accruing from this practice are likely to become part of folk mythology and act as a disincentive to the consultation of original sources.

Koerber *et al.* (1979) describe a 'Neighbourhood Support System' in which neighbourhood mothers were trained as home visitors to families with handicapped children under 3 years of age, but evaluative data includes little more than details of levels of service utilisation. The Texas Tech University (1980) reports on a three-year project more firmly based on the Portage model, which served a total of 80 families of low socio-economic status in a rural area. In addition to standard procedures, family scrapbooks were kept and group meetings of programme families arranged to foster a group project ethos. Evaluation data are weak and impressionistic, however.

In the UK, Wishart *et al.* (1980) used a questionnaire to investigate parental opinions and feelings about the development of their children, comparing the response of parents who had experienced a Portage-type input with that of a group of parents of 'normal' children. Agreement between both parents of a child was high, and positive feelings towards the Portage approach were elicited, although parents of the most severely handicapped preferred full daycare.

Daly (1980) reports on a project servicing seven children, noting high levels of staff attendance, completion of 84 per cent of weekly targets, a 100 per cent parental subjective report that their children progressed faster when on Portage, and details of numbers of skills learned by each child in each area. While Daly's view that 'it would be hard to conclude that the project was anything other than successful' seems fair, many more objective and comparative data are needed before more specific conclusions can be drawn.

A less detailed report emanates from Holland (1981), in whose project the home visits were carried out by health visitors, medical personnel with a community health advisory and preventive role. Only four half-days of in-service training were provided for them. Descriptive and anecdotal information on child progress is given, as are the visitors' subjective views on the success of the project.

Ellender (1983) also eschewed the 'quasi-empirical paradigm'. Data on the progress of individual children is, of course, automatically available from Portage records, and Ellender used questionnaires to compare the views on service provision of Portage with those of non-Portage parents of handicapped children. Additionally, questionnaires were administered to project participants in a 'two-way' evaluation paradigm: the management team had to evaluate their own contribution and that of the supervisior, who evaluated the management team's performance, his own and that of the home teacher, who evaluated the performance of the supervisor, herself and the parent, who evaluated the performance of the home teacher and the child (but not herself). Although Ellender's descriptive statistics do not match Daly's (1980), the subjective responses from parents constituted strong endorsement for the Portage approach. Many children had acquired skills which had not been the subject of activity charts, but whether this is attributable to the Portage input cannot be established on the evidence cited. Ellender's account of parental views is fascinating, but not persuasive from a scientific point of view.

There is a good deal of more robust outcome data on Portage, which will be considered in the section on 'Substantial Evaluation

Research', (pp. 250-261). However, the system is complex and detailed, and it is far from clear which components of the model are critical for progress with which children in which families. For some families, a Portage programme may represent 'behavioural over-kill', with consequent implications for cost-effectiveness. Other studies have shown that group meetings, centre-based training, less rigid requirements of parents and much less frequent supportive visits can have an impact on child progress, at least with some families. It is a pity that these 'lighter' interventions have not taken more consistent care in self-evaluation.

Hester Adrian Research Centre Model Programmes

The Hester Adrian Research Centre (HARC) at the University of Manchester began conducting workshops for the parents of mentally handicapped children in 1971, and in 1973 this became the four-year Parent Involvement Project associated with the names of Cliff Cunningham, Dorothy Jeffree and Roy McConkey (Cunningham and Jeffree, 1975; Jeffree and Cunningham, 1975; Jeffree *et al.*, 1977).

Cunningham, in particular, has been a critic of the 'transplant' model of parent training (transmitting professional skills directly to parents blanket-fashion), and an advocate of the 'consumerist' model (offering flexible training and support appropriate to family needs and exigencies as seen by the parents). He has been rather scornful of, *inter alia*, the behavioural high-technology involved in schemes like Portage.

The HARC centre-based workshops were intended to impart the principles of a teaching model to the parents, which would hopefully enable them to design and effect a wide range of interventions at home. The intention was to help parents utilise time spent with the child more efficiently, rather than creating any expectation that they should spend *more* time with the child: the aim was also to make parents independent of professional support, rather than more reliant on it. The teaching model transmitted was a dilute behavioural one, emphasising observation and assessment of the child, selection and analysis of target task, presentation of task with manipulation of antecedents and consequences, and evaluation of the effects of teaching — all very familiar to a Portage mother. As the HARC team notes: 'without precise objectives, flexibility can become random action'.

The parent training consisted of ten core sessions, with a further session of questions to a 'panel of experts' and a follow-up session ten weeks later. Lectures were given by various professionals, demonstrated on film, video or live, and accompanied by written information. Further teaching and discussions took place in 'tutor groups' of 10–13 parents. Unsupervised practice took place at home and was the subject of verbal feedback from the parents at the next tutor group session. A detailed developmental checklist, later to become the PIP (Parental Involvement Project) Developmental Chart, was produced.

Unfortunately, the only evaluative evidence cited is that the attendance of 82 parents involved averaged approximately 90 per cent, and that parental questionnaires were very favourable. It should also be noted that children aged over 6 years were excluded from the programme, and that the majority of participating parents were middle class. The costs to disadvantaged families attending centre-based workshops are discussed elsewhere.

Subsequently, Jeffree *et al.* (1977) conducted a more structured project, which disseminated teaching games with specific objectives in written form to a large number of parents, but also dealt intensively with a random sample of 20 parents, who attended twelve individual sessions with their children and six evening group sessions. The PIP charts were used to identify individualised learning objectives. Teaching games and techniques were demonstrated with the children by a professional, then the parents took over while the professionals monitored progress. These sessions were video-recorded. Parents then implemented the teaching procedures at home, recording results by writing or on tape.

Analysis of the tapes made it possible to chart a child's progress with respect to multiple baselines. Jeffree *et al.* (1977) assert: 'progress was often confirmed by an accelerated learning curve', but only one example is given.

A number of other workers in the UK have adopted the HARC model or derivations thereof, and likewise present evaluative data of a fairly restricted nature. McCall and Thacker (1977) report on a school-based course, which additionally utilised video demonstration. Attendance was 72 per cent and parental ratings and questionnaire responses were very favourable. A home-school communication system to facilitate linkage of continuing work at home and school was established.

Munro (1979) reported the extension of the HARC model to older children (ages unspecified), and analysed audio-tapes of group discussion training sessions throughout a twelve-week course. Changes in parental analysis of problems and responses were apparent, there being a marked shift from 'care-taker' solutions to 'learning' solutions. No evidence on changed parental or child behaviour at home is offered.

Burton *et al.* (1981) also incorporated video demonstration in a course on language stimulation and behavioural techniques which was introduced to parents by a home visit. Evaluation by questionnaire suggested the parents valued the social support of the group more than the didactic input. Moore *et al.* (1981) report on a shorter course, of six weekly meetings, which included children up to 8 years. Parents used the PIP chart then selected an area and target behaviour which they wished to modify, and thus the course focused much more immediately on a pragmatic task. Evaluation again relied on attendance records and questionnaire responses.

Emerson *et al.* (1981) supplemented centre-based sessions, held weekly for between six and eight weeks, with home visits for further feedback and monitoring. Evaluation was by analysis of pre- and post-programme video-recordings of parents teaching the child a specified task. The initial recordings were viewed and discussed by the group, to whom parents also demonstrated with the child the strategies they were using on a currently targeted task. No changes in parental teaching behaviour were revealed by the method of analysis employed, which may have been inappropriate. Questionnaire responses were of doubtful validity, but many children were reported to have progressed.

Finally, Firth (1982) reports on nine eight to twelve week evening workshops catering for 40 families, including one for families of children aged 8–13. A brief 'textbook' was provided, and parents could borrow books of teaching games. Curriculum content was not sequential, but parents kept written records of child progress. Attendance was good, 75 per cent of families attending all sessions, and many fathers participated. Most targeted problems related to communication, feeding and toileting. Of 78 targets, parent records showed success was achieved at follow-up three to four months later in 46 per cent of cases; partial success was reported in a further 26 per cent, work with younger children proving more successful. (Firth reports that home visiting has proved much more successful in modifying the problems of older children.) Pre–post video-recording for one workshop showed some change in parental teaching behaviour. Firth found group workshops no less time-consuming than home visiting.

Other UK Programmes

Attwood (1978) described a series of evening meetings between a multi-disciplinary professional team and the parents of 25 pre-school handicapped children (the 'Croydon workshops'). Separate workshops were operated for parents of children aged 5–11 years and over 11 years. Lectures and written information, observational checklists and small-group discussions were incorporated. Attendance was good (87 per cent), but no other data are cited.

Subsequent workshops for the parents of children aged 5–11 reduced the numbers of professionals and participating parents (Attwood, 1979), and approximated more closely to the HARC model, including also a good deal of emotional support and counselling. Pre-course assessment was undertaken on a home visit, and 'tutor groups' formed by nature of the child's handicap, and modelling and role-play incorporated. Attendance was 80 per cent, and again no other outcome data are cited beyond subjective impressions.

Bevington *et al.* (1978) describe a school-based course for 13 families. Introductory home visits enabled a needs assessment survey to be carried out. Self-help skills and behaviour problems were the most chosen target areas. Behavioural objectives for the parents on the course were then written, but related only to a multiple-choice test of knowledge. Mastery of these 22 objectives varied from 19 per cent to 100 per cent of parents, depending on the objectives. Areas of course curriculum content needing better teaching were thus identified. Follow-up visits for semi-structured interviews at one and three months post-programme were carried out, and all parents except one reported using the methods taught, but few were keeping records. Later work (Cocks and Gardner, 1979) demonstrated the low validity of reliance on knowledge gains in evaluation, and increased emphasis was placed on back-up modelling sessions at home to promote parental behaviour change. Close links between parent and school were advocated to provide continuous support and co-ordination and compatability of teaching programmes.

A large scale programme for the parents of pre-school Down's syndrome children is reported by Ludlow and Allen (1979). The programme group were home visited and counselled and observed in a clinic playgroup setting. Lectures were given by various professionals and mothers asked to keep records of progress. A minority of children with distant addresses were seen at home and attended an 'ordinary' playgroup. Yearly assessment using Stanford-Binet and the Griffiths Scale was carried out on programme children and two comparison groups of non-intervened and institutionalised children.

Socio-economic status of participant families was wide-ranging but somewhat skewed to the upper end. Intervention and non-intervention groups showed similar rates of decline in developmental quotients, while the institutionalised group did worse. Other data purporting to show better speech and personal–social development in the intervened group are based only on post-test data, and the longitudinal data indicate that the groups were not matched at the outset.

Holland and Hattersley (1980) describe a small-scale centre-based programme, targeted on four children aged 6–10 years, and operating via seven monthly sessions. Attendance was 77 per cent for the behaviourally oriented course. Changes on scores in the Alpern and Boll Developmental Schedule did not reach statistical significance, although the parents *felt* the children had showed some change.

Parent workshops were instigated in combination with home visits, toy library provision and liaison with day nurseries by Pollack and Stewart (1982), but the parents 'took over' the workshops and subsequently ran them autonomously. Parental attendance increased and questionnaire returns (n = 32, 91 per cent) showed 78 per cent of parents were satisfied with the group, particularly valuing the emotional support gained from meeting other parents. The parents seemed a great deal more confident in relating to professionals.

Other US Programmes

A large number of idiosyncratic programmes have emerged in the USA during the 1970s and early 1980s. Fredericks *et al.* (1971) describe school-based training of parents by a single lengthy verbal input, parental observation of the child's teacher in class, and parent practice with their child which was video-recorded and later reviewed with feedback. TV sessions were repeated as necessary and two group meetings of all parents were held. Parents recorded details of the written programme of home teaching and returned these to the school daily. In three schools in three cities, 85 per cent of parents had participated. However, 'since all data are individualised, no group results are reported'.

Benson and Ross (1972) describe a programme in which eleven parents volunteered to act as classroom aides for two hours per week, usually with their own children. Two workshops incorporated verbal instruction, written objectives and activities, provision of materials and live demonstration. Monthly group meetings subsequently served to review progress. Details of child progress are given, but no baseline learning rates are specified for comparison. Parental attendance was almost 100 per cent over an eight week period, and the parents asked for additional teaching tasks to carry out at home.

A media package consisting of a four-part slide–sound programme presented over two weeks is described by Latham and Hofmeister (1973). Delivery was via a non-specialist public health nurse. Workbooks and other materials supplemented the behaviourally oriented curriculum. Half of the 20 experimental parents dropped out of the programme, but the children of the remainder were found to have significantly improved on a progress record at two-month follow-up, while a control group did not do so well. Exact details are sparse in this report, however.

A substantial programme of a quite different kind is reported by Bricker and Bricker (1973, 1976), who aimed to blend Piagetian and behavioural frameworks in the service of pre-school children with a wide range of handicaps, as well as some non-delayed children. Parents were trained roughly in sequence in the areas of language, cognitive, motor and social development. Training was via a mixture of one-to-one tuition and weekly group meetings. Written materials, video-tape and live demonstration were included with feedback on parental imitation. In all, 78 children were involved, aged 6 months to 6 years, from low- and middle-SES families. Supportive home visits were provided every four to six weeks for families unable to attend the centre, and a social worker attached to the programme helped with securing welfare benefits. The Brickers describe themselves as adopting a 'cartographical' approach to evaluation. They offer interesting studies of child development in particular skill areas and contrast between teacher and parent teaching styles, but nothing on tangible programme outcomes. In any event it would be difficult to partial the effect of the parent training component and the centre-based teaching of the children by professionals.

The Early Education Project for young Down's Syndrome children in Canada is described by Kysela *et al.* (1976). A behaviourally oriented home teaching service incorporating parental record-keeping on individualised child programmes is coupled with a classroom component, and again the effects of the two components are not partialled. Parents participated in class-room activities. Case studies are reported.

O'Sheilds (1977) compared the relative effectiveness of three delivery systems with 88 children. A Home Visiting Service by paraprofessionals was the most effective (59 per cent improvement in student performance), with a family training service (46 per cent) and classroom teaching service (45 per cent) less so. The home-visiting service was the most cost-effective.

A very large programme of training for professionals, para-professionals and parents using specially developed written and audio-visual materials and assessment and monitoring procedures is reported by the National Association for Retarded Citizens (1979). It is disappointing that such a large programme, covering virtually the whole of the USA, relied merely on a pre–post parental attitude questionnaire for evaluation. Positive shifts were demonstrated, of course.

Considerably more thorough is the Wyoming Infant Stimu-lation Program (WISP) reported by Jelinek and Flamboe (1979). Both centre-based and home-based intervention for children under 3 years of age were provided in a rural area, home-based until the child was 18 months then school-based until the age of 3 years. In the home programme, home visits of 90 minutes involved weekly activity plans, provision of materials, visitor modelling of teaching tech-niques, and weekly reviews of progress made, rather as in the Portage system. Additionally, a range of written instructional materials was available, a 'co-ordinator' made a supervisory visit every two weeks, and a 'parent network' was established to link families with common problems who lived reasonably near to each other. Pre–post measures on developmental profiles and the Bayley Scales indicate quotient gains of from 83 to 95 and 85 to 103, but full data are not available on all children, and the impact of the school-based programme is not partialled out. Parental involvement was good and high satisfaction expressed.

An interesting programme to help parents with career education for handicapped children is described by Vasa *et al.* (1979), but no evaluative data are included.

Project Sunrise is a home-based parent training programme serving children up to 6 years of age in rural Montana, and is reported by Sexton *et al.* (1980) and the Institute for Habilitative Services (1980). Parents successful in the programme could themselves become paraprofessional home visitors. A toy lending library also operated. Pre–post data on a non-representative sample of 20 of the 60 families served indicated that '95% of children showed gains over the anticipated rate in at least 4 of 5 developmental areas charted', but it is not made clear how these anticipations are arrived at, and very little information on the actual teaching behaviour of the visitors is included. Parental satisfaction data are reported.

An eight-week training programme involving both individual and small-group instruction is reported by Sandler and Coren (1981), who followed this up with weekly parent–teacher meetings and further case review meetings of parents and professionals every six weeks. Modelling and parent practice with video-taped feedback were incorporated, as was daily home–school reporting of parent-recorded progress data. Questionnaire data from 26 high-SES parents indicated high satisfaction levels; the authors acknowledge the inherent methodological weaknesses, but cite no other data.

The Play Program of Kuzovich and Yawkey (1982) focused particularly on the parents' use of play routines. Sixteen low-income families of 'mildly' retarded children received weekly play training procedures and activities in a six-month programme. Toys were loaned and home visitors talked about and demonstrated their use and supplied additional written information. Techniques were role-played and practised in and out of the house. Behavioural objectives were set for each session. Evaluation was preoccupied with the quality of play activity, and much emphasis was placed on questionnaires and inventories, including some given orally to the children. The authors claim that pre–post scores show that the programme group of children increased their imaginative play in home and school situations, but in fact the measures used were weak and only half showed significant changes.

Substantial Evaluation Research

For readers with any powers of concentration left thus far into this heavyweight area, higher quality research will now be considered, reviewing first Portage and then 'other' programmes in the USA, and then the UK in turn.

Portage USA

The original pre-school Portage Project is reported in Shearer and Shearer (1972, 1976), Yavner (1972) and Hillard and Shearer (1976). In 1972 the Shearers gave data for 75 children. The average IQ of the children was 75 (Cattell Infant Intelligence test and Stanford-Binet Intelligence Test), and it was therefore proposed that, on average, a developmental growth rate for project children would be 75 per cent that of children of normal intelligence. Using mental ages, it might be expected that the average gain for project children would be about 6 months in an eight-month period of time. In fact, the average child in the project gained 13 months in an eight-month period — 60 per cent more than a peer of average intelligence. Repeat testing on some children three months later indicated no regression. An average of 128 teaching prescriptions were written per child, and the children were successful on 91 per cent of these.

An experimental study was conducted involving randomly selected childen from the Portage Project (n = 36) and randomly selected children of at least average intelligence from a classroom-based Head Start Program with a 'cultural enrichment' type of input. Pre—post testing results at a nine-month interval on the Stanford-Binet, Cattell and Gesell Developmental Scales and the Alpern-Boll Inventory were subject to multiple ANCOVA controlling for initial IQ, age and practice effects. Portage children did significantly better than comparison children in IQ gains, language, social and academic development, but little improvement in motor co-ordination skills was noted. Using children as their own control, gains on IQ and developmental scales were significant at beyond the 1 per cent probability level. (Also see Peniston, 1975.)

Subsequent reports document the expansion of the project to 150 children (Shearer and Shearer, 1976), and cite an average project child gain in mental age of 15 months in an eight-month period. Parents were beginning to take over programme planning and home visits were gradually faded. A number of parents reported generalising the techniques to other family members, but no data on this area are given. The cost per child in 1976 was $622 per year. A structure for replicating the Portage Model in other areas was established.

Hillard and Shearer (1976) document the extension of the project to 163 children, and Boyd and Stauber (1978) report on subsequent work which took pains to demonstrate mediating behaviour change in the parents. In this latter study, extra emphasis was placed on structuring parental teaching behaviours — on behaviour modification lines. Multiple baseline data are displayed for six parents served by different visitors, with impressive results, although follow-up probes are not recorded for all cases and in one recorded case showed regression. A reliability study incorporating 27 checks on 14 visitors' recording of parental behaviour showed mean agreement of 85 per cent, although reliable recording of parental corrections proved a particular problem. A 'task probe' study checked the teaching behaviours of ten parents in the absence of the visitor, and showed parental teaching behaviours increased from pre-project baselines in five out of six behaviour coding categories, while a control group increased in only one. Significant changes in knowledge were also demonstrated.

Portage-style programme evaluations are reported from Michigan by Barnard and Pfalzer (1979) and from Texas by Cadman (1979). The Michigan Teach Our Tots Early Program (TOTE) added mini-workshops, monthly group meetings for parents and visits to relevant schools to the basic Portage framework. Data are given for a *random* sample of 20 programme children on pre–post testing. Average gains over a period of 10.8 months were 9.4 months in gross motor skills, 8.8 months in fine motor skills, 10.2 months in cognitive skills, 10.3 months in language, 9.0 months in feeding and 11.9 months in socialisation. These results are not as spectacular as the original Shearer findings (although better in motor skills), but are none the less impressive.

Cadman (1979) reports on the progress of 98 children on whom full data were available (out of 203) in the Program for Early Education of Children with Handicaps (PEECH) Project. Parents were trained as paraprofessional home visitors, and training handbooks for both parents and teachers devised. Generalised progress measures used were the Alpern-Boll, Cattell and Stanford-Binet Scales, and the child gains on all measures were significant at the 0.1 per cent level.

Although these results are impressive, as Smith (1984) points out, there is no reason to be optimistic about long-term maintenance of gains. Furthermore, generalisation of application of behavioural techniques outside of specific target-related work between parent and child has not been adequately investigated. Smith criticises Boyd and Stauber's (1978) work for over-emphasis on manipulation of consequences and under-emphasis on antecedents and concurrent factors in the development of parental interaction, which may be critical for generalisation and maintenance.

Portage UK

The two best reported Portage projects in the UK are those in Hampshire and Glamorgan.

The Wessex Health Care Evaluation Research Team (Hampshire) established a Portage scheme in Winchester in 1976. Initial findings on 13 families are reported in Smith *et al.* (1977). Over a six-month period, visitors made 80 per cent of all possible visits, and set activity charts on 65 per cent of visits, much of the default occurring with three families under high stress levels. Over the period, 528 activity charts were returned, 82 per cent attained successfully; and of 471 behavioural objectives set for the children, 71 per cent were attained (44 per cent on the first day). Eleven per cent of the charts required the mother to record her own teaching behaviour. On 60 per cent of a 10 per cent sample of activities charted the visitor had definitely checked (by observation) the acquisition of the target behaviour on a subsequent visit. Parental replies to a questionnaire about visitor behaviour are detailed.

The Smith *et al.* (1977) report continues in voluminous detail. The vast majority (83 per cent) of the parents felt their children's progress had accelerated on the Portage scheme. Child gains on the Portage checklist occurred both among items for which activity charts were set (43 per cent) and for which charts were not set (57 per cent), although *spontaneous* acquisition of skills was much lower in cognitive areas and much higher in self-help areas. Smith *et al.* also feel that 'it is very likely that the D.Q. or I.Q. test item steps for very young children are larger and less sensitive than the equivalent items on the Portage checklist'. For both these reasons, they refuse to countenance normative evaluation measures. This report is highly recommended for its meticulous treatment of evaluation issues. Suggestions for additions to the Portage package are made.

In 1979, the team collected data for a further six-month period, and found children were gaining in checklist items at a very similar rate to 1976 — although parents were spending less time in daily teaching — and similar levels of parents satisfaction were reported (Glossop and Castillo, 1982). However, no evidence that parents were generalising skills outside specific target teaching sessions had been found. Further research on this topic was needed via time-sampling and video-recording, particularly with reference to the control of disruptive behaviour.

A very different approach to evaluation is taken by the Glamorgan team. Revill and Blunden (1977, 1978, 1979) used a time-series design with two groups of children totalling 19 subjects, ranging in age from 8 months to 4 years and in Griffiths Developmental Scale quotients from 8 to 85. Assessment measures were the Griffiths Scale and Portage checklist. Baseline rates were taken over a two-month period for one group and over a four-month period for the other, and measurement during Portage servicing continued for a further four months. Reliability checks showed 94-96 per cent agreement.

For one group, the mean number of Portage checklist skills gained per month increased from 4.3 at baseline to 11.1, and for the other group from 3.7 to 9.5. A total of 306 tasks were set for the 19 children during the four months, considerably fewer than the Wessex team reports, and 88 per cent of these were learned, 67 per cent in one week. Mean gains of points on the Griffiths Scale per two months passed rose from 1.0 to 4.1 for one group, and from 0.4 to 2.7 for the other. Although the children gained many more checklist skills during the project period than during baseline, the majority of these were not directly taught via activity charts. Although the Wessex team might not concur, the most plausible explanation for this would seem to rest in generalisation of Portage skills to other behaviours or some other more general spin-off from participating in the project, even allowing for practice effects and possible lack of generalisation from the test situation.

Clements *et al.* (1980) document the extension of this service to 45 families in a subsequent seven-month period, involving 1057 charts at the rate of 3.4 per case per month (a substantial increase), 66 per cent of which were still completed within one week. A further evaluation is reported in Barna *et al.* (1980), covering 35 children. Mean monthly gains in Griffiths mental ages were disappointing, except for four children whose main handicap was environmental deprivation. For children whose main handicap was visual or cerebral palsy, rates of gain actually fell after introduction of the Portage service. Age of entry to the scheme was unrelated to rates of gain.

From a different area of the UK Buckley (1985a) reports on a Portage service for 14 children, all Down's syndrome, some of whom were visited weekly and some every two weeks. The Portage service was accompanied by a parent-powered reading teaching programme, which is reported elsewhere (Buckley, 1985b). There was sample attrition affecting four children, but for the weekly visited children, Griffiths quotients after two years had increased 1.1 points on average, while for the less frequently visited group they had declined by 3.2 points, despite this group having higher developmental quotients at the start. This difference was not statistically significant, but neither group suffered the eight-point drop reported by Ludlow and Allen (1979). No relationship between gains and age at onset of service was found, but children with fewer and older siblings tended to do better. A similar picture emerged from analysis of Portage checklist items gained. The more frequently visited group acquired a higher proportion of checklist skills in association with specific Portage teaching of that skill. Periods of family stress were associated with declines in progress, unsurprisingly. The parents reported valuing the service, but said that the practical help to the child was more important than support for themselves.

Despite these variable results, Portage services have become widespread in the UK, where the scheme seems almost more popular than in the USA (Bendall *et al.*, 1984; Bendall, 1985). Of 200 schemes reported to be operating, 116 (58 per cent) were clearly based on the Portage Model. Contrary to the US experience, most UK Portage schemes are found in urban, densely populated areas.

Other US Programmes

An early programme reported by Santostefano and Stayton (1967) involved training mothers to teach their retarded children attention control. An experimental group of 28 mothers was exposed to two group meetings, a written manual and daily recording at home. Specific standard materials of a rather abstract nature were provided. The mothers taught the children by gestural prompts, modelling and physical prompts, accompanied with verbalisations. Pre- and post-testing on tasks not directly related to the trained task were undertaken with both experimental and control children, whose scores were not significantly different at pre-test. At post-test, the experimentals were significantly better than the controls on four out of five tasks, irrespective of IQ. Although these results are quite striking, their relevance to everyday life is not immediately clear. The authors argue that attention training of this sort renders the child's cognition more accessible to training by others, although they acknowledge that any systematic training might promote improvement in cognitive functions.

Rose (1974) taught natural and foster parents a number of principles of behaviour modification and how to apply them to their 3–8-year-old retarded children. Group leaders used programmed booklets, modelling and behaviour rehearsal, lectures and discussion, weekly assignments and positive reinforcement, together with parental recording at home. Training in reinforcement, extinction, time-out, modelling, cueing and rehearsal was given of 90-minutes between seven and ten sessions. Supportive home visits were also undertaken. Foster parents were paid expenses, but natural parents had to pay a deposit refundable in the event of good attendance. Following training in eleven small groups, 27 of the 33 families in the programme successfully modified 55 of the 58 behaviours for which plans were initiated. Follow-up of 21 families at three to six months showed all gains but one were maintained, and several had designed new programmes. Natural parents did as well as foster parents, in both cases irrespective of social class.

A related programme is the Parent Training Technology System described by Watson and Bassinger (1974), which involved siblings, peers and teachers as well as parents, but was delivered by home training specialists (although not necessarily in the home). Programmed text and slide/film presentations were supplemented by knowledge tests. Detailed multiple baseline results are cited which appear promising, although the procedures would seem alien to UK professionals.

Tyler and Kogan (1977) developed a series of instruction sessions focused on the enrichment of the mother–child interaction repertoire and utilised immediate feedback to 18 mothers via a radio device ('bug-in-the-ear'). Mother and (pre-school) child behaviour was video-taped and analysed before, immediately following and nine months after the training sessions. Of 216 problem behaviours, 48 decreased immediately after the course, and 40 of these changes were still present nine months later.

A more conventional programme is reported by Baig (1977, 1981). Initially, 23 retarded children aged 4–11 years were involved in the home programme. Statistically significant improvements in three areas of functioning (language, socialisation and independence) were noted, together with gains in mental age and goal attainment scores. Significant differences between experimental and control groups on nine parental teaching strategies were observed.

In 1981 Baig reported the extension of the outreach programme to 42 parents of retarded children aged under 12 years. The programme focused on teaching specific skills, and was successful in helping the children attain goals set by the parents. In addition to specific goal attainment, improvement in other functional behaviours was noted.

The Regional Intervention Program in Nashville is documented by Timm and Rule (1981). Much of the service is offered by parents to other parents. Started in 1969, the programme serves about 66 families each year. Classroom programmes and activities are coupled with work at home, and parents act as classroom aides. When the programme is complete for their own child, parents 'pay back' the time received, up to 230 hours, by helping other children and parents. During payback, parents learn to generalise their newly acquired skills to other children, problems and situations.

Initial training occurs in a structured play setting, establishes contingent attention and ignoring, with a brief reversal phase, then intermittent reinforcement is introduced. Home problems begin to be recorded and then remediated. Additionally, individualised programmes are written and implemented in the centre and home, with recording in both contexts. All children also participate in the classroom programme, as do their siblings. Detailed objectives are set for each family in a 'management by objectives' structure.

The programme is claimed to have 'saved' a number of children from institutionalisation, yielding high cost-benefits. Data are cited on 85 families, supporting claims for generalisation and maintenance of positive behaviour change. However, another 29 families were not considered to have 'completed treatment' and did not do well. The children in these families tended to be older and were more likely to come from non-intact families, but other socio-economic factors did not predict outcome.

A separate follow-up study of 40 families was conducted,

wherein each former non-compliant Regional Intervention Program child was compared with four control peers drawn randomly from the ex-programme child's classroom. Direct observations of parent, child and siblings were made in the home over a four-week period. Behaviour of the ex-programme children was largely pro-social and no different from that of controls. Teacher ratings confirmed this finding for the school setting. No wash-out effect was detected, but the same child age and family intactness effects were noted. The Regional Intervention Program has been replicated in at least ten other sites.

A reinforcement programme in which parents earned lottery tickets and won prizes for the progress made by their handicapped children during home-based intervention is described by Muir and Milan (1982). An ABAB reversal design replicated across three families indicated that the artificial incentive produced clinically significant increases in child progress.

Yet another different approach is reported by Affleck *et al.* (1982), who tested a 'relationship-focused' intervention which attempted to foster adaptive parent–infant and parent–professional relationships with a view to enhancing parent competence in a more generalised way.

The relationship-focused intervention aimed to enhance the quantity and quality of parent–child interaction, rendering the parent more sensitive to cues from the child and the whole relationship more reciprocal. Weekly home visits were made, including in the evenings, and 'the subject matter was largely determined by the parents'. Parental anxieties were discussed, as was the usefulness of other welfare agencies and programmes. Parents were filmed interacting with their children and the films viewed and discussed at home.

Nine-month outcomes are available for 38 programme families and 40 contrast group families. Comparison variables included scores on an inventory of home environment quality, parent–infant interaction observations, and maternal reports of mood disturbance. Results favoured the relationship-oriented programme, whose mothers were significantly more responsive, reciprocal and involved in interaction with their children.

Other UK Programmes

A regime for Down's syndrome neonates was advocated by Brinkworth (1973). It incorporated special diets, exercises and strong sensory and locomotor experiences. Parental handling and affection and widespread social contact were emphasised, together with aids to posture and mobility. The progress of five experimental children was matched with that of a comparison group of twelve, with assessment on the Griffiths Developmental Scales at approximately 6 months of age. The mean developmental quotient of the experimental group was 102, while that of the comparison group was 75. Differences were insignificant only in the locomotor area.

However, the programme input was heavy (weekly home visits of up to four hours, plus written information), although there is reasonable evidence that both groups were representative of the background population, including all social classes. Brinkworth gives little explicit information about curriculum content and teaching methods — thus reducing replicability — or about mediatory change in parental behaviour. Follow-up testing one year later demonstrated lack of maintenance of gains during a period when the families were no longer under direct surveillance, the experimental mean developmental quotient having fallen to 81 compared with 75 for the non-intervention group. The parents remained satisfied with their children's progress, however. Brinkworth's work remains an inspirational classic.

Bidder *et al.* (1975) taught behaviour modification techniques to the mothers of Down's syndrome children, also including them in group discussions dealing with family or personal problems. Behavioural training was conducted in twelve sessions — initially weekly, then increasingly spaced. Tape-recordings and live demonstration, verbal input and group discussions, and maternal recordings were used. Mothers were encouraged to set aside brief sessions at home to teach specific tasks. Matched control and experimental groups were pre- and post-tested on the Griffiths Scales. The experimental group performed significantly better than the control group on the language and performance sub-scales, but differences on the other four sub-scales did not reach statistical significance. Locomotor performance was least improved.

Further work by this team (Bidder *et al.*, 1983) involved the training of parents of eight school-age Down's childen in workshops on language stimulation. Child ages ranged from 5 to 10 years and all had at least 30 words and some phrases at the outset. Both parents participated in the scheme. Four group training sessions were supplemented with telephone contact and/or home visits. Role-play between parent dyads proved effective in changing parent communication behaviour in the centre. Assessment on the language performance and reasoning sub-scales of the Griffiths showed the scores of both experimental and control groups increased, but those of the experimental group increased by a significantly greater amount. Parent recordings at home of length of child utterance substantiated this finding.

Apparently contradictory results were found by Sandow and Clarke (1978) from their study of two matched groups of parents of pre-school retarded children aged 1 year 6 months to 3 years 6 months. One group was visited every two weeks and one every eight weeks. The socio-economic status of the parents showed a degree of top bias. Developmental checklists and specific written behavioural programming were utilised, with loose parental recording. Measures included the Cattell Infant Intelligence Scale, Vineland Social Maturity Scale, Peabody Picture Vocabulary Test and the developmental checklists.

Frequently visited children initially were superior in progress to infrequently visited children, but a subsequent deceleration for the first group was matched by the less frequently visited group showing a later rise in performance. Overall differences after two years were not significant, but the less frequent visiting seemed clearly more cost-effective. The authors discuss possible causative factors most interestingly, but can draw no firm conclusions.

A later paper from the same team (Sandow *et al.*, 1981) reports data from a control group allied with the previous study. Controls showed steady deceleration in performance from the end of the first year onwards, despite admission to school 14 months earlier than either of the other groups. At three-year follow-up, the less frequently visited group's progress had declined again. No relationship between progress and socio-economic status was found. The authors propose that the frequently visited group produced an early Hawthorne effect but then became dependent on the visitor. It is perhaps worth noting that the visits were long (between two and three hours), and the authors are less specific than other workers about their structure. Furthermore, visits held as infrequently as once every eight weeks is an option few other workers have explored. A more useful comparison might have been weekly compared with fortnightly visits, with briefer sessions and more highly structured input (cf. Buckley, 1985a). Nevertheless, these studies do demonstrate the effectiveness (albeit erratic) of the intervention programme over a lengthy period. More refined statistical procedures might have elucidated this further.

A programme for 36 Down's syndrome infants and their parents, incorporating home and centre-based instruction, is reported in Australia by Clunies-Ross (1979). Period of involvement in the project ranged from four months to two years. The curriculum draws on a wide range of manuals, including the DISTAR teaching packages. Specific behavioural objectives are set for individual childen, and assessment is via a developmental checklist, Stanford-Binet, Peabody Picture Vocabulary Test and Reynell Language Scales. Children and parents attend the centre two or three times a week for a total of six hours, and the children receive direct teaching from professionals in addition to the parent-training component, which comprises a ten-week training course, resulting in written home programmes with parental recording. Results showed mean increases in developmental quotients for the children, but the impact of the parent training is not partialled out. However, as Clunies-Ross expresses it, the results 'are in the reverse direction to the developmental trends for Down's children who did not experience systematic early intervention'.

Review

By the mid-1970s, sufficient work of substance had been done in this area of work to justify the production of critical reviews. Callias and Carr (1975) and Cunningham (1975) had contributions of this kind within one book. The lack of information on generalisation and maintenance was noted by Cunningham, who emphasised the need for training to provide socio-emotional support as well as specific skills, expressing his usual distaste for behaviour modification.

A valuably methodical and well-organised review is provided by Baker (1976). Models of parent training are reviewed under the headings of centre-based, school-based and home-based programmes, group training and training through media. Outcome research is reviewed in terms of child change, mediating parental behaviour change, and what aspects of training are critical for such change. Data on characteristics of parents, children, siblings and trainers are reviewed, as is the role of programme incentives.

Baker concludes with a list of 20 guidelines drawn from his review for the optimal structure of training programmes.

Griffin (1979) provides a review of studies, again less confined to work with parents of mentally handicapped children than one might expect from the title. A very brief review by Gath (1979), who notes that evaluation of parent training programmes is complicated by our ignorance of what developmentally delayed children *can do* — i.e. what our expectations should be — nevertheless merits attention.

Training programmes for parents, teachers and nurses are surveyed practically by Callias (1980). Guidelines on recruitment, selection of parents, pre-group contact, group composition and child characteristics, selection and training of tutors, length of course, format of meetings, curriculum content and sequence, training materials and methods, provision for home visits, and procedures for assessment and evaluation are given. Possible problem areas are discussed.

Most recently, Hornby and Singh (1983) review group training methods for parents of mentally retarded children. The authors' own speciality is reflective group counselling (Hornby and Singh, 1982), but their critical review is confined to behavioural studies, in which they find a number of methodological flaws. Relatively few studies are considered, and these are very various and by no means concerned purely with developmentally delayed children.

Training Formats

Much of the preceding discussion has, of course, referred in passing to issues of training format, but here studies which have deliberately contrasted different formats with similar populations can be considered.

An early classic study is that of Tavormina (1975), further reported in Tavormina *et al.* (1976). Fifty-one mothers of diverse socio-economic status, and with retarded children whose mean age was 6½ years, were allocated to behavioural or reflective group training or a control group, allocation being determined purely by considerations of time convenience, but resulting in no significant mismatching. Written manuals, verbal instruction and group discussions over eight weekly sessions were common to both formats. The reflective group focused on reflecting feelings, setting

appropriate limits, providing alternative activities, and the importance of empathy, acceptance and understanding. The behavioural
groups were taught general principles and the application of these
to specific problems identified by the parents.

Assessment measures included an attitude survey of parental
feeling of adequacy, a child behaviour rating scale, coupled with
coded behavioural observations taken during mother–child interaction in a centre playroom, parental ratings of specific problem
behaviours, frequency counts of problem behaviours by mothers,
and a multiple-choice general evaluative questionnaire. Two baseline assessments were made, together with post-programme assessment.

Virtually no change was recorded between the two baseline
measurements. After intervention, a number of checklist sub-
scores showed no change. Those that did change, particularly
relating to child aggression, showed the behavioural group ahead
of the reflective group, who in turn did better than the control
group. Behavioural observations in the centre showed a similar
pattern, as did parental ratings of behaviour problems at home.
However, parental recordings at home showed no differential
change, all groups improving. The two behavioural groups did not
differ in outcome, but the two reflective groups showed greater
variability. Most mothers reported positive feelings towards the
programme, with the behavioural group reporting a significantly
more positive reaction.

It is a pity that this study did not incorporate direct observation
of parental interaction in the home. Many of this multiplicity of
measures are rather weak. However, it is interesting that the
behavioural group did well on measures associated with socio-
emotional support as well as on ratings of behaviour change, while
the reflective counselling did as well as the behavioural groups on
recorded behaviour change in the home. It seems you don't always
get quite what you've paid for. Tavormina's teaching methods were
unsophisticated by modern standards, and an improved replication
of this study would be most valuable, particularly if focusing on
generalisation and maintenance in the home.

Subsequently, Tavormina went on to offer a combination of
behavioural and reflective input to his (ex-) control group.
Questionnaire data indicated this group ended up more satisfied
than the reflective group, but somewhat less satisfied than the
purely behavioural group (Tavormina *et al.*, 1976). Mothers in the

behavioural group asked for even more input on specific skills and techniques, and many mothers asked for fathers to be included.

Substantial comparative work on the impact of written instruction is reported by Baker and Heifetz (1976) and Heifetz (1977a, 1977b, 1980). The READ Project revolves around an assessment booklet and series of instructional manuals specially written for use by parents in teaching language, self-help and play skills and in managing problematic behaviour. The manuals covered selection of target skills, task-analysis, antecedents and consequences, record-keeping and other general information including case studies, illustrations and step-by-step programme outlines.

A comprehensive evaluation was conducted with 160 families of retarded children aged 3–14 years. The families were of wide-ranging and representative socio-economic status, but were volunteers from a total pool of 222, and therefore arguably well motivated. Families were randomly assigned to five groups receiving differing training formats: MO (manual only), MP (manual plus bi-weekly telephone consultations), MG (manuals plus bi-weekly group training meeting), MGV (manuals plus training group plus home visits), and C (control group). The intervention lasted 20 weeks.

Of 128 families assigned to training conditions, 17 dropped out and an additional eleven did not complete post-intervention measures, leaving between 23 and 28 families in each group. All trained parents were encouraged to keep and send in records, and the two groups involving face-to-face contact with professionals showed a significantly higher rate of recording (59 per cent compared with 45 per cent). Parents in these groups carried out substantially more programmes, in more skill areas.

A test of parent knowledge showed that scores for mothers in all groups, except MP, improved significantly, although fathers did much less well, appearing largely uninvolved in MO and MP conditions. Child skills were assessed on a checklist by parents pre- and post-training. The gains in all training conditions were significantly different from those of controls, but not from each other. The parental data revealed improvement in non-targeted skills also, but a much higher proportion of change in targeted skills.

The most extraordinary finding is that, although overall there was little significant difference in outcome between conditions, more detailed analysis shows marked trends in favour of the MO group in absolute effectiveness. This makes the MO condition dramatically the most cost-effective. Heifetz notes that most of the programming was done in the self-help skill area, and that this finding might not generalise to other target skill areas. Few MO and MP parents tackled behaviour problems, although parents in other groups did. It is therefore suggested that face-to-face programming may be necessary for dealing with behaviour problems, which tend to be more complex and idiosyncratic. Furthermore, although MO parents did very well with self-help skill programming, they reported *feeling* less confident than other groups. A follow-up study at one year is reported in the section on maintenance of gains (below, pp. 266-268).

Subsequent comparative studies have tended to be of rather smaller scale. Garner (1979) compared the effectiveness of home-based and centre-based parent education programmes for the parents of 51 handicapped children. Measures of extent of parental involvement and programme effectiveness showed no significant difference between the two training formats.

Hudson (1982) randomly allocated the mothers of 40 developmentally delayed children to four treatment groups: verbal instruction (VI), verbal instruction plus the teaching of behavioural principles (VIB), verbal instruction plus the use of modelling and role-play (VIMR), and a control group (C). Sessions lasted three hours each over ten weeks. The VI group concentrated on a specific behavioural deficit, and the parents were told what to do and required to record the results and return these for scrutiny. The VIB group combined this with generalised instruction by lecture in principles of behaviour analysis. VIMR mothers brought their children with them for the purposes of modelling, practice and feedback.

Outcome measures included a test of knowledge, a test of programming skill for two novel behaviour problems to check on generalisation of knowledge, analysis of brief video-recordings of maternal teaching behaviour, analysis of parent records of child progress on target skills, progress on a developmental checklist (Denver) and a satisfaction questionnaire and scale. No differences between treatment groups were found for the satisfaction measures. On the knowledge and knowledge generalisation tests, and on the developmental checklist, all treatment groups were significantly different from the control groups, but not from each other. For skills application and number of home tasks completed, the

VIMR group performed significantly better than the other experimental groups.

Thus parents given specific task-focused training appear to have learnt general principles incidentally, although Hudson has doubts about the discriminatory capacities of his test. However, he is convinced that modelling and role-play are necessary for effective training. The parents reported equally high levels of satisfaction, no matter what training they received or what they subsequently did or did not do. Doubts about the validity of such measures in terms of implications for child change are thus reinforced.

Brightman *et al.* (1982) compared group and individual training with a control condition for 66 families with retarded children aged 3–13.years. Nine training sessions in both treatment conditions focused on self-help skills, behaviour problem management, and language and play skills in turn. Manuals, training video-tapes, home assignments and home recording were common to both. In the group sessions, training tended to be didactic, but audio-visual media, role-playing, co-consulting and small-group problem-solving were used extensively. Parents in individual training brought their children to practise with, and experienced modelling, practice, and verbal and video feedback.

Measures included a knowledge test, coded observation of videos of parents teaching specimen tasks, child progress on a self-help skills inventory and behaviour problems checklist completed by the parents, and a follow-up tape-recorded interview six months after the intervention. The self-help skills of programme children improved no more than those of controls, but trained families showed a significant decrease in behaviour problems. All parent measures showed gains favouring the experimental groups. However, there were no significant differences between the two experimental groups immediately after the intervention or at follow-up. The authors concluded that the group format is the more cost-effective, requiring half the time of the individual format.

Maintenance

In relation to the amount of work done in this area, the quantity and quality of long-term follow-up data are disappointing. It may be that the difficulties of maintaining gains (or minimising deceleration) are greater with the developmentally delayed than with any other population, but that is hardly an adequate reason for failing to research the issue. Harris (1978) describes some of the problems which have arisen in working with a group of parents of mentally handicapped children over four and a half years. Run on behavioural lines, the group became very dependent on video facilities for basic communication and data-recording. Group meetings and home visits were combined with the provision of a toy library. Difficulties of a single group for parents of children of very different abilities are discussed, as are possible tensions between home and school, but the evidence given is impressionistic.

The results of a longitudinal intervention programme for Down's syndrome infants and their families are given by Hanson (1976) and Hanson and Schwarz (1978). In a home-based programme, the parents of twelve infants were taught gross motor and cognitive adaptive instruction techniques. The children were the first consecutive twelve referred, and the families were of wide-ranging socio-economic status. One child dropped out. Individual programming was begun as early as possible and never later than 6 months of age, via weekly or bi-weekly home visits. Behavioural task-analysed programmes were written, and more general recommendations made. Parents recorded progress data from teaching trials, becoming increasingly independent and using the visitor only as a consultant.

Measures included the Bayley and Gesell Scales, and the Denver and SEED developmental checklists. Visitors checked all parent developmental checklist claims for reliability. Data show dramatically that programme infants reached various developmental milestones a little later than ordinary children but a great deal earlier than normal expectations for non-intervened Down's children. Further longitudinal data beyond three years would be extremely valuable.

The READ project was followed up at 14 months post-intervention by Baker (Baker, 1977; Baker *et al.*, 1980), with 95 of the 100 trained families, using a structured interview, a test of knowledge and a checklist of child self-help skills. Knowledge gains during training were maintained, but had not increased further. Gains in self-help skills were maintained except for a slight loss in the MP condition. Overall, continuation or new programming of any regularity post-intervention was self-reported by only half the families, and there was no significant difference between training formats. Continued improvement in child self-help skills was slight, and few parents had carried a problem behaviour management plan through to completion. However, 86 per cent of families reported that some incidental, informal 'teaching' had occurred during the follow-up period. A total index of degree of follow-through was compiled from the various measures, and on this the MO condition scored significantly lower than the others. The parents ranked 'lack of support' lower than 'lack of time' or child-based factors in explaining their absence of continuance.

A two-year follow-up of a group parent training programme is reported by Uditsky and MacDonald (1981). Training sessions held weekly over eight weeks incorporate verbal and written instruction, written exercises, films and video-tapes, modelling and behavioural rehearsal. Between sessions, home visits for assistance with specific programming are made. Finally, the instructor fades involvement with the family over a three-month period.

Data are reported on 64 parents, divided into groups according to how recently training had taken place. All information was collected by structured interviews and questionnaire. After one year, 75 per cent of parents reported maintenance of improvement in original target behaviours; after two years, the proportion was 83 per cent. Similar proportions of parents reported the existence of other behavioural problems which they had not modified, however. Almost all the parents stopped using formal procedures (recording, charting, etc.) almost immediately the training workshop finished, although about 80 per cent claimed they used 'incidental' procedures even after two years. Only about 10 per cent of parents had set up new programmes. These results are in accord with those of the READ team who used some less expensive interventions.

Uditsky and MacDonald conclude that training should place greater emphasis on simple, incidental, informal techniques and less on specific structured techniques, and provide longer-term support via a more extensive 'contact fading' period. Booster or refresher sessions could be incorporated. These suggestions have yet to be tested.

Social Psychological Factors

Parent training for families of developmentally delayed children has been shown to be effective in many studies with subjects of very various socio-economic status, at least in the short term, although this is less true for children with some other difficulties. However, this general effectiveness might be masking a tendency for the low-SES families to do less well. Buckley's (1985a) finding at two-year follow-up that children from large families with younger siblings and a high incidence of stressing events tended to make less long-term progress may be indicative.

Two studies have specifically investigated this question, in the attempt to elucidate predictive factors in training effectiveness. Brassell (1977) collected longitudinal data in West Carolina on 73 infants with various handicaps (of whom 14 per cent were of normal intelligence), and these data were related to a number of organismic and social–psychological factors. Training was via weekly home visits, wherein visitors had 'considerable latitude in tailoring intervention programmes' according to guidelines laid down by the central multi-disciplinary directorate. Developmental rates on the Bayley Scales were the dependent variable, and the effect of psychosocial factors was examined by ANCOVAs and stepwise regression analyses. The children had been in the programme for an average of ten months.

Initial base rates had low predictive power — the best did not automatically get better. Gender was the most predictive of the organismic variables, females doing better. Degree of mental and motor retardation at the outset were significantly predictive of outcome, but primary diagnosis was not. Intactness of family was also highly predictive, as was parental education level, child's birth order and paternal age. Number of siblings was predictive in terms of motor development, but not mental age. A quarter of the variance in post-intervention progress was accounted for by psychosocial factors as opposed to organic factors. It is interesting to speculate whether similar results would be found with a more structured curriculum.

Predictive factors were extracted from the READ Project's 14-month follow-up data by Clark *et al.* (1982), with outcome variables being mothers' post-training knowledge and degree of follow-through programming, but the analysis was based only on those parents in the two groups who had received face-to-face training. Of the 64 families assigned to these groups, full data were available only on 49.

Significant predictive factors in maternal knowledge at follow-up were a mother's previous group training experience, her educational level, and her previous behaviour modification experience, in that order. Income and social class were less significant predictors. Predictive factors in reported degree of follow-through programming were quite different: mother's age, teaching sessions logged during training and trainer's prediction of degree of follow-through were significant. The authors note that few families in the sample fell in the lowest social group, but raise the possibility that prediction equations could be used to assign families with different characteristics to different training formats, to maximise cost-effectiveness. However, it is obviously important not to assess parental proficiency solely on paper-and-pencil tests of knowledge.

Given the apparent importance of family size and intactness, the role of fathers and siblings may be crucial in sustaining teaching behaviours and child gains in the long term. Weinrott (1974) trained 18 siblings of retarded children as behaviour modifiers in conjunction with a summer camp programme. The trainees, aged 10–18, were trained during a five-day residential period by observation of classes, modelling, didactic presentations, role-playing, video feedback, and practice with a group of retarded children which included their brother or sister. The siblings learned to use a wide range of behavioural techniques with remarkable proficiency. Unfortunately, evaluation was weak. The older children did as well on a knowledge test as their parents, who were trained also, and the parents felt the sibling training had improved the quality of family interaction. No follow-up was available. The impact of parent and sibling training was not partialled. Nevertheless, this remains a pioneering programme.

More recently, Sandler *et al.* (1983) examined the generalised effects on mother, child *and father* of a school-linked parent training programme. Subjects were 21 mothers and 15 fathers of above average socio-economic status, but only mothers were trained, using verbal and written instruction, practice and video feedback. The children had various disabilities and were aged up to 5 years 6 months. Three groups were formed: control, data-keeping and no data-keeping. Assessment before and after a three-month intervention involving group and individual training included an attitude scale, developmental checklist, a test of knowledge and analysis of video-recordings of parent–child interaction.

Post-intervention experimental mothers showed significant knowledge gains compared with controls, but fathers did not. No significant changes in attitude occurred between experimental and control groups for mothers or fathers, and developmental checklist scores showed no difference between experimental and control children. Significant changes in mother–child interaction occurred for mothers only, and then only in two analysis categories for the data-keeping group and one for the non-data group. The outcome data are thus uninspiring, and do little to elucidate further the significance of paternal role.

McConachie and Mitchell (1985) essayed a fine-grain analysis from video-tapes of interaction between 21 mothers and fathers and their young mentally handicapped children, using a standard toy. Delayed children tend to initiate less, respond inconsistently and otherwise prove more difficult in the establishment of smooth interaction. Previous research indicating that the mother and father of a handicapped child tend to interact with the child in very similar ways was confirmed, although mothers tended to be a little more flexible and fathers tended to rely more on physical help. Fathers tended to be less successful in interaction, in terms of child outcomes. The authors warn that training might result in parent 'over-direction' of a child, with negative consequences.

Summary

The evaluation research on training programmes for the parents of children who are mentally retarded or handicapped (otherwise known as developmentally delayed) is voluminous, but very variable in quality. Many of the more rigorous research studies have generated results which are contradictory in detail, although the vast majority claim to demonstrate effectiveness of some kind. Programmes which do not adopt a framework which is in some way behavioural are very much in the minority, as are programmes which concentrate on socio-emotional support for parents at the expense of specific skill training.

Portage programmes have been widely replicated in the USA and UK. A number of weak evaluations merely report attendance rates (all around 80 per cent) and parental satisfaction expressed on questionnaires (invariably positive). Parental ratings of child post-programme improvement also tend to be universally positive.

A more substantive approach to evaluation includes the use of scores on developmental checklists and a variety of norm- and criterion-referenced tests.

The original Wisconsin results showed programme children developing at rates faster than those of 'normal' children, and better than culturally disadvantaged children in a school programme. Control over process variables was demonstrated in a small-scale study. Replications (with additional or slightly varied inputs) showed Portage children improving at rates equivalent to normal children and very significant gains in developmental quotients. In the UK, a baselined study showed dramatic increases in developmental rates from the onset of Portage input. Two subsequent UK replications showed developmental gains respectively equivalent to 'normal' rates and markedly below normal (with environmentally deprived children doing better).

As the Portage approach is usually targeted on pre-school children, a substantial proportion of whom are likely to have Down's syndrome, it is intrinsically more likely to show better results than programmes which include older children, given the developmental deceleration often shown by Down's children. It is regrettable that so little baselined or controlled research has been undertaken in this area.

Workshops of a flexible nature incorporating socio-emotional support and dilute behavioural methods have been operated from the Hester Adrian Research Centre, but evaluation research methods were largely confined to attendance and paper-and-pencil satisfaction measures, both of which were very positive. More substantial later work at HARC has not been well reported. Replications of the HARC Model from a school base and with older children, sometimes incorporating more sophisticated teaching methods, have again demonstrated good attendance and parental PAP satisfaction, and in one study parental recordings showed successful modification of 72 per cent of targeted behaviours. (Although parental teaching behaviour was demonstrated to change in this latter study, this was not achieved in another.)

A wide variety of other programmes have been weakly evaluated. In the UK one programme with very loosely structured input found no difference in developmental rates between programme and comparison groups — both declined, but a further comparison group of institiutionalised children declined even faster. Other programmes have shown merely good attendance, or knowledge gains which were found to be unreliable predictors of behaviour change. Two studies note high levels of parental self-report of programme method usage, but in the case where this was coupled with analysis of progress on developmental checklists, the latter showed no change. In the USA, a number of studies coupled parental training with classroom input and failed to partial effects; two of these studies showed substantial gains in developmental quotients, and another 'normalisation' of the children with no 'wash-out'. Training parents via deployment as classroom aides has been adopted in two studies, and parents used as paraprofessional visitors in another two — with no signs of ill effect in either case. A brief media package programme generated gains in parental behavioural records for the 50 per cent who stayed the course.

More substantial evaluation research is available on a variety of programmes. Training in attention control strategies using specific materials were found effective, with some immediate generalisation, but follow-up data are lacking. Training in behaviour modification for parents of 3–8-year-olds which was both centre- and home-based proved very effective, and effects were sustained at follow-up three to six months later, with some parent skill generalisation reflected in design of new programmes. Direct radio feedback during mother–child interaction was found to reduce 22 per cent of cited child problem behaviours, with good maintenance at nine-months follow-up. A controlled skill-based study for parents of children up to 12 years of age showed changed parental behaviour and gains in developmental quotients. Tangible reinforcement for parents in training has produced gains in child progress, at least in the short run. A loosely structured, home-based programme focusing on parent–child interaction style yielded observational indications of improvement in parent–child relationships, although consequent outcomes were not explored.

In the UK, Brinkworth's stimulation programme for Down's syndrome neonates resulted in normalised developmental quotients for experimental children, 27 points ahead of a comparison group, although input was heavy and of questionable replicability, and follow-up at one year showed substantial wash-out. Training both parents at home and in a centre to accelerate their Down's child's language showed good effects in one controlled study, but a centre-based programme in behaviour modification showed less positive results, only partially reaching significance. Another controlled study found parents visited bi-weekly produced more immediate gains than parents visited bi-monthly, but in the second year the former group decelerated and the latter accelerated to catch up, although both stayed ahead of the controls.

Studies comparing the effectiveness of different training formats yield interesting results. Both behavioural and reflective training produced *some* gains over controls, with the behavioural training doing best, but training was unsophisticated and measures not strong. Distributing well-produced (READ) manuals alone resulted in very satisfactory gains in parental knowledge, but personal contact by visits or group meetings resulted in more parental programming behaviour and involved fathers more. However, child skill gains were not increased by either form of contact, all intervention groups doing better than controls. This finding may be specific to the self-help skills area and well-motivated parents. At one-year follow-up, the MO group showed least persistence of overall programme effects, although knowledge gains had not washed out. Verbal behavioural instruction of a specific or generalised kind resulted in high satisfaction, knowledge gains and improved child skills, but the inclusion of modelling and rehearsal in the training increased parental skill application and programming. Three studies of mixed delivery methods have drawn the tangential conclusion that home visiting is more effective than centre-based training (perhaps especially for older children and those with behaviour problems), but the two studies which directly compared the two formats found few significant differences in outcome. Most, but not all, workers have found centre-based programmes cheaper in *professional* time.

Long-term follow-up data in this area are scant. Aforementioned behaviour modification and interactive training programmes showed good maintenance, but the Brinkworth programme suffered some wash-out. Parent-programmed Down's children have been shown to reach developmental milestones at little less than normal ages from birth to 3 years of age, without deceleration. The READ manuals (see above, pp. 264-5) were incorporated in a programme without follow-up support, and 14 months later parental knowledge and child skills were maintained but not progressing, and only half the families reported new programming, much of this 'informal'. Another one-year follow-up study likewise showed maintenance of gains but little extension to new problem behaviours, despite claims for 'incidental' application

of programme skills. It seems clear that maintenance of programme gains is typical, but continuing acceleration after
withdrawal of programme support is rare. Long-term 'wash-out' in
comparison to controls might therefore occur.

Afore-mentioned studies have differed in their view of the influence of socio-economic factors on parental response to training,
two reporting no effect and others noting family intactness and size
having some influence. There is some evidence that, for a loosely
structured input, family intactness, parent educational level, child
birth order and paternal age can be predictive of training outcome.
(Female children and the less retarded tend to do best.) Another
study found parental educational level predictive of knowledge
gain, but parental age and effort during training much more predictive of degree of post-programme persistence. It seems that
family intactness and size can have some influence in some circum-
stances, and parental age is relevant, but the influence of parent
educational level should not be over-emphasised. Comparative
studies of the impact of socio-economic factors on loosely versus
tightly structured, cognitively versus behaviourally oriented, and
centre-based versus home-based training is still awaited, particularly with respect to maintenance of gains in the long term.

Overall, the research in this area has not been of the quality that
might be expected to be associated with its quantity. The Portage
work has been particularly remiss with respect to baselined, controlled and follow-up studies, and has often failed to demonstrate
control over process variables. It is clear that paper-and-pencil
indications of parental satisfaction are virtually useless as outcome
measures. Behaviourally flavoured training has been by far the
most popular, but some studies of reflective or interactive training
have shown promising results. It may be that these latter are more
susceptible to variance in the skills of their promulgators, and thus
less successfully replicable. Behavioural programmes linked in with
a school programme have done well, and school-based parent
training merits more detailed and discriminatory evaluation, since
a neighbourhood school-based support service might help to
eliminate some of the problems of maintaining gains in the long
term. In retrospect, it seems naive to expect one type of parent
training programme to deal with the enormously varied needs in
this area, and the requirement would seem to be for a co-ordinated
parent training service which can offer a range of different types,
intensities and durations of input according to family need. How-

ever, results to date permit confidence that parent training is efective with developmentaly delayed children, and has much future potential.

References

Affleck, G. *et al.* (1982) 'Promise of Relationship-focussed Early Intervention in Developmental Disabilities', *Journal of Special Education, 16, 4,* 413-30

Attwood, T. (1978) 'The Croydon Workshop for Parents of Pre-school Mentally Handicapped Children', *Child Care Health and Development, 4, 2,* 79-97

Attwood, T. (1979) 'The Croydon Workshop for the Parents of Severely Handicapped School Age Children', *Child Care Health and Development, 5, 3,* 117-88

Baig, K. (1977) *Home Training of Parents and their Trainable Mentally Retarded Children* (Toronto: University of Toronto Press) (E.R.I.C. E.C. 114399)

Baig, K. (1981) 'Parents as Paraprofessionals: A Home Training Approach for Parents of Developmentally Delayed School-age Children', *Special Education in Canada, 55, 4,* 7-9.

Baker, B.L. (1976) 'Parent Involvement in Programming for Developmentally Disabled Children', in L.L. Lloyd (ed.), *Communication Assessment and Intervention Strategies* (Baltimore: University Park Press)

Baker, B.L. (1977) 'Support Systems for the Parent as Therapist', in P. Mittler (ed.), *Research to Practice in Mental Retardation*, vol. 1: *Care and Intervention* (Baltimore: University Park Press)

Baker, B.L. and Heifetz, L.J. (1976) 'The Read Project: Teaching Manuals for Parents of Retarded children', in T.D. Tjossem (ed.), *Intervention Strategies for High Risk Infants and Young Children* (Baltimore: University Park Press)

Baker, B.L. *et al.* (1980) 'Behavioural Training for Parents of Mentally Retarded Children: One-year Follow-up', *American Journal of Mental Deficiency, 85, 1,* 31-8

Barna, S. *et al.* (1980) 'The Progress of Developmentally Delayed Pre-school Children in a Home-training Scheme', *Child Care Health and Development, 6, 3,* 157-64

Barnard, P.E. and Pfalzer, J. (1979) 'A Parent Supportive Early Intervention Public School Programme — That Works', paper presented at Annual International Convention of the Council for Exceptional Children, Dallas (E.R.I.C. EC 115259 ED 171050)

Bendall, S. (1985) 'National Portage Survey — Preliminary Results', in B. Daly *et al* (eds.), *Portage: The Importance of Parents* (Windsor: NFER — Nelson)

Bendell, S. *et al.* (1984) *A National Study of Portage-type Home Teaching Services* (Southampton: Wessex Health Care Evaluation Research Team, University of Southampton)

Benson, J. and Ross, L. (1972) 'Teaching Parents to Teach their Children', *Teaching Exceptional Children, 5,* 30-5

Bevington, P. *et al.* (1978) 'An Approach to the Planning and Evaluation of a Parental Involvement Course', *Child Care Health and Development, 4, 4,* 217-27

Bidder, R.T. *et al.* (1975) 'Benefits to Down's Syndrome Children through Training their Mothers', *Archives of Disease in Childhood, 50,* 383-6

Bidder, R.T. *et al.* (1983) 'Training Parents of School-age Down's Children in Verbal Communication', *Mental Handicap, 11, 1,* 26-7

Boyd, R.D. and Boyd, E.D. (1974) 'Parent Intervention in the Education of the Preschool Handicapped Child', *Mental Retardation, 24, 3,* 17-20

Boyd, R.D. and Stauber, K.A. (1978) *Acquisition and Generalization of Teaching and Child Management Behaviors in Parents of Preschool Handicapped Children: A Comparative Study* (Portage, Wisconsin: Cooperative Educational Service Agency 12) (E.R.I.C. ED 163737 EC 112831)

Brassell, W.R. (1977) 'Intervention with Handicapped Infants: Correlates of Progress', *Mental Retardation, 15*, 18-22

Bricker, D.D. and Bricker, W.A. (1973) 'Infant, Toddler and Preschool Research and Intervention Project Report — Year III', *IMRID Behavioural Science Monograph No. 23* (Nashville, Tennessee: George Peabody College for Teachers) (E.R.I.C. ED 089529 EC 061497)

Bricker, W.A. and Bricker, D.D. (1976) 'The Infant, Toddler and Preschool Research and Intervention Project', in T.D. Tjossem (ed.) *Intervention Strategies for High Risk Infants and Young Children* (Baltimore: University Park Press)

Brightman, R.P. *et al.* (1982) 'Effectiveness of Alternative Parent Training Formats', *Journal of Behavior Therapy and Experimental Psychiatry, 13, 2*, 113-17

Brinkworth, R. (1973) 'The Unfinished Child. Effects of Early Home Training on the Mongol Infant', in A.D.B. Clarke and A.M. Clark (eds.), *Mental Retardation and Behavioural Research* (Edinburgh: Churchill Livingstone)

British Institute of Mental Handicap (1981) *Parental Training (Reading List)* (Kidderminster: BIMH)

Burton, A.E. *et al.* (1981) 'A Workshop for Parents of Preschool Children with Delayed Development: A School Psychological Service Project', *Journal of the Association of Educational Psychologists, 5, 5*, 36-9

Buckley, S. (1985a) 'The Effect of Portage on the Development of Down's Syndrome Children and their Families — An Interim Report', in B. Daly *et al.* (eds.), *Portage: The Importance of Parents* (Windsor: NFER — Nelson)

Buckley, S. (1985b) 'Teaching Parents to Teach Reading to Teach Language: A Project with Down's Syndrome Children and their Parents', in K. Topping and S. Wolfendale (eds.), *Parental Involvement in Children's Reading* (London: Croom Helm/New York: Nichols Publishing Co.)

Cadman, L.A. (1979) *PEECH Outreach Project (A Program for Early Education of Children with Handicaps). 1978-9 Final Report* (Wichita Falls, Texas: Education Service Center Region 9) (E.R.I.C. ED 185783 EC 124028)

Callias, M. (1980) 'Teaching Parents, Teachers and Nurses', in W. Yule and J. Carr (eds.), *Behaviour Modification for the Mentally Handicapped* (London: Croom Helm)

Callias, M. and Carr, J. (1975) Behaviour Modification Programmes in a Community Setting', in C.C. Kiernan and F.P. Woodford (eds), *Behaviour Modification with the Severely Retarded* (Amsterdam: Associated Scientific Publishers)

Chacko, R. (1981) 'Family Involvement in the Training of Mentally Retarded Children: An Indian Example', *Prospects, 11, 4*, 456-9

Clark, D.B. *et al.* (1982) 'Behavioral Training for Parents of Mentally Retarded Children: Prediction of Outcome', *American Journal of Mental Deficiency, 87, 1*, 14-19

Clements, J.C. *et al.* (1980) 'A Home Advisory Service for Pre-school Children with Developmental Delays', *Child Care Health and Development, 6, 1*, 25-33

Clunies-Ross, G.G. (1979) 'Accelerating the Development of Down's Syndrome Infants and Young Children', *Journal of Special Education, 13, 2*, 169-77

Cocks, R.P. and Gardner, J.M. (1979) 'The Role of the Educational Psychologist in the Education of Severely Subnormal Children', *Journal of the Association of Educational Psychologists, 4, 10*, 13-20

Coordinating Office for Regional Resource Centres (1976) *Early Childhood Programs for the Severely Handicapped* (Lexington, Kentucky: CORRC) (E.R.I.C. EC 091339 ED 129039)

Cunningham, C.C. (1975) 'Parents as Therapists and Educators', in C.C. Kiernan and F.P. Woodford (eds.) *Behaviour Modification with the Severely Retarded* (Amsterdam: Associated Scientific Publishers)

Cunningham, C.C. and Jeffree, D.M. (1975) 'The Organisation and Structure of Workshops for Parents of Mentally Handicapped Children', *Bulletin of the British Psychological Society, 28*, 405-11

Daly, B. (1980) 'Evaluation of Portage Home Teaching Pilot Project: 1979-1980', unpublished report, Barking and Dagenham Schools Psychological Service

Ellender, P. (1983) 'A Formative Evaluation of a Voluntary Portage Group', *Occasional Papers of the Division of Educational and Child Psychology, British Psychological Society, 7, 1*, 72-3

Emerson, P. *et al.* (1981) 'Workshops for Parents of Mentally Handicapped Children', *Journal of the Association of Educational Psychologists, 5, 6*, 33-8

Firth, H. (1982) The Effectiveness of Parent Workshops in a Mental Handicap Service', *Child Care Health and Development, 8*, 77-91

Fredericks, H.D.B. *et al.* (1971) 'Parents Educate their Trainable Children', *Mental Retardation*, pp. 24-6

Garner, A.Y.S. (1979) 'An Examination of Two Delivery Models with Regard to Program Effectiveness and Extent of Parent Involvement', unpublished doctoral dissertation, New Mexico State University (E.R.I.C. EC 123796)

Gath, A. (1979) 'Parents as Therapists of Mentally Handicapped Children', *Journal of Child Psychology and Psychiatry, 20, 2*, 161-5

Glossop, C. and Castillo, M. (1982) 'Summary of Present and Future Research into the Portage Model', in R.J. Cameron (ed.), *Working Together: Portage in the U.K.* (Windsor: NFER – Nelson)

Griffin, M.W. (1979) 'Training Parents of Retarded Children as Behaviour Therapists: A Review', *Australian Journal of Mental Retardation 5, 5*, 18-27

Hanson, M.J. (1976) 'Evaluation of Training Procedures Used in a Parent-implemented Intervention Program for Down's Syndrome Infants', *AAESPH Review, 1, 7*, 36-52 (E.R.I.C. EC 092840)

Hanson, M.J. and Schwarz, R.H. (1978) 'Results of a Longitudinal Intervention Program for Down's Syndrome Infants and their Families', *Education and Training of the Mentally Retarded, 13, 4*, 403-7

Harris, J. (1978) 'Working with Parents of Mentally Handicapped Children on a Longterm Basis', *Child Care Health and Development, 4, 2*, 121-30

Heifetz, L.J. (1977a) 'Professional Preciousness and the Evaluation of Parent Training Strategies', in P. Mittler (ed.), *Research to Practice in Mental Retardation*, vol. 1: *Care and Intervention* (Baltimore: University Park Press)

Heifetz, L.J. (1977b) 'Behavioural Training for Parents of Retarded Children: Alternative Formats Based on Instructional Manuals', *American Journal of Mental Deficiency, 82, 2*, 194-203

Heifetz, L.J. (1977b) 'Behavioral Training for Parents of Retarded Children: the Network of Services for Retarded Children', in R.R. Abidin (ed.), *Parent Education and Intervention Handbook* (Springfield, Illinois: C.C. Thomas)

Hillard, J. and Shearer, M. (1976) 'The Portage Project', *Bureau Memorandum, 17, 2*, 4-8 (E.R.I.C. EC 081918)

Holland, F.L.U. and Noaks, J.C. (1982) 'Portage in Mid Glamorgan', *Journal of the Association of Educational Psychologists, 5, 9*, 32-7

Holland, J. (1981) 'The Lancaster Portage Project: A Home Based Service for Developmentally Delayed Young Children and their Families', *Health Visitor, 54*, 486-8

Holland, J.M. and Hattersley, J. (1980) 'Parent Support Groups for the Families of Mentally Handicapped Children', *Child Care Health and Development, 6*, 165-73

Hornby, G. and Singh, N.N. (1982) 'Reflective Group Counselling for Parents of

Mentally Retarded Children', *British Journal of Mental Subnormality, 28,* 71-6

Hornby, G. and Singh, N.N. (1983) 'Group Training for Parents of Mentally Retarded Children: A Review and Methodological Analysis of Behavioural Studies', *Child Care Health and Development, 9, 4,* 199-213

Hudson, A.M. (1982) 'Training Parents of Developmentally Handicapped Children: A Component Analysis', *Behavior Therapy, 13,* 325-33

Institute for Habilitative Services (1980) *Project Sunrise: Handicapped Children's Early Education Program: Third Year Demonstration. Final Report 1979-1980* (Billings, Montana: IHS, Eastern Montana College) (E.R.I.C. EC 132419 ED 199942)

Jeffree, D.M. and Cunningham, C.C. (1975) 'Workshops for Parents of Young Mentally Handicapped Children', in D.A.A. Primrose (ed.), *Proceedings of the 3rd Congress of the International Association for the Scientific Study of Mental Deficiency* (Warsaw: Polish Medical Publishers)

Jeffree, D.M. *et al.* (1977) 'A Parental Involvement Project', in P. Mittler (ed.), *Reserch to Practice in Mental Retardation,* vol. 1: *Care and Intervention* (Baltimore: University Park Press)

Jelinek, J.A. and Flamboe, T.C. (1979) 'The Wyoming Infant Stimulation Programme — Go WISP, Young Baby, Go WISP', paper presented at the Annual International Convention of the Council for Exceptional Children, Dallas (E.R.I.C. EC 115299 ED 171090)

Koerber, C. *et al.* (1979) *Neighborhood Support Systems for Infants, July 1976–December 1979. Final Report* (Somerville, Massachusets: NSSI) (E.R.I.C. EC 131739)

Kuzovich, C.A. and Yawkey, T.D. (1982) 'Play Programs at Home to Stimulate Growth', paper presented to the Conference of the Association for Childhood Education International, Atlanta (E.R.I.C. EC 150031 ED 221007)

Kysela, G.M. *et al.* (1976) 'The Early Education Project 1', paper presented to the Canadian Psychological Association, Toronto (E.R.I.C. ED 141995 EC 101353)

Latham, G. and Hofmeister, A. (1973) 'A Mediated Training Program for Parents of the Preschool Mentally Retarded', *Exceptional Children, 39,* 472-3

Ludlow, J.R. and Allen, L.M. (1979) 'The Effect of Early Intervention and Pre-school Stimulus on the Development of the Down's Syndrome Child', *Journal of Mental Deficiency Research, 23,* 29-44

McCall, C. and Thacker, J. (1977) 'A Parent Workshop in the School', *Special Education: Forward Trends, 4, 4,* 20-1

McConachie, H. (1983) 'Examples of Partnership in Europe', in P. Mittler and H. McConachie (eds.), *Parents, Professionals and Mentally Handicapped People* (London: Croom Helm)

McConachie, H. and Mitchell, D.R. (1985) 'Parents Teaching their Young Mentally Handicapped Children', *Journal of Child Psychology and Psychiatry, 26, 3,* 389-405

Mittler, P. and McConachie, H. (eds.) (1983) *Parents, Professionals and Mentally Handicapped People: Approaches to Partnership* (London: Croom Helm)

Moore, S. *et al.* (1981) 'A Workshop for Parents of Young Handicapped Children', *Journal of the Association of Educational Psychologists, 5, 5,* 40-4

Muir, K.A. and Milan, M.A. (1982) 'Parent Reinforcement for Child Achievement: The Use of a Lottery to Maximise Parent Training Effects', *Journal of Applied Behavior Analysis, 15, 3,* 455-60

Munro, J.K. (1979) 'Living with a Child who is Mentally Retarded: A Course in Parent Education', *Australian Journal of Mental Retardation, 5, 8,* 303-6

National Association for Retarded Citizens (1979) *Training to Facilititate the Education of the Severely Handicapped. Final Report* (Arlington, Texas: NARC) (E.R.I.C. ED 182954 EC 123232)

Noone, J.J. (1980) *Model Programs Serving the Developmentally Disabled* (Washington, DC: Joseph P. Kennedy Jnr Foundation) (E.R.I.C. ED 189825 EC 124556)

O'Shields, D.C. (1977) 'Program Effectiveness, Efficiency and Cost Effectiveness of Delivery Systems to the Severely/Profoundly Handicapped', unpublished doctoral dissertation, University of Alabama (E.R.I.C. EC 114302)

Peniston, E. (1975) *An Evaluation of the Portage Project: A Comparison of a Home-visit Program for Multiply Handicapped Preschoolers and a Head Start Program* (Petersburg, Virginia: Southside Virginia Training Center) (E.R.I.C. EC 073764 ED 112570)

Pollack, G. and Stewart, J. (1982) 'Group Work with Parents of "Special Needs" Children — A Second Look', *Journal of the Association of Educational Psychologists, 5, 10,* 40-2

Revill, S. and Blunden, R. (1977) *Home Training of Pre-school Children with Developmental Delay: Report of the Development and Evaluation of the Portage Service in South Glamorgan* (Cardiff: Applied Research Unit, Ely Hospital)

Revill, S. and Blunden, R. (1978) *Home Training of Pre-school Children with Developmental Delay (Report of the Development and Evaluation of the Portage Service in Ceredigion Health District, Dyfed)* (Cardiff: Applied Reserch Unit, Ely Hospital)

Revill, S. and Blunden, R. (1979) 'A Home Training Service for Pre-school Developmentally Handicapped Children', *Behaviour Research and Therapy, 17,* 207-14

Rose, S.D. (1974) 'Training Parents in Groups as Behavior Modifiers of their Mentally Retarded Children', *Journal of Behaviour Therapy and Experimental Psychiatry, 5,* 135-40

Sandler, A. and Coren, A. (1981) 'Integrated Instruction at Home and School: Parents' Perspective', *Education and Training of the Mentally Retarded, 16, 3,* 183-7

Sandler, A. *et al.* (1983) 'A Training Program for Parents of Handicapped Preschool Children: Effect upon Mother, Father and Child', *Exceptional Children, 49, 4,* 355-8

Sandow, S.A. and Clarke, A.D.B. (1978) 'Home Intervention with Parents of Severely Subnormal Pre-school Children: An Interim Report', *Child Care Health and Development, 4,* 29-39

Sandow, S.A., *et al.* (1981) 'Home Intervention with Parents of Severely Subnormal Pre-school Children: A Final Report', *Child Care Health and Development, 7, 3,* 135-44

Santostefano, S. and Stayton, S. (1967) 'Training the Preschool Retarded Child in Focussing Attention: A Program for Parents', *American Journal of Orthopsychiatry, 37,* 732-43

Sexton, R.P. *et al.* (1980) *The Project Sunrise Model: A Home Based Parent Teaching Program Designed to Serve Handicapped Children Ages Birth to Six Living in Rural Areas of Montana* (revised edition) (Billings, Montana: Institute for Habilitative Services, Eastern Montana College) (E.R.I.C. ED 197531 EC 131733)

Shearer, M.S. and Shearer, D.E. (1972) 'The Portage Project: A Model for Early Childhood Education', *Exceptional Children, 39, 3,* 210-17

Shearer, D.E. and Shearer, M.S. (1976) 'The Portage Project: A Model for Early Childhood Intervention', in T.D. Tjossem (ed.), *Intervention Strategies for High Risk Infants and Young Children* (Baltimore: University Park Press)

Smith, J. (1984) 'The Parent–Child Teaching Interaction: A Measure of Effectiveness', in A. Dessent (ed.) *What is Important about Portage?* (Windsor: NFER — Nelson)

Smith, J. *et al.* (1977) *The Wessex Portage Project: A Home Teaching Service for*

Families with a Pre-school Mentally Handicapped Child (Report no. 125) (Winchester, Hampshire: Wessex Health Care Evaluation Research Team)

Stock, J.R. *et al.* (1975) *Selection and Validation of Model Early Childhood Projects: Final Report* (Columbus, Ohio: Columbus Laboratories) (E.R.I.C. EC 080581 ED 115049)

Tavormina, J.B. (1975) 'Relative Effectiveness of Behavioral and Reflective Group Counseling with Parents of Mentally Retarded Children', *Journal of Consulting and Clinical Psychology, 43*, 22-31

Tavormina, J.B. *et al.* (1976) 'Participant Evaluations of the Effectiveness of their Parent Counseling Groups', *Mental Retardation, 14*, 8-9

Texax Tech University (1980) *Project Family Link 1. Year III Final Report, 1979-1980* (Lubbock, Texas: Texas Tech University) (E.R.I.C. ED 205364 RC 012882)

Timm, M. and Rule, S. (1981) 'R.I.P.: A Cost-effective Parent-implemented Program for Young Handicapped Children', *Early Child Development and Care, 7, 2*, 147-63

Tyler, N.B. and Kogan, K.L. (1977) 'Reduction of Stress between Mothers and their Handicapped Children', *American Journal of Occupational Therapy, 31, 3*, 151-5

Tymchuk, A.J. (1975) 'Training Parent Therapists', *Mental Retardation, 13, 5*, 19-22

Uditsky, B. and McDonald, L. (1981) 'Behavioral Training for Parents of Developmentally-delayed Children: A Two Year Follow-up', *Journal of Practical Approaches to Developmental Handicap, 5, 1*, 5-8

Vasa, S.F. *et al.* (1979) *Career Education for the Handicapped Child: A Guide to Parent Education Programming. Information Series No. 180* (Columbus, Ohio: National Centre for Research in Vocational Education, Ohio State University) (E.R.I.C. EC 124466 ED 179772)

Watson, L.S. and Bassinger, J.F. (1974) 'Parent Training Technology: A Potential Service Delivery System', *Mental Retardation, 12*, 3-10

Weinrott, M.R. (1974) 'A Training Program in Behavior Modification for Siblings of the Retarded', *American Journal of Orthopsychiatry, 44, 3*, 362-75

Wishart, M.C. *et al.* (1980) 'Parental Responses to their Developmentally Delayed Children and the South Glamorgan Home Advisory Service', *Child Care Health and Development, 6*, 361-76

Yavner, M. (1972) *The Portage Project — A Home Approach to the Early Education of Multiply Handicapped Children in a Rural Area* (Portage, Wisconsin: Cooperative Educational Service Agency)

Further Reading

Baker, B.L. (1984) 'Intervention with Families with Young Severely Handicapped Children', in J. Blacher (ed.), *Severely Handicapped Young Children and their Families* (London and New York: Academic Press)

Cunningham, C.C. (1985) 'Training and Education Approaches for Parents of Children with Special Needs', *British Journal of Medical Psychology, 58*, 285-305

McConachie, H. (1986) *Parents and Young Mentally Handicapped Children: A Review of Research Issues* (London: Croom Helm)

12 PHYSICAL AND MULTIPLE HANDICAP

Many children with physical disabilities have other handicaps, and some of the programmes considered in Chapter 11, 'Developmental Delay', included a minority of children who also had physical handicaps. In this chapter, we will consider programmes for children whose primary disability is physical, programmes for children a majority of whom are physically handicapped, and programmes catering on a broad front for children with a great variety and multiplicity of handicaps.

Physical Handicap

An early study of the effectiveness of training parents of brain-injured children was carried out by Salzinger *et al.* (1970). One group of seven families and another of eight were trained. Various self- and programme-selection procedures operated, but interested parents seemed more likely to be experiencing problematic child behaviour. Child ages ranged from 3 to 11 years. Many were hyperactive and threw tantrums. Training involved a written manual (including a reading test to make sure a parent could understand it), small group instruction on taking baseline observations, lectures and discussions, a written test on manual content, and didactic instruction on programming.

Evaluation was by parental recording, observation in centre and at home, and a repeat test of knowledge. Of the 15 parents, four carried out the designed programmes and all were successful in modifying the target behaviour(s). Four other parents implemented only part of the programme, with correspondingly limited success. Seven of the parents did not try to carry out the programmes or completely bungled them, and experienced no change in child behaviour. The authors acknowledge the crudeness of their teaching methods, which are doubtless related to their finding that parents of low educational level did least well.

A group approach to teaching behaviour modification principles and techniques to mothers of children with a wide variety of physical handicaps is reported by Fishman and Fishman (1975).

The diagnoses of the 17 children in the study included spina bifida, hydrocephalus, cerebral palsy, epilepsy and other more obscure conditions. The mothers were seen in two groups for ten weekly sessions of 90 minutes, involving verbal instruction, discussion, film, programmed text and other written handouts, behavioural rehearsal, role-playing, modelling, and positive reinforcement.

Outcome measures were mainly based on pre–post interviews with mother and child and a parental satisfaction questionnaire. Attendance was good (87 per cent), but the techniques were implemented by only 12 of the 17 mothers. All the programming mothers were successful in improving child behaviour. The mothers also felt they could communicate with and praise their children much more than before.

Gentry (1976) provides a most useful review of training parents as modifiers of somatic disorders. The author notes that behavioural techniques have been applied to three different kinds of heart problem, hypertension, asthma, chronic pain, headaches, spasms associated with cerebral palsy, wry neck, neurodermatitis, epilepsy, diarrhoea and benign vocal nodules. Studies with children, however, had been restricted to those suffering from asthma, headaches, scratching and spasms resulting from cerebral palsy.

Case studies demonstrating reduction of asthmatic and severe scratching behaviour by parental non-attention to it and positive reinforcement of incompatible behaviour are reviewed. A simple response–cost procedure had eliminated severe headache in an adolescent, who had to write a detailed report on each headache before receiving any attention. (Parents were the primary change agent in all these studies.) In another study, parents were used to maintain a successful programme of behavioural treatment initiated in hospital for an asthmatic, who was subjected to time-out when he had an asthmatic 'attack'. The author is optimistic about the potential of such methods.

Interesting work with children showing 'failure to thrive' is reported by Drotar (1981), who notes that the condition generates substantial stress in the care-givers. A home-based, family-centred programme involves family members in assessing how family influences disrupt nurturance and encourages them to develop alternative strategies. Stress management techniques and analysis of family relationship problems are included. Infants are assessed at six-month intervals on intellectual development, play behaviour, language competence and attachment, and monthly home obser-vations are made of parent–child interaction. Follow-up data at one year from small samples of infants from low-income families show improved rates of weight gain and more positive attachment behaviour.

Epstein *et al.* (1981) report a treatment programme for 19 diabetic children aged 8–12 years, which involved instruction on medication, diet and exercise and the use of a token economy and praise by the parents. Training took place in three groups during eight sessions of 90 minutes each spread over twelve weeks, together with a follow-up two months later. Written instructions with cloze and other tests played a large part, and separate modules were available for parent and child. Parents paid a $35 deposit, some of which was returned contingent on attendance at meetings. Contracts were also established with the children. The target behaviour was production of negative glucose urine tests. Telephone contact was also made with parents and children weekly. Mean percentage of negative glucose tests increased from baseline in all three groups by at least two standard deviations.

Wide-span Programmes

Early work with the parents of multiply handicapped youngsters aged 14 to 21 is reported by Feldman *et al.* (1975). The children had previously been in special educational placements for the brain-injured or emotionally disturbed, and had a wide range of learning and behaviour problems. About a quarter of the parents were involved in a course designed jointly to explore each child's profile of skills and review objectives, and methods for helping, followed by more specific training in behaviour modification. All the parents implemented a behavioural programme at home, but further outcome data are descriptive.

A paediatric clinic in a general hospital was the setting of a parent education programme for children with a miscellany of problems, described by Morris *et al.* (1976), who had commenced work of this kind in 1973. A playroom was staffed and equipped, and a twelve session structured curriculum for children aged 2–3 devised. The mainly black and Hispanic parents received an individual tutoring session every two months, using role-play, to enable the parents to teach the child curriculum skills at home.

Concepts relating to child development and reinforcement were included. Parents were asked to work at home daily for 15–20 minutes using materials supplied by the programme.

Sixty per cent of the eligible parents entered the programme, but only half of these completed it. Older parents were found to be significantly more likely to complete training, as were parents who lived nearby. Other demographic variables proved insignificant. Tests of intelligence (Cattell/Stanford-Binet) were conducted at six-month intervals, and increases in IQ significant at the 0.01 level found. At six-month follow-up these gains were maintained. Parental feedback questionnaires were positive. The authors concluded that raising children is not just a question of 'doing what comes naturally', and that parent training can be demonstrated to be of benefit to children. The usefulness of pre-/post-natal and paediatric clinics as a communication line with mothers is emphasised.

A programme for the parents of children aged 2 weeks to 4 years, including children with brain damage/cerebral palsy (44 per cent), Down's syndrome (25 per cent), hydrocephalus (7 per cent), and blindness (3 per cent), is described by Drezek (1976). Over half the parents were Mexican-American (44 per cent) or black (12 per cent). An initial series of four one-hour sessions covered the skill profile of the child and introductory information, and this was followed by a further four sessions in which three families at a time met in a group with several professionals, who trained them by verbal instruction and modelling. Additionally, there were large group evening meetings devoted to Parent Effectiveness Training (see Chapter 4, 'Ordinary Children'). Some parents took their involvement further, and were provided with welfare, marriage or other counselling, while others became parent representatives on the advisory board.

The total services offered in this project included centre-based daycare, nursery and therapy programmes. The home programme, however, operated via weekly visits at which specific exercises were taught to mother and child; emphasis was also placed on the quality of interaction. Child curriculum was drawn from Portage and Nisonger (O'Connell, 1975).

Over a period of six months in the programme, Denver and Portage checklist scores rose very significantly (0.001 level), and qualitative changes in child behaviour were noted on video-recordings. The quality of parent–child interaction also seemed to improve. It is a pity that this large, multi-faceted and comprehensive programme was not more thoroughly evaluated.

In a completely different vein, Neman *et al.* (1977) carried out a survey of parents who had undertaken sensori-motor patterning therapy programmes in their home. The parents had carried out work under the supervision of the breakaway American Academy of Human Development (AAHD), rather than the original Doman-Delacato techniques of the Institute for the Achievement of Human Potential (the similarities between the two nevertheless being greater than their differences). The 'patterning' method itself has been the subject of considerable professional controversy, and the stringent requirements of programme implementation at home have been said to be detrimental to family stability. Originally designed for the brain-injured, Doman-Delacato techniques have subsequently been prescribed for a much wider population, children said to show signs of 'neurological disorganisation'.

Evaluations of the effectiveness of 'patterning' largely confine themselves to programmes where therapy was carried out in places other than the home, and while the original results of Doman and Delacato were supportive of their methods, a majority of studies by other investigators have failed to replicate their findings (Neman *et al.*, 1973, 1975). The 1977 National Association for Retarded Citizens survey looked at the beliefs of 274 parent respondents from a sample of 559 families in four major cities who had carried out AAHD-style 'patterning' at home.

The children of most of the responding parents had been diagnostically categorised, with proportions as follows: brain damage (52 per cent), learning or reading disability (22 per cent), visual impairment (6 per cent), mobility impairment (12 per cent), mental retardation (4 per cent), and miscellaneous (4 per cent). The parents responding were generally supportive of the programme: 91 per cent felt there had been *some* effect, 86 per cent would recommend the programme to another family, 83 per cent would do it all over again if necessary, and 61 per cent definitely thought the improvements seen would never have happened without the programme. 'Much positive improvement' was reported by 58 per cent of parents and 'slight improvement' by a further 30 per cent.

A deleterious effect on family relationships was noted by between 2 per cent and 11 per cent of respondents, depending on the relationship, with the mother's relationships with the rest of the family suffering most. Greater numbers reported improved family relationships. The improvements the parents reported seeing in the children were extremely various and parents seemed to find it difficult to be specific. A sub-study using data supplied by the AAHD indicated that non-respondents were considerably more likely to have failed to implement a programme correctly or succesfully. Thus the representativeness of the sample is in doubt and, of course, the questionable validity of evaluation via grateful testimonials from parents has been repeatedly noted. Nor can these results be generalised to other institutions offering 'patterning' training.

A programme which sounds similar (but isn't) is EXTEND: Exercises to Encourage Development (Thurmon, 1980). This project was targeted upon children who survived in ordinary classes but showed developmental lags in motor skills, perception or language. After an initial detailed assessment and 'diagnosis', meetings between parent, teacher and programme co-ordinator were held every two weeks. Individualised 'lessons' were designed, materials provided for these to be carried out at home, and parental recordings instituted.

For evaluation purposes, experimental, control and placebo groups (n = 22–4) were established, the placebo group receiving extra attention from a volunteer (high school student) tutor. Pre–post testing on the Meeting Street School Screening Test showed the EXTEND group significantly ahead of placebo or control groups at the 0.01 level, consistently in fine and gross motor skills, less consistently in visual motor skills, and erratically from year to year in language skills.

Bricker (1980) reports on a programme for Down's syndrome, cerebral palsied, behaviour problem, sensorily impaired and other handicapped pre-school children. Multiple services were offered, including a wide range of ordinary and special 'pre-school' classroom options, as well as the home-based option servicing families who lived a long way from the centre. All participating parents had some support, but the home programme in particular offered weekly visits by home teachers who proposed activities, modelled their implementation and encouraged parental recording. Some additional group meetings occurred, and welfare counselling and other advocacy was also in-built. Evaluation by pre–post assessment on norm- and criterion-referenced tests showed some significant improvements, but not in developmental quotients, i.e. the children were not accelerated beyond 'normal' rates. Also, data for the home programme group are unfortunately not separately reported.

Project KIDS (Kindling Individual Development Systems) is described by Turner and Rogers (1981). A pre-school programme for handicapped children from birth to 6 years of age, it offers centre-based professional teaching and an independent home-based twice-weekly visiting service which has catered for 118 children. Children with a wide range of mental, physical and multiple handicaps are served, and in the home programme the most frequent primary handicaps are developmental delay and cerebral palsy. Families of very various socio-economic status are served, of which 41 per cent are black and 15 per cent Hispanic.

Child progress is assessed by criterion-referenced curriculum-based assessment and developmental checklists, together with some normative testing and sampling of parent perceptions. Significant gains were made by children on developmental checklists, but gains on norm-referenced tests were less than half normal rates on average, although a ceiling effect operated on the Bayley Scale for some of the older children. The use of a 'theoretical control group', consisting of the projections of expected development given by an independent panel of experts, is described. Inter-expert reliability findings are reported at coefficients of 0.92 to 0.96, but the authors are secretive about the outcome of the comparison of project gains with 'theoretical control' scores. In any event, there is no separate reportage of outcomes for the home programme group.

Fromboluti (1982) reports on the DEBT (Developmental Education Birth through Two) project, catering for a wide span of disabilities — speech, hearing, visual, emotional and physical problems as well as developmental delay. Initial assessment and data-collection from parents precedes the development of an individual education plan, which is implemented via weekly home visits, supplemented by larger group discussions. If both parents are in full-time employment, the home teacher works directly with the child wherever the child is to be found.

A study of 103 children who had completed the DEBT programme used scores on a detailed developmental checklist compensated to control for maturation. Impressive gains are noted irrespective of degree of handicap in the areas of receptive and expressive language, social development and fine motor skills, with lesser gains in gross motor skills. Children graduating from the programme at the age of 3 proceed to ordinary educational placements at a much higher rate than might be expected, half of them requiring no extra help. Subsequent outreach developments carried the programme into other communities and rural areas, and for this various manuals were written (see 'Resources Directory', pp. 319-337). Further details of, or a reference to, the compensation formula would have been welcome.

A series of programmes for groups of parents of school-aged physically handicapped, hearing-impaired, and mildly and moderately mentally handicapped children in New Zealand is reported by Hornby and Murray (1983). The courses typically involved two-hour sessions, held every six to eight weeks, of lecture presentation, written information, home assignments and small group discussion, combining reflective and behavioural techniques. Evaluation measures did not extend beyond post-programme questionnaires and attendance rates. The latter varied from 71 to 85 per cent, and questionnaire responses were as positive as is usually the case. Considerable detail of organisational features is given.

Summary

Early work on training parents of brain-injured children in operant procedures was of limited success. More sophisticated teaching methods raised implementation rates to 70 per cent. Single case studies have documented successful training of this kind to reduce asthmatic, headache and scratching problems. Operant techniques coupled with token economy and contracting proved effective with 8–12-year-olds in controlling diabetes. From a different theoretical perspective, a project offering training in family relationship and stress management produced some positive outcomes at twelve-month follow-up with families of infants showing 'failure to thrive'.

Programmes catering for a wide range of diverse handicaps are reviewed. A training programme in a paediatric clinic had a high drop-out rate, but resulted in marked child acceleration for the remainder, which was maintained six months later. The evidence on the effectiveness of centre-based sensori-motor patterning (Doman–Delacato) is conflicting, and there is little on the effectiveness of the procedures at home. However, a (non-random) sample of parents responding to a survey reported largely positive effects.

The EXTEND project, involving centre-based parent training in educational tasks conducted at home, resulted in erratic but encouraging gains. The KIDS home-visiting project seems to have yielded rather disappointing gains. However, the DEBT programme, operating on a similar basis, produced impressive gains, accelerating children at well beyond expected rates.

It seems that programmes specifically for children with physical handicaps have been largely behavioural, with results improving in line with methods. There seems no reason why this approach should not be extended to a wide range of somatic conditions. Programmes with other theoretical orientations warrant exploration. Wide-span programmes for children with diverse handicaps have tended to be educational in orientation, with emphasis on curriculum skills. Centre-based and home-visiting programmes have been equally common. Three programmes offering multiple services have failed to partial out the effect of the home component in the evaluation. The best programmes have demonstrated both effectiveness and cost-effectiveness, but a small minority of reported results are disappointing.

Few data on short- or long-term follow-up are reported, and there is very little information on generalisation or demonstration of control over process variables. This might be expected in a field where relatively little work has taken place, but it is alarming that a number of the studies (particularly of wide-span programmes) offer so little detail of process that replicability is questionable. Nevertheless, there is great potential here, and it is interesting that the best programmes manage to work effectively with parents of children with very diverse difficulties, contrary to the expectations of some workers in other fields, such as developmental delay.

References

Bricker, D. (1980) *Handicapped Children's Early Education Program, Division of Innovation and Development. Final Report 1977-1980* (Eugene, Oregon: Center on Human Development, Oregon University) (E.R.I.C. ED 206148 EC 140002)

Drezek, W. (1976) *The Infant–Parent Training Program* (Austin, Texas: Travis County Mental Retardation Center) (E.R.I.C. ED 132816 EC 092707)

Drotar, D. (1981) 'Family Centered Intervention with Infant Failure to Thrive', paper presented at annual meeting of Americal Psychological Association, Los

Angeles (E.R.I.C. ED 208960, PS 012469)

Epstein, L.H. *et al.* (1981) 'The Effects of Targeting Improvements in Urine Glucose on Metabolic Control in Children with Insulin Dependent Diabetes', *Journal of Applied Behavior Analysis, 14*, 4, 365-75

Feldman, M.A. *et al.* (1975) 'Parents and Professionals: A Partnership in Special Education', *Exceptional Children, 41*, 551-4

Fishman, C.A. and Fishman, D.B. (1975) 'A Group Training Program in Behaviour Modification for Mothers of Children with Birth Defects: An Exploratory Study', *Child Psychiatry and Human Development, 6, 1*, 3-14

Fromboluti, C.S. (1982) 'A Pioneer Program', *American Education, 18, 5*, 20-4

Gentry, W.D. (1976) 'Parents as Modifiers of Somatic Disorders', in E.J. Mash *et al.* (eds.) *Behavior Modification Approaches to Parenting* (New York: Brunner/Mazel)

Hornby, G. and Murray, R. (1983) 'Group Programmes for Parents of Children with Various Handicaps', *Child Care Health and Development, 9*, 4, 185-98

Morris, A.G. *et al.* (1976) 'Educational Intervention for Preschool Children in a Pediatric Clinic', *Pediatrics, 57*, 5, 765-8

Neman, R. *et al.* (1973) *Sensori-motor Training Project: Final Report* (Arlington, Texas: National Association for Retarded Citizens)

Neman, R. *et al.* (1975) 'Experimental Evaluation of Sensorimotor Patterning Used with Mentally Retarded Children', *American Journal of Mental Deficiency, 79, 4*, 372-84

Neman, R. *et al.* (1977) 'A Survey of Parents Using Sensorimotor Home Training Programs', *Education and Training of the Mentally Retarded, 12*, 109-18

O'Connell, C.Y. (1975) 'The Challenge of Parent Education', *Exceptional Children, 41*, 554-7

Salzinger, K. *et al.* (1970) 'Training Parents of Brain-injured Children in the Use of Operant Conditioning Procedures', *Behaviour Therapy, 1*, 4-32

Thurmon, C. (1980) 'EXTEND: Exercises to Encourage Development. A Program of Parent Involvement', paper presented at Annual International Convention of the Council for Exceptional Children, Philadelphia (E.R.I.C. ED 188423 EC 124383)

Turner, R. and Rogers, A.M. (1981) 'Project KIDS: Infant Education for the Handicapped in an Urban Public School System', *Journal of the Division for Early Childhood, 2*, 40-51

13 SUMMARY

Much as we may dream of distilling over 600 research reports into a single exquisite pearl of wisdom, life is not like that. The fields of study are too disparate, and the needs of workers in them far from homogeneous. Nor can we be sure that the non-reportage of poor results has equally affected all areas.

What *is* clear is that the quality and quantity of research varies dramatically from area to area. In Table 13.1, an attempt has been made to indicate the frequency of use by area of different types of research methodology. Figures do not refer to single studies, but to particular methodologies used in single studies. Thus a study with multiple outcome measures of quite different kinds might appear several times, while a study with multiple outcome measures all of the same kind would only appear once. Studies offering only generalised description do not apper in the table at all.

Caveats have already been stated about probable bias in the selection and retrieval of items for this review. In addition, the categories adopted for Table 13.1 are not all-encompassing, and some levering has been necessary to cram the data in somehow. A degree of arbitrariness must be forgiven. Other outcomes have been omitted, e.g. sociometric data, parameters of physical development, improved aid usage, social skills functioning, school attendance, grade retention and special education placement rates, adjustment in employment, and so on. The generalisation column has been collapsed, and incorporates several forms of generalisation: across environmental contexts, to other children (especially siblings), new applications and developments of skills taught to parents, and direct effects on other areas of child skill, for instance.

Even more contentiously, it is argued that the evaluative methodologies are arranged from left to right in Table 13.1 very roughly in order of increasing tangibility or substantiveness. If this approximation can be accepted, it becomes possible to develop an index of the quality of research in an area by weighting follow-up data more than child change data more than parent change data more than descriptive data, summing and standardising by the number of observations. Then, considering frequency of data

Table 13.1: Evaluation Methodologies in Parent Education: Summary Chart

Area	Subsection	Descriptive Data — Attendance Rate	Descriptive Data — Consumer Satisfaction	Descriptive Data — Participation Rate	Parental Change — Attitude	Parental Change — Knowledge	Parental Change — Self-report	Parental Change — Self-record	Parental Change — Observation-centre	Parental Change — Observation-home	Parent Records target behaviour — Pre-post	Parent Records target behaviour — Baseline	Parent Records target behaviour — Control	Parent rating	Self-report	Child Change — Observation-home	Child Change — Observation-else where	Child Change — Attitude/Self-concept	Criterion-referenced — Pre-post	Criterion-referenced — Baseline	Criterion-referenced — Control	Norm-referenced — c.f. norms	Norm-referenced — Baseline	Norm-referenced — Control	Generalisation	Follow-up (<6 mo)	Follow-up (>6 mo)
Parental Involvement in School	Nursery	6																			1	2		3			3
	Primary		4	5		2	1															7		1			
	Secondary & General		2	1					2													1					
Home-School Reporting		2	2	1								5							1	5	3	1	2	3	6		1
Ordinary Children	Miscellaneous		2	1	1	2	1		2	1						1		2					3		3			2
	Early Stimulation				2		2		2									1				2	2		2			
	Academic/Reading			1			1															1	1					
	Gifted						1																					1
	General Parenting		3	1	6	2	4				1			2					1			1					1
Disadvantaged Children	Head/Home Start	1		1			4			1							2				1	4		4	3	1	4
	Gordon																1				1	1		1		1	1
	Levenstein	2	1						1	1						1	1				1	9		8	3	1	4
	High/Scope								2	2						2	2	1			2	4		4		4	3
	DARCEE								1	1											1	4		2			3
	Honig & Lally						1										1	1			1	2		5			2
	Karnes																					5		1	3		
	Schaefer		2	4	1				3						1		4				1	9		9	2	1	1
	miscell. N. America		2					1		6							1				4	9		9	3	2	2
	UK & Europe	1		2	1		3	1						1				1			3	5		5	3	3	2
	HIPPY - Israel		1						1								3				2	2		2	3	3	3
	Australia	1	1				4		1	1						1						2					

Table 13.1: continued

Area	Subsection	Attendance Rate	Consumer Satisfaction	Participation Rate	Attitude	Knowledge	Self-report	Self-record	Obs-centre	Obs-home	Parent Records: Pre-post	Parent Records: Baseline	Parent Records: Control	Parent rating	Self-report	Obs-home	Obs-else where	Attitude/Self-concept	Criterion: Pre-post	Criterion: Baseline	Criterion: Control	Norm: c.f. norms	Norm: Baseline	Norm: Control	Generalisation	Follow-up (<9 mo)	Follow-up (>9 mo)
		Descriptive Data			Parental Change											Child Change											
Ethnic Minorities	N. American Indian	1	1		1														1			1		3			1
	Hispanic		1	3					3	4		4		3		4		3	5	2		10	4	19	9	4	4
Learning Difficulties	Reading	1			1																			2			
	Perceptual	1																	1	1	1				1	1	
	Spelling								3										1		1				1		
	Multiple/Various					1	1			4	1				1												1
Behaviour Problems	Child Abuse								2	4	1					4	1								1	3	1
	Non-behavioural			3	2		3	1	3	5	1			3		1	1								1	3	1
	Behavioural vs not				1		3		2	2	1					1									1	1	2
	Specific programmes		2	1	1		1	1	6	6	1	6	4	2		8	4								5	4	4
	Training Format				1	4		2	6	9	1	4	3	1		9	4								1	6	1
	Generalisation								2	4		3				6	3								10	1	4
	Maintenance								1	3		2	1			3	3								1		7
	Social Factors								1	1	1	2	1	2	1	2	1								1		2
	Therapist training								2								2										
Language Dysfunction	Compensatory				1		1	1	1								2							2	2	2	2
	Specific Dysfunction		1				1	1	1	2	1	1					2							1	2	1	
	Developmental Delay						1	1	1	3	1	1				4	2							1	1	1	
	Autism					1	1	1	5	5	1	2	1	1	1	3	4		4		1	2			2		4
Sensory Impairment	Hearing		1									2				2						2	1			1	
	Vision	1							2			2	2		1						1	2		2			

Area	Subsection	Attendance Rate	Consumer Satisfaction	Participation Rate	Attitude	Knowledge	Self-report	Self-record	Observation-centre	Observation-home	PR Pre-post	PR Baseline	PR Control	Parent rating	Self-report	Observation-home	Observation-else where	Attitude/Self-concept	Crit Pre-post	Crit Baseline	Crit Control	c.f. norms	Norm Baseline	Norm Control	Generalisation	Follow-up (<6 mo)	Follow-up (>6 mo)
		Descriptive Data			Parental Change						Child Change																
											Parent Records target behaviour								Criterion-referenced			Norm-referenced					
Developmental Delay	Portage		3	1				1		2	1	7		2					3	2	2	5	1	1	3	2	
	HARC	4	5						2	2	1	1														1	
	Other UK	4	3	1	1	4			4		1	3	3	3	2		1		2	1	3	1		5	1		3
	Other US	1	6	2	1	5	2	1	7	6	5	7		1	2	1		1	4	1	3	4			5	2	5
Physical & Multiple Handicap	Physical Handicap		1		2	1				1		3			1	1	1		1			1					1
	Wide Span	1	3	1			1							1		1			4		1	3					1

formats together with the weighted index, categorisation of areas
as in Table 13.2 is possible.

However approximate and arbitrary, and obviously open to
debate, it is nevertheless hoped that this structure will give the
reader a framework of reference which may be helpful in assimi-
lating an otherwise rather indigestible mass of information.

The tables indicate deployment of methodologies, not frequency of positive results. Indications of positivity of outcomes are
best retrieved from the written area summaries. However, the
tables do clearly show some considerable gaps which need
addressing by future action research work. It is clear that work on
parent education in the areas of behaviour problems, developmental
delay and disadvantaged children is the most advanced, followed
by work on learning difficulties and language dysfunction.

Although some areas have been the subject of very little
research, almost all have at least one positive outcome.

The whole point of this wide-ranging survey is that methods of
service delivery and evaluation effective in one area may be trans-
ferrable to other areas in an earlier state of development. There is
absolutely no doubt that parent education can not only be highly
effective, but highly cost-effective, if done properly. Hopefully,
this cross-disciplinary overview will stimulate the more rapid dissemination of effective practice.

Table 13.2: Stages of Development in Parent Education

Category 1: Adequate Quantity of Good Quality Evidence (methods of known
effectiveness merely need applying)

Parental involvement in school	—	Nurseries
Home–school reporting		
Ordinary children	—	Early stimulation
Ordinary children	—	Academic/reading
Disadvantaged children	—	Home Start
	—	Levenstein
	—	DARCEE
	—	UK programmes
	—	HIPPY
Learning difficulties	—	Reading
Behaviour problems	—	Non-behavioural methods
	—	Behavioural vs not
	—	Specific programmes
	—	Training format
	—	Generalisation
	—	Maintenance

Language dysfunction	—	Specific dysfunctions
	—	Developmental delay
	—	Autism
Sensory impairment	—	Hearing
Developmental delay	—	Portage
	—	Other UK programmes
	—	Other US programmes
Physical and multiple handicap	—	Physical handicap
	—	Wide-span programmes

Category 2: Adequate Quality but Not Enough Quantity (replication and extension required)

Parent involvement in school	—	Primary schools
Disadvantaged children	—	Gordon
	—	High/Scope
	—	Honig/Lally FDRP
	—	Karnes
	—	Schaefer IERP
	—	Miscell. N. American
Ethnic minorities	—	Hispanic
Learning difficulties	—	Perceptual
	—	Spelling
	—	Multiple/various
Behaviour problems	—	Child abuse
	—	Social factors
	—	Therapist training
Language dysfunction	—	Compensatory

Category 3: Adequate Quantity but Not Enough Quality (better research designs needed)

Ordinary children	—	General parenting
Developmental delay	—	HARC

Category 4: Neither Quantity Nor Quality Adequate (field ripe for development)

Parental involvement in school	—	Secondary and general
Ordinary children	—	Gifted
	—	Miscellaneous
Disadvantaged children	—	Australia
Ethnic minorities	—	N. American Indian
Sensory impairment	—	Vision

14 PROJECT PLANNING

Many implications for the planning of projects have already emerged from the literature review. However, the indications for planning do not always point in the same direction. Thus, for instance, we have some evidence that home visiting improves the effectiveness of parent education programmes for disadvantaged children, while on the other hand its use does not necessarily improve the effectiveness of programmes for children with learning difficulties.

Innumerable variables are at work in the operation of parent education programmes: social, psychological, organisational, locational and financial — plus, of course, the impact of sheer determination. It would be naive to expect one 'ideal' form of organisation to cover all eventualities. The management of a successful programme is the art of rapidly discovering the most propitious aptitude × treatment interactions at all levels, then trying to keep the whole thing in balance by constant juggling.

For the moment, we can review some of the literature on planning considerations, and look to the development of a 'planning guide', which will outline the options, or points of planning decision. This should enable programme planners to make decisions more consciously and help clarify any points at which they may be unwittingly deciding not to make a decision.

However, even given such a structured outline, there is no subtitute for experience. The newcomer will have to review the known facts, make a series of best guesses as to what form of organisation to adopt, ensure that it is carefully evaluated, and modify it as necessary subsequently. Modifications can be in the direction of a lighter-weight or more substantial intervention — and will themselves need evaluating. Initially, it is desirable to go for a degree of organisational 'over-kill' in your first project. If you start small and keep it tight you are much more likely to have a successful first project. This is not only essential for you, to keep your motivation high, but also for the community, since if word spreads on the neighbourhood grapevine that your project is a waste of time, you will have severe recruitment difficulties for a subsequent project, no matter how much you have modified and improved the format.

For the same reasons, it is foolish to attack the biggest problems first. To target your first project on the *most* disadvantaged, the severest learning difficulties, the most handicapped children, etc., is simply to ask for trouble. Of course that may be where the crying need is that motivated you to set up the project in the first place, but you need some experience with smaller fry before hurling yourself at the big stuff. Projects are like schools: they need to be both led and managed, and for this to occur effectively, project leaders must be able to manage their own time and their own stress levels.

Literature on Planning

A particularly useful source is the Portage manual (Boyd and Herwig, 1980), which includes sections on planning individual programmes, planning and implementing home visits, using behavioural objectives and developing lesson plans. Stevens (1976) reviews three programme strategies (visiting, group meetings, combined methods) and discusses research evidence on which parents might benefit from which method in which situation. Garland (1978) offers a Skills Inventory for Teachers (SIFT), listing behaviours and skills requisite for a parent educator working with the families of very young handicapped children. Ratings may be completed by self, peer or supervisor, and cover eleven relevant skill areas. Heward and Dardig (1978) review strategies in planning, conducting and evaluating programmes.

The Nisonger *Program Manager's Manual* (Wnek *et al.*, 1980) covers initial assessment, developing individualised programmes, generating home activities, and periodic evaluation. Elgas (1981) gives details of procedures for recruiting and supervising home visitors and planning home visit activities. A useful overview is given by Wolfendale (1985). LaCrosse (1982) discusses different types of programme format in HCEEP (Handicapped Children's Early Education Program) projects. Work with fathers and the role of parent counselling is considered. Klenke *et al.* (1975) offer a guide to a simulation–information exercise designed to increase parental understanding of the Wisconsin Design for Reading Skill Development, a school-based but parent-involved reading programme. Evaluation procedures involving assessment of parental knowledge of the programme and understanding of their role in it are included in the materials. As a device for 'improving home–school–community relations', these materials appear on the surface to be a little short on subtlety.

A useful paper by Baker (1976) summarises research and offers these guidelines:

1. seek some homogeneity in child functioning and types of problem;
2. seek some diversity in parents' background;
3. have two trainers in the group — preferably of different genders — at least one must be experienced;
4. schedule some evening meetings to involve fathers;
5. schedule meetings in easily accessible locations;
6. provide supervision/creche for children, or (if possible) include them in the training;
7. encourage single parents to bring a friend;
8. have an organised plan for training sessions but be prepared to depart from it if necessary;
9. present objectives of training clearly at the outset — what you will and will not do, what will be expected of parents;
10. state parameters of programme clearly at outset (number of sessions, schedule of inputs);
11. involve parents in assessing their children and selecting targets (thereby shaping them into record keeping);
12. begin with skills parents want to teach and child is ready to learn;
13. minimise lectures, use action-oriented inputs such as modelling and role-playing;
14. practice in training everything you expect parents to do at home;
15. provide written information in advance, so trainer time is used to model and give feedback rather than to provide information;
16. only ask for as much record keeping as is really needed;
17. model your interest in record keeping by reviewing records carefully with parents;
18. structure occasions for parents to discuss with one another;
19. provide incentives for parental attendance and programming;
20. provide ways for parents to give feedback about the training programme — and respond to it!

A similar list is offered by Turner and Rogers (1981), who emphasise starting on a small scale, involving local community figures, using existing organisational infrastructures within the neighbourhood of the target group and existing local community resources, selecting teachers with a wide range of skills, expecting the ecology of the handicapped child to impact the programme, anticipating some resistance from professionals who feel their territory is being encroached on, reviewing the experience of other programmes and building in evaluation.

Another useful paper dealing with planning issues is that of Wyckoff (1980). The relative merits of group versus individual instruction are discussed, and problems of training and monitoring reviewed. There is an interesting debate on screening potential programme parents for psychopathology and 'locus of control'. Practical issues of recruitment and meeting, decisions on curriculum content, format of training methodology and maintaining established gains are all covered.

Kruger (1975), in a review of 'education for parenthood', proposed the following 'standards' for an effective parent programme:

1. comprehensive — curriculum specified, priority ordered, strategies and resources identified;
2. competency-based — involving demonstrable knowledge and behaviours, with staff training and evaluation built in;
3. experience-based — involving observation and participation and realistic field activities to ensure generalisation of principles;
4. flexible — a modular curriculum may be necessary to meet the needs of special groups or situations, and cater for aptitude × treatment interaction effects;
5. interdisciplinary — since parenthood is multi-disciplinary;
6. universal — implying generalisability to the rest of the family and the community;
7. continuous — preventive in nature rather than being seen as a response to critical incidents or needs, and giving parents skills to meet future needs;
8. cost-effective;
9. multi-goal.

The reader may be forgiven for thinking that our *school* systems fall well short of these standards in many respects. Being relatively new, parent programmes have to try harder.

Eldridge Cleaver once said that if you're not part of the solution, you're part of the problem. Tentative project leaders may too readily see the recruited parents as 'a problem', and the programme as a remedial intervention rather than an independent positive input. Shearer and Shearer (1977) give a list of ways in which parents can be part of the solution, describing parental roles in programmes as administrators, disseminators, staff members, teachers, recruiters, curriculum developers, counsellors, skill assessors and evaluator/record keepers. Several concrete examples of practice are then given.

Particular attention should be paid to the training methods adopted. Reliance on 'normal' didactic methods is usually fatal, as many high schools have discovered (while continuing to assume that this implies a defect in the children). Shively *et al.* (1975) studied the relative effectiveness of written instruction at three levels of difficulty (8-, 11- and 14-year level) with two types of illustration (decorative and instructional) on parents' ability to complete a prescribed set of home-teaching activities. Even with the easiest reading materials, 25 per cent of the parents could not carry out the described activity, and the use of instructional illustrations made things worse.

Even with undergraduate students serving as paraprofessional reading tutors, Gueldenpfenning (1976) found that training them by lecturing improved their emission of pre-specified tutor behaviours by 33 per cent from baseline, while modelling improved performance by 238 per cent and role-playing by 250 per cent. The author's seven 'essential tutoring skills' are also interesting: (i) specifying — informing tutee of material to be covered, tasks and consequences of task completion, (ii) signalling — asking questions, giving direction and prompting at relevant points; (iii) recognition — indicating rather than criticising errors; (iv) reinforcing — praising correct responses; (v) correcting — prompting the tutee to self-correct errors; (vi) data-collection — recording tutee performance; and (vii) enthusiasm — varying loudness, rhythm, pacing and pauses in voice when interacting with tutee.

In similar vein, O'Dell (1976) found a lengthy verbal theoretical pre-training, prior to a behavioural workshop experience, did not improve the effectiveness of the workshop on multiple outcome measures. In fact, the small differences found favoured the briefer training. On the other hand, programmes which are totally focused on a small number of concrete behavioural outcomes may result in failure by the programme participants to generalise those skills.

Doleys *et al.* (1976) took this further, comparing the effect of verbal and written instruction plus modelling plus role-play with the impact of an extended training which also included feedback from the group and self-rating from audio-recordings. The extended training produced the more marked changes in parental behaviour.

It has been suggested that programme participants who tend to see events influenced by factors outside themselves (external locus of control) respond better to directive teaching methods than those with an internal locus, who respond better to non-directive tuition (Abramowitz *et al.*, 1974). Brewer *et al.* (1981) manipulated presentation formats with 'internal' and 'external' groups in a behaviourally oriented training programme for parents (32 mothers, four fathers, all group leaders female, participants mostly middle class). Matching locus of control to presentation mode did indeed significantly raise parent management skills. On measures of changed child behaviour, 'directed externals' did best and 'directed internals' worst, while internals and externals did equally well in non-directive groups. However, general parental attitudes were most enhanced by participation in the less directive groups. This leaves programme designers in a fine quandary, of course, and emphasises the need to be very clear about ultimate programme objectives.

In addition to 'personality' factors, social factors may influence the outcome of the training programme. Reisinger *et al.* (1976) found treatment failure connected to marital problems, and Strain *et al.* (1980) found single parent families more likely to drop out of training than intact families, and less able to sustain treatment effects. Martin (1977) studied the effects of fathers' involvement in training, and concluded it made little difference, but outcome measures were weak.

Webster-Stratton (1985) compared families with a father present and involved with the child to families with no father figure present or involved, in terms of response to a behavioural parent training programme. In the father-involved group, fathers attended nearly as many programme sessions as mothers. Subsequently, mothers in both groups and fathers in one reported significant and equivalent attitudinal and child behaviour improvements post-programme. However, at one-year follow-up, the father-involved group had maintained and generalised behavioural improvements much better than the other group. Webster-Stratton concludes that community support or 'booster sessions' may be necessary for single parents.

A more immediate problem than maintenance of gains may be attrition *during* the programme. Stile (1978) found home-centred projects tended to suffer less from attrition than centre-based projects. This phenomenon reflects the fact that centre-based projects only appear to be cheaper in professional time (and therefore more likely to be cost-effective, *ceteris paribus*) because they shift programme participation costs from the professionals on to the parents. Financial and time costs of travelling and stress from disturbance of routine activities to attend meetings at times and places fixed to suit some group compromise all constitute disincentives to attend.

Siegert and Yates (1980) provide an excellent discussion of these matters in their paper comparing individual home-based, individual centre-based and group delivery systems. The three systems were found to be equally effective in this case, and although operations costs favoured group delivery, opportunity costs and client cost favoured in-home delivery. The authors also note that the relationship between cost and effectiveness should not be expected to be linear, extrapolatable or generalisable. More of the same isn't necessarily better.

Finally, attention must be paid to generalisation. The classic papers here are Stokes and Baer (1977) and Koegel *et al.* (1978) — essential reading for all those who hope for an enduring impact from their parent training programmes.

A schematisation of project planning is given in Tables 14.1 and 14.2. Remember, review the options, start small, keep it tight, modify as necessary, and make time for evaluation. Failure is bad for your mental health.

Table 14.1: Programme Planning — Outline Steps

Preparation

1.	Needs assessment	8.	Location
2.	Context	9.	Socio-emotional support
3.	Objectives	10.	Curriculum content
4.	Target Group	11.	Target setting
5.	Selection	12.	Materials and resources
6.	Recruitment	13.	Duration and frequency
7.	Teaching staff		

Teaching Methods

14.	Verbal input	20.	Prompting and cueing
15.	Written/visual input	21.	Practice
16.	Discussion/questions	22.	Feedback
17.	Social grouping	23.	Reinforcement
18.	Modelling	24.	Contracting
19.	Role-play/rehearsal		

Follow-up

25.	Staff supervision	28.	Generalisation
26.	Parent monitoring	29.	Maintenance
27.	Fading	30.	Evaluation

Table 14.2: Programme Planning Guide

Step	Options	Questions/issues
	PREPARATION	
Needs *assessment*	Informal contact	What bias does this introduce?
	Advice from community leaders	Are they really in touch?
	Questionnaires	Open-ended or multiple-choice?
	Discussion groups	Bias to verbal parents
	Interviews — individual	Can volunteer parents do this?
	Interviews — group	As for discussion groups
	Home visits	Who's got the time?
Context *(issues to* *consider)*	*Community*	
	Size of community	
	Size of catchment area	
	Density of population	
	Socio-economic status	
	Ethnic minorities	
	Ease of access to centre	

Table 14.2: continued

Step	Options	Questions/issues
	School Aims/policies of the hierarchy Responsiveness of staff Organisation problems Attainment levels Awareness of programme goals Parental response to school	Are you upsetting the boss? Have they been briefed? Crumbling curriculum? Hyper-authoritarian? Are you shoring up a rotten system? Ignorance breeds anxiety — brief colleagues What current levels/type of involvement?
	Resources Time Money Buildings Travel Materials Clerical support Other support	Ensure no duplication of other programmes Budget for enthusiasm and determination Beware other events (Christmas, summer holidays, etc.) Room? Seating? Power? Refreshments? Practice space? Storage? Creche space and staffing? Paper and card? Audio-visual and reprographic equipment? Got a typewriter? Typist? Telephone? Stamps? Transport? (incl. for parents) Who supports the project leader?
Objectives	Specify behavioural objectives for: project leader; project staff; parents; children; teachers; other	Consider behavioural excesses and deficits
Target group	How many? What age? What ability? Degree of handicap? Organisational context? Parental 'co-operativeness'? Socio-economic status Language problems?	Think how many you can manage, and halve it Can early intervention be sustained? Can late intervention be effective? Seek some homogeneity Ease of access/monitoring How to predict? Consider family stresses How to communicate?

Selection	Any 'screening' of participants? —	What are family strengths?
	mothers	Costs to *family* of involvement?
	fathers	Distance from centre?
	siblings	Parental work hours?
	relatives	Parental language levels?
	foster-parents	Parental literacy levels?
	surrogate parents	Previous parental experience?
	(childcare staff or	Needs of other children in
	volunteers)	family?
		Family interaction?
		Other stresses (what can be done to minimise the impact of these)?
Recruitment	Via informal personal contact	Does this happen with the parents you want?
	Via home visits	Project staff or welfare/liaison agency?
	Via volunteer parents contacting	Consider their role in the community nexus
	Promotional introductory meeting	Will the parents you want come?
	Press, radio, TV coverage	Are you that interesting? Ready to be swamped?
	Public notices	Who will/can read them?
	Via open evenings or social events	Do the parents you want, come?
	Introductory letter	How detailed should pre-course information be?
	Detailed invitation	Direct mail or hand delivery?
	Reply slip	Letters must be simple, informal, positive
	Written reminder	Ditto
	Reminder via children	Who will lose it, unless you can ...
	Energise children to nag parents	Advance meeting of target children?
		Have children write invitation letters?
	Telephone contact	
		Consider: ancillary attractions to maximise turn-out; inviting siblings, grandparents, volunteers as surrogates where necessary
Teaching staff	Professionals	
	Paraprofessionals	
	Volunteers	What experience and

Table 14.2: continued

Step	Options	Questions/issues
	Students Programme graduates	qualifications? What screening and selection process? Who trains the teachers, and how? Supply teaching reference manuals? Teacher/family staffing ratios? Time availability of staff? How release staff from other tasks? How cover when staff ill, etc.? Can staff experiment on own family?
Location	Homes Simulated home Other centre Mobile facility Residential centre Streets, playground, shops, etc. Summer school or camp	For individual or group meetings Parents' room, flat, etc. School/university/laboratory Mobile home/laboratory For intensive courses To test generalisation For multiple experiences consider: effect of time of day; need for creche for children; need/facility for refreshments
Socio-emotional support	Counselling elements? Psychodynamic elements? Discuss family dynamics/ support? Solicit/vent parental anxieties? Boost parental confidence Identify stressors Explore feelings of guilt	Consider: is this a necessary precursor? is it a specified objective? how to promote self-disclosure? Methodology: information input; group discussion; brainstorming problem solutions; assertion training; establish parent 'network'; refer to other agencies
Curriculum	Language skills Cognitive sills Academic skills Social skills Motor skills Self-help skills General childcare and development Problem-solving	Consider: how finely to task-analyse? how to individualise? how to make it fun? how to make it idiot-proof? Include: parental consultation on curriculum; parental choice in curriculum; units

Behaviour management
Emotional development

Broad or narrow focus?
Structured or unstructured?
Content or method focus?
Materials or interaction focus?
Conceptual or activity focus?
Set tasks or incidental
methods?
General skills or specific
behaviour?
Standardised or individualised?
Didactic or experiential?
Behavioural or reflective?
Positive or interactive?
Naturalistic or technical?

or modules? (specify criteria
for progression) tuition in
recording/self-recording (for
monitoring parents and
establishing baselines for
problem definition and
evaluation)

Consider: likely popular appeal
of method? are you biting
off more than you can
chew?

Target setting

Are targets to be set?
Individualised or standardised?
Pre-sequenced or free
selection?

Procedure for recording
targets?
Procedure for recording
progress?
Procedure for reviewing
progress?

This alone may create change
Individual Educational Plan?
Use developmental checklist?

Precision teaching format?

Keep it simple

Materials and resources

Books
Pamphlets
Instruction sheets
Workbooks
Diagrams/cartoons
Slide
Film
Video, audio-tapes
TV programmes off-air
Games
Toys
Physical aids
Speech trainers
Combined kits
Supplementary materials

Written lesson plan
Written lesson script

How to sequence?
Have parents make in
workshops?
Have volunteers make?
Instruct parents re materials
already in the home?
Establish toy/book library?
Estalish book/toy shop or
exchange?
Explore existing loan agencies,
libraries, etc.?
Materials for training
pamphlets?
Materials for recording/
monitoring?
Folders, etc., to transport
materials?
Exhibition of materials at group
training meeting?

Table 14.2: continued

Step	Options	Questions/issues
		Child selection of materials? Child preparation of some materials
Duration and frequency	Length of meetings Frequency of meetings Duration of project Time of day Time of year	Consider: optimum timetabling for parents and professionals? how long a no-contact gap dare you leave? (existing programmes have ranged from 3 × 20 min. meetings in 1 week to weekly meetings over 4 years)

TEACHING METHODS

Step	Options	Questions/issues
Verbal input	Talks Lectures Audio-tapes (distance) Telephone messages (recorded or live)	Consider: how directive? use of humour? linguistic complexity? individual/group/both?
Visual input	TV programme off-air Video- audio-tape Diagrams/cartoons Slide/film Observation of others Projective pictures	Availability of ohp, flipchart, blackboard, etc. Availability of TV monitor, aerial point, video-recorder, audio-recorder, extension loud speaker, slide/film projector, distance from power point, blackout facilities Is everything working and compatible? Test
Written input	Manual/pamphlet Programmed texts Workbooks/exercises Case studies/vignettes Sequenced instruction sheets Lesson scripts Professional assessment information	Readability? Pre- or post-meeting? Mail cost for distance teaching? Specific or general? Incorporating a quiz? Incorporating a reading test? Parents collect sequenced material from school?
Discussion/questions	Whole group Small group Individual	Structure/topics for group? Key points for individuals? Who is the group leader/facilitator?

	Quizzes Problem-solving Self-analysis and report Active listening Communication games Individual counselling	Ensured there is a clear purpose?
Social grouping	One-to-one Small group — one tutor Small group — plural tutors Large group — several tutors as aides in classroom/ workshop Children present or not? Siblings present or not? Relatives present or not?	Separate events of a more 'social' nature? Developing parent neighbourhood network for socio-emotional support? 'Family fun' nights? Ensured there is a clear purpose?

Modelling	Live
	    teacher: teacher role-play
	    teacher: parent role-play
	    teacher: experienced child
	    teacher: target child
	    experienced parent: own
	    child
	Video
	Film
	Audio
	Observation in classroom
	Observation in playroom
	    (?clandestinely)
	Field trips for observation
	    (schools, community,
	    events)
		Should model be perfect and
		distant or incorporate flaws
		used as teaching points?
		Incorporating an initial
		demonstration of how *not* to
		do it?
		Train novice professionals/
		students simultaneously to
		give parents confidence?
		Can parents who are
		'participant observers' in
		school act as paid aides?
		Ensured social reinforcement
		well modelled?
		Ensured importance of parents
		providing good model at
		home stressed?

Role-play rehearsal	Parent–teacher Parent–parent Parent–surrogate child Parent–own child Combination	Ensure: space for privacy; access to appropriate materials; incorporate desensitisation and task analysis as necessary; incorporate role reversal

Table 14.2: continued

Step	Options	Questions/issues
Prompting and cueing	Verbal Gestural Physical Sound Light 'Bug-in-the-ear'	Have you the equipment, money to purchase it, expertise to use it, standby or cover arrangements when it breaks down? Parental/child reaction to technology?
Practice	In-centre In-home Immediately Revision Homework assignments	Consider the same issues as for Role-play/Rehearsal, plus: Specific requirement re number/length of teaching sessions? Practice in recording? Practice in classroom as aide? Practice as apprentice to experienced parent? Practice on visits/trips?
Feedback	Verbal Video Audio Individual or group? From professionals Other parents Self-rating From target children	Consider: how detailed (a loose rating or within a micro-teaching format) Parents can be asked to demonstrate strategies in use to other parents, or just report to the group
Reinforcement	For children and/or parents: Gestural, light, sound, signal Edibles Other tangibles Verbal praise 'Bug-in-the-ear' Social reinforcement (non-verbal) Tokens or points Favourite activities Certificates, badges, prizes Opportunity to work as paid aide Lottery tickets Use of facilities after hours Paid expenses Paid stipend	Dispensed in group or individually? Discriminate long- vs short-term reinforcers? Establish reinforcement 'menu'? Individually contracted or standardised? On all behaviours or only some? Home–school reports for extra reinforcement at school? What about siblings and children whose parents declined the programme? Switch to lower-cost, naturalistic reinforces as soon as maintenance of behaviour allows

Exchangeable vouchers
Help in seeking welfare benefits
Day trips
Extra leave

Response cost measures:

Refundable deposits
Token participation fee
Postpone feedback visits
Loss of previously written
    cheque
Variety of child response costs

Contracting	Parent and programme
	Child and programme
	Parent, child and programme
	
	Verbally
	By signing list
	By singing contract form
	Contract copies to all parties
		Organisational aspects and
		    committments must be
		    made *very* clear, including
		    in writing
		Performance criteria for
		    continuance could be
		    specified, especially re
		    attendance
		Penalty clause (loss of deposit,
		    etc.)?

FOLLOW-UP

*Staff
supervision/
support*
	Monitoring of staff by:
	
	Written reports
	Written records/ratings
	Self-recording
	Audio and/or video-recording
	Individual meetings with
	    supervisor
	Group meetings with supervisor
	Home visits by supervisor for
	    parental feedback and/or
	    direct observation
	Telephone interviews
	Parental questionnaires
	
	Supervisor reports to
	    management team or
	    project leader
		Specify frequency and duration
		    of monitoring
		    arrangements, and contract
		    bilaterally from the outset.
		    Ensure staff receive
		    feedback, especially
		    positive! Beware
		    unreliability of medium of
		    feedback does not generate
		    critical confrontation
		
		Little fleas have bigger fleas ...

*Parent/child
monitoring
support*
	Observational home visits —
	    from professional/
	    paraprofessionals/
		Consider:
		Length and time of visits
		Building in a disincentive to

Table 14.2: continued

Step	Options	Questions/issues
	volunteers who are programme graduates Teacher–parent meeting at centre (weekly or occasional, individual or group) Regular telephone calls Contact offered at parental request	'lose' records Check for forged records Have parents mutually audio-/video-record in centre Specify who scrutinises records and how often Make this clear from the outset Watch for 'extinction bursts' in the children — much early support may be needed
	Self-recording (diary, cards, charts) Periodic parent ratings 'Family scrapbook' Time-sampling Audio- and video-recording Self-counting (wrist counter) (all records returned for scrutiny)	Where home–school record cards used, ensure parents receive feedback from monitoring of these in school Home–school diaries keep the records together, but if you lose one, you lose the lot
	Check child's workbook Assignments 'marked' at school Specific tasks set and checked Probes by teacher with child	
	Video-/audio-recording at centre Parents report back to group Revision sessions at centre Booster holiday schools Test programming skills on new objectives Check generalisation to school, etc.	
Fading	Increase objective step size Reduce frequency of reinforcement Reduce frequency of monitoring Introduce random/intermittent reinforcement/monitoring Monitor samples of days/families, etc. Promote generalisation of parent skills Promote parental takeover of organisation	Be honest with families about the reason/purpose for this Be prepared to deal with very varied reactions!

Generalisation	Ensure some training in home setting	Home and centre are a world apart
	Some training in community settings?	The biggest problem may be in the supermarket
	Check input from father, relatives, siblings, neighbours, etc.	Check care-taker generalisation
	Check curriculum structure *promotes* generalisation	Have you taught set tasks, specific skills or principles?
	Institute generalisation probes by professionals outside of home	Perhaps at school
	Check any gains *not* targeted	Developmental checklist good for this
	Check parental ability to design new programmes, and monitor them	But on an objective of *their* choice
	Have parents act as tutors in outreach programmes to consolidate their own skills	Teaching is a good way of learning/consolidating, *and* boosting confidence
Maintenance (long term)	Occasional 'booster shots' or follow-up sessions	Do not adopt the 'wrap up the programme and hope' approach
	Holiday schools/reunions	Be clear about maintenance strategies from the start
	Ongoing informal support groups	And tell the parents this is a programme objective, for the idea of doing something consistently over time may be novel to them
	Parent neighbourhood networks	
	Continuing home–school report	
	Continuing contact with school to ensure compatibility of objectives/methods	Time spent getting the effects of your first programme to hang on in there is probably better spent then on rushing ahead with a second programme
	Reinforce formal/informal new programming	
	Set parents long-term targets	
	Conduct follow-up assessments	
	Conduct follow-up interviews	
	Incorporate self-management training in planning, goal-setting using cues for self-prompting, and self-monitoring	
Evaluation	Ensure clear and full description of programme is available	Has programme met process objectives?
	Attendance rates	Also check teacher behaviour: visits made, records and activity charts completed, objectives set. Reliability checks?
	Participation rates	
	Consumer satisfaction	

Table 14.2: continued

Step	Options	Questions/issues
	Parental change	
	Attitude change	To what? How to measure?
	Knowledge gain	Tests: cloze, multi-choice, open-ended?
	Self-report/Interview	Individual/group/by telephone?
	Self-recording	Keep it simple — provide aids
	Observation in centre	Analysis of parental interaction
	Observation in home	style?
	Child change	
	Attitude change	Verbal or written?
	Parental report	Verbal or written?
	Reports from teachers, or others	Verbal or written?
	Parental rating	Tests at home or school?
	Child self-records	How to gather teacher observations?
	Parent records target behaviours	Use of audio/video analysis?
	with baseline	
	with control group	
	Child observation	
	centre	Use of time-sampling?
	home	How to assess affective outcomes?
	Criterion-referenced tests	Parents to evaluate
	pre-post	professionals' performance?
	baseline	(rating, questionnaires)
	control groups	What form of statistical analysis?
	Norm-referenced tests	How to feed results back to
	norm comparison	parents?
	pre-post	Use older siblings as control
	baseline	group?
	control groups	Multiple baseline or reversal design across subjects?
		Analyse with reference to socio-economic status and/or participation rates?
		Placebo group receiving alternative programme?
		Developmental checklists?
		Probes analysed by accuracy/ fluency?

Generalisation: situational to other children to new problems to untargeted skills Follow-up short term long term	Use school records/reports/ exam results? Check on siblings, even friends? Test programming skill on new objectives? Wide-span assessment needed for this Take care with sample attrition Ensure tracking information kept up to date Use grade retention and special education placement rates, unemployment and crime rates

Note: Don't forget to calculate programme unit costs and estimate cost-effectiveness.

References

Abramowitz, C.V. *et al.* (1974) 'Differential Effectiveness of Directive and Non-directive Group Therapies as a Function of Client Internal–External Control', *Journal of Consulting and Clinical Psychology, 42*, 849-53

Baker, B.L. (1976) 'Parent Involvement in Programming for Developmentally Disabled Children', in L.L. Lloyd (ed.), *Communication Assessment and Intervention Strategies* (Baltimore, Maryland: University Park Press)

Boyd, R.D. and Herwig, J. (eds.) (1980) *Serving Handicapped Children in Home-based Head Start: A Guide for Home Visitors and Others Working with Handicapped Children and their Families in the Home* (Portage, Wisconsin: Cooperative Educational Service Agency 12) (E.R.I.C. EC 132496 ED 199991)

Brewer, S. *et al.* (1981) 'The Effects of Matching Locus of Control and Presentation Mode in Parent Training', *Psychology in the Schools, 18*, 482-8

Doleys, D.M. *et al.* (1976) 'Parent Training Techniques: Effects of Lecture Role-playing Followed by Feedback and Self-recording', *Journal of Behavior Therapy and Experimental Psychiatry, 7*, 359-62

Elgas, P. (1981) *Home Based Information Packet* (Urbana, Illinois: CDA Services and Resource Center) (E.R.I.C. ED 207695 PS 012413)

Garland, C.W. (1978) *Skills Inventory for Teachers (SIFT)* (Williamsburg, Virginia: Child Development Resources) (E.R.I.C. EC 130143)

Gueldenpfenning, J. (1976) 'The Relative Effectiveness of Lecturing, Modeling, and Role Playing in Training Paraprofessional Reading Tutors', in J. Willis and D. Giles (eds), *Great Experiments in Behavior Modification* (Indianapolis, Indiana: Hackett Publishing Co.)

Heward, W.L. and Dardig, J.C. (1978) 'In-service for Parents of Special Needs Children', *Viewpoints in Teaching and Learning, 54, 4*, 127-37

Klenke, W.H. *et al.* (1975) *Simformation 1: Introducing Parents to the Wisconsin*

Reading Design (Madison, Wisconsin: Wisconsin University) (E.R.I.C. ED 205940 CS 006249)

Koegel, R.L. *et al.* (1978) 'Generalisation of Parent-training Results', *Journal of Applied Behavior Analysis, 11, 1,* 95-109

Kruger, W.S. (1975) 'Education for Parenthood and School-age Parents', *Journal of School Health, 55,* 292-5

LaCrosse, E. (1982) *Parent Involvement* (Monmouth, Oregon: Western States Technical Assistance Resource) (E.R.I.C. EC 150040)

Martin, B. (1977) 'Brief Family Intervention: Effectiveness and the Importance of Including the Father', *Journal of Consulting and Clinical Psychology, 45,* 1002-10

O'Dell, S. (1976) 'A Comparison of Parent Training Techniques in Child Behavior Modification', *Dissertation Abstracts International, 36* (8-B) 4173-4

Reisinger, J.J. *et al.* (1976) 'Toddler Management Training: Generalization and Marital Status', *Journal of Behavioral Therapy and Experimental Psychiatry, 7,* 335-40

Shearer, M.S. and Shearer, D.E. (1977) 'Parent Involvement', in J.B. Jordan *et al.* (eds.), *Early Childhood Education for Exceptional Children* (Reston, Virginia: Council for Exceptional Children)

Shively, J.E. *et al.* (1975) *Study of Effectiveness of Materials for Appalachian Parents* (Charleston, West Virginia: Appalachia Educational Laboratory) (E.R.I.C. ED 127025 PS 008734)

Siegert, F.E. and Yates, B.T. (1980) 'Behavioral Child Management Cost-effectiveness' *Evaluation and the Health Professions, 3, 2,* 123-52

Stevens, J.H. (1976) *Training Parents as Home Teachers: A Review of Research* (E.R.I.C. ED 147014 PS 009656)

Stile, S.W. (1978) 'Attrition Factors in a Home-based Service Delivery Model for Parents of Handicapped Children', unpublished doctoral dissertation, Utah State University

Stokes, T.F. and Baer, D.M. (1977) 'An Implicit Technology of Generalization', *Journal of Applied Behavior Analysis, 10,* 349-67

Strain, P.S. *et al.* (1980) 'An Examination of Child and Family Demographic Variables Related to Generalized Behaviour Change during Oppositional Child Training', *Behavior Modification, 5,* 15-25

Turner, R. and Rogers, A.M. (1981) 'Project KIDS: Infant Education for the Handicapped in an Urban Public School System', *Journal of the Division for Early Childhood, 2,* 40-51

Webster-Stratton, C. (1985) 'The Effects of Father Involvement in Parent Training for Conduct Problem Children', *Journal of Child Psychology and Psychiatry, 26, 5,* 801-10

Wnek, L. *et al.* (1980) *Parent Infant Programme: Program Manager's Manual* (Columbus, Ohio: Nisonger Center, Ohio State University) (E.R.I.C. ED 222003 EC 150071)

Wolfendale, S. (1985) 'Planning Parental Involvement in Reading', in K. Topping and S. Wolfendale (eds.), *Parental Involvement in Children's Reading* (London: Croom Helm/New York: Nichols, Publishing Co.)

Wyckoff, J.L. (1980) 'Parent Education Programs: Ready, Set, Go!', in M.J. Fine (ed.), *Handbook on Parent Education* (New York: Academic Press)

15 RESOURCES DIRECTORY

A huge volume of readers, manuals, guides, films, videos, audio-tapes, kits of materials, worksheets and other paraphernalia now exists, associated with a variety of parent training ventures. Where such materials have already been referred to in the text, details of them will not necessarily be repeated here. An excellent first source for those new to the area is the chapter on 'Parental Involvement' by Marsha and David Shearer in the J.B. Jordan *et al.* (eds.) text of 1977 (*Early Childhood Education for Exceptional Children*, published in Reston, Virginia, by the Council for Exceptional Children). This includes examples of a variety of resource materials and lists of sources of some of the more obscure items.

However, as our review of 'planning' considerations should have made clear, to attach any great faith to the power of teaching materials, especially written ones, would be misguided. The overall structure of the training programme and the quality of organisation and interaction within it are likely to be far more crucial to success. Many written materials are of high readability levels, and auto-matically debar usage by parents of limited educational back-ground. Manuals may vary from the highly specific to the barely focused, and their readability may range from the level of an average 10-year-old to that of a college graduate. Reviews of parent training manuals will be found in:

Andrasik, F. and Murphy, W.D. (1977) 'Assessing the Readability of Thirty-nine Behavior Modification Training Manuals and Primers', *Journals of Applied Behavior Analysis, 2,* 2-5
Bernal, M.E. and North, J.A. (1978) 'A Survey of Parent Training Manuals', *Journal of Applied Behavior Analysis, 11, 4,* 533-44

The effect of readability was explored in an experimental com-parison by Shively *et al.* (1975), who field-tested materials of three readability levels (8, 11 and 14 years) and two illustrative formats (instructional versus decorative illustrations) with the parents of 700 children. On the outcome criterion of parental ability to demonstrate mastery of the requisite teaching behaviour in the presence of a home visitor, even with the materials which were easiest to read, 25 per cent of the parents still failed. The incorporation of 'instructional' illustrations seemed to make matters worse! The simplest reading texts with purely decorative illustrations proved most effective. Parental educational background emerged as a very strong factor in parental competence. Further details will be found in:

Shively, J.E. *et al.* (1975) *Study of Effectiveness of Materials for Appalachian Parents* (Charleston, West Virginia: Appalachia Educational Laboratory) (E.R.I.C. ED 127025 PS 008734)

For all the resources listed below, inclusion does not imply endorsement. For all, in unthinking hands the materials will prove worse than useless.

Parental Involvement in School

Advisory Centre of Education (undated) *How You Can Help Your Local School: Information Sheet* (London: ACE)

Auerbach, A.B. (1968) *Parents Learn Through Discussion: Principles and Practices of Parent Group Education* (New York: Wiley)

Bailard, V. and Strong, R. (1964) *Parent–Teacher Conferences* (New York: McGraw-Hill)

Bell, T.H. (1976) *Active Parent Concern: A New Home Guide to Help Your Child in School* (Englewood Cliffs, New Jersey: Prentice-Hall)

Berger, E.H. (1981) *Parents as Partners in Education: The School and Home Working Together* (St Louis, Missouri: C.V. Mosby)

Brandt, R.S. (1979) *Partners: Parents and Schools* (Alexandria, Virginia: Association for Supervision and Curriculum Development)

Bratt, P. (1979) *Title I: An Opportunity for Growth. (A Handbook Designed to Introduce, Inform and Instruct Parents about Title I)* (Washington, D.C.: Office of State Superintendent of Public Instruction, Olympia) (E.R.I.C. ED 189225 UD 020718)

Collins, C.H. *et al.* (1982) *The Home–School Connection: Selected Partnership Programs in Large Cities* (Boston, Massachusets: Institute for Responsive Education)

Criscuolo, N.P. (1973) 'Ways to Involve Parents in Expanding Reading Services to Children', *Reading*, 7, *1*, 11-14

Croft, D.J. (1979) *Parents and Teachers: A Resource Book for Home, School and Community Relations* (Belmont, California: Wadsworth Publishing Co.)

E.R.I.C. Clearinghouse on Elementary and Early Childhood Education (College of Education, University of Illinois, Urbana, Illinois 61801). (i) *Family/School Relationships: An ERIC Abstract Bibliography* (1978); (ii) *Parental Involvement in Education* (1979) (bibliography compiled by M. Henniger)

Family Matters, Distribution Center, 7 Research Park, Cornell University, Ithaca, New York NY 14850. *Leaders' Guides* for six-session workshop for parents, workshops for teachers, home visitors and group leaders

Friedlander, J. *et al.* (1981) *Early Reading Development: A Bibliography* (London: Harper & Row). See section on 'Parental Involvement'

Gilkerson, E. (1972) *Teacher–Child–Parent Relationships* (New York: Early Childhood Education Council of New York)

Gordon, I.J. and Breivogel, W.T. (1976) *Building Effective Home–School Relationships* (Boston: Allyn & Bacon)

de Groot, J. (ed.) (1979) *Education for All People: A Grassroots Primer* (Boston, Massachusets: Institute for Responsive Education)

Hailstone, E. (1984) *Stay-away Parents: How to Draw Them In* (London: Home and School Council). Available from the Campaign for the Advancement of State Education, 58 Wrinklemarsh Road, London SE3

Kroth, R.L. (1975) *Communicating with Parents of Exceptional Children* (Denver, Colorado: Love Publishing)

Lombana, J.H. (1983) *Home–School Partnerships: Guidelines and Strategies for Educators* (New York: Grune & Stratton)

Miller, M.S. and Baker, S.S. (1976) *Straight Talk to Parents* (New York: Stein & Day)

Morrison, G.S. (1978) *Parent Involvement in the Home, School and Community* (Columbus, Ohio: Charles E. Merrill)

Nedler, S.E. and McAfee, O.D. (1979) *Working with Parents* (Belmont, California: Wadsworth Publishing Co.)

Newman, S. (1971) *Guidelines to Parent–Teacher Cooperation in Early Childhood Education* (New York: Book-Lab Inc.)

Newmark, G. (1976) *This School Belongs to You and Me* (New York: Hart Publishing)

Parent Cooperative Preschools International, 20551 Lakeshore Road, Baie d'Urfe, Quebec H9X 1R3. Parental involvement guideline package, including booklets and bibliography

Rich, D. and Mattox, B. (1976) *101 Activities for Building More Effective School–Community Involvement* (Washington, DC: Home and School Institute, Trinity College)

Rubin, R.I. (1979) *Parent Involvement Results for the Six Parent Roles in the Parent Education Follow Through Program* (Chapel Hill, North Carolina: School of Education, North Carolina University) (E.R.I.C. ED 168720 PS 010489)

Rutherford, R. and Edgar, E. (1979) *Teachers and Parents: A Guide to Interaction and Cooperation* (Boston, Massachusets: Allyn & Bacon)

Tizard, B. *et al.* (1981) *Involving Parents in Nursery and Infant Schools: A Source Book for Teachers* (London: Grant McIntyre)

Films

The Parent/Teacher Intro/Motivator (Olympus Publishing Co., 1670 East 13th South, Salt Lake City, Utah, UT 84105)

Teachers, Parents and Children: Growth Through Cooperation (Davidson Films, 164 Turnstead Avenue, San Anselmo, California CA 94960)

Home–school Reporting

Very few materials are necessary in this straightforward and cost-effective area

Schumaker, J.B. *et al.* (1977) *Managing Behavior, Part 9: A Home-based School Achievement System* (Lawrence, Kansas: H. & H. Enterprises Inc.) (E.R.I.C. EC 093012)

Ordinary Children

Early Stimulation

Bell, T.H. (1973) *Your Child's Intellect: A Guide to Home-based Preschool Education* (Salt Lake City, Utah: Olympus Publishing Co.)

Board of Cooperative Educational Services of Nassau County (1976) *While You're At It: 200 Ways to Help Children Learn* (Englewood Cliffs, New Jersey: Prentice-Hall)

Caplan, F. (1977) *The Parenting Adviser* (New York: Anchor Press)

Cole, A. *et al.* (1972) *I Saw a Purple Cow and 100 Other Recipes for Learning* (Boston, Massachusets: Little, Brown & Co.)

D'Audney, W. (1975) *Calendar of Developmental Activities for Preschoolers* (Omaha, Nebraska: University of Nebraska Medical Center)

Evans, J. and Ilfield, E. (1982) *Good Beginnings: Parenting in the Early Years* (Michigan: High/Scope Press). Available in the UK from the National Children's Bureau, 8 Wakley St, London EC1V 7QE

Flemming, B.M. *et al.* (1977) *Resources for Creative Teaching in Early Childhood Education* (New York: Harcourt Brace Jovanovich)

Garvey, C. (1982) *Play* (London: Fontana)

Garvey, C. (1984) *Children's Talk* (London: Fontana)

Gordon, I.J. (1970) *Baby Learning through Baby Play: A Parent's Guide for the First Two Years* (New York: St Martin's Press)

Gordon, I. (1972) *Child Learning through Child Play: Learning Activities for Two and Three Year Olds* (New York: St Martin's Press)

Gotts, E.E. (1977) *Home Visitor's Kit* (New York: Human Sciences Press)

Harben, G. and Cross, L. (1975) *Early Childhood Curriculum Materials — An Annotated Bibliography* (Washington, DC: US Department of Health, Education and Welfare)

Kaye, K. (1984) *The Mental and Social Life of Babies: How Parents Create Persons* (London: Methuen)

Koch, J. (1982) *Superbaby: Over 300 Exercises and Games to Stimulate Your Baby's Intellectual, Physical and Emotional Development* (London: Orbis). In the US: Total Baby Development (New York: Wallaby Pocket Books, 1978)

Lally, J.R. and Gordon, I.J. (1977) *Learning Games for Infants and Toddlers* (Syracuse, New York: New Readers Press)

Marzallo, J. and Lloyd, J. (1972) *Learning Through Play* (New York: Harper & Row)

Matterson, E.M. (1975) *Play with a Purpose for Under-sevens* (Harmondsworth: Penguin)

Moreno, S. (1975) *Parents — Teach Your Children to Learn Before They Go to School* (San Diego: Moreno Educational Co.)

Nimnicht, G.P. *et al.* (1971) *Parent Guide: How to Play Learning Games with a Preschool Child* (Morristown, New Jersey: General Learning Products)

Olympus Publishing Co., 1679 East 13th South, Salt Lake City, Utah, UT 84105: (i) *The In-Service Training Package* (home-based); (ii) *The Parent Training Package*

Painter, G. (1971) *Teach Your Baby* (New York: Simon & Schuster)

Papalia, D.E. and Olds, S.W. (1975) *A Child's World* (New York: McGraw-Hill)

Rabinowitz, M. *et al.* (1973) *In the Beginning: A Parent Guide of Activities and Experiences for Infants from Birth to Six Months* (New Orleans, Missouri: Parent–Child Development Center)

Stein, S.B. (1976) *New Parents' Guide to Early Learning* (New York: New American Library)

Tizard, B. and Hughes, M. (1984) *Young Children Learning: Talking and Thinking at Home and at School* (London: Fontana)

Toy Libraries Association (1983) *The Good Toy Guide* (London: Inter-action)

White, B.L. (1975) *The First Three Years of Life* (Englewood Cliffs, New Jersey: Prentice-Hall)

Later Learning

Belton, S. and Terborgh, C. (1972) *Sparks: Activities to Help Children Learn at Home* (New York: Behavioral Publications)

Braga, J. and Braga, L. (1978) *Children and Adults: Activities for Growing Together* (Englewood Cliffs, New Jersey: Prentice-Hall)

Caldwell, B. *et al.* (1972) *Home Teaching Activities* (Little Rock, Arkansas: Center for Early Development in Education)

Carson, J. (1975) *The Role of Parents as Teachers* (Philadelphia: Temple University)

Cole, A. *et al.* (1970) *Recipes for Fun* (Northfield, Illinois: Parents as Resources)

Cratty, B.J. (1971) *Active Learning Games to Enhance Academic Abilities* (Englewood Cliffs, New Jersey: Prentice-Hall)

Dumas, E. and Schminki, C.W. (1971) *Math Activities for Child Involvement* (Boston: Allyn & Bacon)

Institute of Family Home Education (1974) *Brushing Up on Parenthood.* From IFHE PO Box 539, Provo, Utah UT 84601; includes 16 audio-tapes and manual

Macht, J. (1975) *Teaching Our Children* (New York: Wiley)

Moreno, S. (1975) *Teaching Ideas for Parents to Use with their Children* (San Diego: Moreno Educational Co.). In Spanish and English

Wade, B. (1984) *Story at Home and School* (Birmingham: Faculty of Education, University of Birmingham). Contains a section on teaching resources

Wile, E.M. (1978) *What to Teach Your Child* (Elizabethtown, Pennsylvania: Continental Press)

General Parenting

Abidin, R.R. (1976) *Parenting Skills Workbook* (New York: Human Sciences Press)

Abraham, W. (1976) *Living with Preschoolers* (Phoenix, Arizona: O'Sullivan Woodside)

Active Parenting Inc., 2996 Grandview Avenue, Atlanta, Georgia GA 30305. Video-based materials in Dreikurs, Adlerian format

Appalachia Educational Laboratory, Division of Childhood and Parenting, PO Box 1348, Charleston, West Virginia 25325. Video materials, a directory of video materials, activity plans, home visitors' kit, etc.

Babcock, D.E. and Keepers, T.D. (1976) *Raising Kids O.K.* (New York: Grove Press)

Baruch, D.W. (1949) *New Ways in Discipline* (New York: McGraw-Hill)

Berne, E. (1964) *Games People Play* (New York: Grove Press)

Berne, E. (1973) *What Do You Say After You Say Hello?* (New York: Bantam Books)

Biller, H. and Meredith, D. (1975) *Father Power* (New York: Anchor Books)

Birmingham Education Committee (1981) *Child Development and Family Related Courses.* A guide for teachers

Braga, J. and Braga, L. (1974) *Growing with Children* (Englewood Cliffs, New Jersey: Prentice-Hall)

Brazleton, T.B. (1975) *Toddlers and Parents* (New York: Dell Publishing. Harmondsworth: Penguin (1979))

Briggs, D. C. (1975) *Your Child's Self-esteem* (Garden City, New York: Dolphin Books)

Callahan, S.C. (1974) *Parenting Principles and Politics of Parenthood* (Baltimore, Maryland: Penguin Publishing)

Catholic Marriage Advisory Council (1979) *Resources for Relationships.* Teaching materials (London: CMAC)

Chess, S. *et al.* (1977) *Your Child is a Person: A Psychological Approach to Parenthood without Guilt* (New York: Penguin)

Child Care Resource and Referral Inc. 1312 N.W. 7th St, Rochester, Minnesota 55901. Various materials and equipment in a lending library

Child Study Press, 853 Broadway, New York, 10003. Selective annotated bibliography on family life and child development

Christopherson, E.R. (1977) *Little People: Guidelines for Common Sense Rearing* (Lawrence, Kansas: H. and H. Enterprises)

Clarke-Stewart, K.A. (1978) 'Popular Primers for Parents', *American Psychologist, 33*, 359-69

Community Education Development Centre, Stoke School, Briton Rd, Coventry CV2 4LF. Materials including leaflets, booklets, flip charts

Della-Piana, G. (1973) *How to Talk with Children (and Other People)* (New York: Wiley)

Development Education Centre, Gillett Centre, Selly Oak Colleges, Bristol Rd, Birmingham B29 6LE. Resources for teaching about child development and the family

Dinkmeyer, D. and McKay, G.D. (1976) *Systematic Training for Effective Parenting* (Circle Pines, Minnesota: American Guidance Service). Includes leader's manual, parents' handbook, brochures, posters and audio-tapes

Dodson, F. (1970) *How to Parent* (New York: Signet Books)

Dodson, F. (1975) *How to Father* (New York: Signet Books)

Donovan, F.R. (1967) *Wild Kids* (Harrisburg, Pennsylvania: Stackpole Books)

Dreikurs, R. (1964) *Children: The Challenge* (Des Moines, Iowa: Meredith Press)

Dreikurs, R. (1970) *Parents' Guide to Good Discipline* (New York: Dutton)

Education Development Center (1976) *Exploring Childhood: Program Overview and Catalog of Materials* (Newton, Massachusets: EDC)

Eimers, R. and Artchson, R. (1977) *Effective Parents, Responsible Children: A Guide to Confident Parenting* (New York: McGraw-Hill)

Endres, J.B. and Rockwell, R.E. (1980) *Food, Nutrition, and the Young Child* (St. Louis, Missouri: C.V. Mosby)

Fraiberg, S.H. (1968) *The Magic Years: Understanding and Handling Problems of Early Childhood* (New York: Scribner's)

Freed, A.M. (1971) *T.A. for Kids* (Los Angeles: Jalmar Press)

Freed, A.M. (1973) *T.A. for Tots* (Los Angeles: Jalmar Press)

Gersh, M. (1966) *How to Raise Children at Home in Your Spare Time* (Greenwich, Connecticut: Fawcett Publications Inc.)

Ginott, H.G. (1965) *Between Parent and Child* (New York: Macmillan)

Ginott, H.G. (1969) *Between Parent and Teenager* (New York: Macmillan)

Gloucester Association for Family Life, 2 College St, Gloucester. Four publications

Gordon, S. (1975) *Let's Make Sex a Household Word: A Guide for Parents and Children* (New York: John Day)

Gordon, S. and Wollin, M. (1975) *Parenting: A Guide for Young People* (New York: William H. Sadler)

Gordon, T. (1975) *P.E.T.: Parent Effectiveness Training* (New York: P.H. Wyden (hb) and New American Library (pb)). Manual, tapes and instructional materials from: Effectiveness Training, 531 Stevens Avenue, Solana Beach, California 92705

Greene, B.F. *et al.* (1977) *Shopping with Children: Advice for Parents* (San Rafael, California: Academic Therapy). Also see: Clark, H.B. *et al.* (1977) 'A Parent Advice Package for Family Shopping Trips: Development and Evaluation',

Journal of Applied Behavior Analysis, 10, 605-24

Harris, T.A. (1969) *I'm O.K. — Your're O.K.* (New York: Harper & Row (hb) and Aron Books (pb)

Health Education Council, 78 New Oxford St, London WC1A 1AH. Bibliographies of publications and resources

Hesterly, S.O. (1974) *The Parent Package* (Berkeley, California: Transactional Publications). Including leader's manual with exercises and activities

Hope, K. and Young, N. (1976) *The Source Book for Single Mothers* (New York: New American Library)

Howard, M. (1975) *Only Human: Teen-age Pregnancy and Parenthood* (New York: Seabury Press)

Inner London Education Authority, Essendine Teachers' Centre, Essendine Rd, London W9 2LR. Resources for child development courses including films

James, M. (1974) *Transactional Analysis for Mums and Dads* (Reading, Massachusets: Addison-Wesley)

James, M. and Jongeward, D. (1971) *Born to Win* (Reading, Massachusets: Addison-Wesley)

Jolly, H. (1977) *The Book of Child Care: A Complete Guide for To-day's Parents* (London: Sphere Books)

Kennedy, C.E. *et al.* (1978) *Resource Catalog for Foster Parent Education* (Manhattan, Kansas: Kansas State University)

Knox, L. (1978) *Parents are People Too* (Nashville, Tennessee: Intersect)

Lane, M.B. (1975) *Education for Parenting* (Washington, D.C.: National Association for the Education of Young Children)

Levin, P. (1974) *Becoming the Way We Are* (Berkeley, California: Transactional Publications)

Ligon, E.M. *et al.* (1976) *Let Me Introduce Myself: The First 30 Months of Life — A Guide for the Parents of Infant Children* (Schenectady, New York: Character Res)

McDearmid, N.J. *et al.* (1975) *Loving and Learning* (New York: Harcourt Brace Jovanovich)

Maddox, B. (1975) *The Half Parent* (New York: Signet Books)

Markun, P.M. (1973) *Parenting* (Washington, D.C.: Association for Childhood Education International)

National Alliance Concerned with Teenage Parents, 7315 Wisconsin Avenue, Washington, DC 20014. Parenting guide

National Association for Maternal and Child Welfare, Tavistock House North, Tavistock Square, London WC1H 9JG. Parentcraft education teaching aides

National Children's Bureau, 8 Wakley St, London EC1V 7QE. A variety of booklists and filmlists pertaining to child development

Open University, Centre for Continuing Education, Walton Hall, Milton Keynes MK7 6AA. Four parenthood courses covering different stages of childhood, plus sundry other materials

Parenting Materials Information Center, Southwest Educational Development Laboratory, 211 E. 7th St., Austin, Texas 78701. A listing of resource materials held by PMIC

Peterson, K. and Vermeire, G. (1976) *Since You Care: A Parenting Skills Training Manual* (Erie, Pennsylvania: Council on Prevention of Alcoholism and Drug Abuse)

Putney, S. and Putney, G. (1964) *The Adjusted American* (New York: Harper & Row)

Rowan, B. (1975) *Tuning in to Your Child* (Atlanta, Georgia: Humanics Press)

Royal College of Midwives, 15 Mansfield St, London W1M 0BE. Selected reading lists on parentcraft education

Royal College of Nursing, Henrietta Place, London W1M 0AB. Bibliographies on parentcraft

Salk, L. (1973) *What Every Child Would Like His Parent to Know* (New York: Warner)

Schools Council, previously at Newcombe House, 5 Notting Hill Gate, London W11 3JB. Many relevant curriculum development projects

Shure, M.B. and Spivack, G. (1978) *Problem-solving Techniques in Childrearing* San Francisco, California: Jossey-Bass)

Simon, S.B. and Olds, S.W. (1976) *Helping Your Child Learn Right from Wrong: A Guide to Values Clarification* (New York: Simon & Schuster)

Smith, H.W. (1978) *Survival Handbook for Preschool Mothers* (Chicago: Follett)

Smith, J.M. and Smith, D.E.P. (1966) *Child Management* (Ann Arbor, Michigan: Ann Arbor Publishers)

Smith, L. (1980) *Feed Your Kids Right* (New York: Dell Books)

Spock, B. (1955) *Dr. Spock Talks with Mothers* (Boston, Massachusets: Houghton-Mifflin)

Spock, B. (1962) *Problems of Parents* (New York: Fawcett)

Spock, B. (1974) *Raising Children in a Difficult Time* (New York: W.W. Norton)

Spock, B. (1977) *Baby and Child Care* (New York: Pocket Books) (original edn. 1945)

Steiner, C.M. (1974) *Scripts People Live* (New York: Bantam Books)

Stone, L.J. and Church, J. (1979) *Childhood and Adolescence* (New York: Random House)

US Department of Health Education and Welfare. Various relevant publications, including an annotated bibliography on parenting (OHDS 78-30134) and a 'reader's guide' for parents of children with difficulties (HSA 77-5290), from the US Government Printing Office, Washington DC 20402

Wagonseller, B.R. *et al.* (1977) *The Art of Parenting* (Champaign, Illinois: Research Press) Includes leader's guide and various modular materials

Weisberger, E. (1975) *Your Child and You: How to Manage Growing-up Problems in the Years One to Five* (New York: E.P. Dutton & Co.)

Films

Association for Childhood Education International, 3615 Wisconsin Avenue N.W., Washington DC 20016. Publishes a review of films of teaching and parenting, as well as various other valuable guides

Modern Talking Pictures Services Inc., 5000 Park St. North, St Petersburg, Florida 33709. Offer a number of relevant items.

Parents' Magazine Films Inc, 52 Vanderbilt Avenue, New York 10017. A well-structured set of 32 films available

Further reviews and evaluations of relevant films are available from:

National Association for the Education of Young Children, 1834 Connecticut Avenue N.W., Washington DC 20009

Administration for Children, Youth and Families, Office of Human Development Services, US Department of Health Education and Welfare, PO Box 1182, Washington DC 20013

Appalachia Educational Laboratory Inc., Division of Early Childhood, PO Box 1348, Charleston, West Virginia 25325

Disadvantaged Children

Ashby, G. *et al.* (1979) *Evaluation of the Span Parent Workshops and the Operation of Span Groups* (Brisbane: Department of Education, Queensland University) (E.R.I.C. ED 183253 PS 011224). Appendices include Span Programme materials

Badger, E.D. and Edufax Inc. (1971) *Teaching Guide: Toddler Learning Program* (Paoli, Pennsylvania: Instructor Learning Corporation)

DARCEE Materials

Elgas, P. (1981) *Home Based Information Packet* (Urbana, Illinois: CDA Services and Resources Center) (E.R.I.C. ED 207695 PS 012413). Includes annotated bibliographies of publications and resource materials

Forrester, B.J. *et al.* (1971) *Home Visiting with Mothers of Infants* (Nashville, Tennessee: George Peabody College for Teachers)

Giesy, R. (ed.) (1970) *A Guide for Home Visitors* (Nashville, Tennessee: George Peabody College for Teachers)

Gray, S.W. *et al.* (1966) *Before First Grade* (New York: Teachers College Press, Columbia University) A manual for teachers of young children

von Nieda, J. *et al.* (1976) *No-cost, Low-cost Playthings: Toys for Fun and Learning* (Nashville, Tennessee: George Peabody College for Teachers)

Florida Materials

Gordon, I.J. and Lally, J.R. (1967) *Intellectual Stimulation for Infants and Toddlers* (Gainesville, Florida: University of Florida)

Gordon, I.J. (1970) *Baby Learning through Baby Play* (New York: St Martin's Press)

Gordon, I.J. *et al.* (1972) *Child Learning through Child Play* (New York: St Martin's Press)

Gordon, I.J. *et al.* (1975) *Parent Oriented Home-based Early Childhood Education Program. Research Report* (Gainesville, Florida: University of Florida) (E.R.I.C. ED 148466 PS 009678). Contains an extensive annotated listing of aids related to parent oriented early childhood education, including printed, video, film and slide materials

High/Scope Materials

Wittes, G. and Radin, N. (1969) three manuals all published in San Rafael, California, by Dimensions: *Helping Your Child to Learn: The Learning through Play Approach*; *Helping Your Child to Learn: The Nurturance Approach*; *Helping Your Child to Learn: The Reinforcement Approach*. Also see: Lambie, D.Z. *et al.* (1974) Home Teaching with Mothers and Infants (Ypsilanti, Michigan: HIGH/SCOPE Educational Research Foundation)

Home Start Materials

Head Start Sound–Slide Films (1974). Obtainable from: Educational and Development Corporation, PO Box 1435, Arlington, Virginia 22210

Home Start Curriculum Guide (Millville, Utah: Millville Home Start Training Center)

Home Start: A Partnership with Parents (1977). A slide and audio-cassette relating to Home Start Training centers, from: Children First Inc., 525 School Street S.W., Suite 303, Washington DC 20024

FDRP Materials

Honig, A.S. and Lally, J.R. (1972) *Infant Caregiving: A Design for Training* (New York: Media Products)

Honig, A.S. and Lally, J.R. (1973) *Preparing the Child for Learning.* Five colour
filmstrips — via *Parents' Magazine*
Lally, J.R. *et al.* (1973) 'Training Paraprofessionals for Work with Infants and
Toddlers', *Young Children, 28,* 173-82.

HIPPY Materials

Lombard, A. (1981) *Success Begins at Home: Educational Foundations for
Preschoolers* (Lexington, Massachusets: D.C. Heath & Co.). Includes
appendices with examples of workbook activities for 4/5/6-year-olds
Office of Child Development (1974) *A Guide to Planning and Operating
Home-based Child Development Programs* (Washington, D.C.: US Department
of Health Education and Welfare)
Pugh, G. and De'Ath, E. (1984) *The Needs of Parents: Practice and Policy in
Parent Education* (London: Macmillan, for National Children's Bureau). Has
appendices on relevant examinations, organisations and resources, including
written and audio-visual material
Pushaw, D. (ed.) (1969) *Teach Your Child to Talk: A Parent Handbook* (Cincinatti,
Ohio: CDBCO Standard Publishing Co.)
Quillian, B.F. and Rogers, K.S. (1972) *Nine Model Programs for Young Children:
Program Summaries for Potential Implementation* (vol. 1) (St Ann, Missouri:
National Coordination Center for Early Childhood Education) (E.R.I.C. ED
129402 PS 008721). Includes implementation of some home-based programmes,
although most are centre-based direct-taught
Shively, J.E. *et al.* (1975) *Study of Effectiveness Materials for Appalachian Parents*
(Charleston, West Virginia: Appalachian Education Laboratory) (E.R.I.C. ED
127025 PS 008734). Materials of different readability levels and illustrative style
Strathclyde Experiment in Education Videotapes, noted in: E. Wilkinson *et al.*
(1978) *Strathclyde Experiment in Education: Govan Project* (Glasgow:
Department of Education, University of Glasgow)
VIP Demonstration Center, Verbal Interaction Project, 5 Broadway, Freeport, New
York 11520. Has a great deal of general and specialised information, including:
manual for replication of the MCH Program, film and other audio-visual
material, the Toy Demonstrator's visiting handbook

Ethnic Minorities

Comer, J.P. and Poussaint, A.F. (1975) *Black Child Care: How to Bring up a
Healthy Black Child in America* (New York: Simon & Schuster, (hb) and Pocket
Books (pb, 19765))
Garcia, A. (1972) 'Developing Questioning Children: A Parent Program', *Teem
Exchange, 2, 2,* 3-7. A description of a programme for Mexican Americans
Harrison-Ross, P. and Wyden, B. (1974) *The Black Child: A Parent's Guide to
Raising Happy and Healthy Children* (New York: Berkeley Publishing)
Henderson, R.W. (1976) 'Application of Social Learning Principles in a Field
Setting', *Exceptional Children,* pp. 53-5. A description of a programme for
Papago Indians
McLaughlin, C.J. (1976) *The Black Parents' Handbook: A Guide to Healthy
Pregnancy, Birth and Child Care* (New York: Harcourt Brace Jovanovich)
Ross, P.H. and Wyden, B. (1973) *The Black Child — A Parent's Guide* (New York:
Peter H. Wyden Inc.). Also see above

Learning Difficulties

A substantial select annotated bibliography of written, film and video materials for training parents to accelerate their children's reading skills will be found in:

Topping, K. and Wolfendale, S. (eds.) (1985) *Parental Involvement in Children's Reading* (London: Croom Helm New York: Nichols Publishing Co.)

Nothing from this key source will be repeated here. In addition to this, readers may wish to consult:

Bert, D.K. (1977) *Parent Readiness Education Project (PREP) Manual* (Detroit, Michigan: PREP, Redford Union School District)

Gambrell, L.B. and Wilson, R.M. (1980) *28 Ways to Help Your Child be a Better Reader* (Paoli, Pennsylvania: Instructor/McGraw-Hill)

Glazer, S.M. (ed.) (1979) *Home Ideas for Reading* (Newark, Delaware: International Reading Association)

Graham, A. (1985) *Help Your Child with Maths* (London: Fontana)

Hayes, R.P. and Stevenson, M.G. (1980) *Teaching the Emotional Disturbed/ Learning Disabled Child: a Practical Guide for Teachers, Administrators and Parents* (Washington, DC: Acropolis Books) (E.R.I.C. EC 132008)

Klenke, W.H. *et al.* (1975) *Simformation 1: Introducing Parents to the Wisconsin Reading Design* (Madison, Wisconsin: University of Wisconsin) (E.R.I.C. ED 205940 CS 006249)

Larrich, N. (1975) *A Parent's Guide to Children's Reading* (New York: Bantam Books)

McElderry, J.S. and Escobedo, L.E. (1979) *Tools for Learning: Activities for Young Childen with Special Needs* (Denver, Colorado: Love Publishing)

Mather, J. (1976) *Learning Can Be Child's Play: How Parents Can Help Slower-than-average Preschool Children Learn and Develop through Play Exercises* (Nashville, Tennessee: Abingdon Press)

Quinsenberry, N.L. (1977) 'Involving Parents in Reading: An Annotated Bibliography', *The Reading Teacher*, *31*, *1*, 34-40

Rosner, J. (1979) *Helping Children Overcome Learning Difficulties — A Step-by-Step Guide for Parents and Teachers* (New York: Walker & Co.)

Stott, D. (1974) *The Parent as Teacher: A Guide for Parents of Children with Learning Difficulties* (London: University of London Press)

Vukelich, C. (1984) 'Parents' Role in the Reading Process: A Review of Practical Suggestions and Ways to Communicate with Parents', *The Reading Teacher*, *37*, *6*, 472-7

Young, P. and Tyre, C. (1985) *Teach Your Child to Read* (London: Fontana)

Zifferblatt, S.M. (1970) *You Can Help Your Child Improve Study and Homework Behaviours* *(Champaign, Illinois: Research Press)*

Audio-visual

Helping Your Child to Read (1984) (London: British Broadcasting Corporation). Laser video disc

Behaviour Problems

Alvord, J.R. (1973) *Home Token Economy: An Incentive Program for Children and Their Parents* (Champaign, Illinois: Research Press)

Arkell, R.N. *et al.* (1976) 'Readability and Parental Behavior Modification Literature', *Behavior Therapy, 7,* 265-6

Becker, W.C. (1971) *Parents are Teachers: A Child Management Program* (Champaign, Illinois: Research Press)

Becker, W.C. (1976) *Parents are Teachers: Group Leader Guide* (Champaign, Illinois: Research Press)

Brockway, B.S. (1974) *Training in Child Management: A Family Approach* (Dubuque, Iowa: Kendall/Hunt)

Carter, R.D. (1972) *Help! These Kids Are Driving Me Crazy* (Champaign, Illinois: Research Press)

Clark-Hall, M. *et al.* (1976) *Responsive Parent Training Manual: A Manual for Training Parents to Use an Applied Behavior Analysis Approach in Managing Behavior* (Lawrence, Kansas: H. & H. Enterprises)

Collier, P.F. and Tarte, R.D. (1977) *Practically Painless Parenting: A Token-reward System for Child Rearing* (Chicago: Henry Regneey Co.)

Csapo, M. (1975) *Beat the Hassle — A Survival Kit for Teenagers and Their Parents* (Vancouver, BC: Center for Human Development and Research)

Csapo, M. (1978) *Pocketful of Praises — A Handbook for Parents* (3rd edn.) (Vancouver: Center for Human Development and Research)

Dardig, J.C. and Heward, W.L. (1976) *Sign Here: A Contracting Book for Children and Their Parents* (Kalamazoo, Michigan: Behaviordelia)

Dardig, J.C. *et al.* (1977) *Sign Here: Leader's Manual* (Kalamazoo, Michigan: Behaviordelia)

DeRisi, W.J. and Butz, G. (1975) *Writing Behavioral Contracts: A Case Simulation Practice Manual* (Champaign, Illinois: Research Press)

Feingold, B.F. and Feingold, H.S. (1979) *The Feingold Cook-book for Hyperactive Children* (New York: Random House)

Glasgow, R.E. and Rosen, G.M. (1978) 'Behavioral Bibliotherapy: A Review of Self-Help Behavior Therapy Manuals', *Psychological Bulletin, 85,* 1-23

Graubard, P.S. (1977) *Positive Parenthood: Solving Parent–Child Conflicts through Behavior Modification* (New York: Bobs-Merrill Co.)

Hall, R.V. (1975) *Managing Behavior (Parts 1-4)* (2nd edn.) (Lawrence, Kansas: H. & H. Enterprises)

Homme, L. and Tosti, D. (1971) *Behavior Technology: Motivation and Contingency Management* (San Rafael, California: Individual Learning Systems Inc.)

Krumboltz, J.D. and Krumboltz, H.B. (1972) *Changing Children's Behavior* (Englewood Cliffs, New Jersey: Prentice-Hall)

McIntire, R.W. (1970) *For Love of Children: Behavioral Psychology for Parents* (Del Mar, California: CRM Books)

McIntire, R.W. (1975) *Child Psychology: A Behavioral Approach to Everyday Problems* (Kalamazoo, Michigan: Behaviordelia)

Madsen, C.K. and Madsen, C.H. (1972) *Parents/Children/Discipline: A Positive Approach* (Boston, Massachusets: Allyn & Bacon)

Patterson, G.R. (1975) *Families: Applications of Social Learning to Family Life* (Champaign, Illinois: Research Press)

Patterson, G.R. and Forgatch, M. (1976) *Family Living Series: Parts 1 and 2* (Champaign, Illinois: Research Press). A set of eight audio-tapes

Patterson, G.R. and Gullion, M.E. (1976) *Living with Children: New Methods for Parents and Teachers* (3rd edn.) (Champaign, Illinois: Research Press)

Patterson, G.R. *et al.* (1975) *A Social Learning Approach to Family Intervention: Families with Aggressive Children* (Eugene, Oregon: Castalia Publishing Co.)

Peine, N.A. and Howarth, R. (1975) *Children and Parents* (Harmondsworth: Penguin)

Reid, J.B. *Childhood Aggression: A Social Learning Approach to Family Therapy.*

Film documenting a behavioural intervention with an aggressive boy: Research Press, PO Box 31772, Champaign, Illinois 61820

Rettig, E.B. (1973) *A.B.C.s for Parents An Educational Workshop in Behavior Modification* (Van Nuys, California: Associates for Behavior Change)

Rinn, R.C. and Markle, A. (1977) *Positive Parenting* (Cambridge, Massachusets: Research Media Inc.)

Rutherford, R.B. (1975) 'Establishing Behavioral Contracts with Delinquent Adolescents', *Federal Probation, 42,* 64-9

Rutherford, R.B. and Bower, K.B. (1976) 'Behavioral Contracting in Conjoint Family Therapy', *Family Therapy, 2,* 215-26

Sadler, O.W. and Seyden, T. (1974) *Groups for Parents: A Guide for Teaching Child Management to Parents* (Brandon, Vermont: Clinical Psychology Publishing Co.)

Sloane, H.N. (1976) *Behaviour Guide Series: Stop that Fighting, Dinner's Ready, Not Till Your Room's Clean, No More Whining, Because I Said So* (Fountain Valley, California: Telesis)

Smith, J.M. and Smith, D.E.P. (1976) *Child Management: A Program for Parents and Teachers* (Champaign, Illinois: Research Press)

Spees. E. *et al. Parent Training Manual,* Illinois Department of Child and Family Services, 1 N. Old State Capitol Plaza, Springfield, Illinois, 62706

Tymchuk, A.J. (1974) *Behavior Modification with Children: A Clinical Training Manual* (Springfield, Illinois: Charles C. Thomas)

Valett, R.E. (1969) *Modifying Children's Behavior: A Guide for Parents and Professionals* (Belmont, California: Fearon Publishers)

Wheldll, K. *et al.* (1983) *Seven Supertactics for Superparents* (Windsor: NFER — Nelson)

Williams, D.L. and Jaffa, E.B. (1971) *Ice Cream, Poker Chips and Very Goods: A Behavior Modification Manual for Parents* (College Park, Maryland: Maryland Book Exchange)

Wolfe, D. *et al.* (1981) *A Child Management Program for Abusive Parents: Procedures for Developing a Child Abuse Intervention Program* (Orlando, Florida: Anna Publishing)

Language Dysfunction

Conant, S. *et al.* (1983) *Teaching Language-Disabled Children* (Cambridge, Massachusets: Brookline Books)

Cooper, J. *et al.* (1978) *Helping Language Development: A Developmental Programme for Children with Early Language Handicaps* (London: Edward Arnold/New York: St Martin's Press)

Eisenon, J. (1976) *Is Your Child's Speech Normal?* (Reading, Massachusets: Addison Wesley)

Gillham, B. (1979) *The First Words Language Programme* (London: Allen & Unwin/Baltimore, Maryland: University Park Press)

Gillham, B. (1982) *Two Words Together* (London and Boston, Massachusetts: Allen & Unwin)

Harris, J. (1976) *Teaching Speech to a Non-verbal Child* (Lawrence, Kansas: H. & H. Enterprises)

Hastings, P. and Hayes, B. (1981) *Encouraging Language Development* (London: Croom Helm/Cambridge, Massachusets: Brookline Books)

Irwin, A. (1980) *Stammering: Practical Help for All Ages* (Harmondsworth: Penguin/New York: Walker & Co.)

Karnes, M. (1968) *Helping Young Children Develop Language Skills: A Book of*

Activities (Reston, Virginia: Council for Exceptional Children)

Kozloff, M.A. (1974) *Reaching the Autistic Child: A Parent Training Program* Champaign, Illinois: Research Press)

Lovaas, O.I. *et al.* (1978) *Teaching Slow Children Fast* (publisher unknown)

McConkey, R. and Price, P. (1985) *Let's Talk: Learning Language in Everyday Settings* (London: Souvenir Press)

Pushaw, D. (ed.) (1969) *Teach Your Child to Talk: A Parent Handbook* (Cincinatti, Ohio: CDBCO Standard Publishing Co.)

Schumaker, J.B. and Sherman, J.A. (1978) 'Parents as Intervention Agents', in R.L. Schiefelbusch (ed.) *Language Intervention Strategies* (Baltimore: University Park Press)

Shere, M.O. (1961) *Speech and Language Training for the Cerebral Palsied Child* (Danville, Illinois: Interstate Publishers) (E.R.I.C. EC 023019)

Simpson, R.L. (1978) *Parenting the Exceptional Child* (Kansas: University of Kansas Press). For parents of autistic children; includes tape/slide

Wing, L. (1980) *Autistic Children: A Guide for Parents* (London: Constable/Secaucus, New Jersey: Citadel (1974))

Audio-visual

Helping Language Development (Windsor: NFER — Nelson). Twenty-minute 16mm colour film

Sensory Impairment

Clark, T.C. and Watkins, S. (1978) *The SKI–HI Model: A Comprehensive Model for Identification, Language Facilitation, and Family Support for Hearing Handicapped Children through Home Management* (Utah: Logan College of Education, Utah State University) (E.R.I.C. ED 162451 EC 112418). Gives sufficient detail to enable replication

McConnell, F. and Horton, K.B. (1970) *A Home Teaching Program for Parents of Very Young Deaf Children: Final Report* (Nashville, Tennessee: School of Medicine, Vanderbilt University) (E.R.I.C. ED 039664)

Nolan, M. and Tucker, I.G. (1981) *The Hearing Impaired Child and the Family* (London: Souvenir Press/New York: State Mutual Book)

Robinson, L.W. (1980) *Project ForSight: Replication Manual* (Austin, Texas: Texas School for the Blind) (E.R.I.C. ED 209814 EC 140328). Includes lists of written and audio-visual materials

Rossett, A. (1974) 'Special Strategies for a Special Problem: Improving Communication between Hearing Impaired Adolescents and Their Parents', *Volta Review*, 76, 231-8. Material available from: National Center on Educational Media and Materials for the Handicapped, Ohio State University, 220 West 12th St, Columbus, Ohio 43210

Scott, E. *et al.* (1977) *Can't Your Child See?* (Baltimore, Maryland: University Park Press)

Developmental Delay

Babington, C.H. (1981) *Parenting and the Retarded Child* (Springfield, Illinois: Charles C. Thomas)

Baker, B.L. *et al.* (1976) *Steps to Independence: A Skill Training Series for Children with Special Needs* (Champaign, Illinois: Research Press). Seven titles: *Early Self-help Skills, Intermediate Self-help Skills, Advanced Self-help Skills, Toilet Training, Speech and Language Levels I and II, Behavior Problems.* A training guide is also available

Baldwin, V.L. *et al.* (1973) *Isn't It Time He Outgrew This? Or, A Training Program for Parents of Retarded Children* (Springfield, Illinois: Charles C. Thomas)

Boyd, R.D. and Herwig, J. (1980) *Serving Handicapped Children in Home-based Head Start: A Guide for Home Visitors and Others Working with Handicapped Children and Their Families in the Home* (Portage, Wisconsin: Cooperative Educational Services Agency 12) (E.R.I.C. ED 199991 EC 132496)

Boyd, R.D. *et al.* (1977) *Portage Parent Program* (Portage, Wisconsin: Cooperative Educational Services Agency 12). *Instructor's Manual* and *Parent Readings.* See also: *Portage Home Training Handbook*; *Portage Guide to Early Education* (S. Bluma *et al.*). Available in the UK from NFER — Nelson, Windsor

Cadman, L.A. (1979) *PEECH Outreach Project* (Wichita Falls, Texas: Education Service Center, Region 9) (E.R.I.C. ED 185783 EC 124028)

Carr, J. (1980) *Helping Your Handicapped Child: A Step-by-Step Guide to Everyday Problems* (Harmondsworth: Penguin)

Chapel Hill Training Outreach Project, Kaplan School Supply Corporation, 600 Jonestown Road, Winston-Salem, North Carolina 27103. A variety of materials are available

Cunningham, C.C. and Sloper, P. (1978) *Helping Your Handicapped Baby* (London: Souvenir Press/New York: State Mutual Book)

Cunningham, C.C. (1982) *Down's Syndrome: An Introduction for Parents* (London: Souvenir Press/Cambridge, Massachusets: Brookline Books)

Dougan, T. *et al.* (eds.) (1979) *We Have Been There — A Guidebook for Parents of People with Mental Retardation* (Salt Lake City, Utah: Dougan, Isabell and Vyas Associates)

Doyle, P.B. *et al.* (1979) *Helping the Severely Handicapped Child: A Guide for Parents and Children* (New York: Thomas Y. Crowell Co.)

Fraser, L. (1973) *A Cup of Kindness: A Book for Parents of Retarded Children* (Seattle, Washington: Bernie Straub Publishing Co.)

Goodman, L. *et al.* (1971) 'The Parent's Role in Sex Education for the Retarded', *Mental Retardation, 9, 1,* 43-5

Gordon, S. (1975) *Living Fully: A Guide for Young People with a Handicap, Their Parents, Their Teachers and Professionals* (New York: John Day & Co.)

Hannam, J. (1980) *Parents and Mentally Handicapped Children* (Harmondsworth: Penguin)

Hanson, M.J. (1977) *Teaching Your Down's Syndrome Infant* (Baltimore, Maryland: University Park Press)

Howard, W.L. *et al.* (1979) *Working with Parents of Handicapped Children* (Columbus, Ohio: Charles E. Merrill)

Jeffree, D.M. (1976) *Let Me Speak* (London: Souvenir Press)

Jeffree, D.M. and Skeffington, M. (1980) *Let Me Read* (London: Souvenir Press)

Jeffree, D.M. *et al.* (1977) *Let Me Play* (London: Souvenir Press)

Jeffree, D.M. *et al.* (1977) *Teaching the Handicapped Child* (London: Souvenir Press/New Jersey: Spectrum Books (1982)). Dorothy Jeffree and co-workers have produced two further volumes, *Let's Make Toys* and *Let's Join In*, both published by Souvenir Press, London, in the UK and in New York by State Mutual Book. The HARC Parental Involvement Project Development Charts are available from Hodder & Stoughton, London

Jobling, M. (1975) *Helping the Handicapped Child: No. 1 in the Family* (Windsor: NFER)

Johnson, V.M. and Werner, R.A. (1975) *A Step-by-Step Learning Guide for*

Retarded Infants and Children (Syracuse, New York: Syracuse University Press)

Kirk, S.A. (1968) *You and Your Retarded Child: A Manual for Parents of Retarded Children* (Pacific Books)

Klein, M.D. *et al.* (1981) *Parent's Guide: Classroom Involvement, Communication Training, Resources* (Topeka: Kansas Neurological Institute) Media package including video available (E.R.I.C. EC 140315).

Lear, R. (1977) *Play Helps: Toys and Activities for Handicapped Children* (London: Heinemann/ Philadelphia, Pennsylvania: International Ideas)

McCormack, M. (1978) *A Mentally Handicapped Child in the Family: A Guide for Parents* (Publisher unknown)

Marshall, M. (1982) *Parents and the Handicapped Child* (London: MacRae)

Michaelis, C.T. (1983) *Coping with Handicapped Infants and Children* (London: Edward Arnold)

Newson, E. and Hipgrave, T. (1982) *Getting Through to Your Handicapped Child* (Cambridge: Cambridge University Press)

Pader, O.F. (1981) *A Guide and Handbook for Parents of Mentally Retarded Children* (Springfield, Illinois: Charles C. Thomas)

Perske, R. (1973) *New Directions for Parents of Persons who are Retarded* (Nashville, Tennessee: Abingdon Press)

Purser, A. (1981) *You and Your Handicapped Child* (London: Allen & Unwin)

Revill, S. and Blunden, R. (1984) *A Manual for Implementing a Portage Home Training Service for Developmentally Handicapped Pre-school Children* (Windsor: NFER — Nelson) The British version of Portage manual

Riddick, B. (1982) *Toys and Play for* Helm/Dover, New Hampshire; Longwood)

Stone, J. and Taylor, F. (1977) *A Handbook for Parents of a Handicapped Child* (London: Arrow Books)

Watson, L.S. (1972) *How to Use Behavior Modification with Mentally Retarded and Autistic Children: A Program for Administrators, Teachers, Parents and Nurses* (Libertyville, Illinois: Behavior Modification Technology)

Watson, L.S. (1973) *Child Behavior Modification: A Manual for Teachers, Nurses and Parents* (New York and Oxford: Pergamon Press)

Weber, S.J. *et al.* (1975) *The Portage Guide to Home Teaching* (Portage, Wisconsin: Cooperative Educational Service Agency 12) (E.R.I.C. ED 189785 EC 124509)

Whelan, E. and Speake, B. (1979) *Learning to Cope* (London: Souvenir Press)

White, M. and East, K. *Wessex Revised Portage Language Checklist* (Windsor: NFER — Nelson)

Wnek, L. *et al.* (1980) *Parent Infant Program: Program Manager's Manual* (Columbus, Ohio: Nisonger Center, Ohio State University) (E.R.I.C. ED 222003 EC 150071)

Audio-visual

We've Been There — We Can Help, Stanfield Film Associates, PO Box 1983, Santa Monica, California 90406. Filmstrip and associated package

Video training kits from: St Michael's House, Upper Kilmacud Road, Stillorgan, Co. Dublin, Ireland. Titles include: *Let's Play, Putting Two Words Together, Learning to Pretend, Community Education Kit, Preventing Handicap, Friendship Scheme*

Physical and Multiple Handicap

Anderson, E. and Spain, B. (1977) *The Child with Spina Bifida* (London and New

York: Methuen)

Cutler, B.C. (1981) *Unravelling the Special Education Maze: An Action Guide for Parents* (Champaign, Illinois: Research Press)

DEBT (Developmental Education, Birth Through Two). For information, contact Director, DEBT Program, Lubbock Independent School District, 1628 19th St, Lubbock, Texas 79401

Finnie, N. (1974) *Handling the Young Cerebral Palsied Child at Home* (London: Heinemann)

Hutinger, P.L. *et al.* (1977) *Have Wagon, Will Travel. Sharing Centers for Rural Handicapped Infants, Toddlers and Their Parents* (Macomb, Illinois: Western Illinois University) (E.R.I.C. ED 180159 EC 122401)

Hutinger, P.L. *et al.* (1978) *Toy Workshops for Parents: Bridging a Gap* (Macomb, Illinois: Western Illinois University) (E.R.I.C. ED 180173 EC 122415)

Landsown, R. (1980) *More Than Sympathy: The Everyday Needs of Sick and Handicapped Children* (London: Tavistock/New York: Methuen)

Miezio, P.M. (1983) *Parenting Children with Disabilities: A Professional Source for Physicians and Guides for Parents* (Dekker)

Mitchell, D. (1982) *Your Child is Different* (London and Boston: Unwin)

Newson, E. and Hipgrave, T. (1982) *Getting Through to Your Handicapped Child* (Cambridge and New York: Cambridge University Press)

The Parent Education Curriculum of Family School. Available from: The Family Support Center, 2 Bailey Road, Yeadon, Pennsylvania 19050

The Parent-to-Parent Program Organizational Handbook. Available from: The University Affiliated Facility, The University of Georgia, 850 College Station Road, Athens, Georgia 30610

Russell, P. (1983) *The Wheelchair Child* (2nd edn.) (London: Souvenir Press/Englewood Cliffs, New Jersey: Prentice-Hall (1984))

Audio-visual

McGraw-Hill Films, 100 Fifteenth Street, Del Mar, California 92014. A number of films available in this area

Manuals Purely for Professionals

Bradley, R.C. (1971) *Parent–Teacher Interviews* (Wolfe City, Texas: University Press)

Bromwich, R. (1981) *Working with Parents and Infants: An Interactional Approach* (Baltimore, Maryland: University Park Press)

Bryce, M. and Lloyd, J.C. (1981) *Treating Families in the Home* (Springfield, Illinois: Charles C. Thomas)

Chinn, P.C. *et al.* (1978) *Two-way Talking with Parents of Special Children: A Process of Positive Communication* (St Louis, Missouri: C.V. Mosby)

Cunningham, C. and Davis, H. (1985) *Working with Parents: Frameworks for Collaboration* (Milton Keynes: Open University Press)

Griffiths, M. and Russell, P. (1985) *Working Together with Handicapped Children* (London: Souvenir Press)

Harris, S.L. (1983) *Families of the Developmentally Disabled: A Guide to Behavioral Interventions* (New York and Oxford: Pergamon)

Hefferman, H. and Todd, V.E. (1961) *Elementary Teachers' Guide to Working with Parents* (West Nyack, New York: Parker Publishing)

Heward, W.L. *et al.* (1979) *Working with Parents of Handicapped Children* (Columbus, Ohio: Charles E. Merrill)

Kroth, R.L. (1975) *Communicating with Parents of Exceptional Children: Improving Parent–Teacher Relations* (Denver, Colorado: Love Publishing)

Kroth, R.L. and Simpson, R.L. (1975) *Parent Conferences as a Teaching Strategy* (Denver, Colorado: Love Publishing)

McConkey, R. (1985) *Working with Parents: A Practical Guide for Teachers and Therapists* (London: Croom Helm/Cambridge, Massachusets: Brookline Books)

Miller, W.H. (1975) *Systematic Parent Training: Procedures, Cases, and Issues* (Champaign, Illinois: Research Press)

Miller, W.H. and Miller, N.B. (1978) *Therapist's Guidebook* (Champaign, Illinois: Research Press)

Mittler, P. and McConachie, H. (1983) *Parents, Professionals and Mentally Handicapped People: Approaches to Partnership* (London: Croom Helm/Cambridge, Massachusets: Brookline Books)

Myers, S.P. *et al.* (1981) *Teacher's Guide to Family Involvement* (Topeka, Kansas: Kansas Neurological Institute) (E.R.I.C. EC 140314)

Noland, R.L. (1978) *Counselling Parents of the Mentally Retarded* (Springfield, Illinois: Charles C. Thomas)

Paul, J.L. (ed.) (1981) *Understanding and Working with Parents of Children with Special Needs* (New York: Holt Rinehart & Winston)

Perkins, E.A. *et al.* (1980) *Helping the Retarded* (Kidderminster, Worcestershire: British Institute of Mental Handicap)

Seligmann, J. (1980) *Strategies for Helping Parents of Exceptional Children: A Guide for Teachers* (London: Collier Macmillan)

Smith, J.M. and Smith, D.E.P. (1976) *Child Management: A Program for Parents and Teachers: Discussion Guide* (Champaign, Illinois: Research Press)

Webster, E.J. (1977) *Counselling with Parents of Handicapped Children* (London and New York: Grune & Stratton)

Wikler, L. *et al.* (1976) *Behavior Modification Parent Groups: A Training Manual for Professionals* (Thorofare, New Jersey: Charles B. Slack)

A variety of other materials are available from voluntary and specialist organisations, especially those dealing with particular handicaps. Recent listings of UK national organisations concerned with handicap will be found in:

Griffiths, M. and Russell, P. (1985) *Working Together with Handicapped Children* (London: Souvenir Press)

Organisations concerned with parent–school links of a more general kind are described in:

Wolfendale, S. (1983) *Parental Participation in Children's Development and Education* (London: Gordon & Breach)

In the USA, such listings are available from a number of recent texts. It may also be useful to readers to contact the Family Resource Coalition, which produces a listing of family resource organisations and an annotated bibliography of resource materials: FRC, 230 N. Michigan Avenue, Suite 1625, Chicago, Illinois, 60601.

Further Reading

Annotated Bibliography for Child and Family Programs (US Department of Health Education and Welfare: Administration for Children, Youth and

Families) (OHDS 78-31118). Available from: Superintendent of Documents, US Government Printing Office, Washington, DC 20402

Lillie, D.L. and Trohanis, P.L. (eds.) (1976) *Teaching Parents to Teach* (New York: Walker)

Mash, E.J. *et al.* (eds.) (1976) *Behaviour Modification and Families* (2 vols) (New York: Brunner/Mazel)

Maybanks, S. and Bryce, M. (1979) *Home-based Services For Children and Families: Policy, Practice and Research* (Springfield, Illinois: Charles C. Thomas)

Parenting: A Bibliography. Available from: Parenting Materials Information Center, Southwest Educational Development Laboratory, 211 East Seventh St, Austin, Texas 78701

Reif, T.F. and Stollak, G.E. (1972) *Sensitivity to Young Children: Training and Its Effects* (East Lansing, Michigan: Michigan State University Press)

School Psychology Review (1981), special issue on: *Services to Families and Parental Involvement with Interventions,* vol. 10, no. 1, winter 1981. Available from: NASP Publications, 10 Overland Drive, Stratford, Connecticut 06497

INDEX